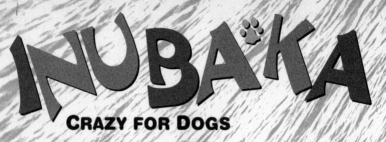

INUBAKA

CRAZY FOR DOGS

8

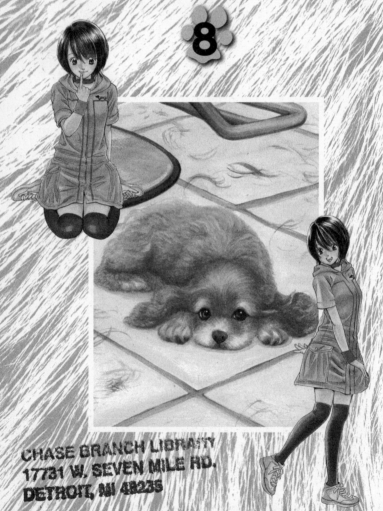

YUKIYA SAKURAGI

Contents

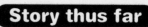

Story thus far

Teppei is the manager of the recently opened pet shop Woofles. He intended to breed his black Labrador Noa with a champion dog, but instead Noa was "taken advantage of" by an unknown and unfixed male dog!

The unknown dog's owner was Suguri Miyauchi and her dog was a mutt named Lupin. Suguri is now working at Woofles to make up for her dog's actions.

Suguri's enthusiasm is more than a little unique. She has eaten dog food (and said it was tasty), caught dog poop with her bare hands, and caused dogs to have "happy pee" in her presence. Teppei is starting to realize that Suguri is indeed a very special girl.

Woofles has a new employee named Momoko Takeuchi. She specializes in grooming and is truly an asset to the team. She's yet another stray taken in by the big-hearted Teppei.

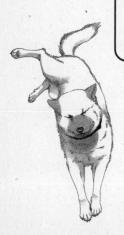

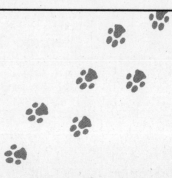

CHARACTERS

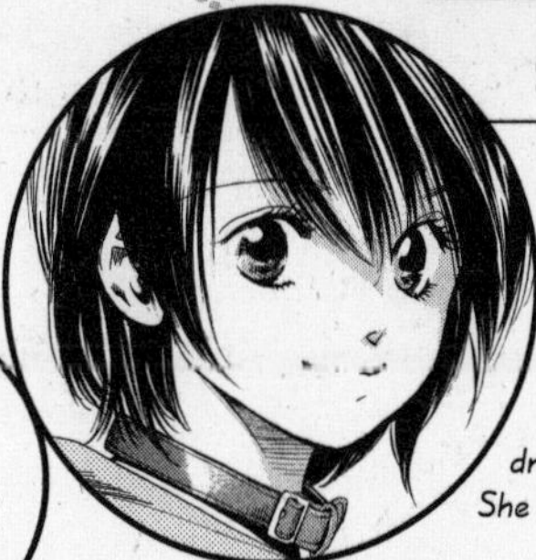

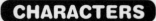

Suguri Miyauchi

She seems to possess an almost supernatural connection with dogs. When she approaches them they often urinate with great excitement! She is crazy for dogs and can catch their droppings with her bare hands. She is currently a trainee at the Woofles Pet Shop.

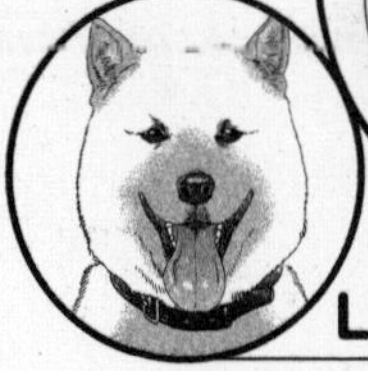

Lupin

♂ *Mutt (mongrel)*

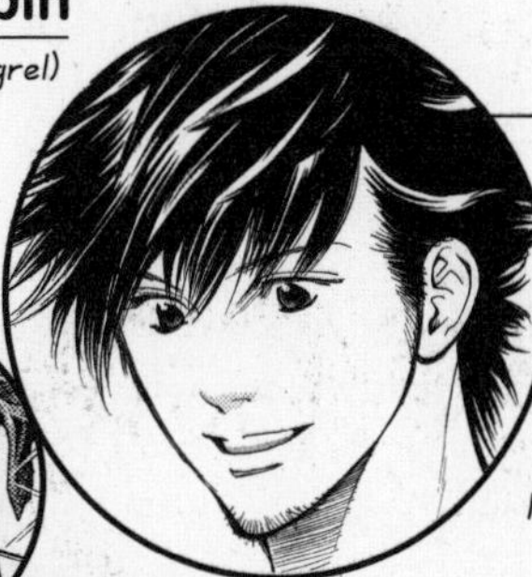

Teppei Iida

He is the manager of the recently opened pet shop Woofles. He is aware of Suguri's special ability and has hired her to work in his shop. He also lets Suguri and Kentaro crash with him.

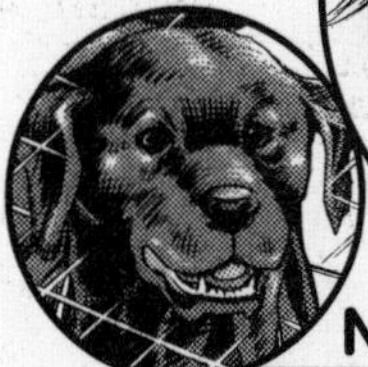

Noa

♀ *Labrador retriever*

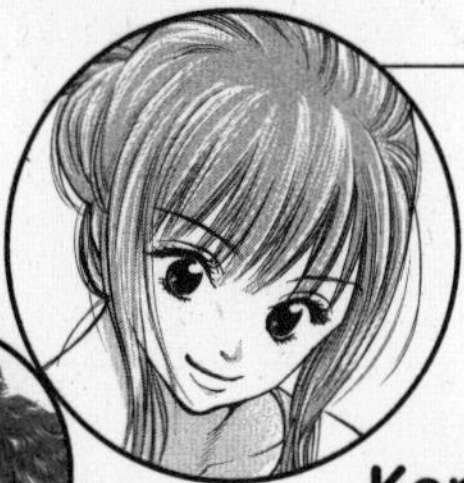

Momoko Takeuchi

Woofles Pet Shop (second location) pet groomer. At first she was a girl with many problems and she rarely smiled. But after meeting Suguri, she's changed and the two are now best friends.

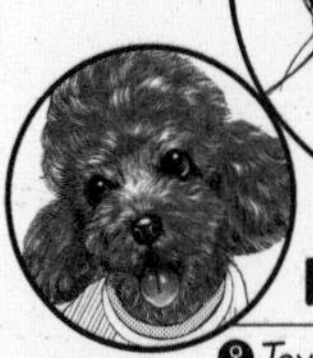

Mel

♀ *Toy Poodle*

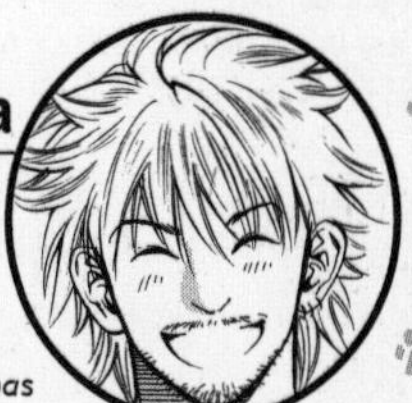

Kentaro Osada

A wannabe musician and buddy of Teppei's from high school. Teppei saved Kentaro when he was a down-and-out beggar. He has a crush on the piano instructor Kanako, but not her dog...

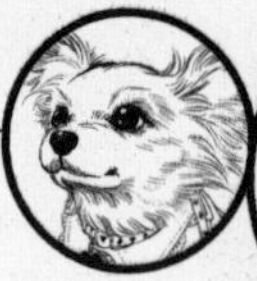

Melon

♂ Chihuahua

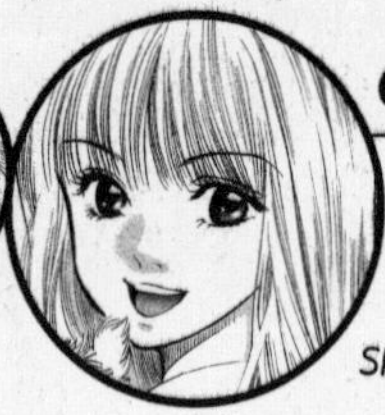

Chizuru Sawamura

She adopted a Chihuahua, Melon, after her long-time pet Golden Retriever Ricky alerted her that he was ill. She works at a hostess bar to repay Melon's medical fees.

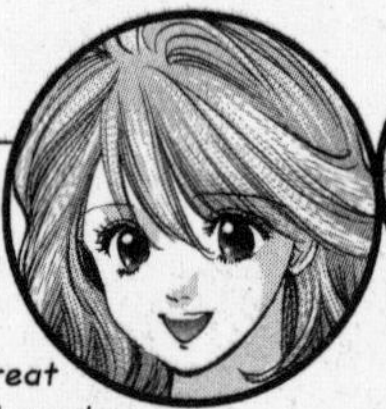

Kanako Mori

She teaches piano on the second floor of the same building as Woofles. Her love for her dog, Czerny, is so great that it surprises even Suguri!

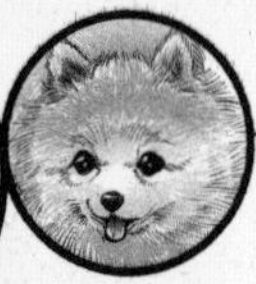

Czerny

♀ Pomeranian

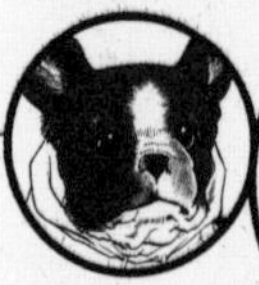

Zidane

♂ French bulldog

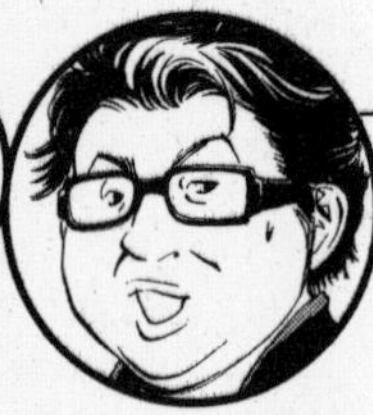

Hiroshi Akiba

Pop-idol otaku turned dog otaku. His dream is to publish a photo collection of his dog, Zidane. He is a government employee.

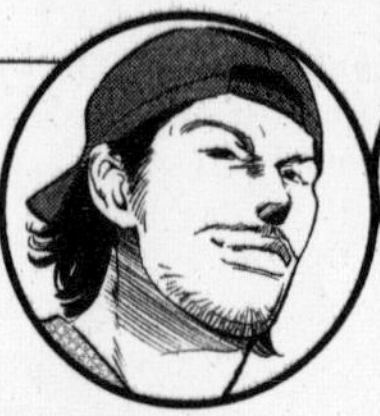

JIN

A mysterious self-employed "entrepreneur." His speech is unpolished and sometimes blunt, but kindness and compassion show through when he's with dogs. Being a student of Kanako-sensei's piano class shows that there are unexpected sides of him.

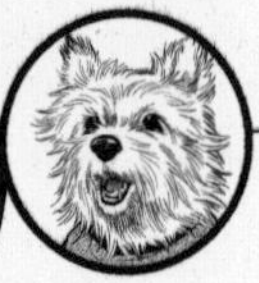

Mosh

♂ West Highland White Terrier

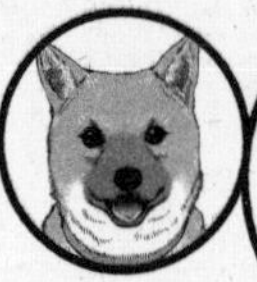

Chanta

♀ Shiba

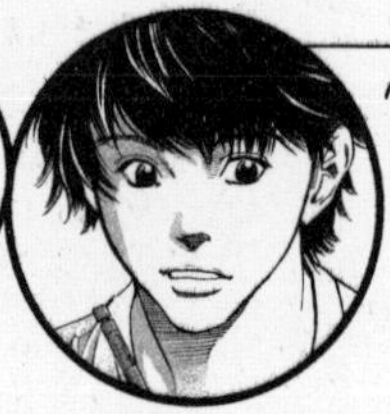

Kim

A Korean friend of Kentaro. He had a phobia of dogs, but he has been working hard to get over it in order to get close to Suguri, whom he has a crush on. He bought a Shiba dog!

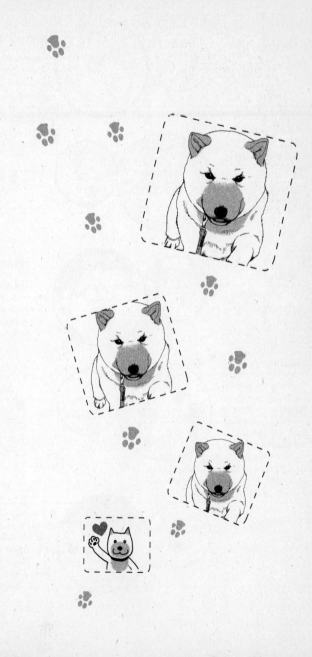

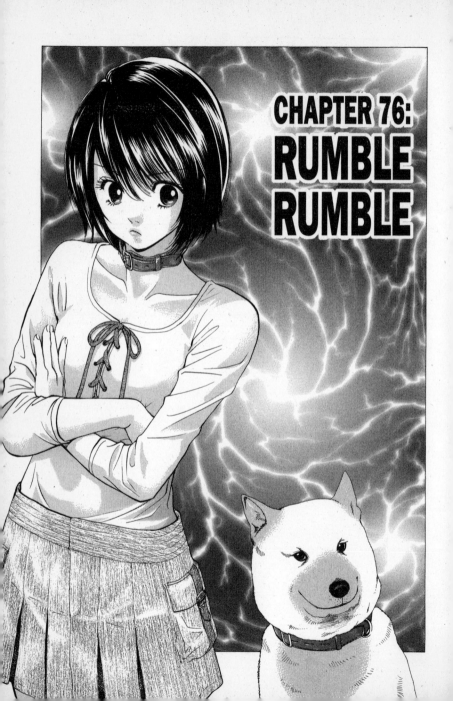

CHAPTER 76:
RUMBLE
RUMBLE

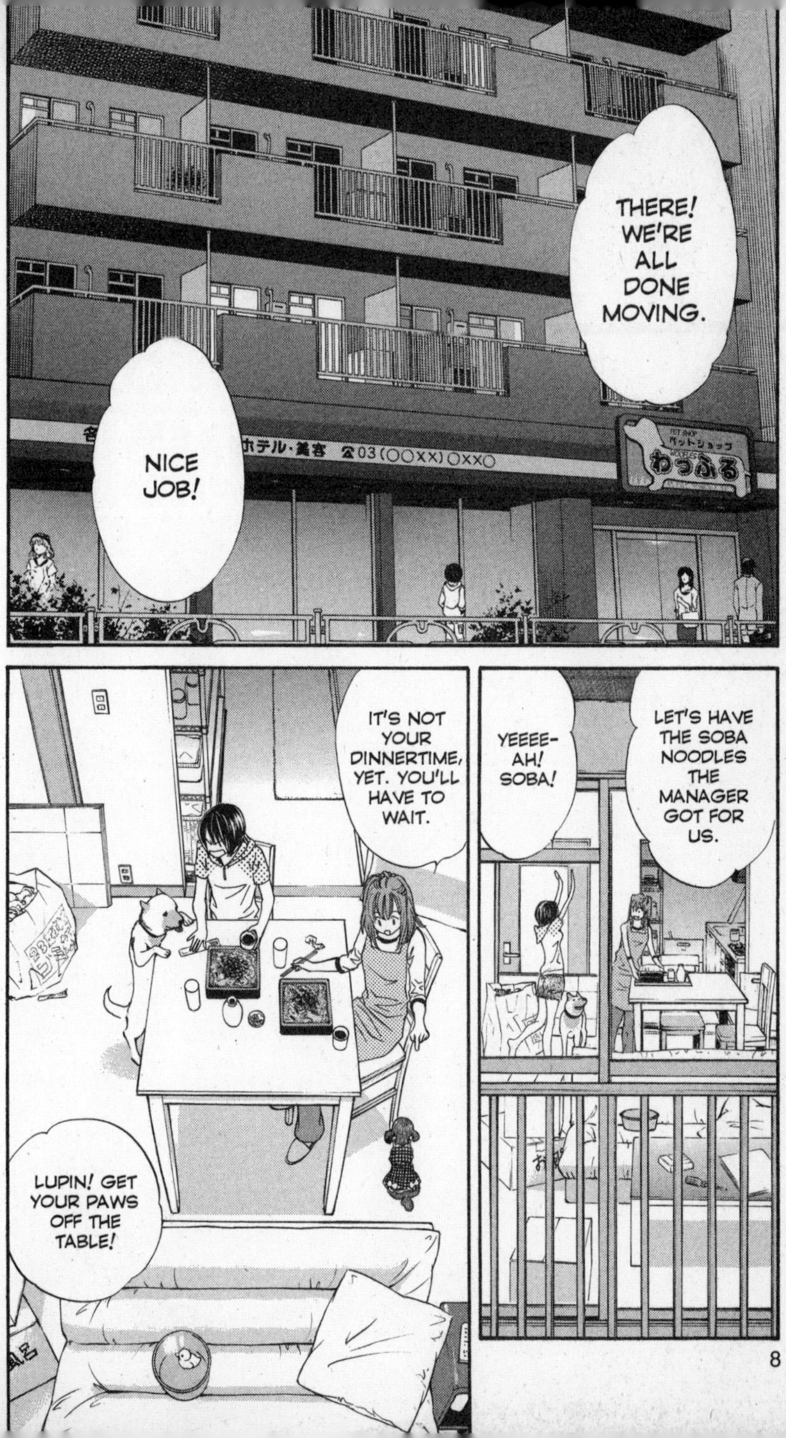
THERE! WE'RE ALL DONE MOVING.
NICE JOB!
ペットショップ
わっふる
ホテル・美容 ☎03(○○XX)○XX○
LET'S HAVE THE SOBA NOODLES THE MANAGER GOT FOR US.
YEEEE-AH! SOBA!
IT'S NOT YOUR DINNERTIME, YET. YOU'LL HAVE TO WAIT.
LUPIN! GET YOUR PAWS OFF THE TABLE!

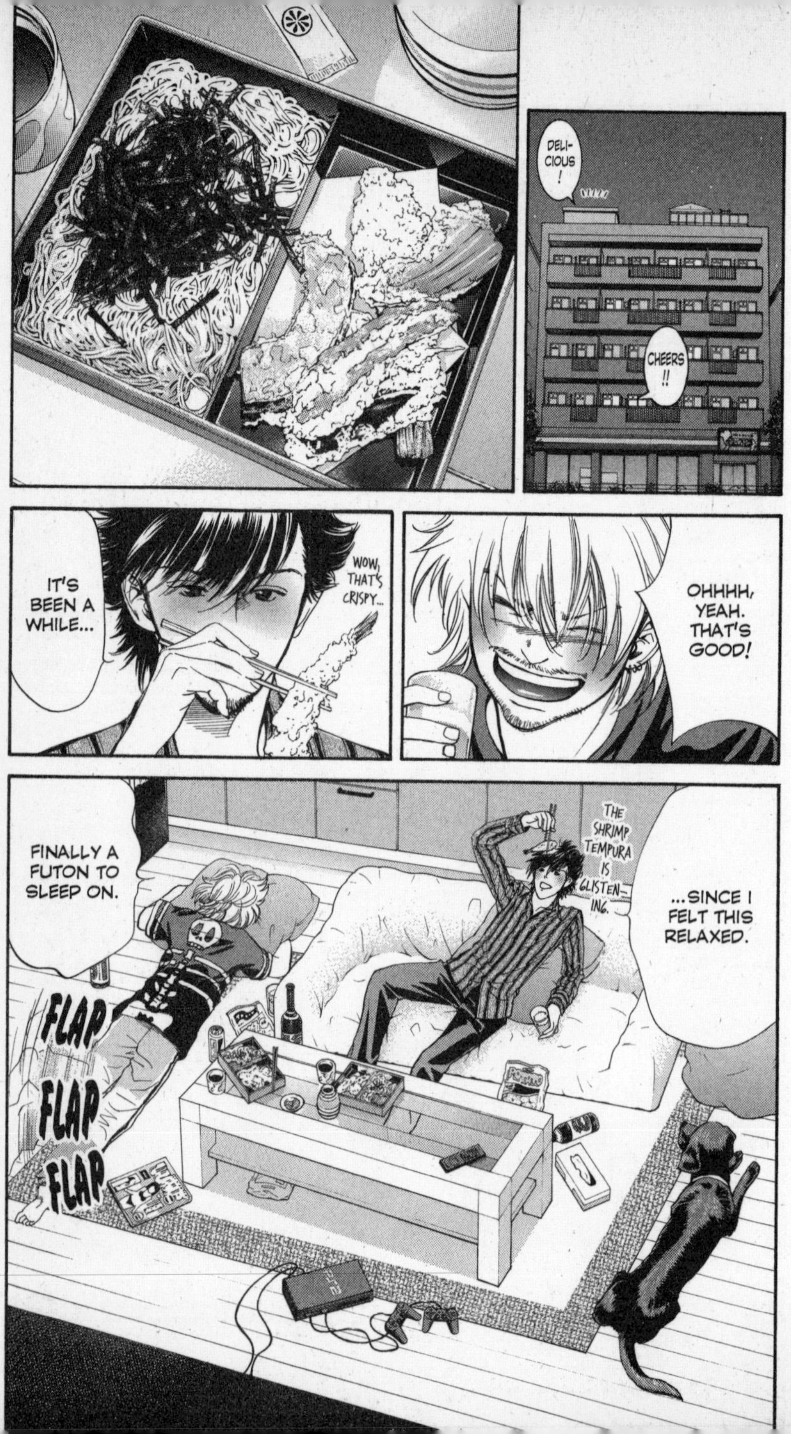
DELI-CIOUS!
CHEERS!!
OHHHH, YEAH. THAT'S GOOD!
WOW, THAT'S CRISPY...
IT'S BEEN A WHILE...
...SINCE I FELT THIS RELAXED.
THE SHRIMP TEMPURA IS GLISTEN-ING.
FINALLY A FUTON TO SLEEP ON.
FLAP
FLAP
FLAP

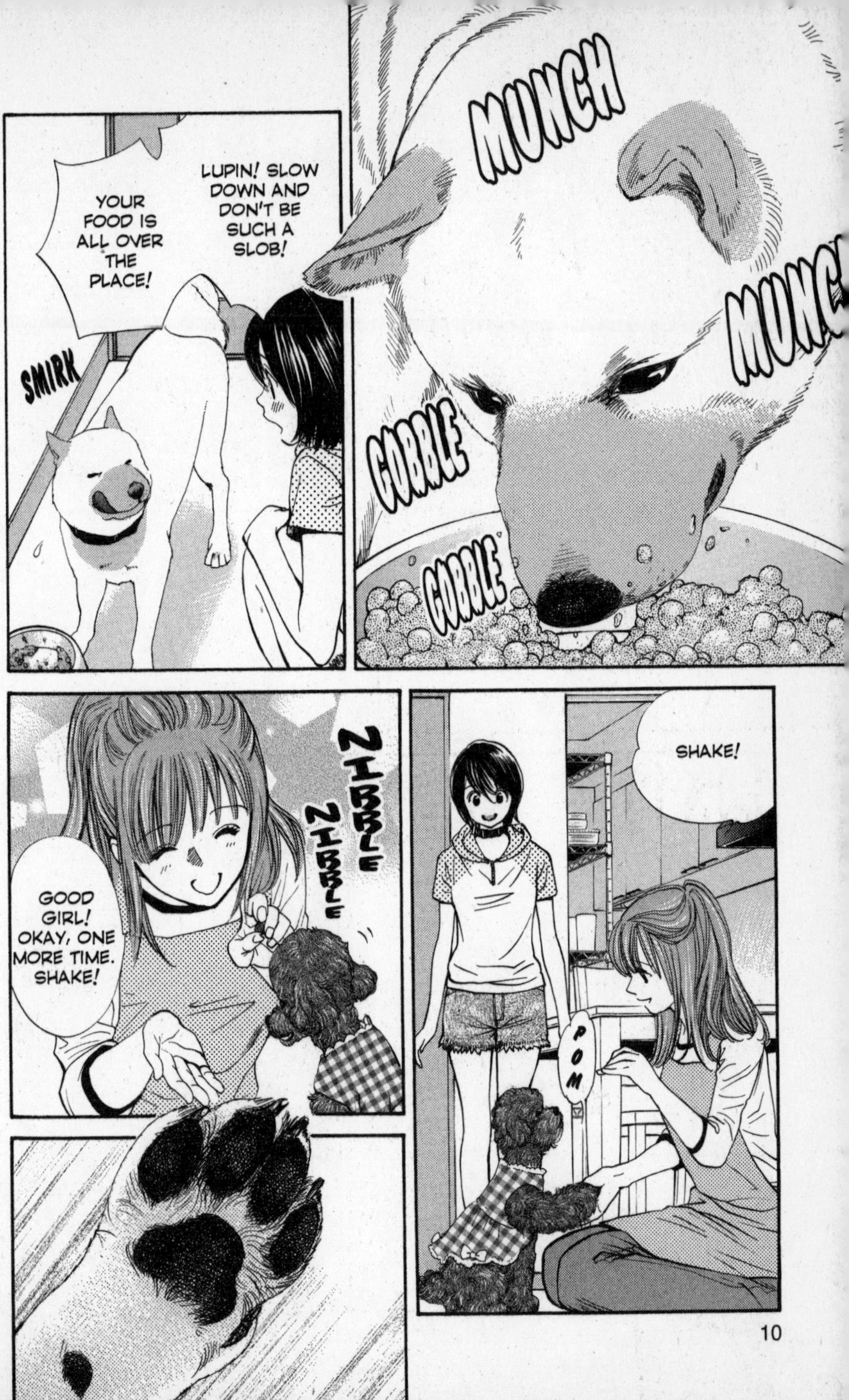
MUNCH
MUNC
GOBBLE
GOBBLE
LUPIN! SLOW DOWN AND DON'T BE SUCH A SLOB!
YOUR FOOD IS ALL OVER THE PLACE!
SMIRK
SHAKE!
POM
NIBBLE NIBBLE
GOOD GIRL! OKAY, ONE MORE TIME. SHAKE!

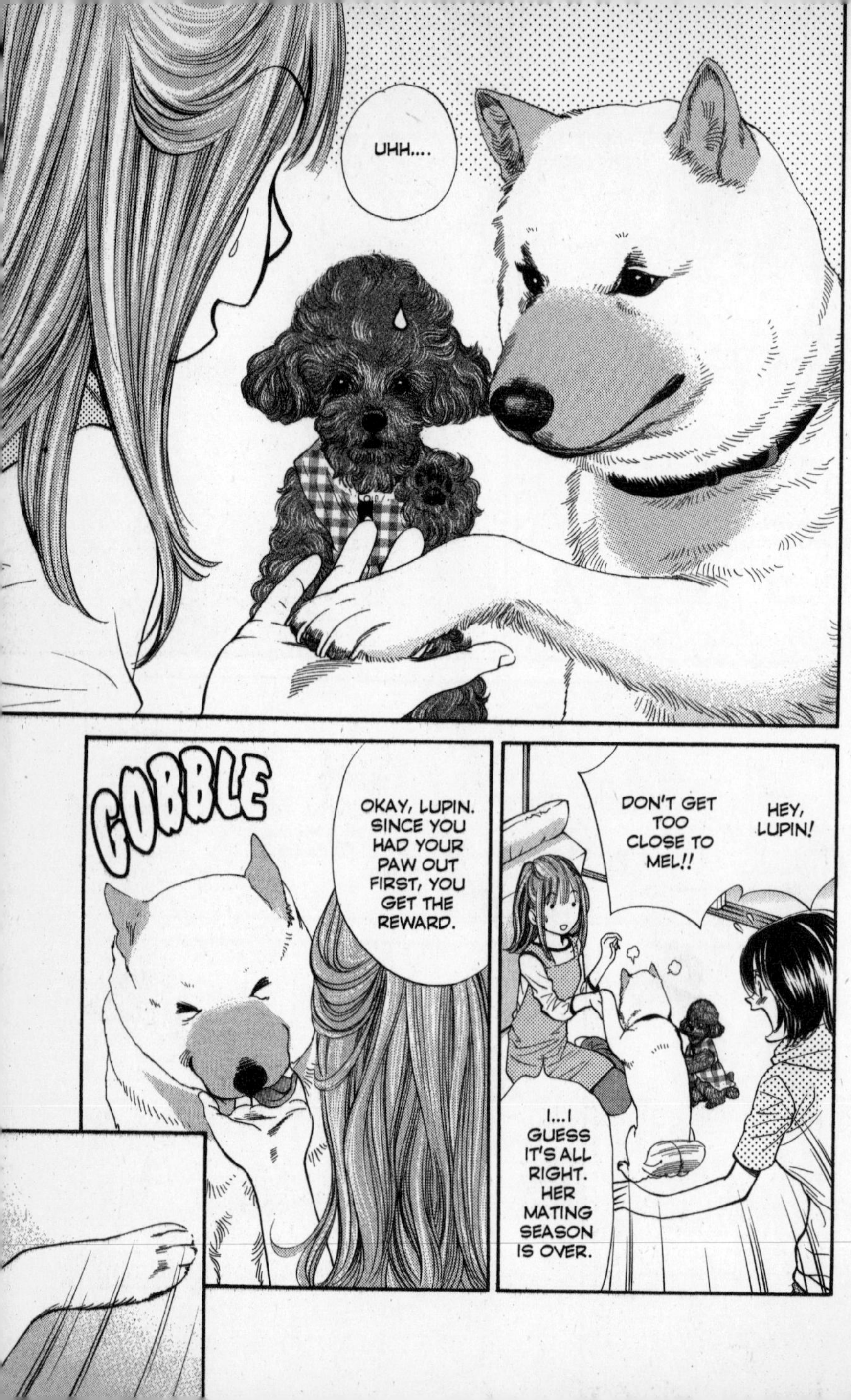
UHH....
HEY, LUPIN!
DON'T GET TOO CLOSE TO MEL!!
I...I GUESS IT'S ALL RIGHT. HER MATING SEASON IS OVER.
OKAY, LUPIN. SINCE YOU HAD YOUR PAW OUT FIRST, YOU GET THE REWARD.
GOBBLE

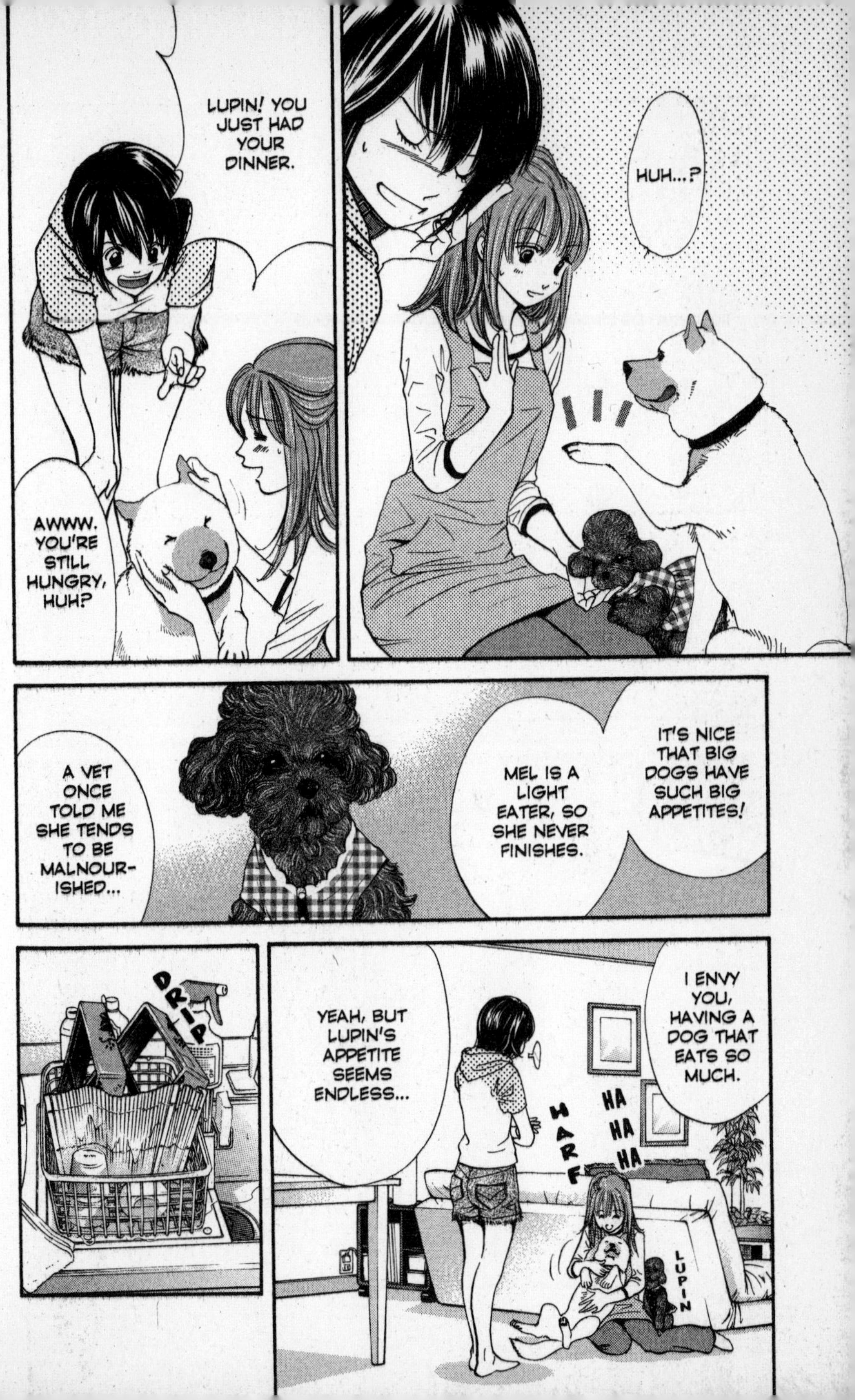
HUH...?
LUPIN! YOU JUST HAD YOUR DINNER.
AWWW. YOU'RE STILL HUNGRY, HUH?
IT'S NICE THAT BIG DOGS HAVE SUCH BIG APPETITES!
MEL IS A LIGHT EATER, SO SHE NEVER FINISHES.
A VET ONCE TOLD ME SHE TENDS TO BE MALNOUR-ISHED...
I ENVY YOU, HAVING A DOG THAT EATS SO MUCH.
HA HA HA
HARF
LUPIN
YEAH, BUT LUPIN'S APPETITE SEEMS ENDLESS...
DRIP

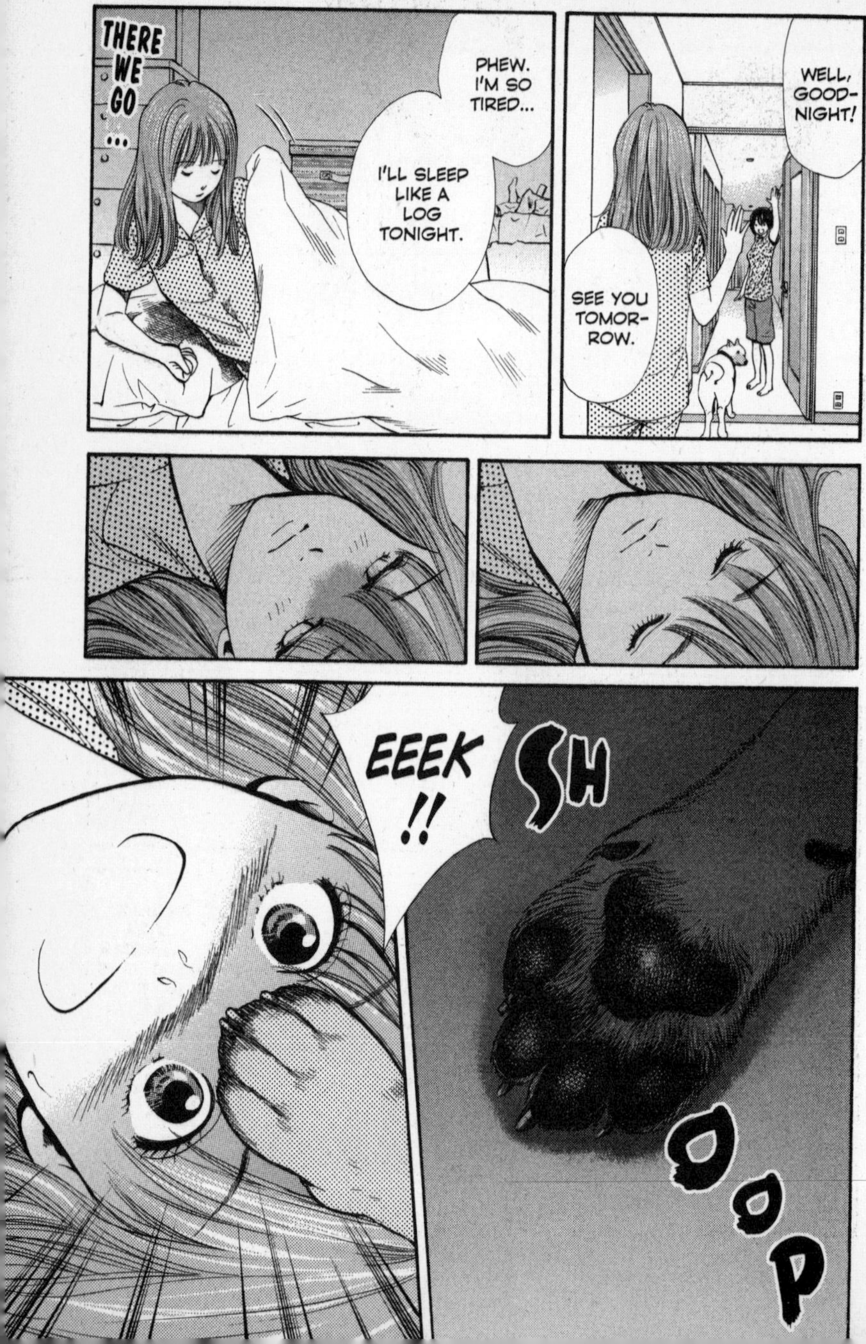
WELL, GOODNIGHT!
SEE YOU TOMORROW.
PHEW. I'M SO TIRED...
I'LL SLEEP LIKE A LOG TONIGHT.
THERE WE GO...
SHOOP
EEEK!!

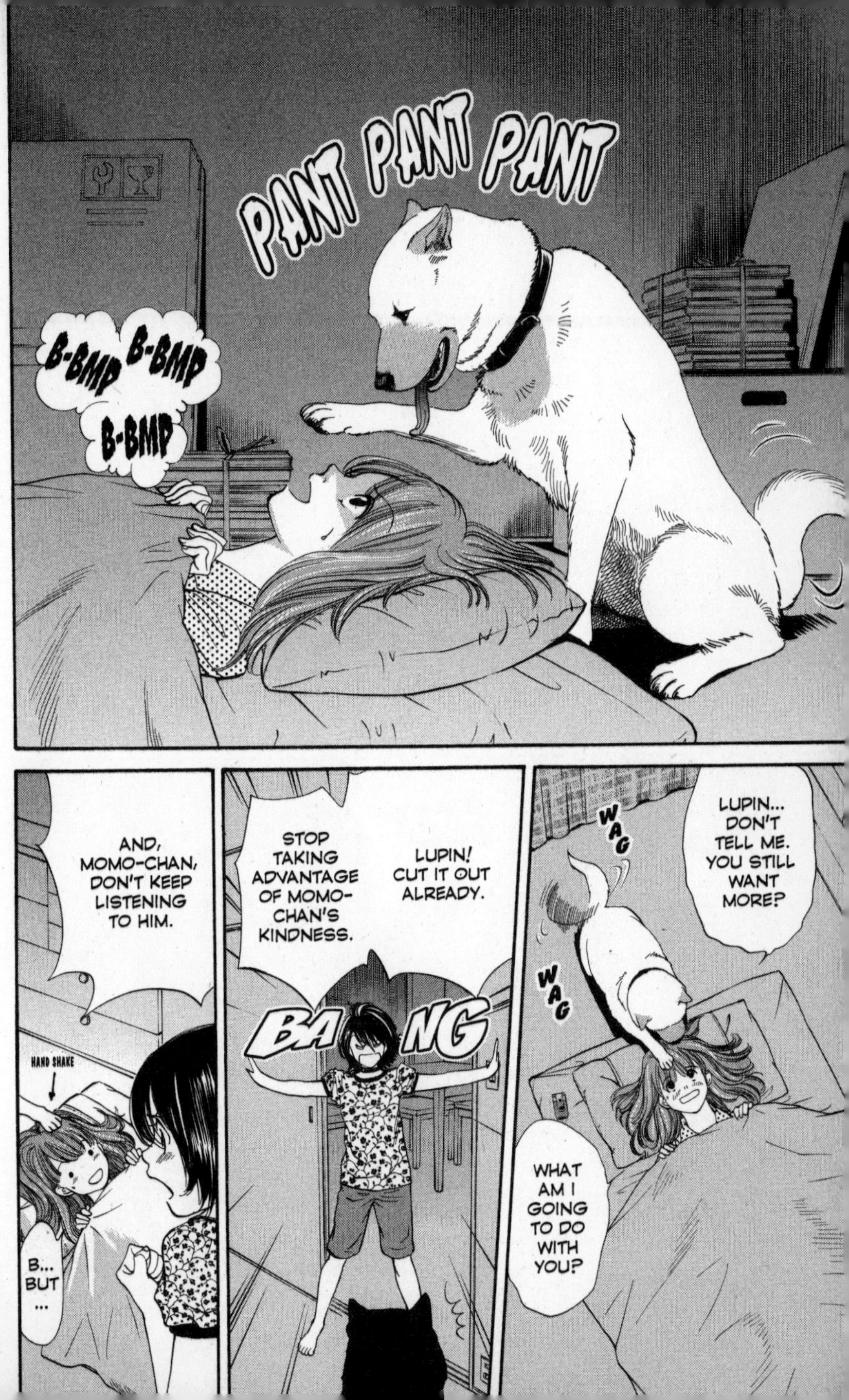
PANT PANT PANT
B-BMP B-BMP
B-BMP
LUPIN... DON'T TELL ME. YOU STILL WANT MORE?
WAG
WAG
WHAT AM I GOING TO DO WITH YOU?
LUPIN! CUT IT OUT ALREADY.
STOP TAKING ADVANTAGE OF MOMO-CHAN'S KINDNESS.
BANG
AND, MOMO-CHAN, DON'T KEEP LISTENING TO HIM.
HAND SHAKE
B... BUT ...

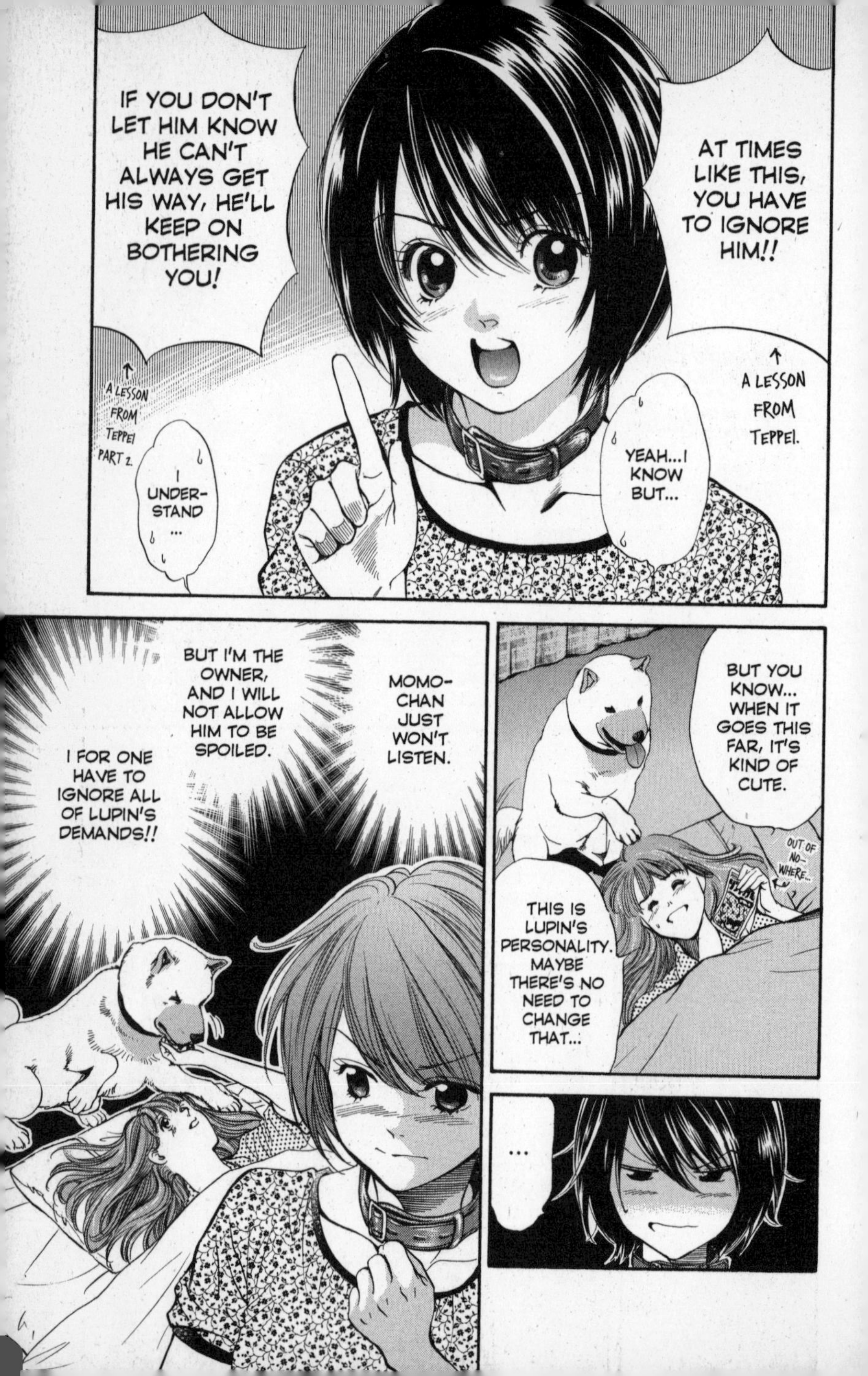

AT TIMES LIKE THIS, YOU HAVE TO IGNORE HIM!!
A LESSON FROM TEPPEI.
YEAH...I KNOW BUT...
IF YOU DON'T LET HIM KNOW HE CAN'T ALWAYS GET HIS WAY, HE'LL KEEP ON BOTHERING YOU!
A LESSON FROM TEPPEI PART 2.
I UNDER-STAND...
BUT YOU KNOW... WHEN IT GOES THIS FAR, IT'S KIND OF CUTE.
OUT OF NO-WHERE...
THIS IS LUPIN'S PERSONALITY. MAYBE THERE'S NO NEED TO CHANGE THAT...
...
MOMO-CHAN JUST WON'T LISTEN.
BUT I'M THE OWNER, AND I WILL NOT ALLOW HIM TO BE SPOILED.
I FOR ONE HAVE TO IGNORE ALL OF LUPIN'S DEMANDS!!

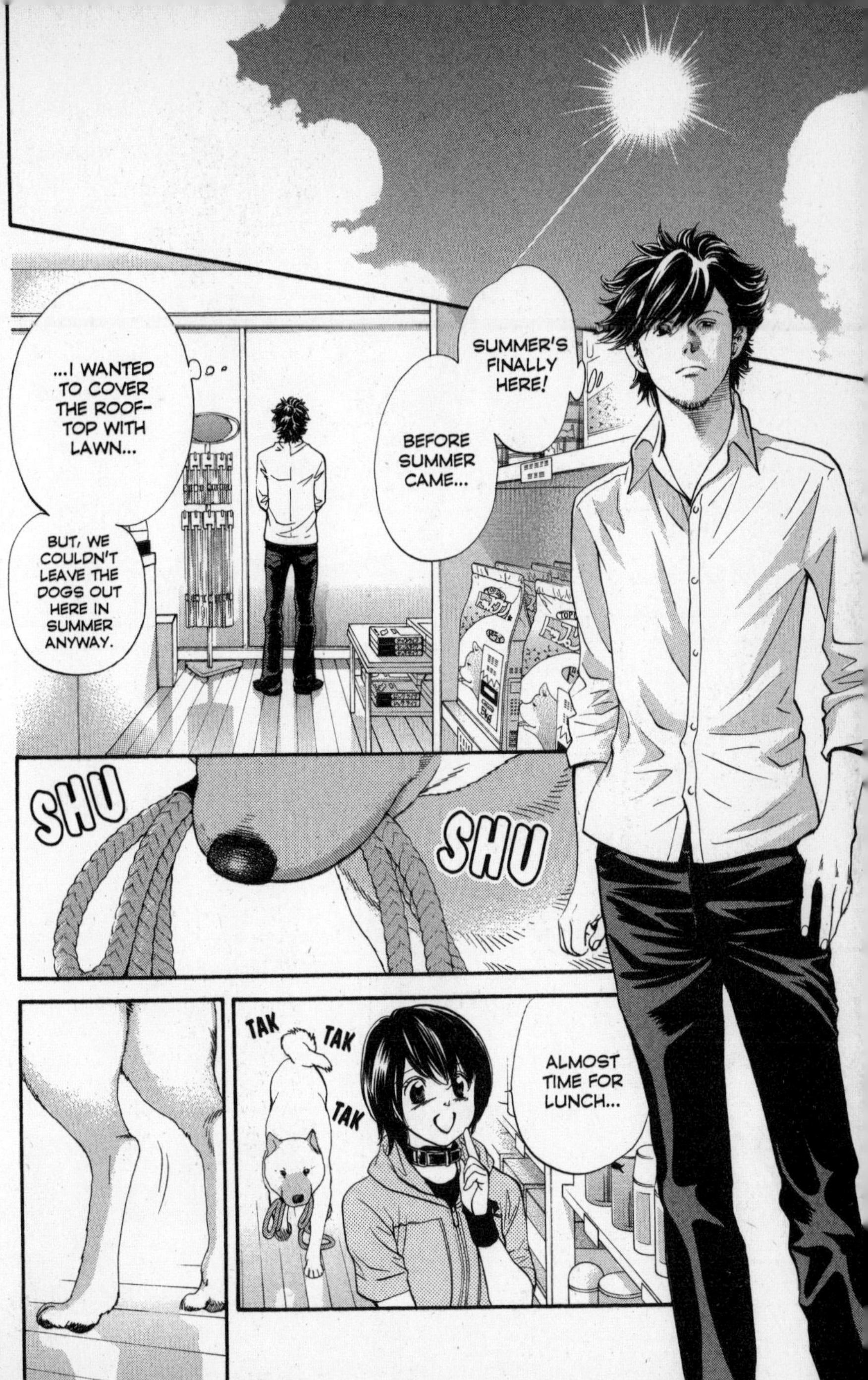
SUMMER'S FINALLY HERE!
BEFORE SUMMER CAME...
...I WANTED TO COVER THE ROOF-TOP WITH LAWN...
BUT, WE COULDN'T LEAVE THE DOGS OUT HERE IN SUMMER ANYWAY.
SHU
SHU
ALMOST TIME FOR LUNCH...
TAK
TAK
TAK

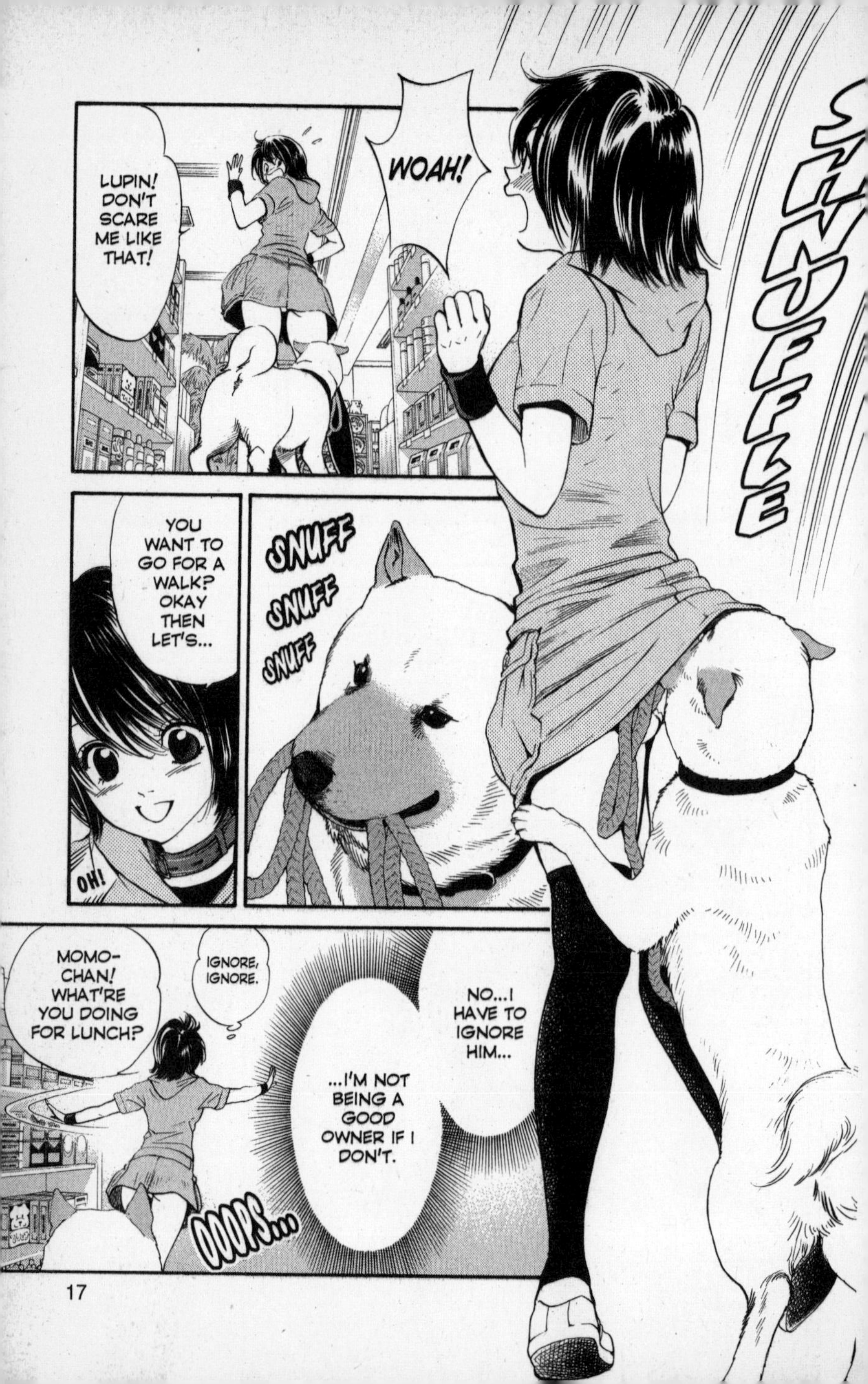
WOAH!
SHNUFFLE
LUPIN! DON'T SCARE ME LIKE THAT!
SNUFF
SNUFF
SNUFF
YOU WANT TO GO FOR A WALK? OKAY THEN LET'S...
OH!
NO...I HAVE TO IGNORE HIM...
...I'M NOT BEING A GOOD OWNER IF I DON'T.
IGNORE, IGNORE.
MOMO-CHAN! WHAT'RE YOU DOING FOR LUNCH?
OOOPS...

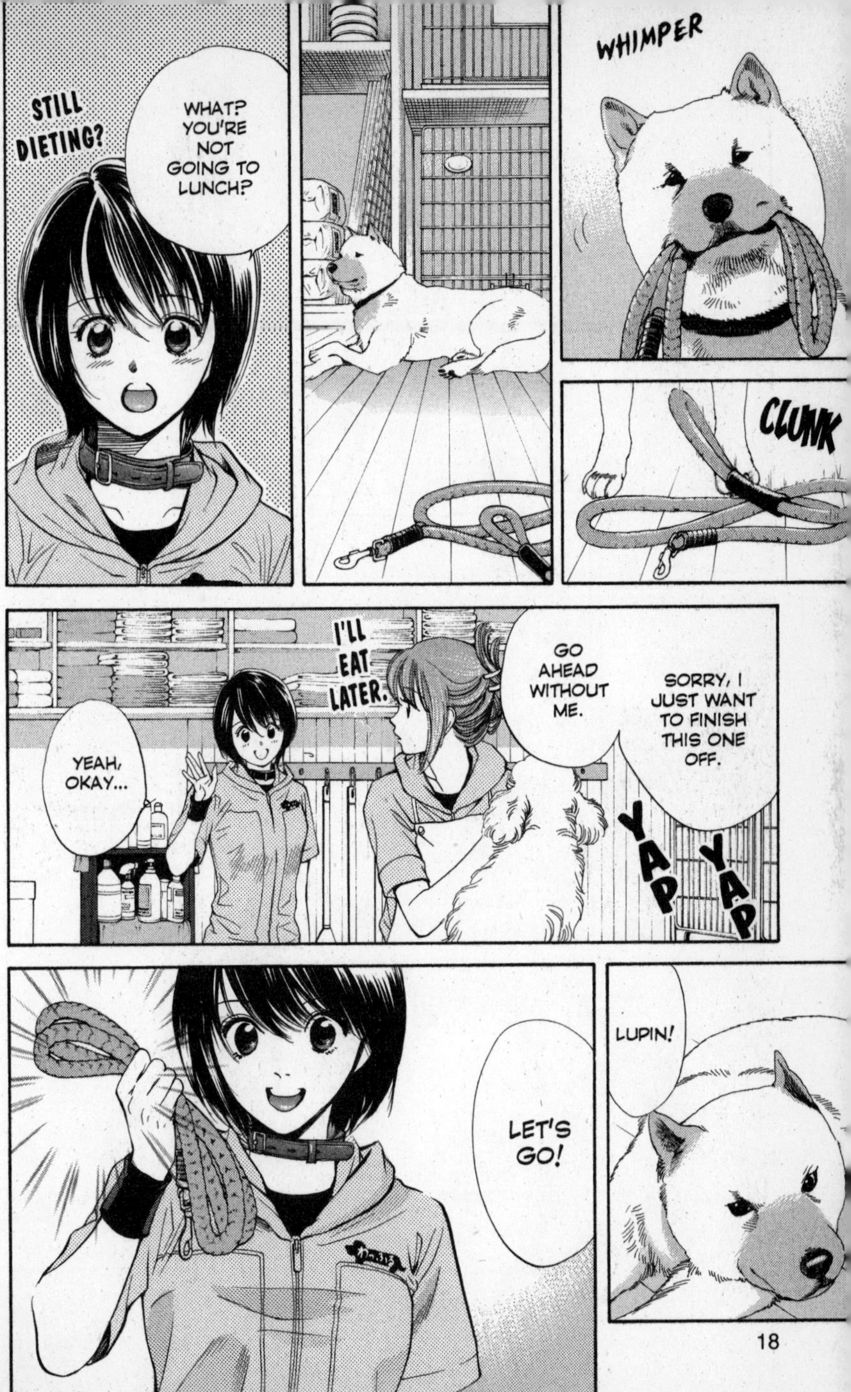
WHIMPER
CLUNK
WHAT? YOU'RE NOT GOING TO LUNCH?
STILL DIETING?
SORRY, I JUST WANT TO FINISH THIS ONE OFF.
GO AHEAD WITHOUT ME.
I'LL EAT LATER.
YAP YAP
YEAH, OKAY...
LUPIN!
LET'S GO!

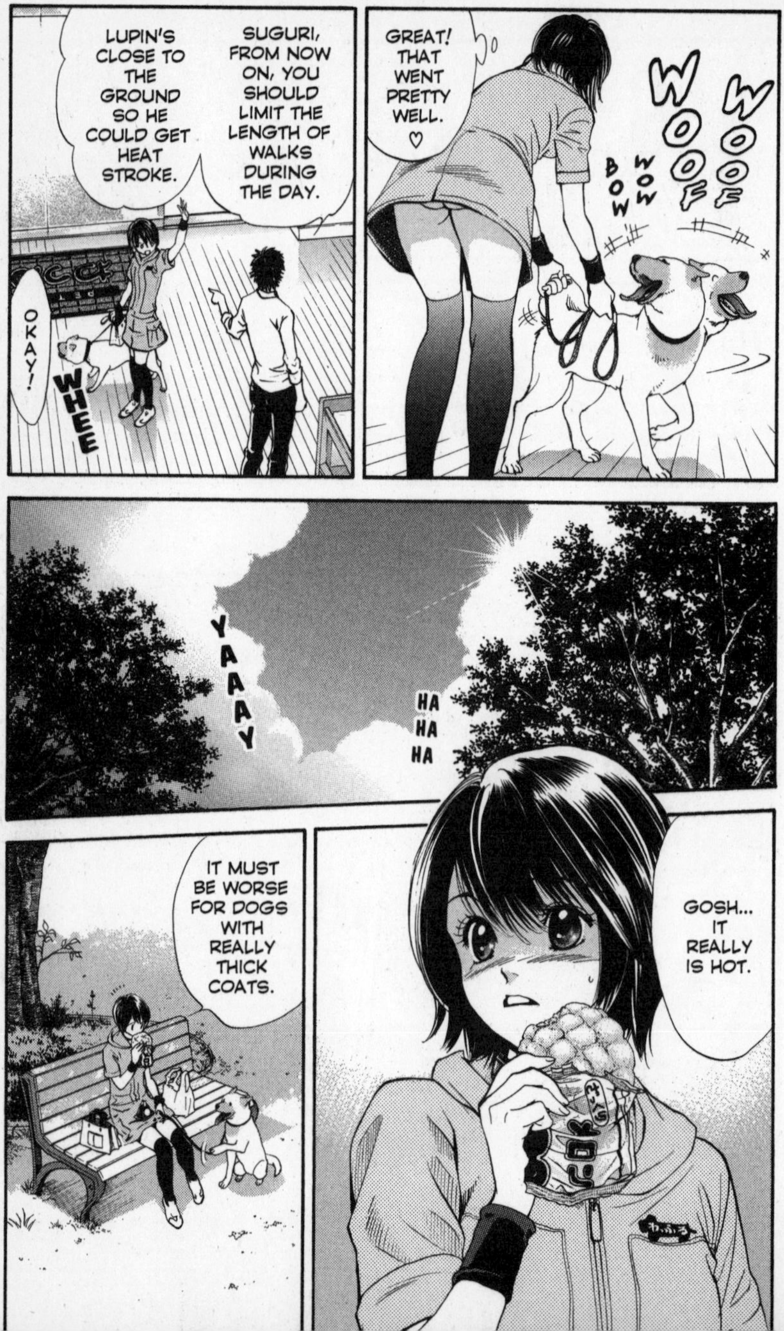
GREAT! THAT WENT PRETTY WELL. ♡
WOOF WOOF
BOW WOW
SUGURI, FROM NOW ON, YOU SHOULD LIMIT THE LENGTH OF WALKS DURING THE DAY.
LUPIN'S CLOSE TO THE GROUND SO HE COULD GET HEAT STROKE.
OKAY!
WHEE
YAAAY
HA HA HA
GOSH... IT REALLY IS HOT.
IT MUST BE WORSE FOR DOGS WITH REALLY THICK COATS.

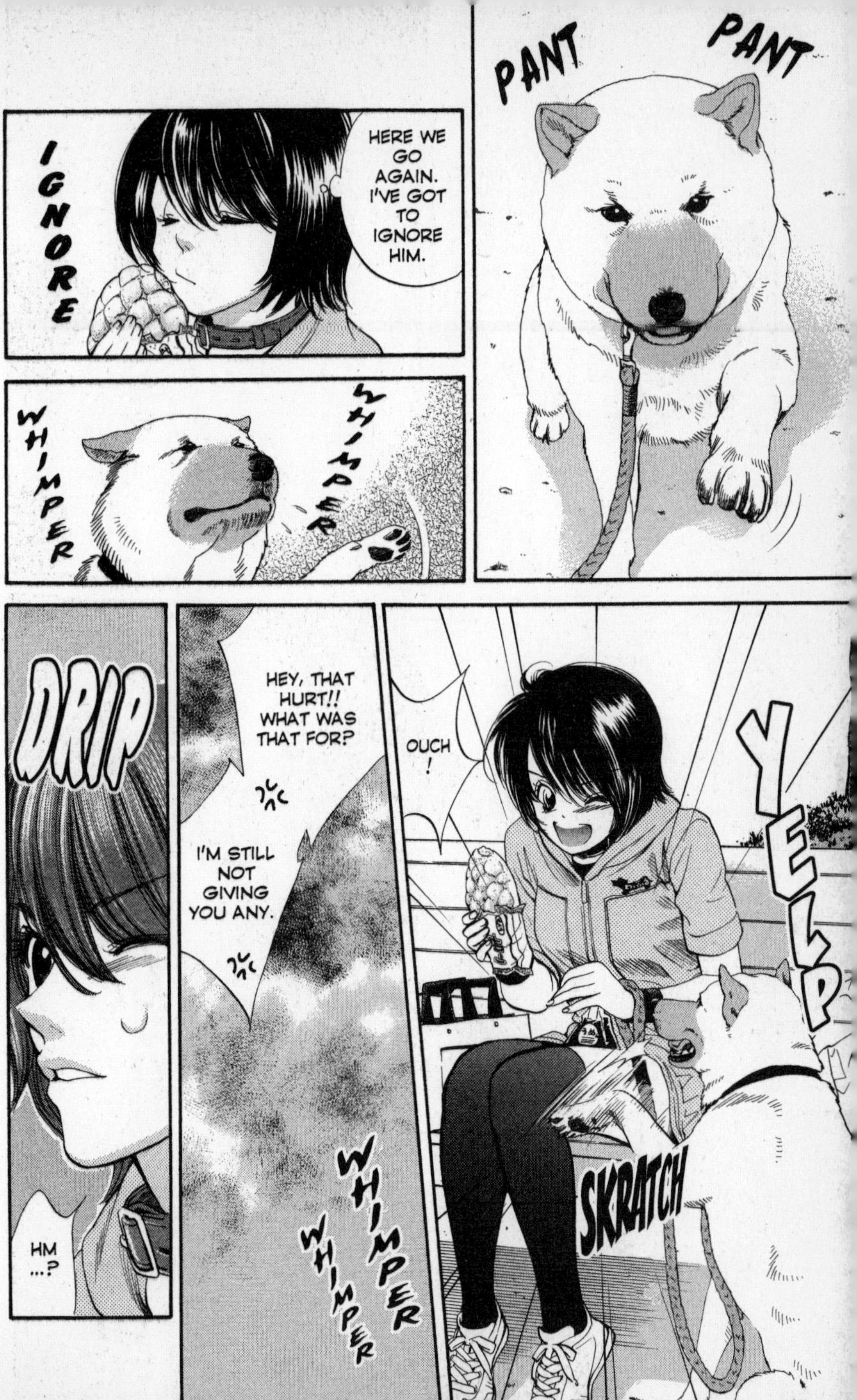
PANT
PANT
IGNORE
HERE WE GO AGAIN. I'VE GOT TO IGNORE HIM.
WHIMPER
WHIMPER
YELP
OUCH!
SKRATCH
HEY, THAT HURT!! WHAT WAS THAT FOR?
I'M STILL NOT GIVING YOU ANY.
WHIMPER
WHIMPER
DRIP
HM ...?

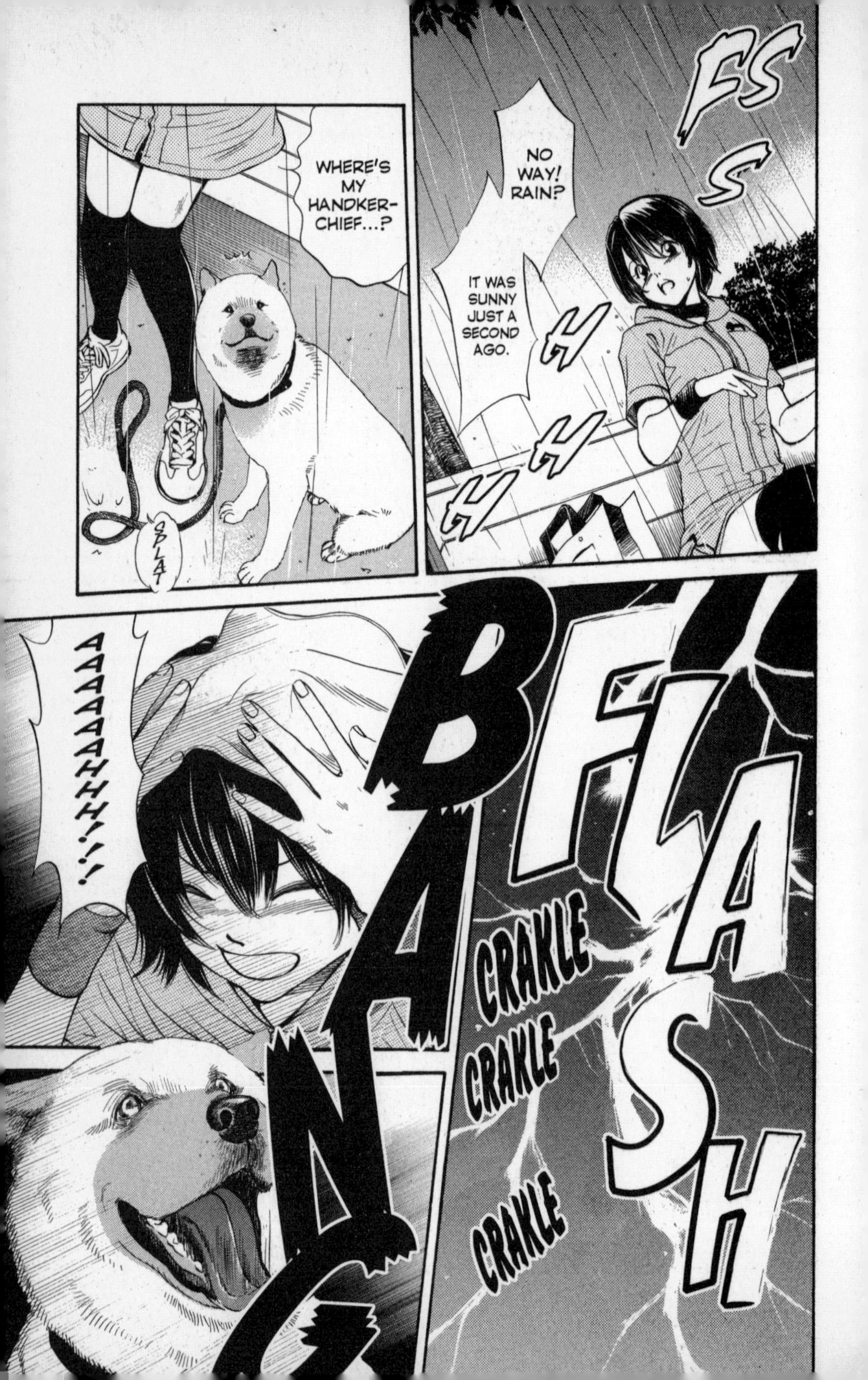
FSSS
NO WAY! RAIN?
IT WAS SUNNY JUST A SECOND AGO.
HHH
WHERE'S MY HANDKER-CHIEF...?
SPLAT
FLASH
CRAKLE
CRAKLE
CRAKLE
AAAAAAAHHH!!!

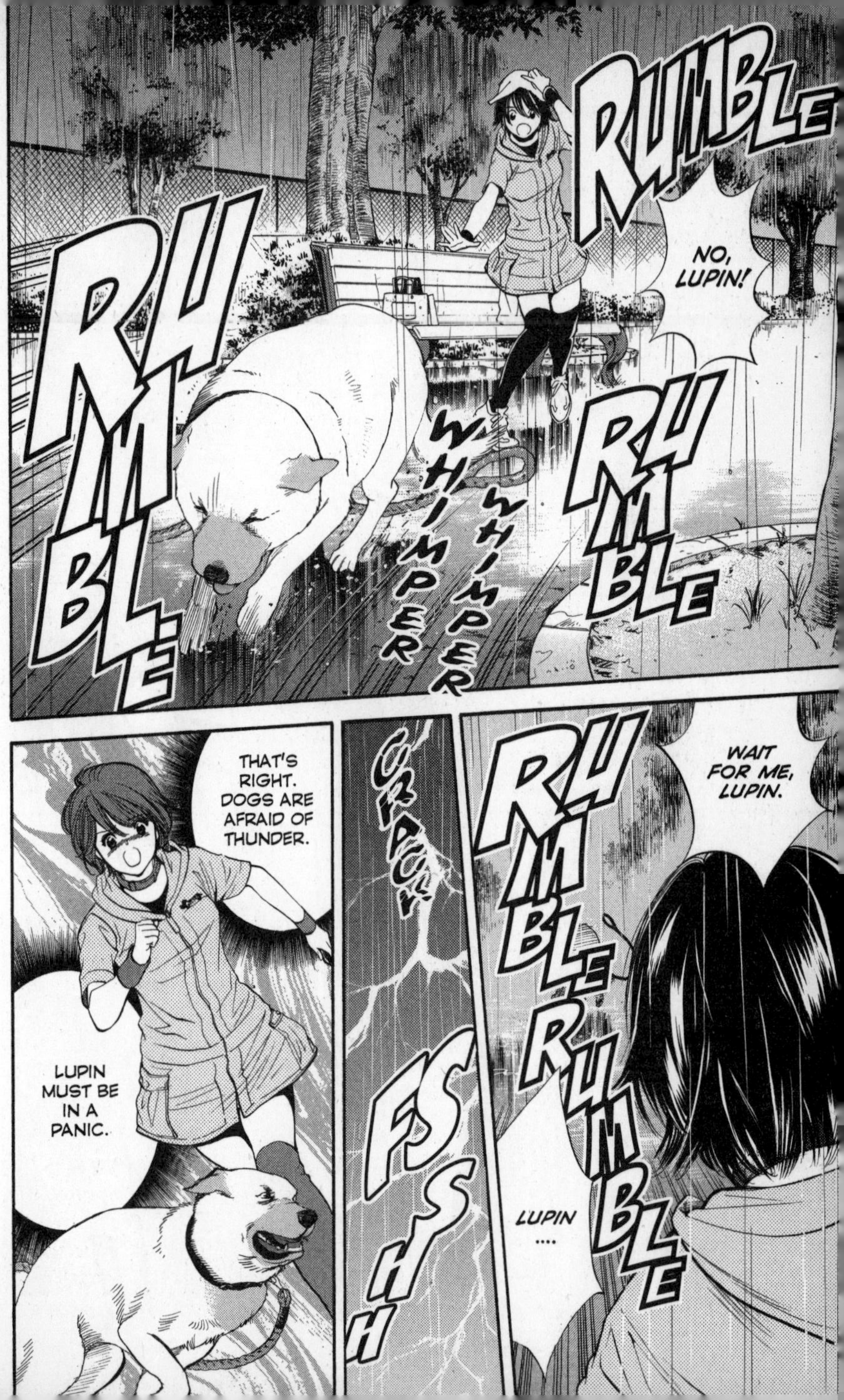
RUMBLE
NO, LUPIN!
RUMBLE
WHIMPER
WHIMPER
RUMBLE
WAIT FOR ME, LUPIN.
RUMBLE RUMBLE
LUPIN ....
CRACK
FSSHH
THAT'S RIGHT. DOGS ARE AFRAID OF THUNDER.
LUPIN MUST BE IN A PANIC..

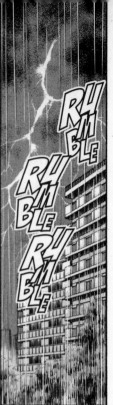

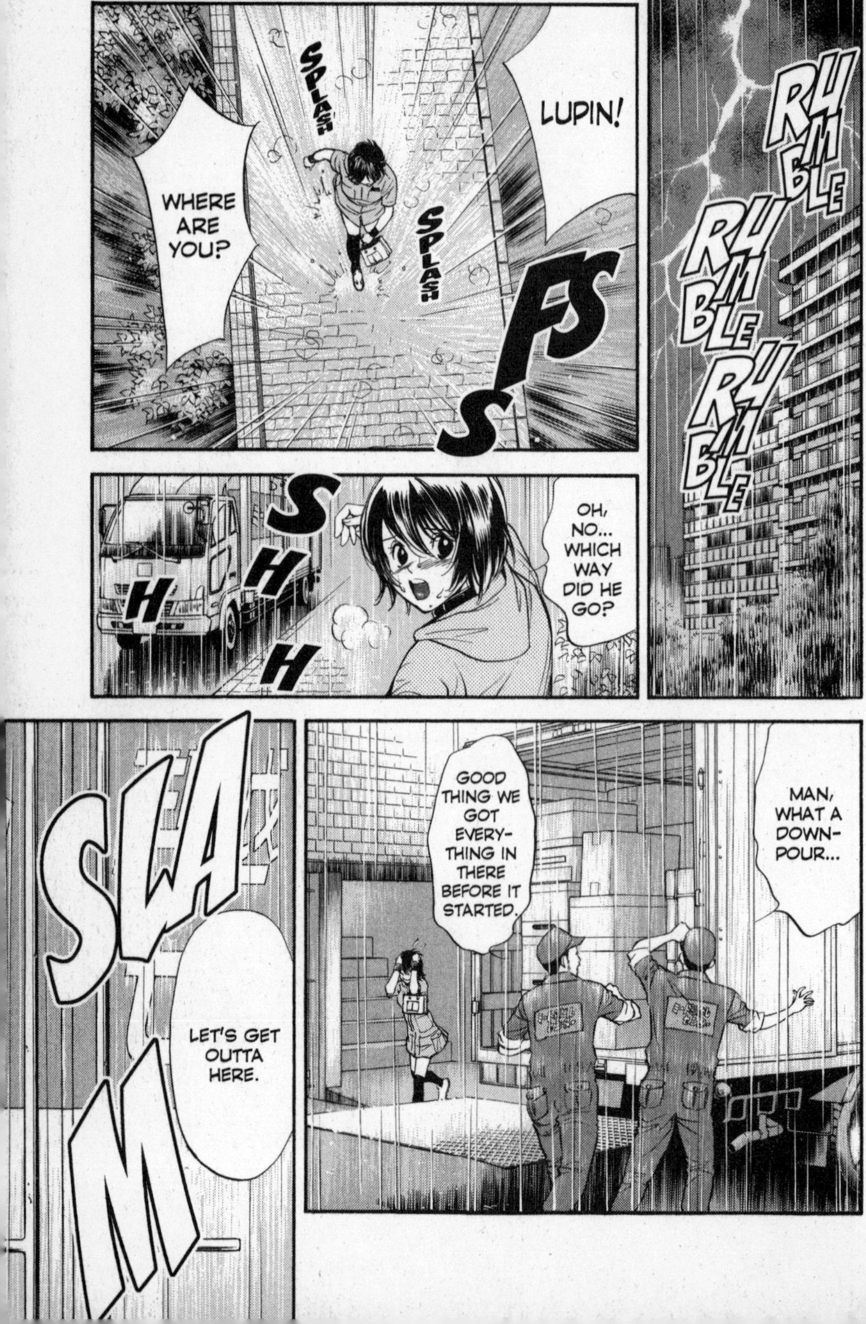
RUMBLE
RUMBLE
RUMBLE
LUPIN!
SPLASH
SPLASH
WHERE ARE YOU?
FSS
OH, NO... WHICH WAY DID HE GO?
SHHH
MAN, WHAT A DOWN-POUR...
GOOD THING WE GOT EVERY-THING IN THERE BEFORE IT STARTED.
SLAM
LET'S GET OUTTA HERE.

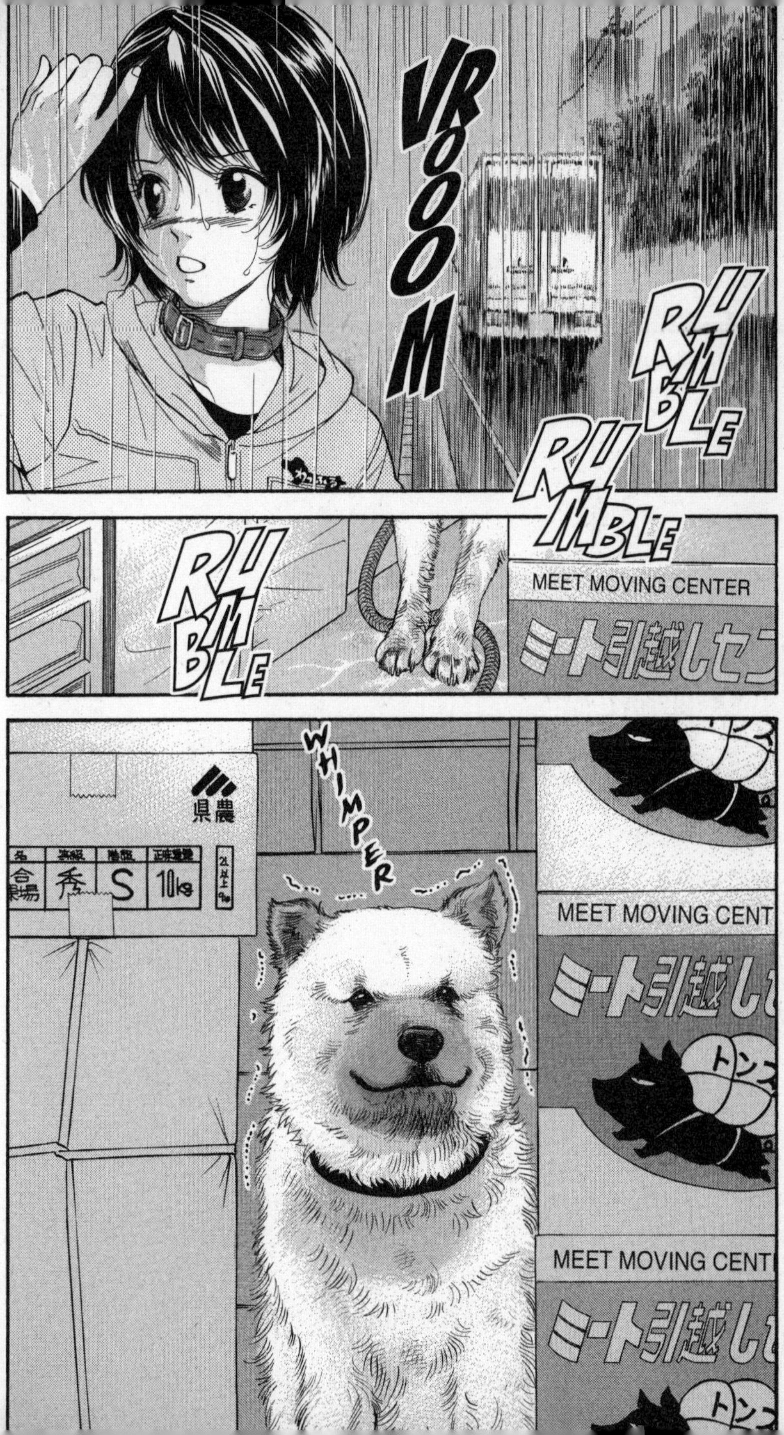
VROOOOM
RUMBLE
RUMBLE
RUMBLE
MEET MOVING CENTER
ミート引越しセン
県農
秀
S
10kg
WHIMPER
MEET MOVING CENT
MEET MOVING CENT

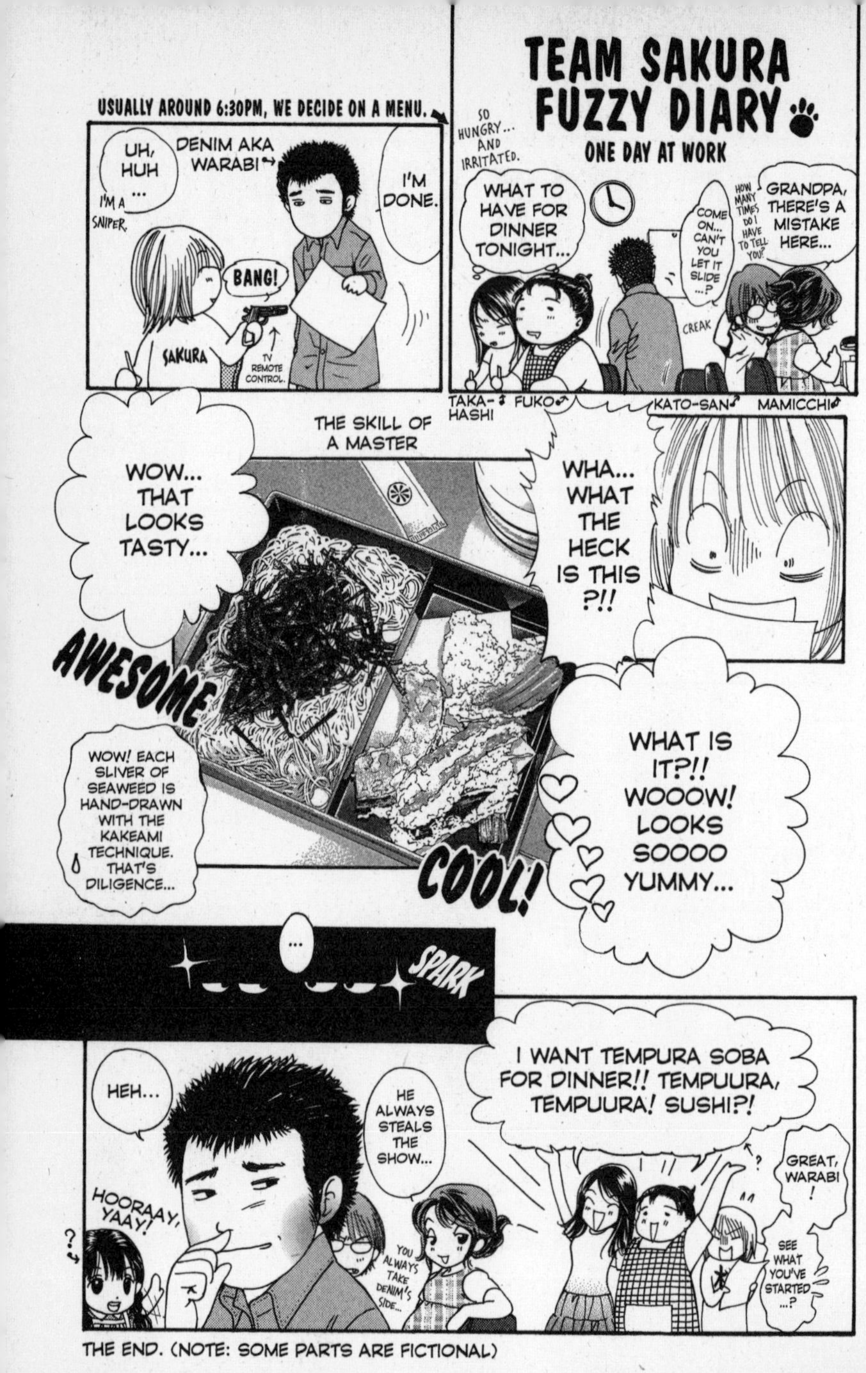
TEAM SAKURA FUZZY DIARY
ONE DAY AT WORK
GRANDPA, THERE'S A MISTAKE HERE...
HOW MANY TIMES DO I HAVE TO TELL YOU?
COME ON... CAN'T YOU LET IT SLIDE...?
SO HUNGRY... AND IRRITATED.
WHAT TO HAVE FOR DINNER TONIGHT...
CREAK
MAMICCHI
KATO-SAN
FUKO
TAKA-HASHI
USUALLY AROUND 6:30PM, WE DECIDE ON A MENU.
I'M DONE.
DENIM AKA WARABI
UH, HUH ...
I'M A SNIPER.
BANG!
TV REMOTE CONTROL.
SAKURA
WHA... WHAT THE HECK IS THIS ?!!
THE SKILL OF A MASTER
WOW... THAT LOOKS TASTY...
AWESOME
WHAT IS IT?!! WOOOW! LOOKS SOOOO YUMMY...
COOL!
WOW! EACH SLIVER OF SEAWEED IS HAND-DRAWN WITH THE KAKEAMI TECHNIQUE. THAT'S DILIGENCE...
SPARK
...
I WANT TEMPURA SOBA FOR DINNER!! TEMPUURA, TEMPUURA! SUSHI?!
GREAT, WARABI !
SEE WHAT YOU'VE STARTED ...?
?
HE ALWAYS STEALS THE SHOW...
YOU ALWAYS TAKE DENIM'S SIDE...
HEH...
HOORAAY, YAAY!
?

THE END. (NOTE: SOME PARTS ARE FICTIONAL)

CHAPTER 77 SEPARATION

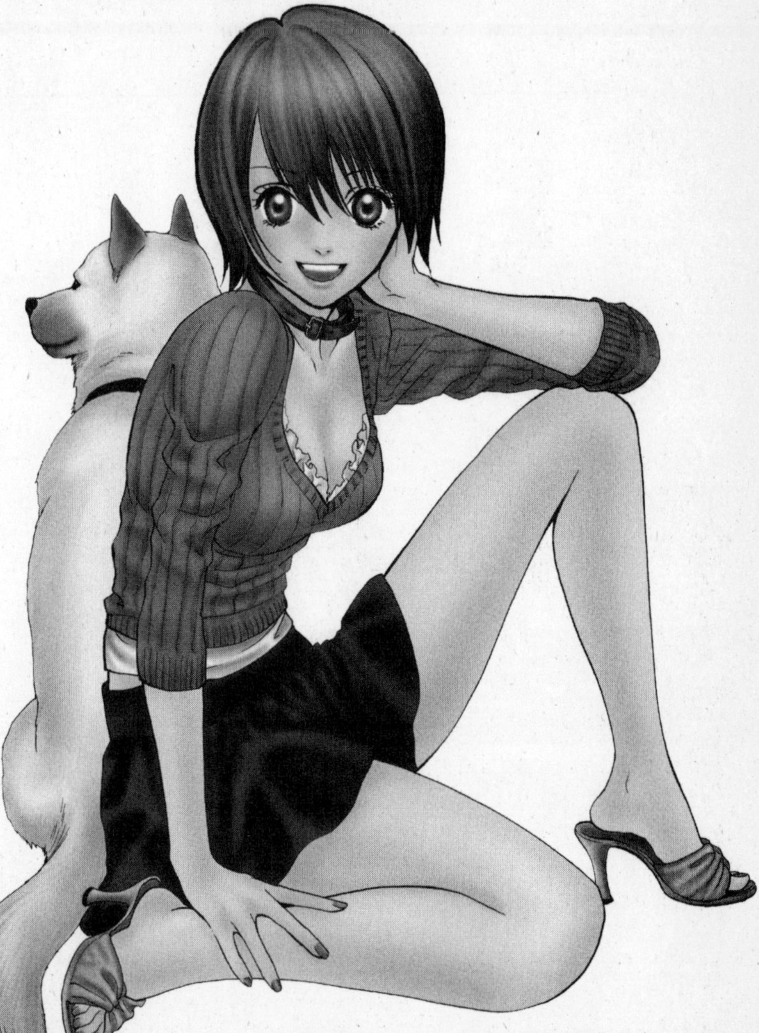

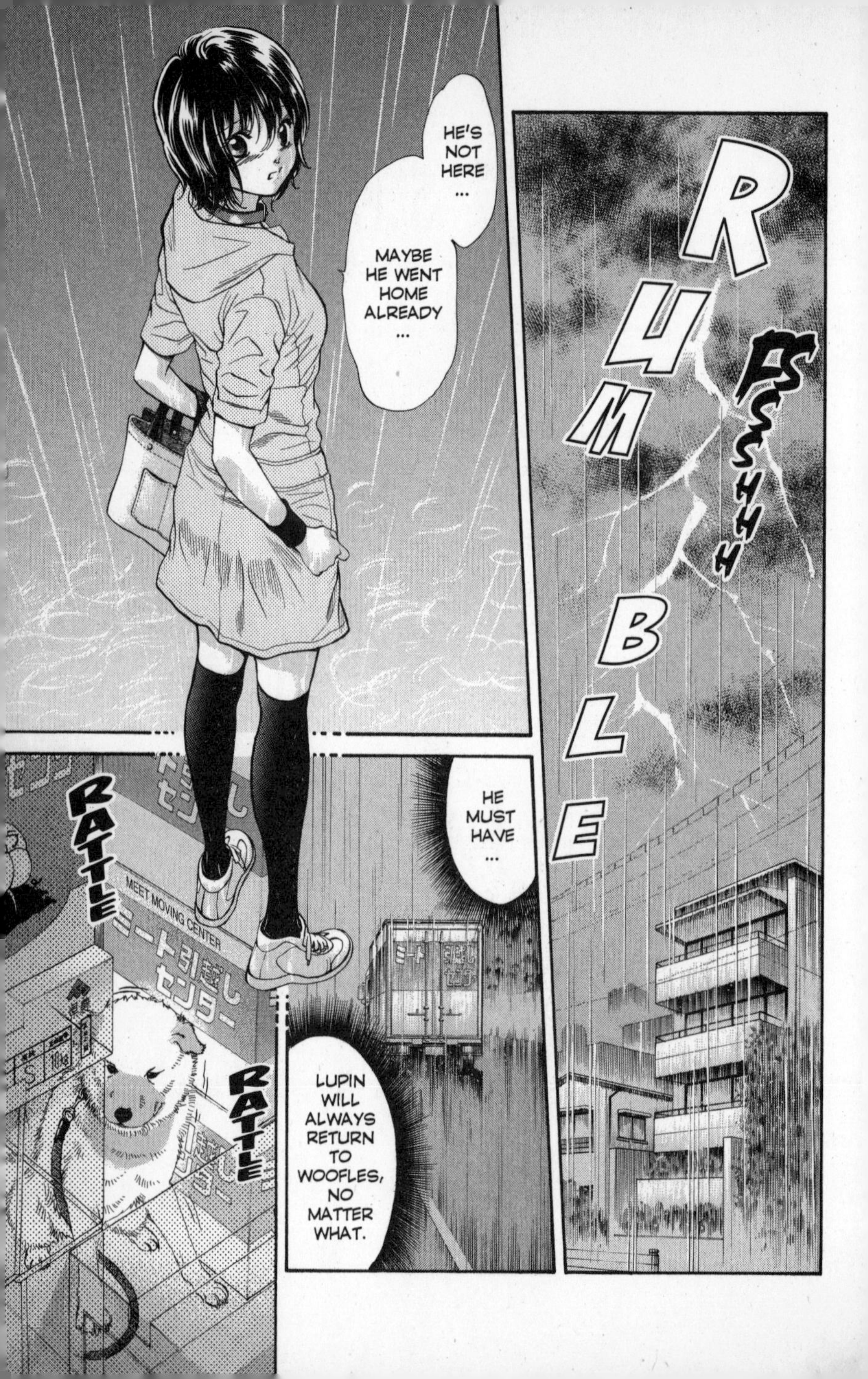
RUMBLE
PSSHHH
HE'S NOT HERE ...
MAYBE HE WENT HOME ALREADY ...
HE MUST HAVE ...
LUPIN WILL ALWAYS RETURN TO WOOFLES, NO MATTER WHAT.
RATTLE
RATTLE
MEET MOVING CENTER
ミート引越しセンター

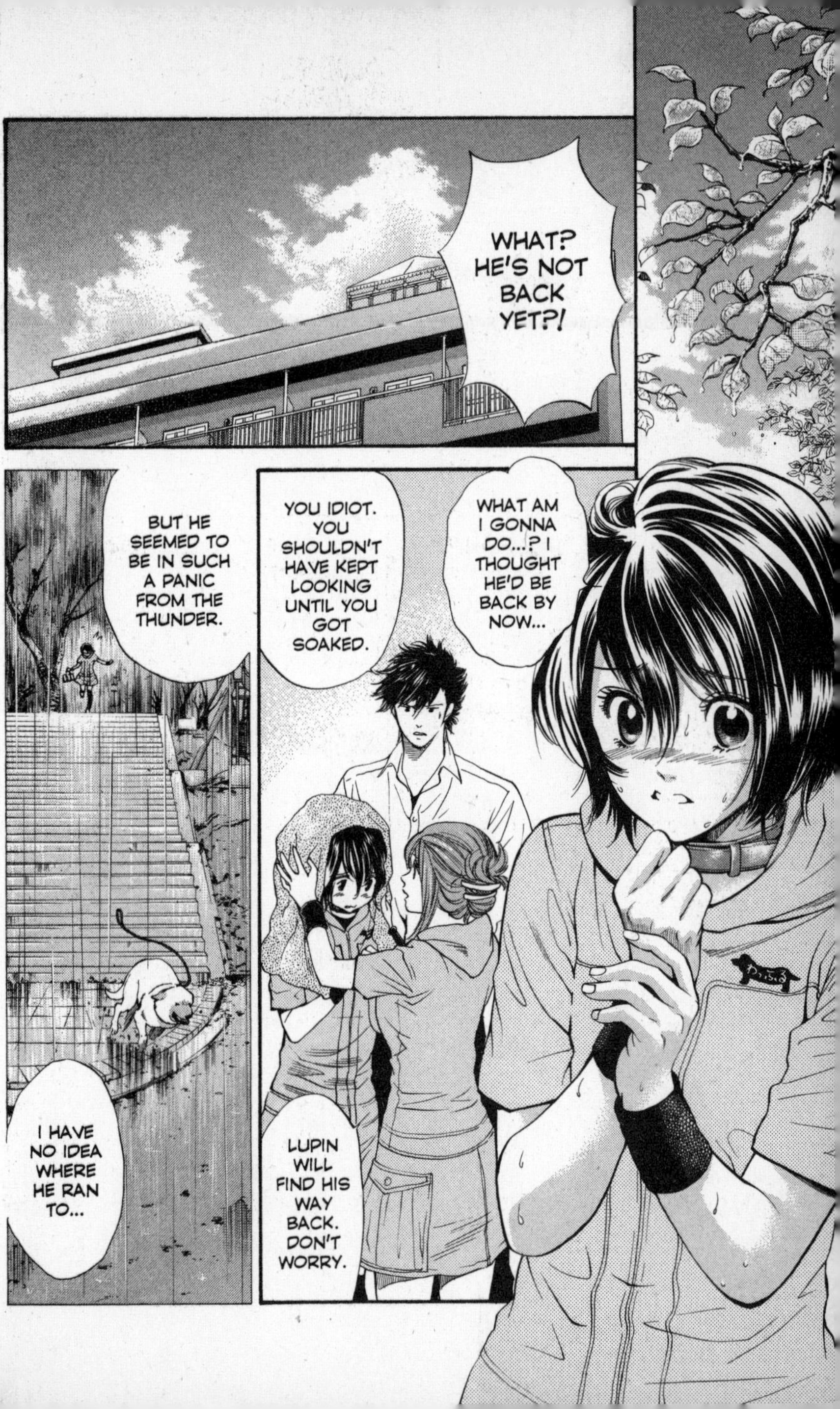
WHAT? HE'S NOT BACK YET?!
WHAT AM I GONNA DO...? I THOUGHT HE'D BE BACK BY NOW...
YOU IDIOT. YOU SHOULDN'T HAVE KEPT LOOKING UNTIL YOU GOT SOAKED.
LUPIN WILL FIND HIS WAY BACK. DON'T WORRY.
BUT HE SEEMED TO BE IN SUCH A PANIC FROM THE THUNDER.
I HAVE NO IDEA WHERE HE RAN TO...

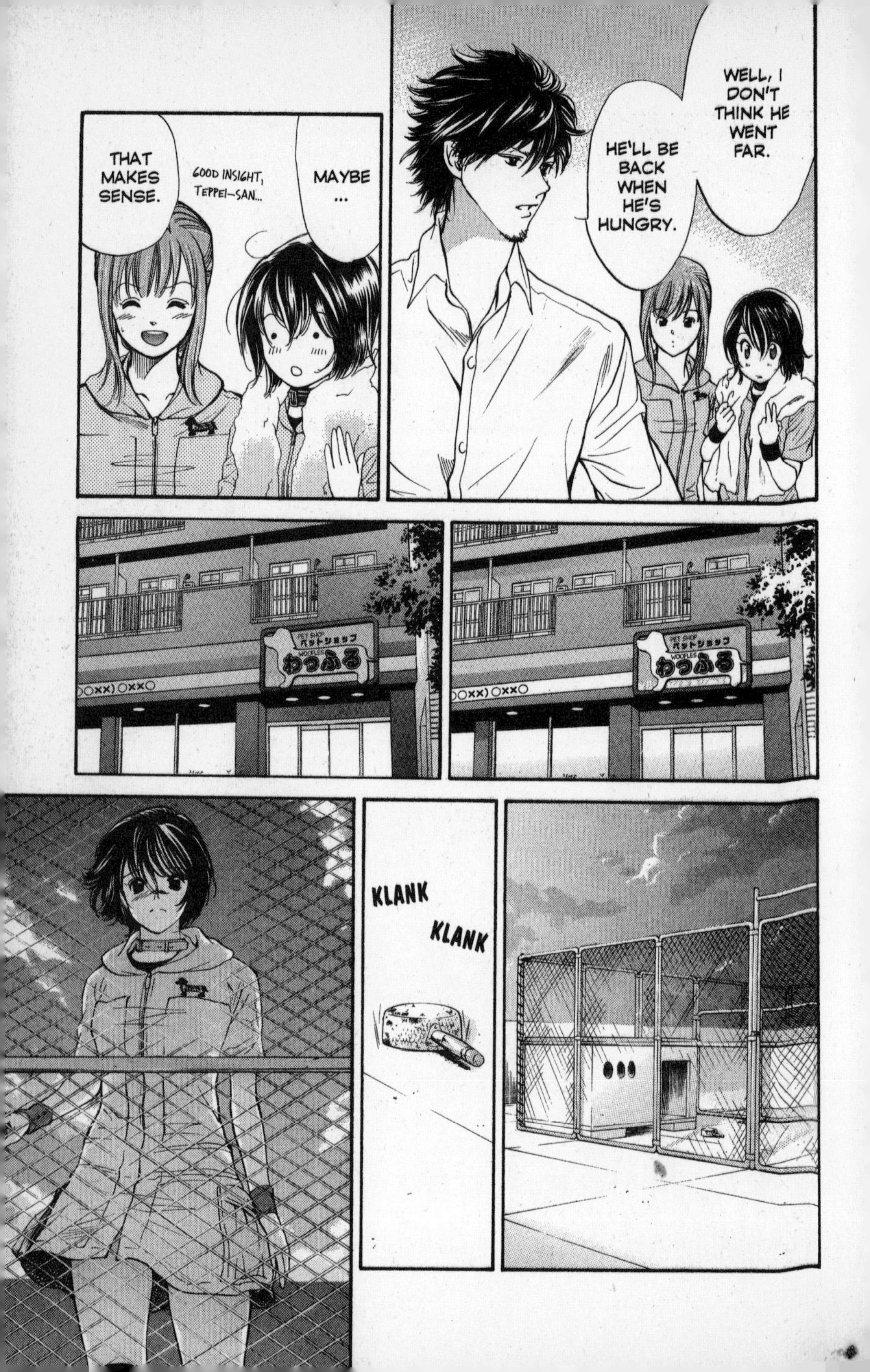
WELL, I DON'T THINK HE WENT FAR.
HE'LL BE BACK WHEN HE'S HUNGRY.
MAYBE ...
GOOD INSIGHT, TEPPEI-SAN...
THAT MAKES SENSE.
PET SHOP ペットショップ WOOFLES わっふる
KLANK
KLANK

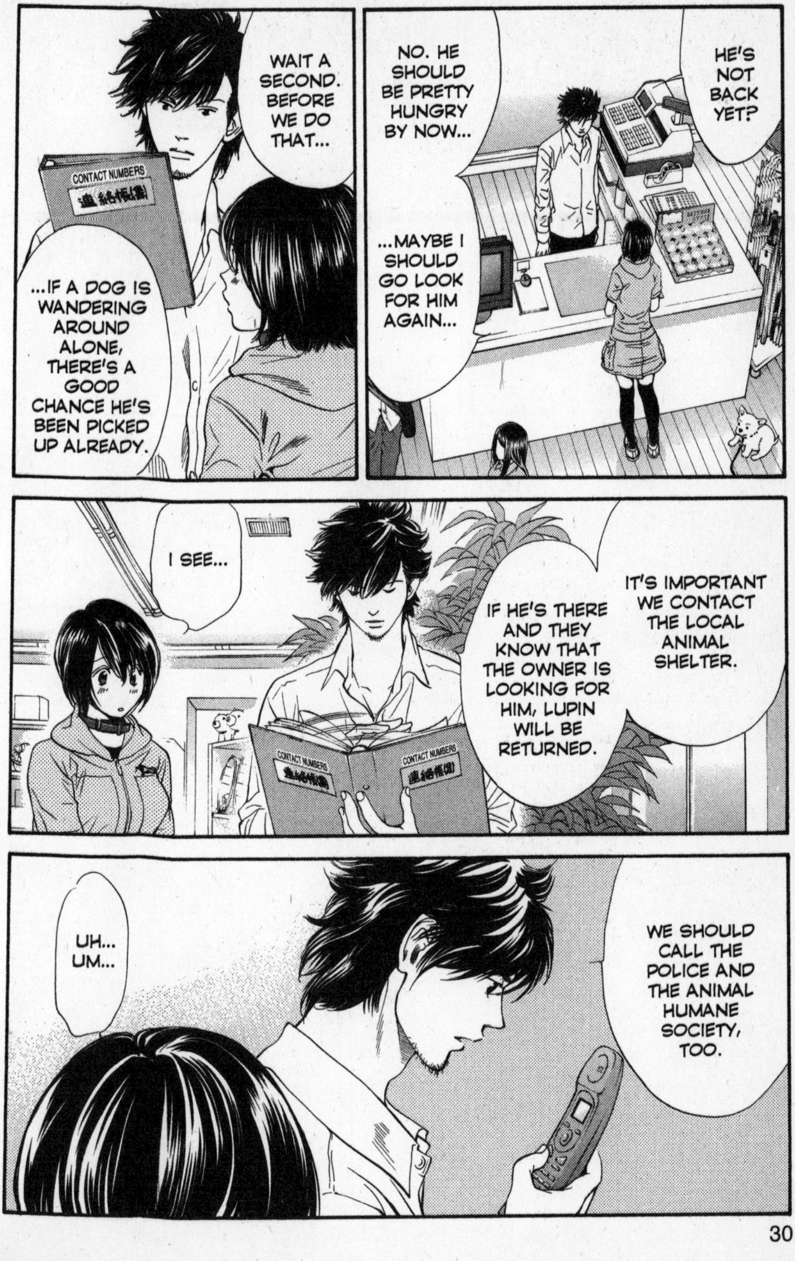
HE'S NOT BACK YET?
NO. HE SHOULD BE PRETTY HUNGRY BY NOW...
...MAYBE I SHOULD GO LOOK FOR HIM AGAIN...
WAIT A SECOND. BEFORE WE DO THAT...
CONTACT NUMBERS
...IF A DOG IS WANDERING AROUND ALONE, THERE'S A GOOD CHANCE HE'S BEEN PICKED UP ALREADY.
IT'S IMPORTANT WE CONTACT THE LOCAL ANIMAL SHELTER.
IF HE'S THERE AND THEY KNOW THAT THE OWNER IS LOOKING FOR HIM, LUPIN WILL BE RETURNED.
CONTACT NUMBERS
I SEE...
WE SHOULD CALL THE POLICE AND THE ANIMAL HUMANE SOCIETY, TOO.
UH... UM...

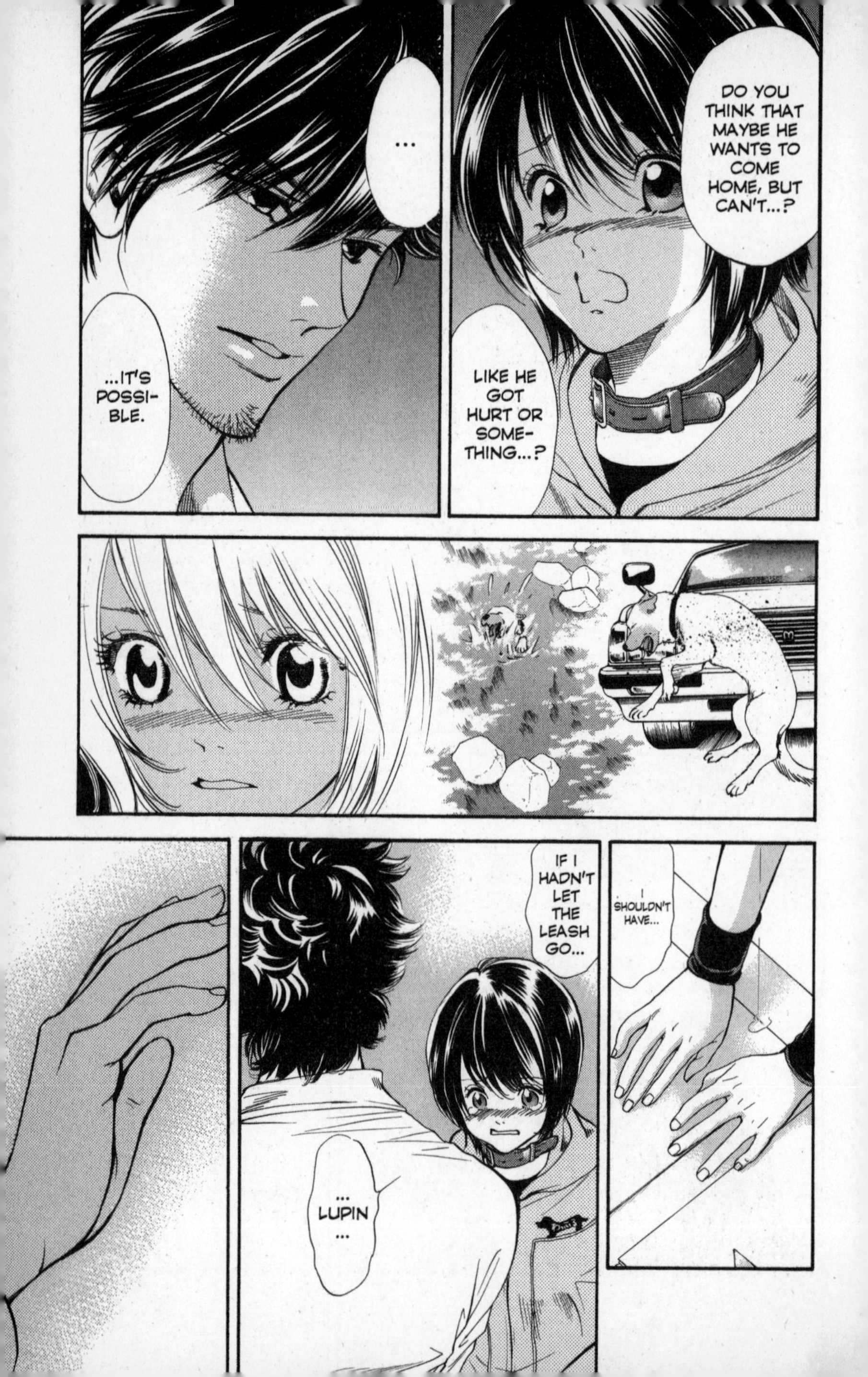
DO YOU THINK THAT MAYBE HE WANTS TO COME HOME, BUT CAN'T...?
LIKE HE GOT HURT OR SOMETHING...?
...
...IT'S POSSIBLE.
I SHOULDN'T HAVE...
IF I HADN'T LET THE LEASH GO...
... LUPIN ...

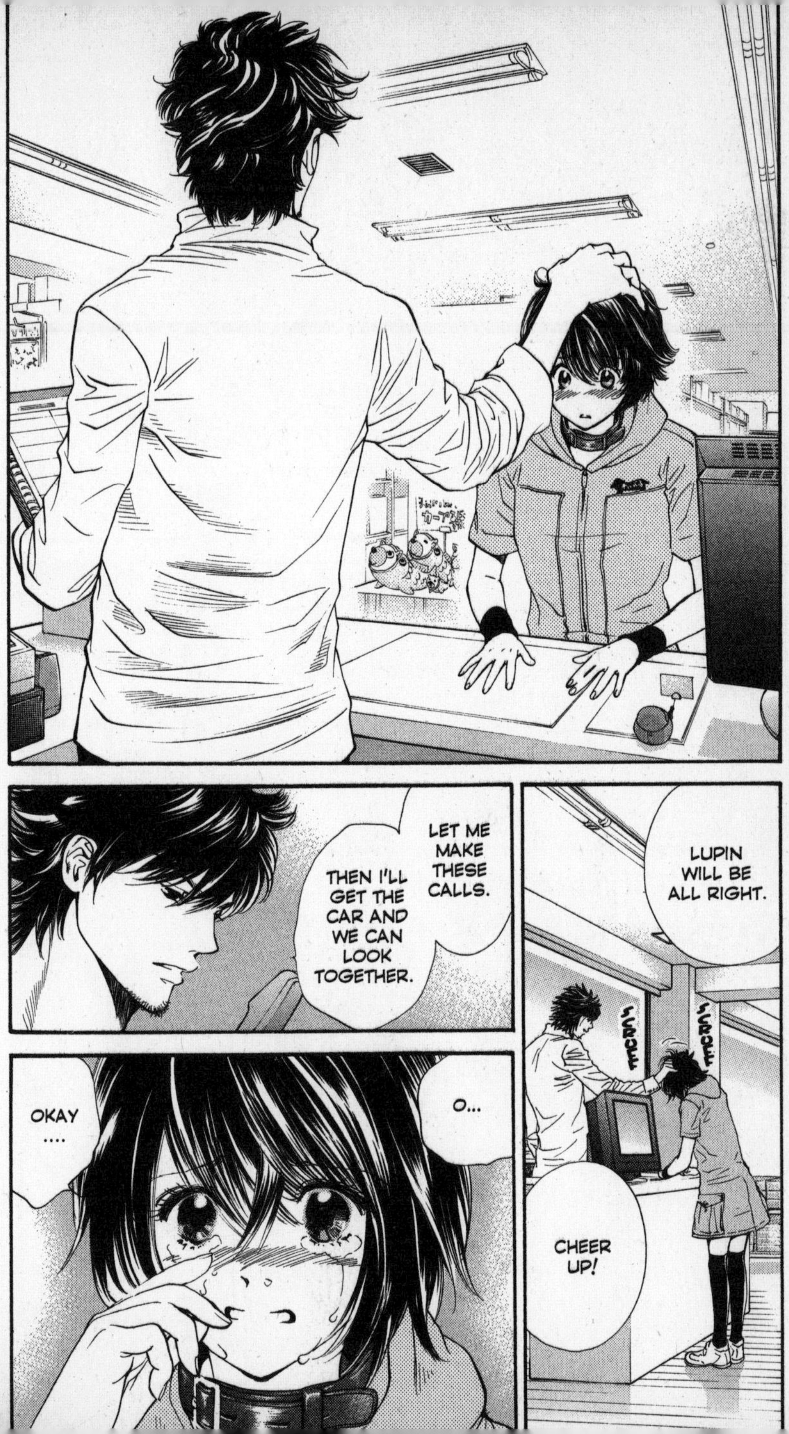
LUPIN WILL BE ALL RIGHT.
SCRUFF
SCRUFF
CHEER UP!
LET ME MAKE THESE CALLS.
THEN I'LL GET THE CAR AND WE CAN LOOK TOGETHER.
O...
OKAY ....

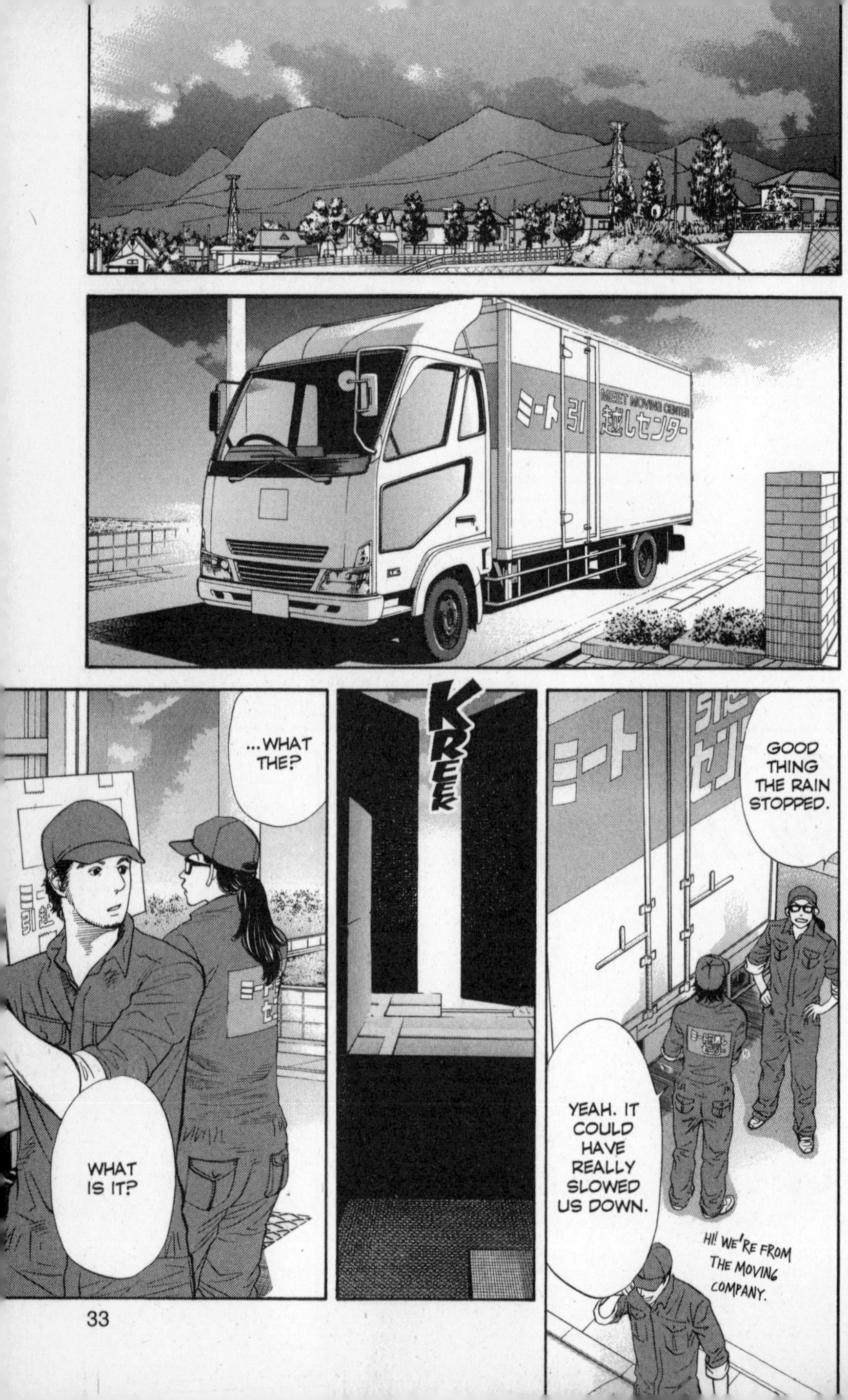
MEET MOVING CENTER
ミート引越しセンター
GOOD THING THE RAIN STOPPED.
YEAH. IT COULD HAVE REALLY SLOWED US DOWN.
HI! WE'RE FROM THE MOVING COMPANY.
KREEK
...WHAT THE?
WHAT IS IT?

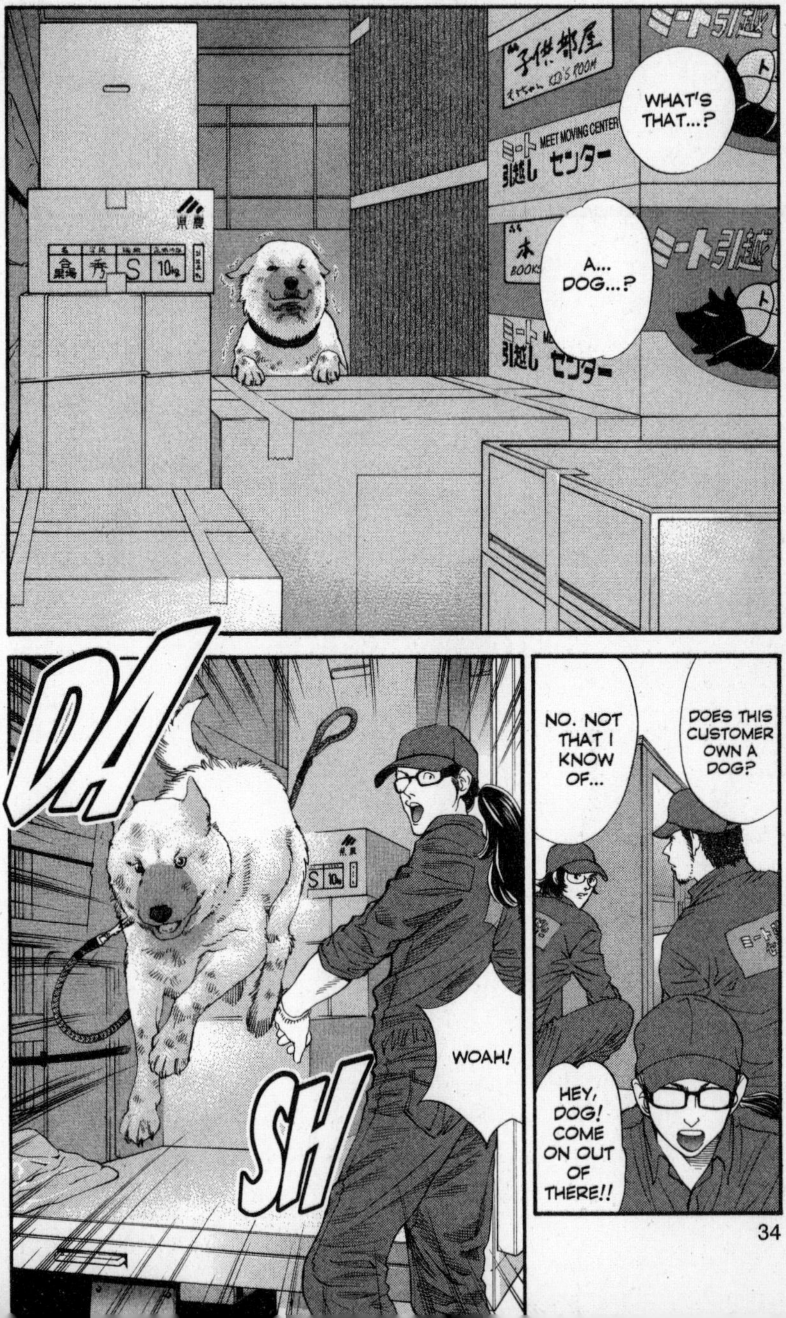
子供部屋
KID'S ROOM
MEET MOVING CENTER
ミート引越しセンター
本
BOOKS
WHAT'S THAT...?
A... DOG...?
DOES THIS CUSTOMER OWN A DOG?
NO. NOT THAT I KNOW OF...
HEY, DOG! COME ON OUT OF THERE!!
DA
WOAH!
SH

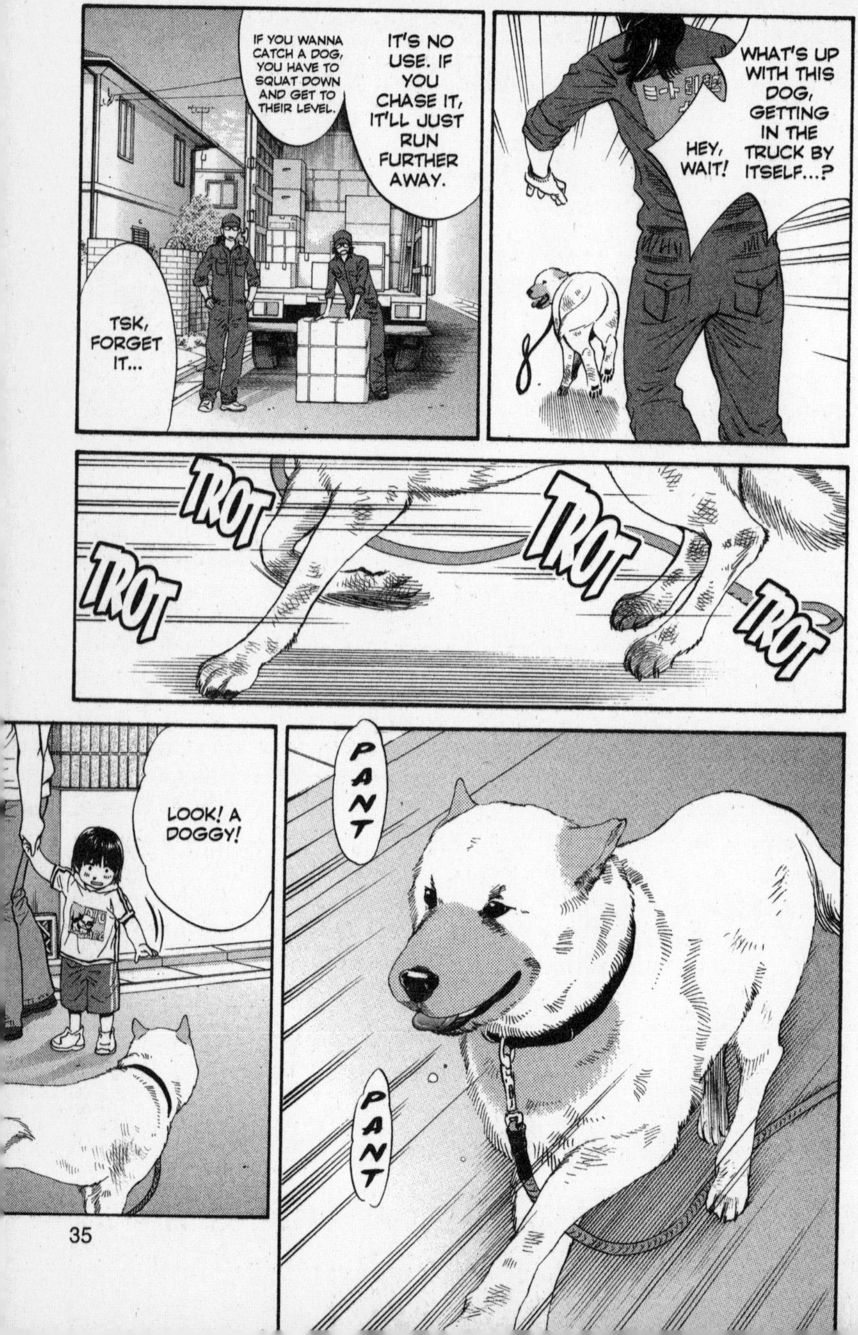
WHAT'S UP WITH THIS DOG, GETTING IN THE TRUCK BY ITSELF...?
HEY, WAIT!
IT'S NO USE. IF YOU CHASE IT, IT'LL JUST RUN FURTHER AWAY.
IF YOU WANNA CATCH A DOG, YOU HAVE TO SQUAT DOWN AND GET TO THEIR LEVEL.
TSK, FORGET IT...
TROT
TROT
TROT
TROT
PANT
PANT
LOOK! A DOGGY!

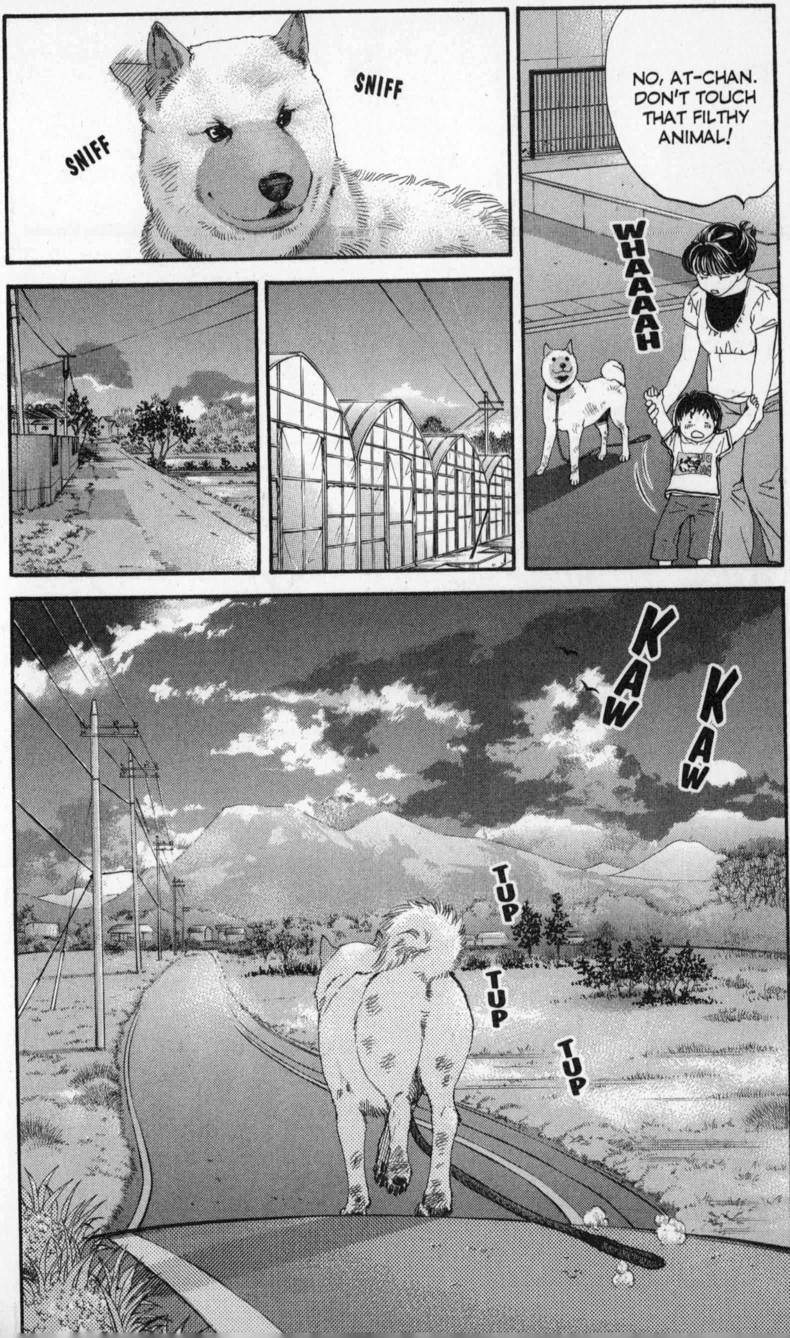
NO, AT-CHAN. DON'T TOUCH THAT FILTHY ANIMAL!
WHAAAAAH
SNIFF
SNIFF
KAW
KAW
TUP
TUP
TUP

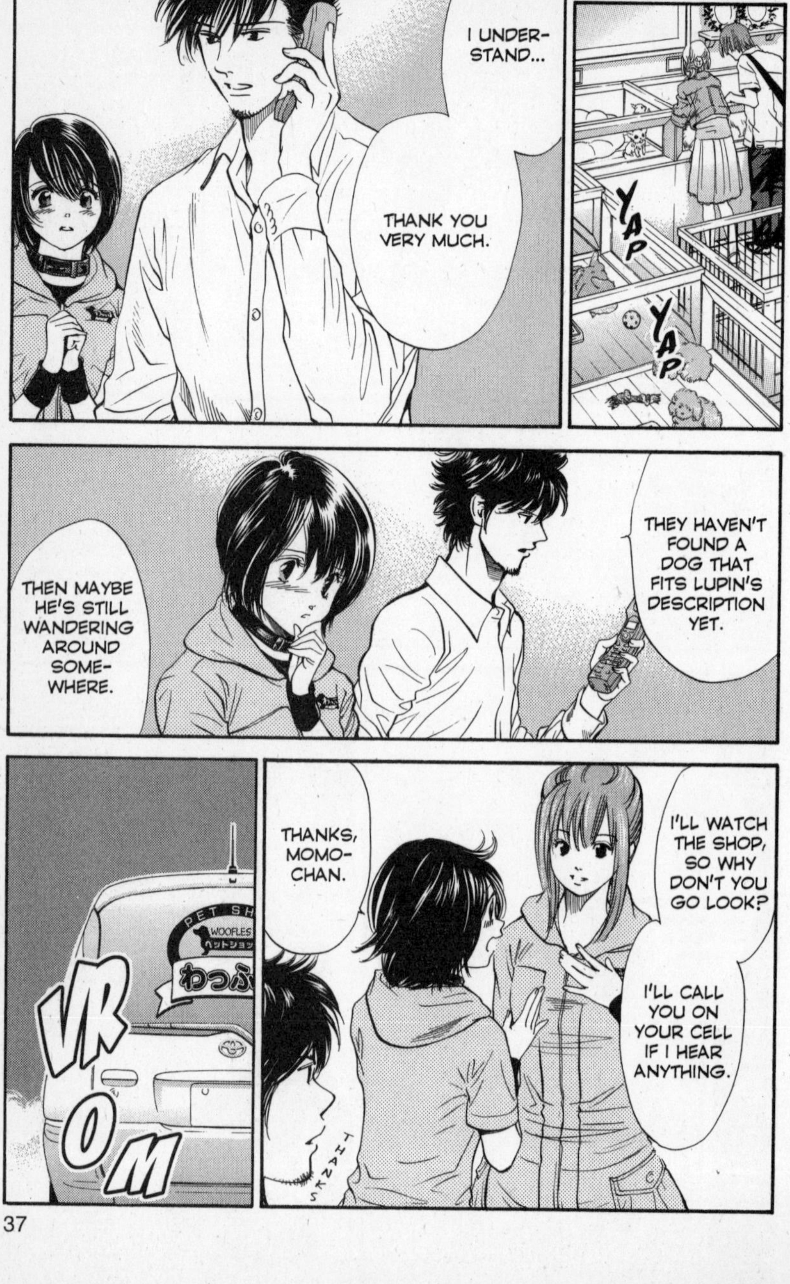
YAP
YAP
YAP
I UNDER-STAND...
THANK YOU VERY MUCH.
THEY HAVEN'T FOUND A DOG THAT FITS LUPIN'S DESCRIPTION YET.
THEN MAYBE HE'S STILL WANDERING AROUND SOME-WHERE.
I'LL WATCH THE SHOP, SO WHY DON'T YOU GO LOOK?
I'LL CALL YOU ON YOUR CELL IF I HEAR ANYTHING.
THANKS, MOMO-CHAN.
THANKS
WOOFLES
VROOM

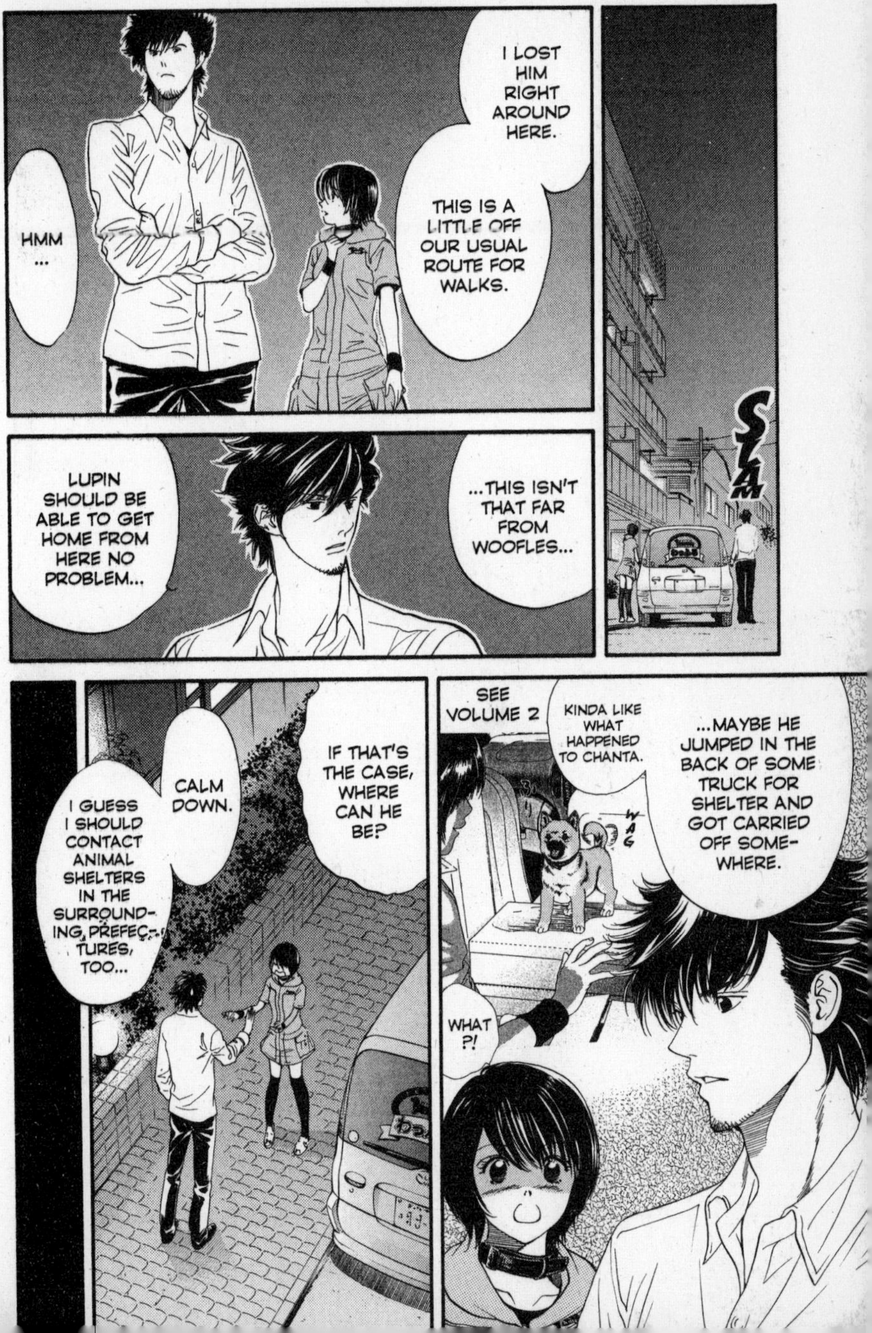
SLAM
I LOST HIM RIGHT AROUND HERE.
THIS IS A LITTLE OFF OUR USUAL ROUTE FOR WALKS.
HMM ...
...THIS ISN'T THAT FAR FROM WOOFLES...
LUPIN SHOULD BE ABLE TO GET HOME FROM HERE NO PROBLEM...
...MAYBE HE JUMPED IN THE BACK OF SOME TRUCK FOR SHELTER AND GOT CARRIED OFF SOME-WHERE.
KINDA LIKE WHAT HAPPENED TO CHANTA.
SEE VOLUME 2
WAG
WHAT ?!
IF THAT'S THE CASE, WHERE CAN HE BE?
CALM DOWN.
I GUESS I SHOULD CONTACT ANIMAL SHELTERS IN THE SURROUNDING PREFECTURES, TOO...

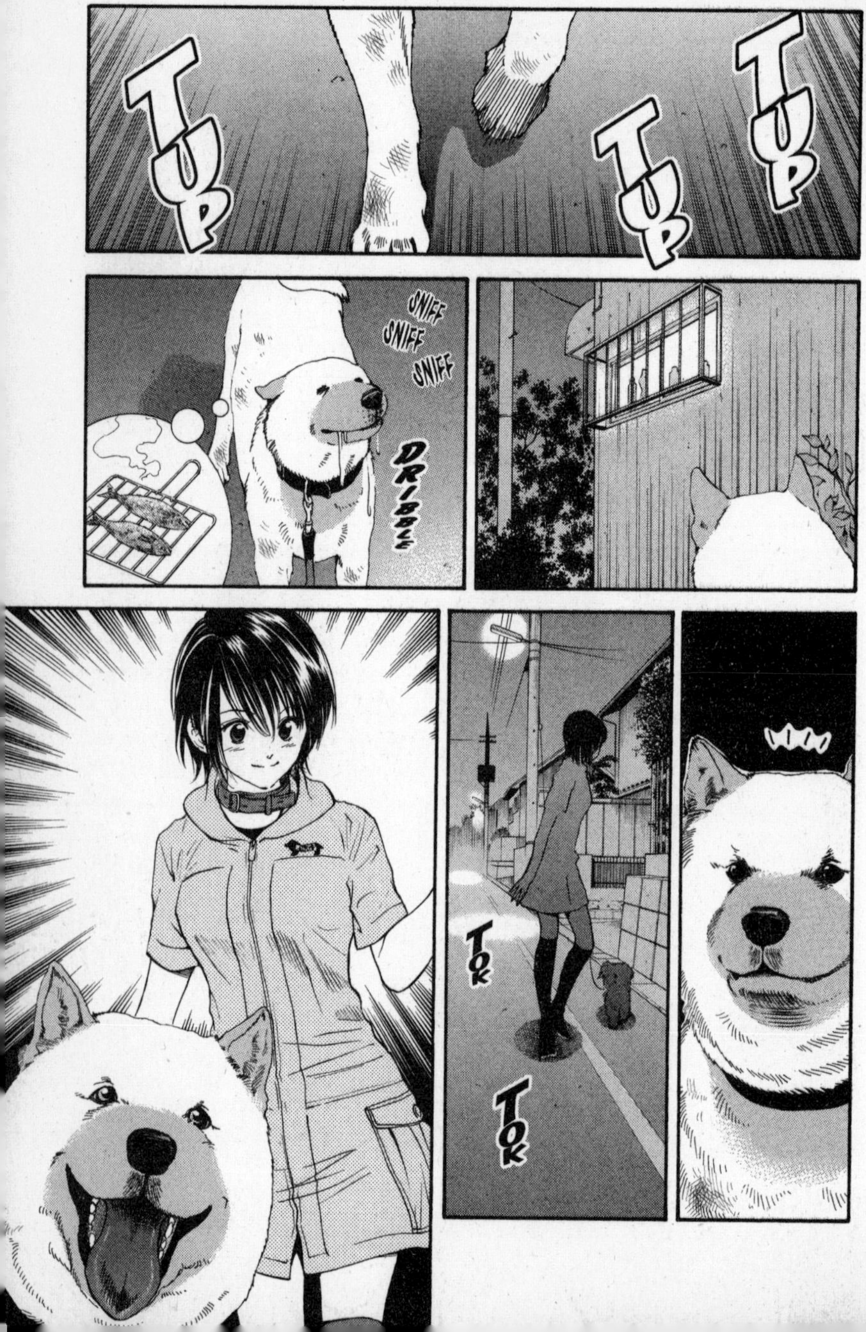
TUP
TUP
TUP
SNIFF
SNIFF
SNIFF
DRIBBLE
TOK
TOK

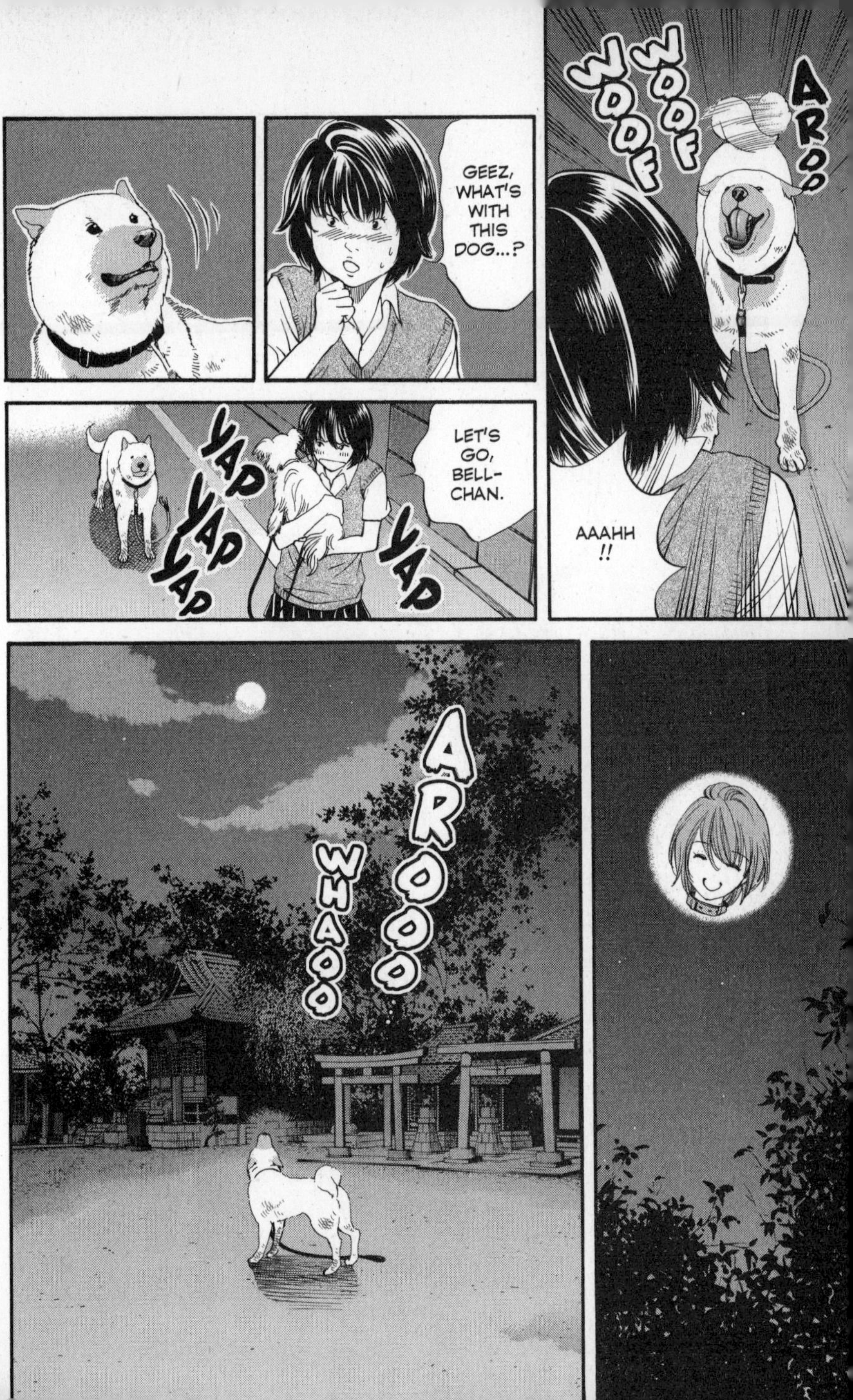
AROO
WOOF
WOOF
AAAHH !!
GEEZ, WHAT'S WITH THIS DOG...?
LET'S GO, BELL-CHAN.
YAP
YAP
YAP
YAP
AROOO
WHAOO

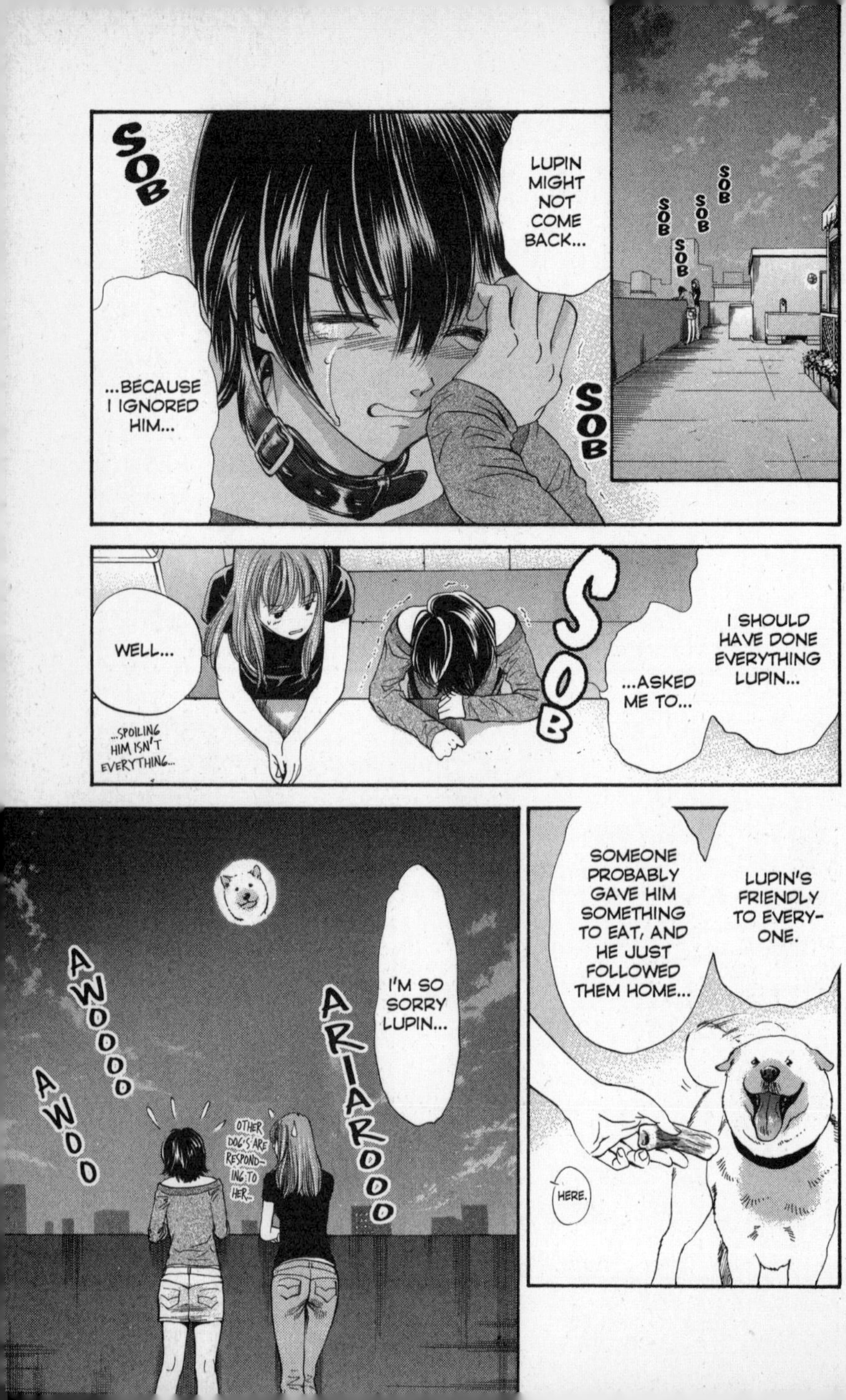
SOB
SOB
SOB
SOB
LUPIN MIGHT NOT COME BACK...
SOB
...BECAUSE I IGNORED HIM...
SOB
I SHOULD HAVE DONE EVERYTHING LUPIN...
...ASKED ME TO...
SOB
WELL...
...SPOILING HIM ISN'T EVERYTHING...
LUPIN'S FRIENDLY TO EVERY-ONE.
SOMEONE PROBABLY GAVE HIM SOMETHING TO EAT, AND HE JUST FOLLOWED THEM HOME...
HERE.
I'M SO SORRY LUPIN...
ARIAROOOO
AWOOOOO
AWOO
OTHER DOG'S ARE RESPOND-ING TO HER...

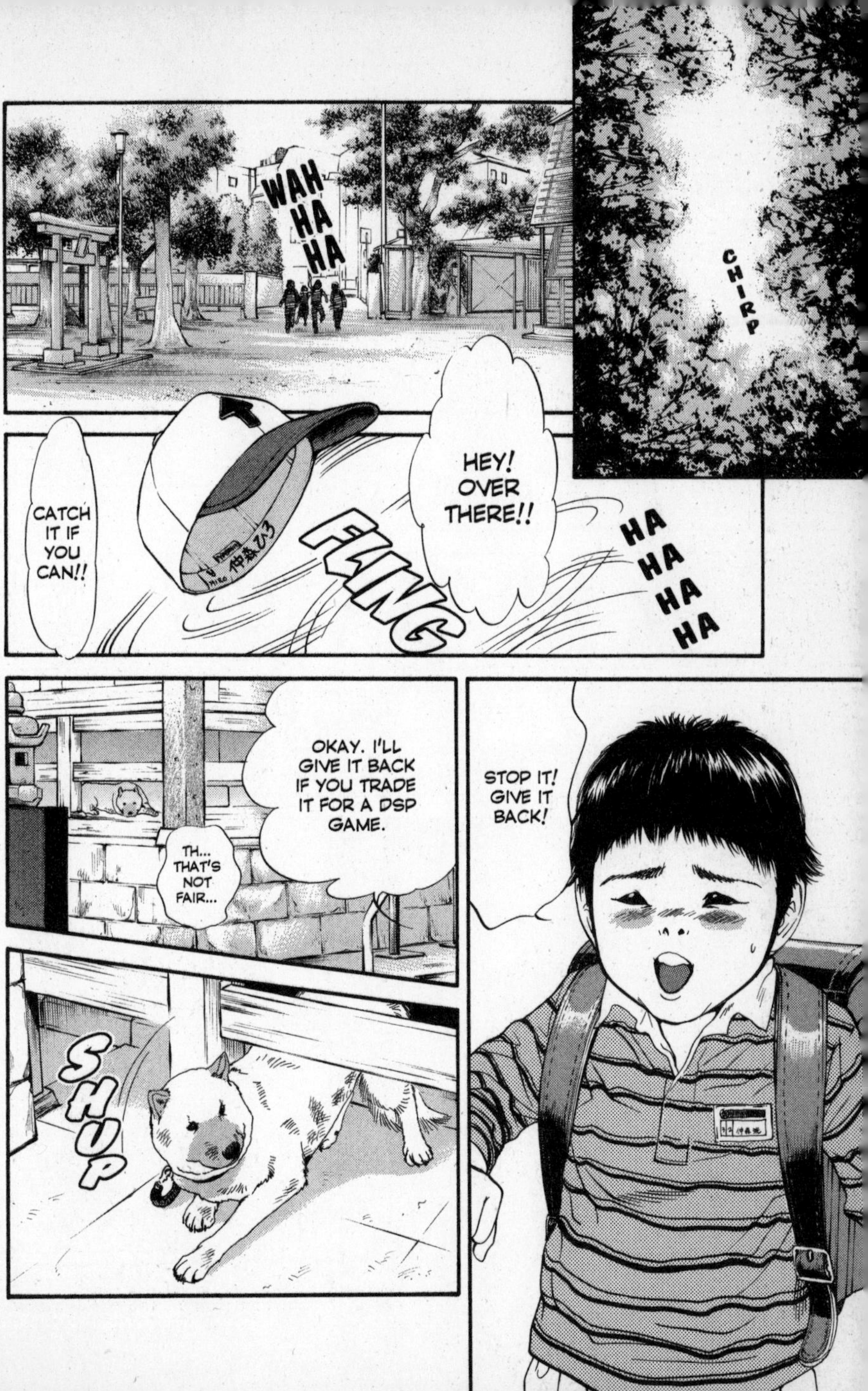
CHIRP
WAH HA HA
HA HA HA HA
HEY! OVER THERE!!
FLING
CATCH IT IF YOU CAN!!
STOP IT! GIVE IT BACK!
OKAY. I'LL GIVE IT BACK IF YOU TRADE IT FOR A DSP GAME.
TH... THAT'S NOT FAIR...
SHUP

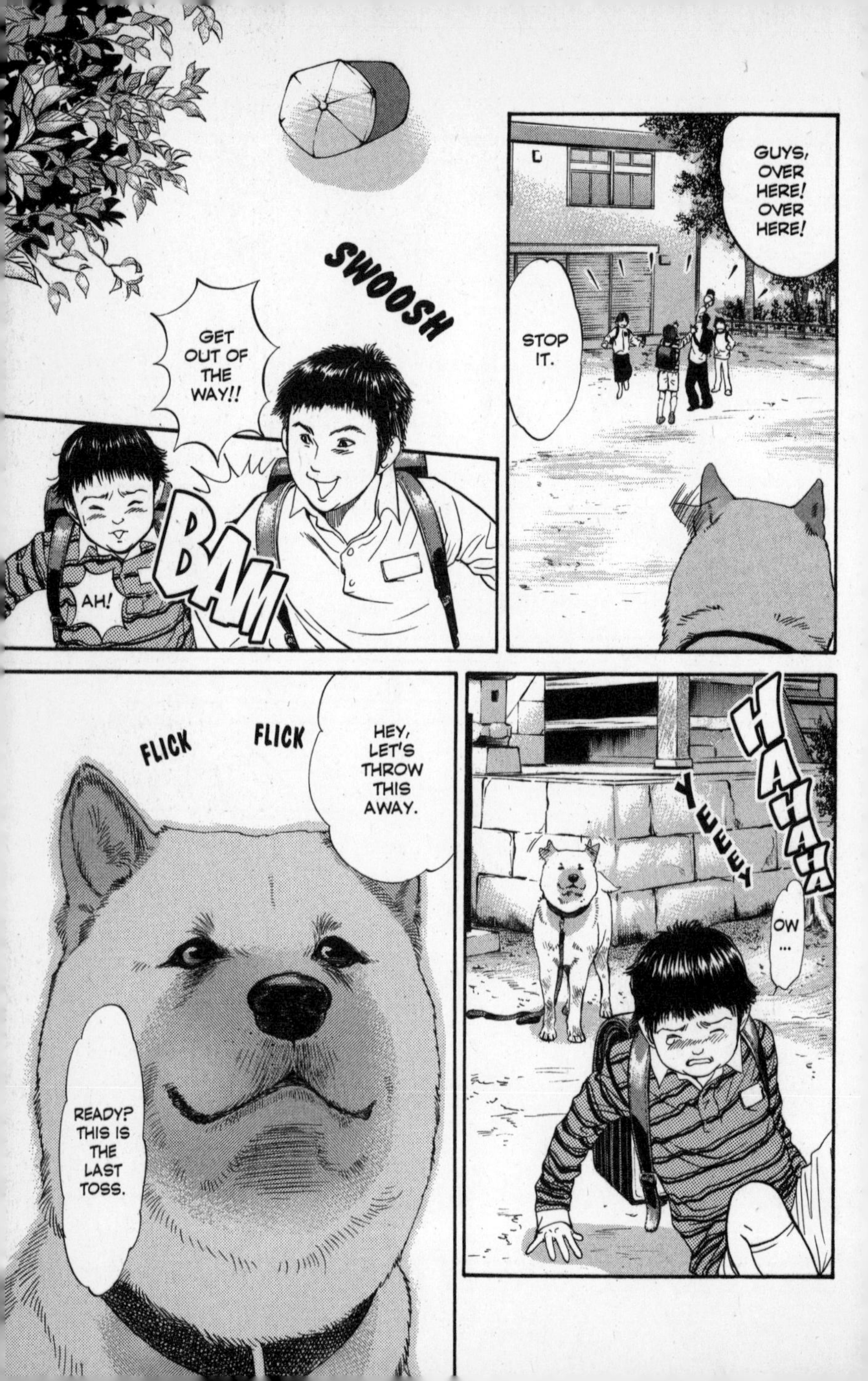
GUYS, OVER HERE! OVER HERE!
STOP IT.
SWOOSH
GET OUT OF THE WAY!!
BAM
AH!
HAHAHA
YEEEEY
OW ...
HEY, LET'S THROW THIS AWAY.
FLICK
FLICK
READY? THIS IS THE LAST TOSS.

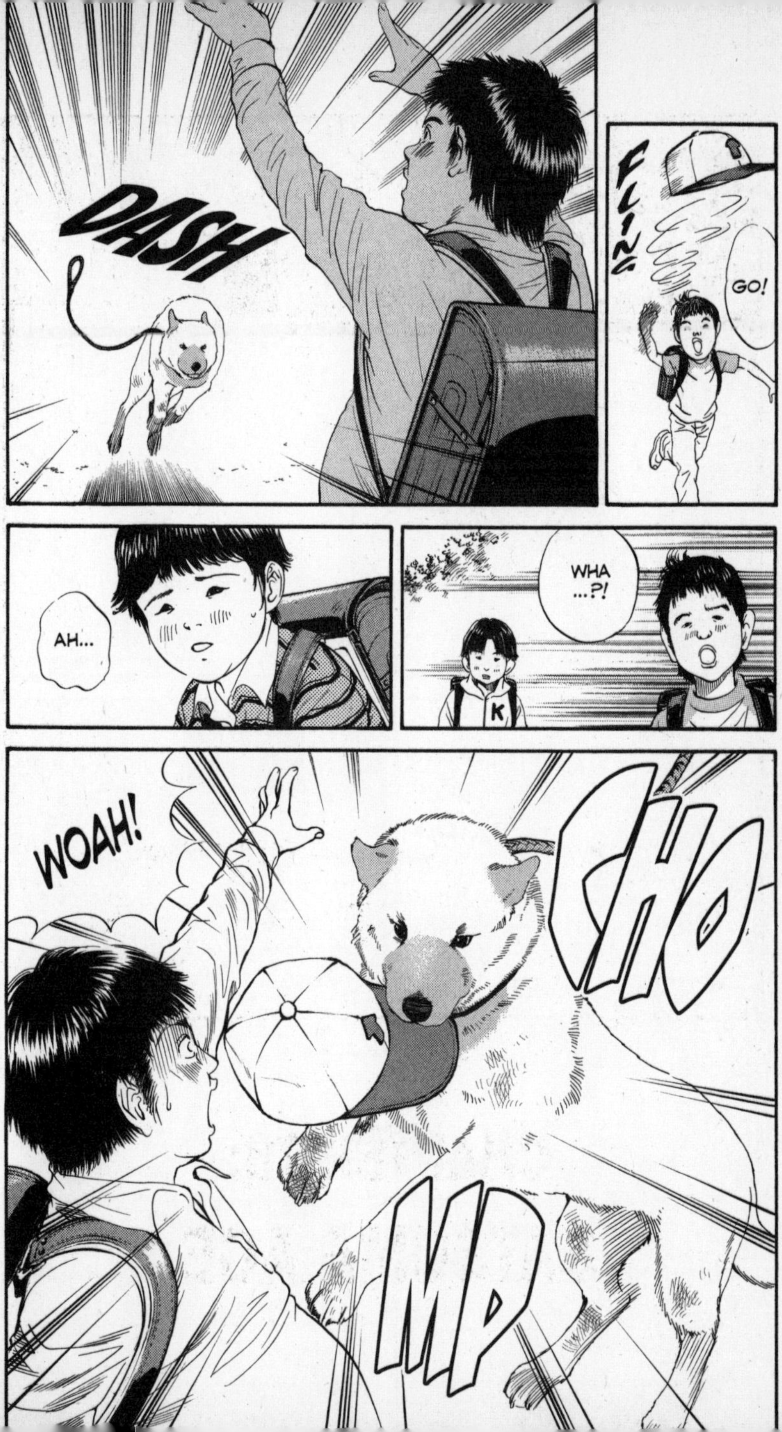
FLING
GO!
DASH
WHA ...?!
AH...
WOAH!
CHOMP

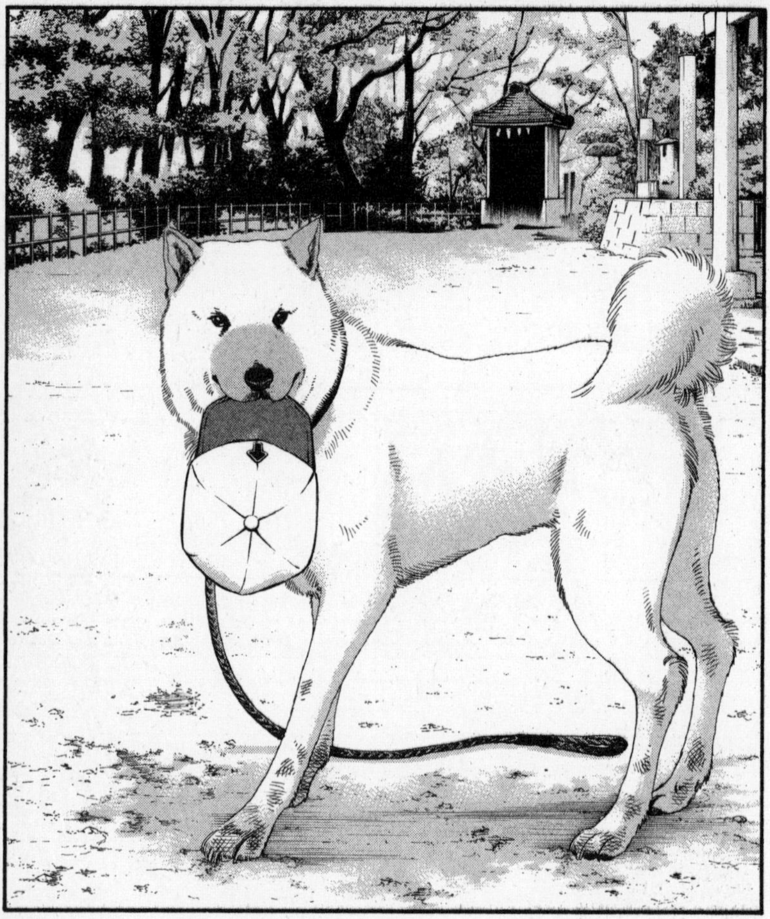

CHAPTER 78:
SATSUMA AGE

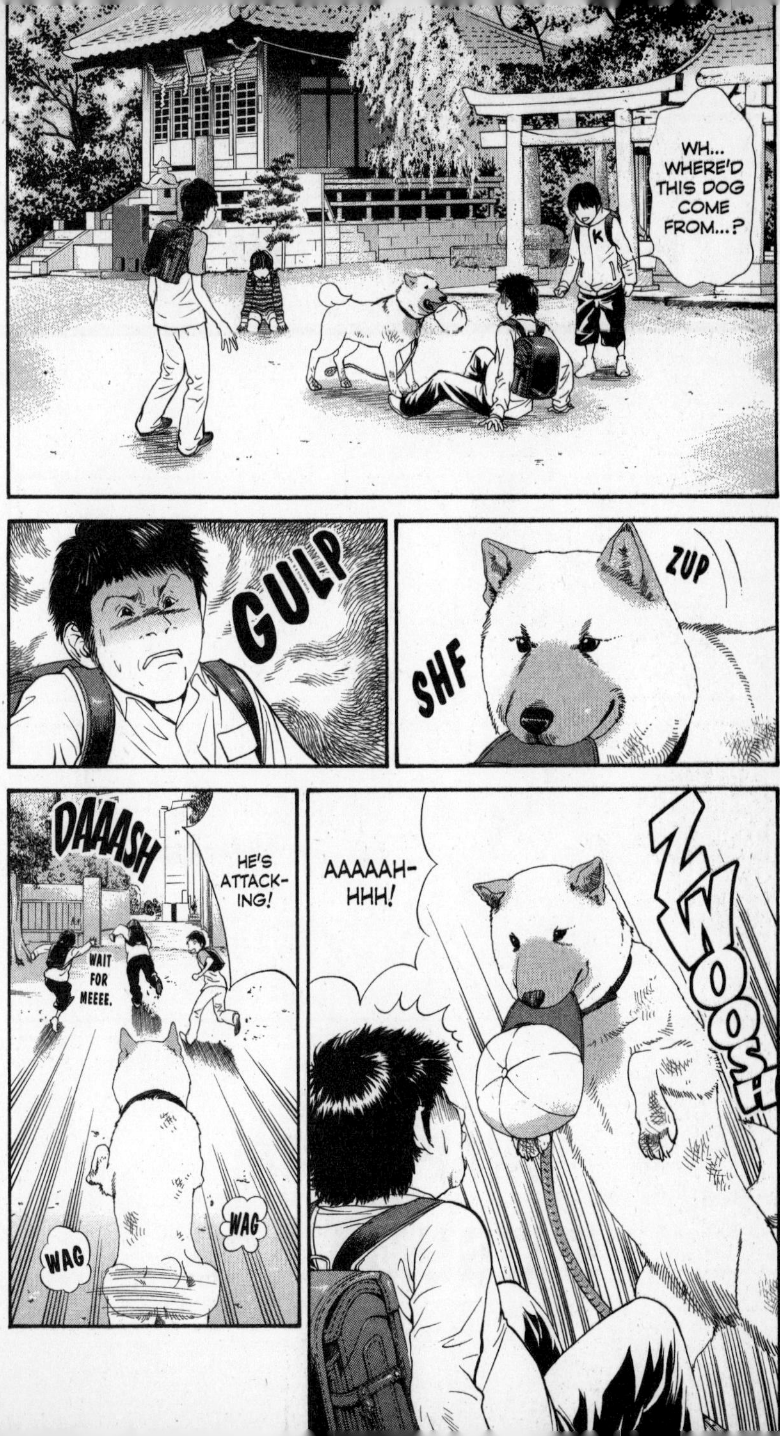
WH... WHERE'D THIS DOG COME FROM...?
ZUP
SHF
GULP
ZWOOSH
AAAAAH-HHH!
DAAASH
HE'S ATTACK-ING!
WAIT FOR MEEEE.
WAG
WAG

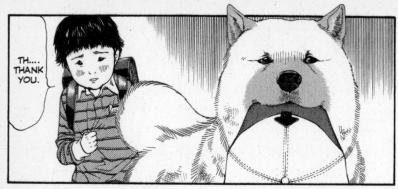

TH....
THANK
YOU.

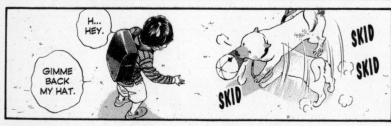

H...
HEY.

GIMME
BACK
MY HAT.

SKID
SKID

SKID

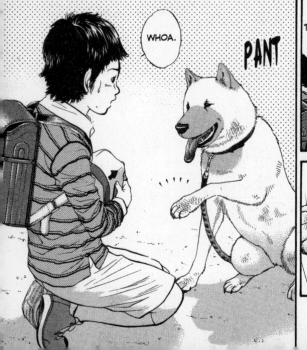

WHOA.

PANT

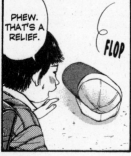

PHEW.
THAT'S A
RELIEF.

FLOP

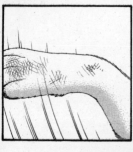

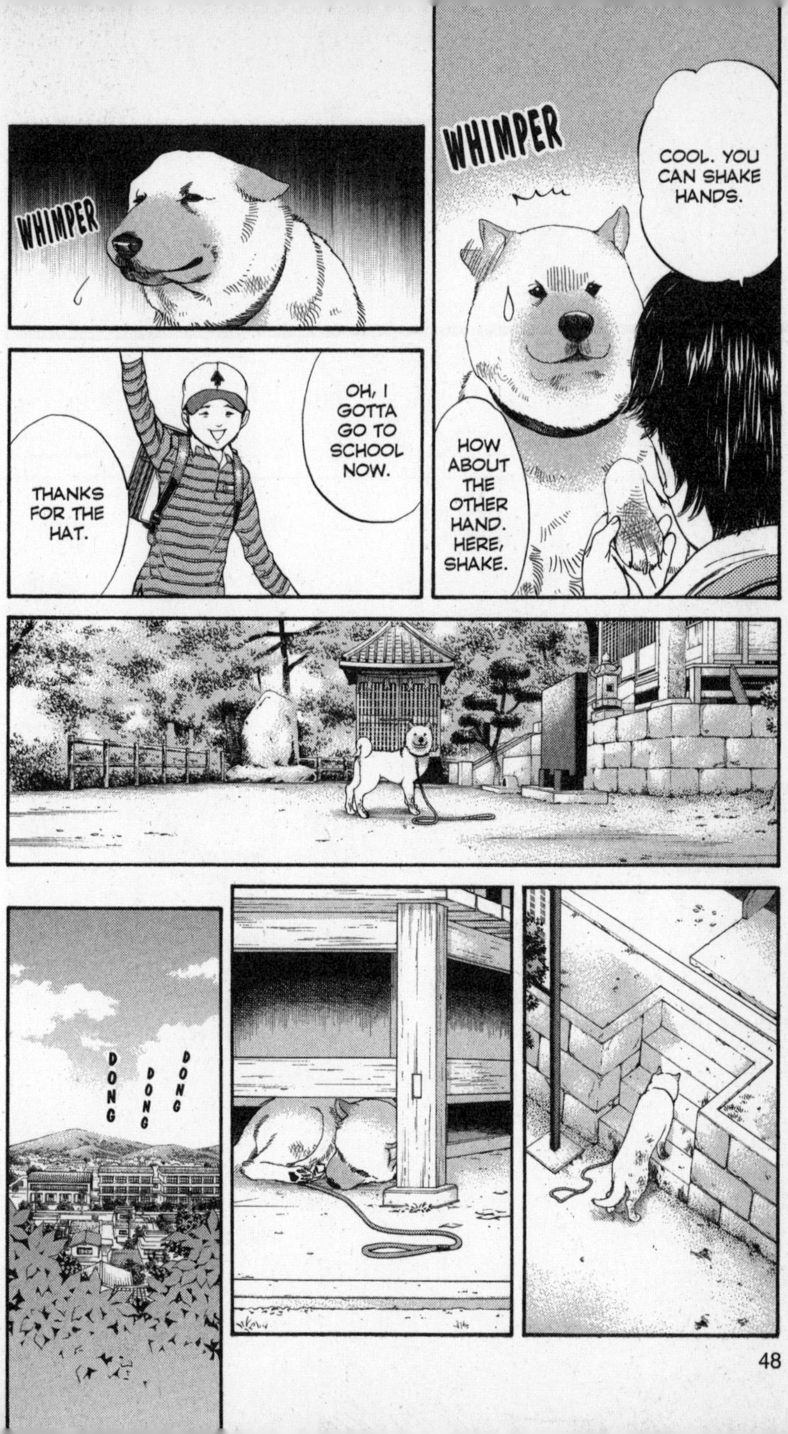

COOL. YOU CAN SHAKE HANDS.
WHIMPER
HOW ABOUT THE OTHER HAND. HERE, SHAKE.
WHIMPER
OH, I GOTTA GO TO SCHOOL NOW.
THANKS FOR THE HAT.
DONG
DONG
DONG

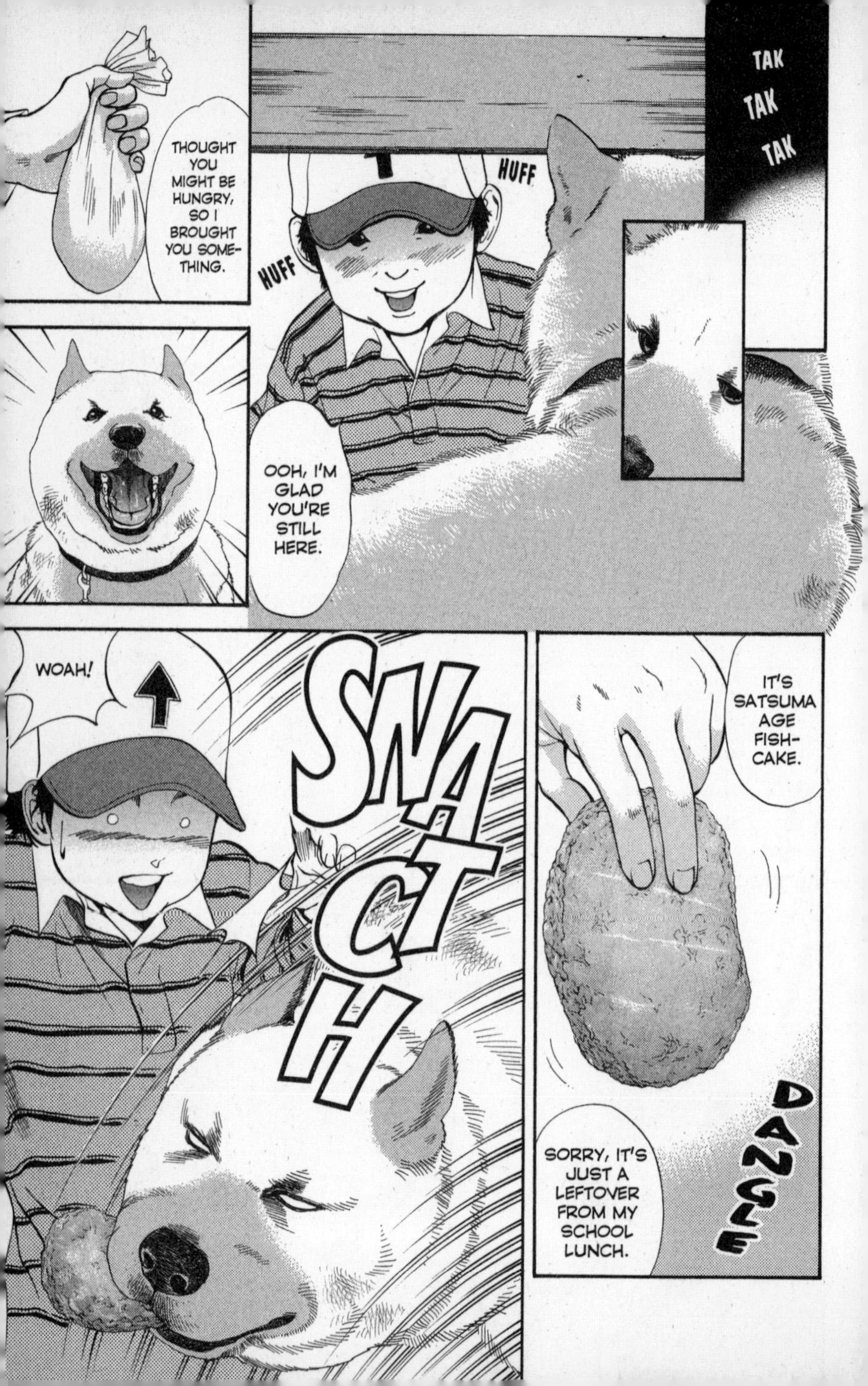
TAK TAK TAK
HUFF
HUFF
OOH, I'M GLAD YOU'RE STILL HERE.
THOUGHT YOU MIGHT BE HUNGRY, SO I BROUGHT YOU SOME-THING.
IT'S SATSUMA AGE FISH-CAKE.
SORRY, IT'S JUST A LEFTOVER FROM MY SCHOOL LUNCH.
DANGLE
SNATCH
WOAH!

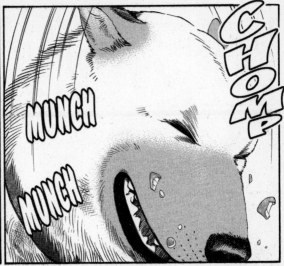

WOW...

THAT FISHCAKE MUST BE REALLY GOOD.

MUNCH MUNCH

CHOMP

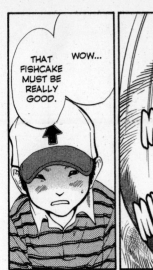

THAT'S RIGHT. I SHOULDN'T JUST CALL YOU "DOG." I HAVE TO GIVE YOU A NAME.

HA-HA-HA-HA

WHIMPER WHIMPER

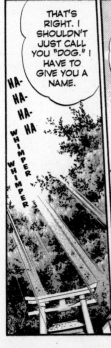

CUT IT OUT, DOG, IT TICKLES...

THAT TICKLES.

WEIRD, HE SMELLS LIKE NATTO.

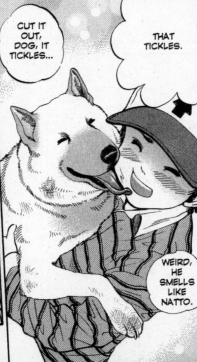

LAP

SORRY. I DON'T HAVE ANY MORE. TOMOR-ROW, OKAY...?

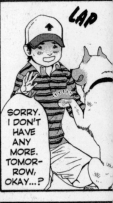

LICK

AH...

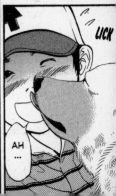

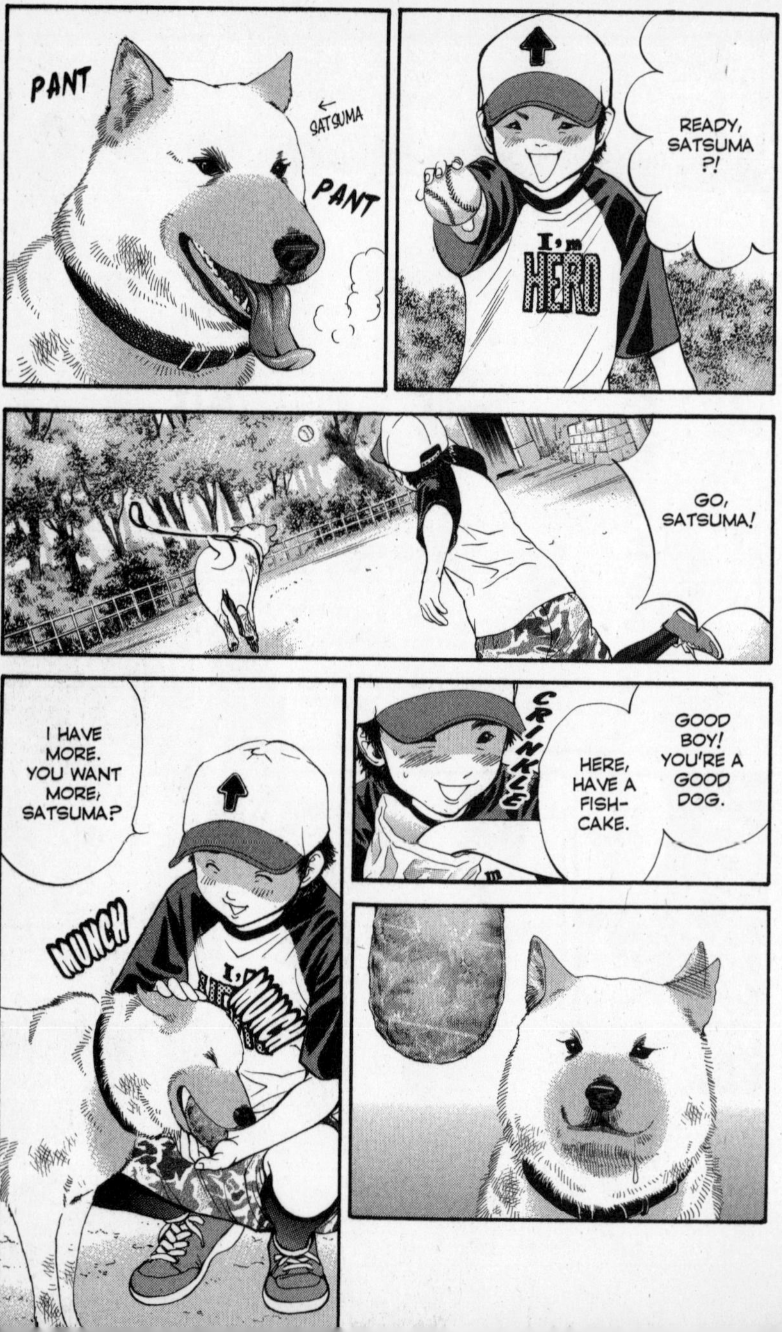
READY, SATSUMA?!
I'm HERO
PANT
← SATSUMA
PANT
GO, SATSUMA!
GOOD BOY! YOU'RE A GOOD DOG.
HERE, HAVE A FISH-CAKE.
CRINKLE
I HAVE MORE. YOU WANT MORE, SATSUMA?
MUNCH
MUNCH

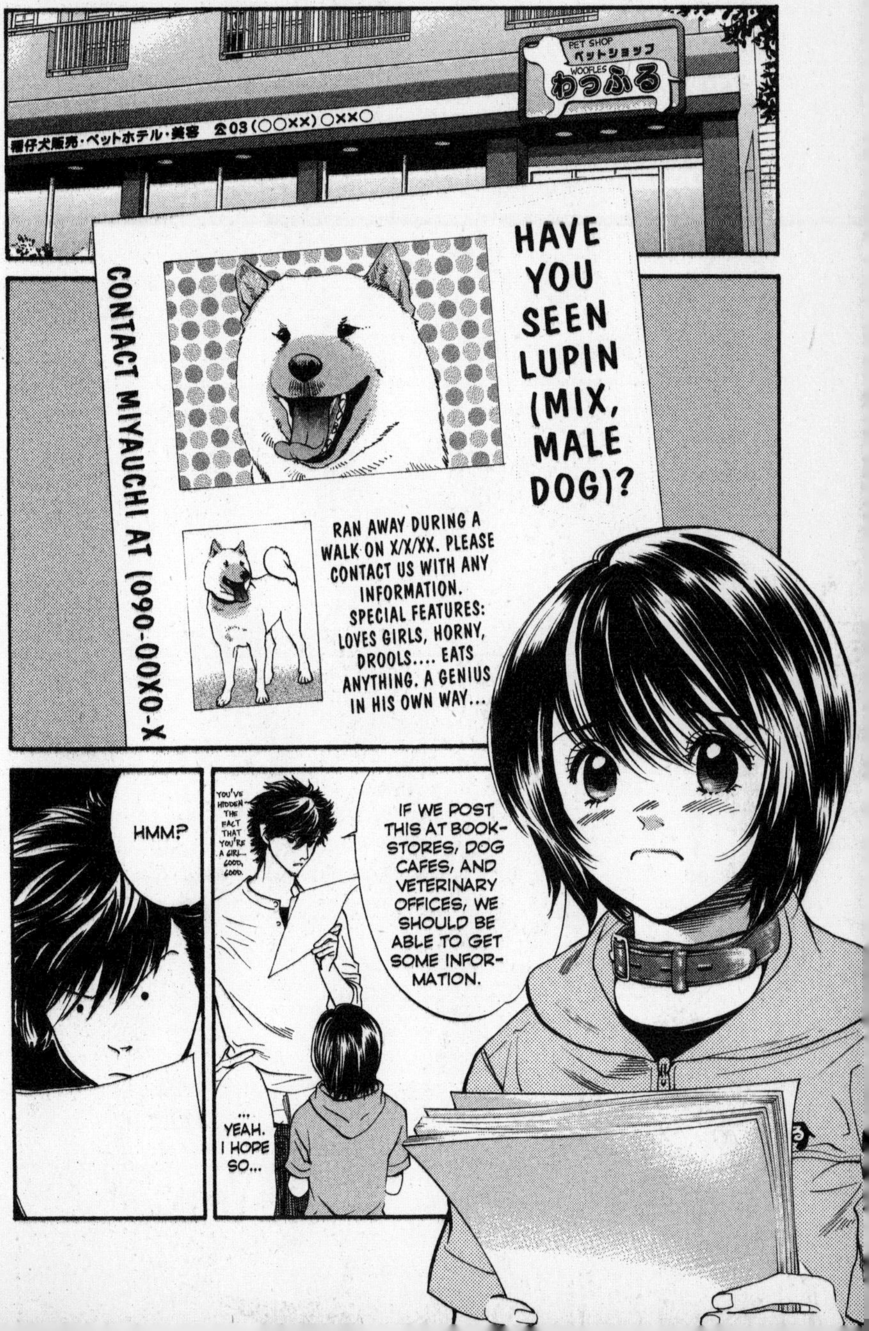
PET SHOP
ペットショップ
WOOFLES
わつふる
仔犬販売・ペットホテル・美容 ☎03(○○××)○××○
HAVE YOU SEEN LUPIN (MIX, MALE DOG)?
RAN AWAY DURING A WALK ON X/X/XX. PLEASE CONTACT US WITH ANY INFORMATION. SPECIAL FEATURES: LOVES GIRLS, HORNY, DROOLS.... EATS ANYTHING. A GENIUS IN HIS OWN WAY...
CONTACT MIYAUCHI AT (090-00X0-X
IF WE POST THIS AT BOOKSTORES, DOG CAFES, AND VETERINARY OFFICES, WE SHOULD BE ABLE TO GET SOME INFORMATION.
YOU'VE HIDDEN THE FACT THAT YOU'RE A GIRL... GOOD, GOOD.
... YEAH. I HOPE SO...
HMM?

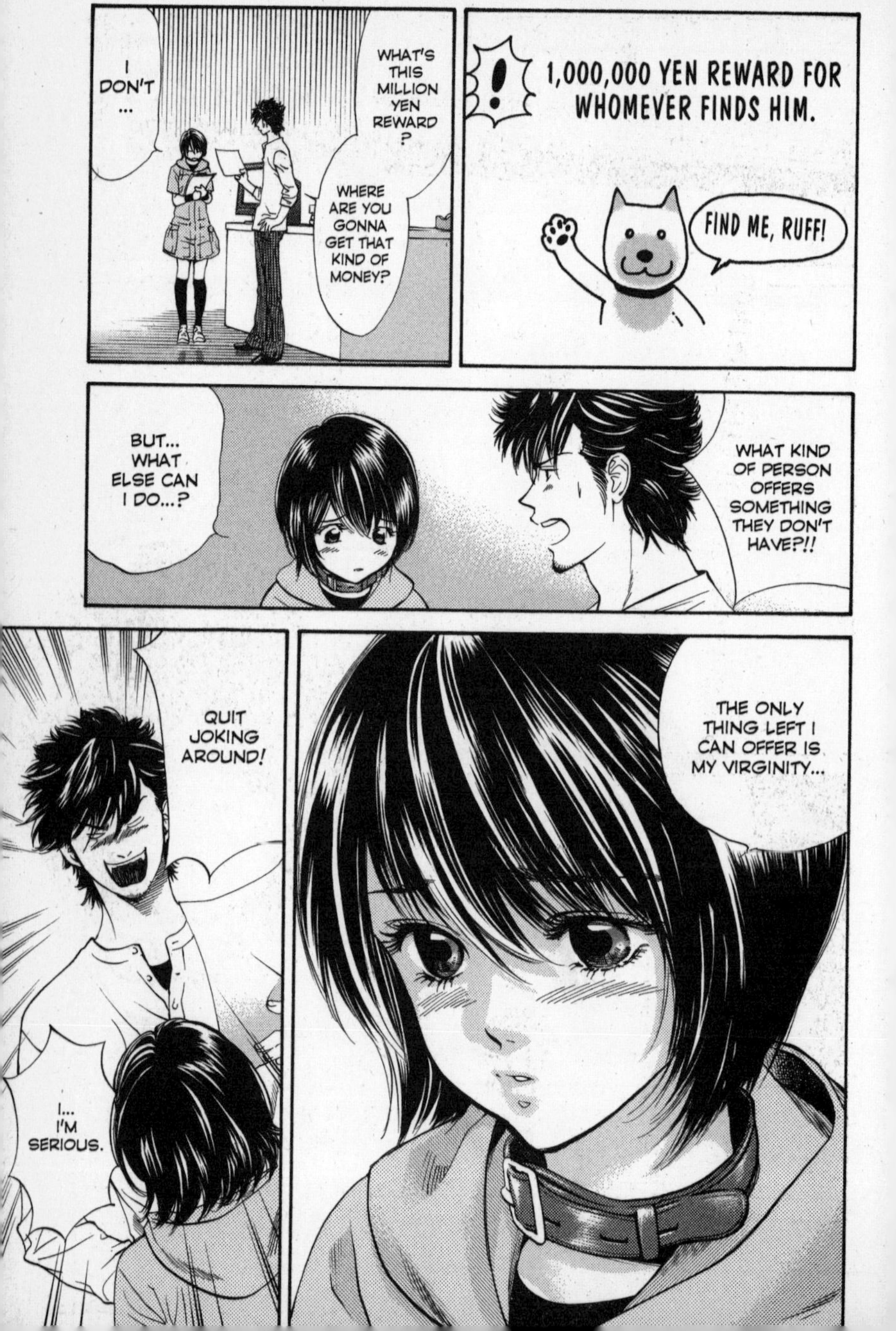

!
1,000,000 YEN REWARD FOR WHOMEVER FINDS HIM.
FIND ME, RUFF!
WHAT'S THIS MILLION YEN REWARD?
WHERE ARE YOU GONNA GET THAT KIND OF MONEY?
I DON'T ...
WHAT KIND OF PERSON OFFERS SOMETHING THEY DON'T HAVE?!!
BUT... WHAT ELSE CAN I DO...?
THE ONLY THING LEFT I CAN OFFER IS MY VIRGINITY...
QUIT JOKING AROUND!
I... I'M SERIOUS.

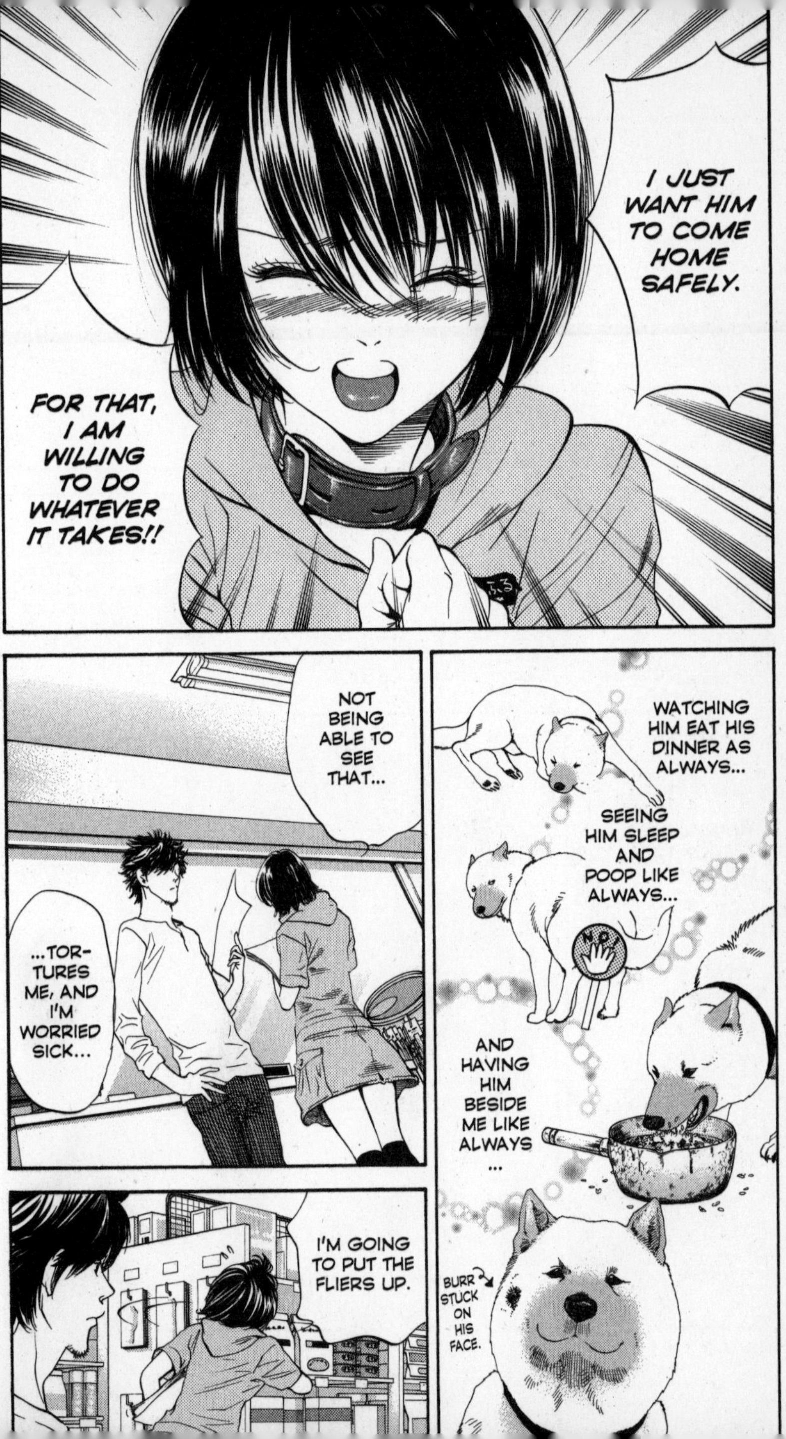
I JUST WANT HIM TO COME HOME SAFELY.
FOR THAT, I AM WILLING TO DO WHATEVER IT TAKES!!
WATCHING HIM EAT HIS DINNER AS ALWAYS...
SEEING HIM SLEEP AND POOP LIKE ALWAYS...
AND HAVING HIM BESIDE ME LIKE ALWAYS ...
BURR STUCK ON HIS FACE.
NOT BEING ABLE TO SEE THAT...
...TORTURES ME, AND I'M WORRIED SICK...
I'M GOING TO PUT THE FLIERS UP.

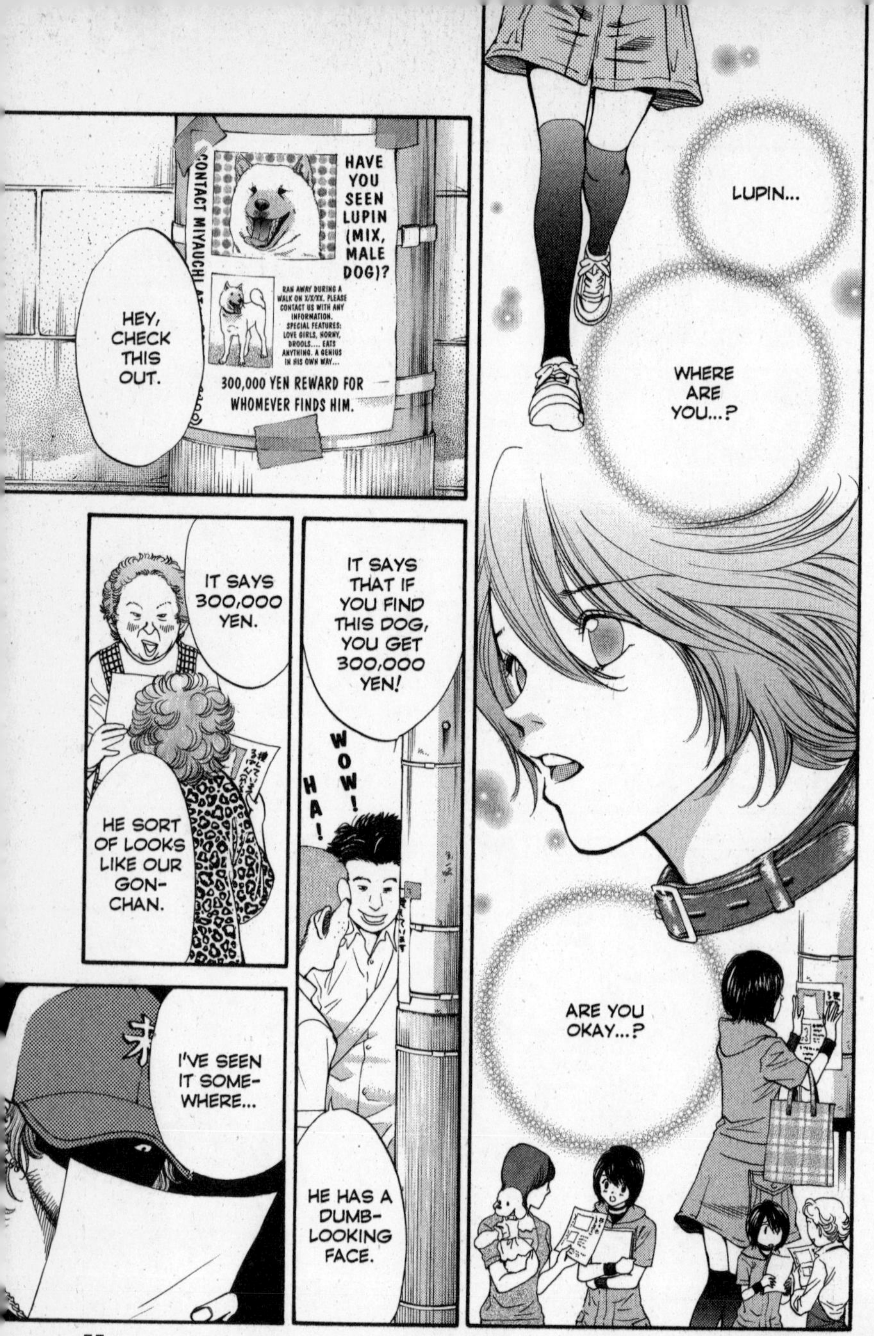
LUPIN...
WHERE ARE YOU...?
ARE YOU OKAY...?
CONTACT MIYAUCHI AT
HAVE YOU SEEN LUPIN (MIX, MALE DOG)?
RAN AWAY DURING A WALK ON X/X/XX. PLEASE CONTACT US WITH ANY INFORMATION. SPECIAL FEATURES: LOVE GIRLS, HORNY, DROOLS.... EATS ANYTHING. A GENIUS IN HIS OWN WAY...
300,000 YEN REWARD FOR WHOMEVER FINDS HIM.
HEY, CHECK THIS OUT.
IT SAYS THAT IF YOU FIND THIS DOG, YOU GET 300,000 YEN!
WOW!
HA!
HE HAS A DUMB-LOOKING FACE.
IT SAYS 300,000 YEN.
HE SORT OF LOOKS LIKE OUR GON-CHAN.
I'VE SEEN IT SOMEWHERE...

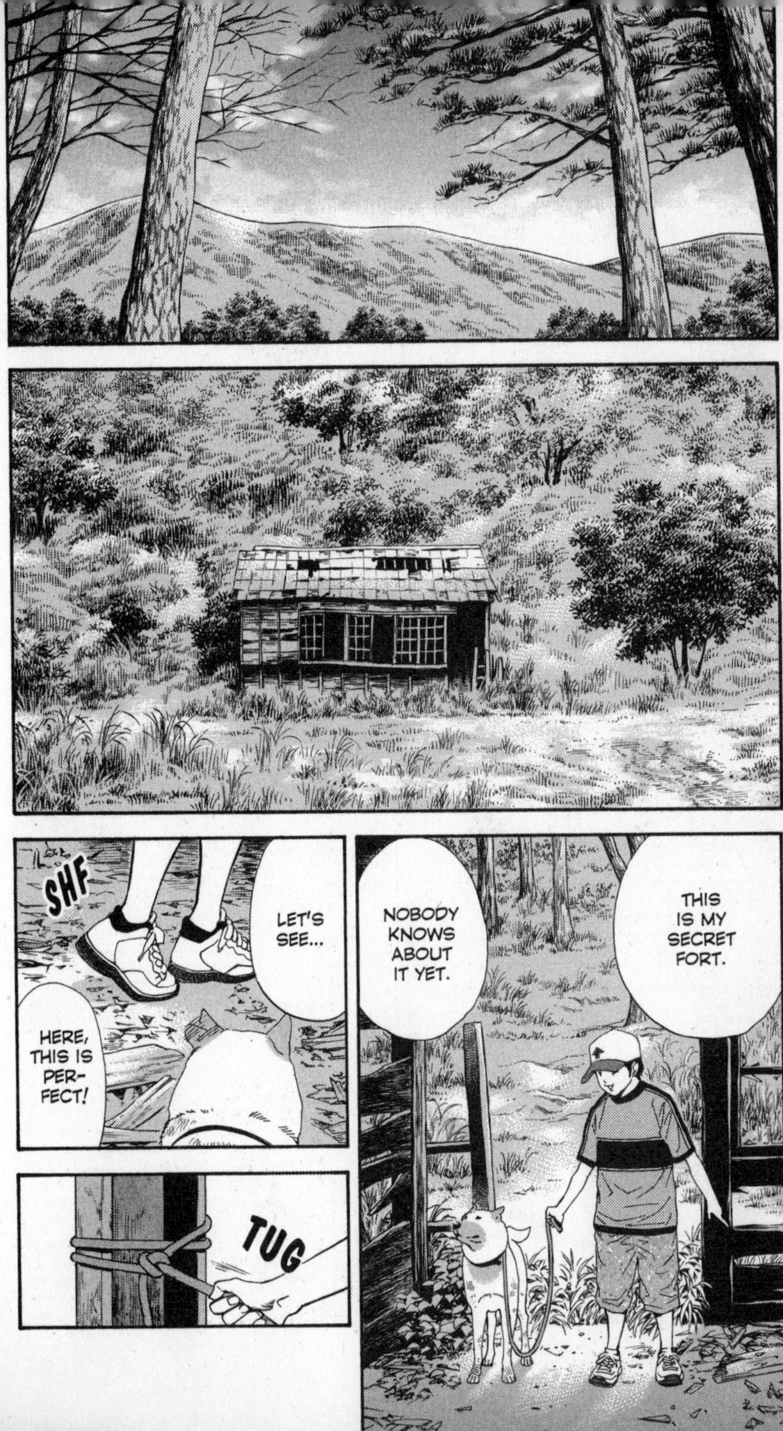
THIS IS MY SECRET FORT.
NOBODY KNOWS ABOUT IT YET.
LET'S SEE...
SHF
HERE, THIS IS PER-FECT!
TUG

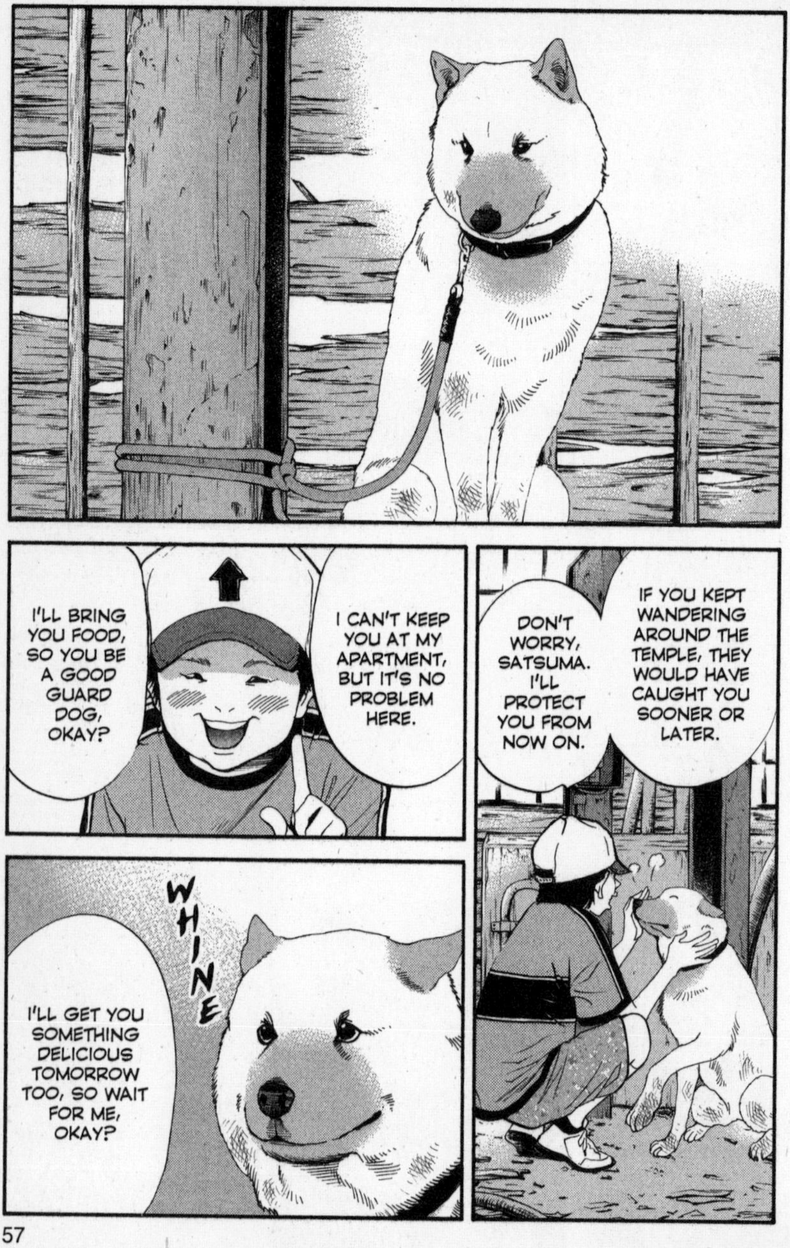
IF YOU KEPT WANDERING AROUND THE TEMPLE, THEY WOULD HAVE CAUGHT YOU SOONER OR LATER.
DON'T WORRY, SATSUMA. I'LL PROTECT YOU FROM NOW ON.
I CAN'T KEEP YOU AT MY APARTMENT, BUT IT'S NO PROBLEM HERE.
I'LL BRING YOU FOOD, SO YOU BE A GOOD GUARD DOG, OKAY?
WHINE
I'LL GET YOU SOMETHING DELICIOUS TOMORROW TOO, SO WAIT FOR ME, OKAY?

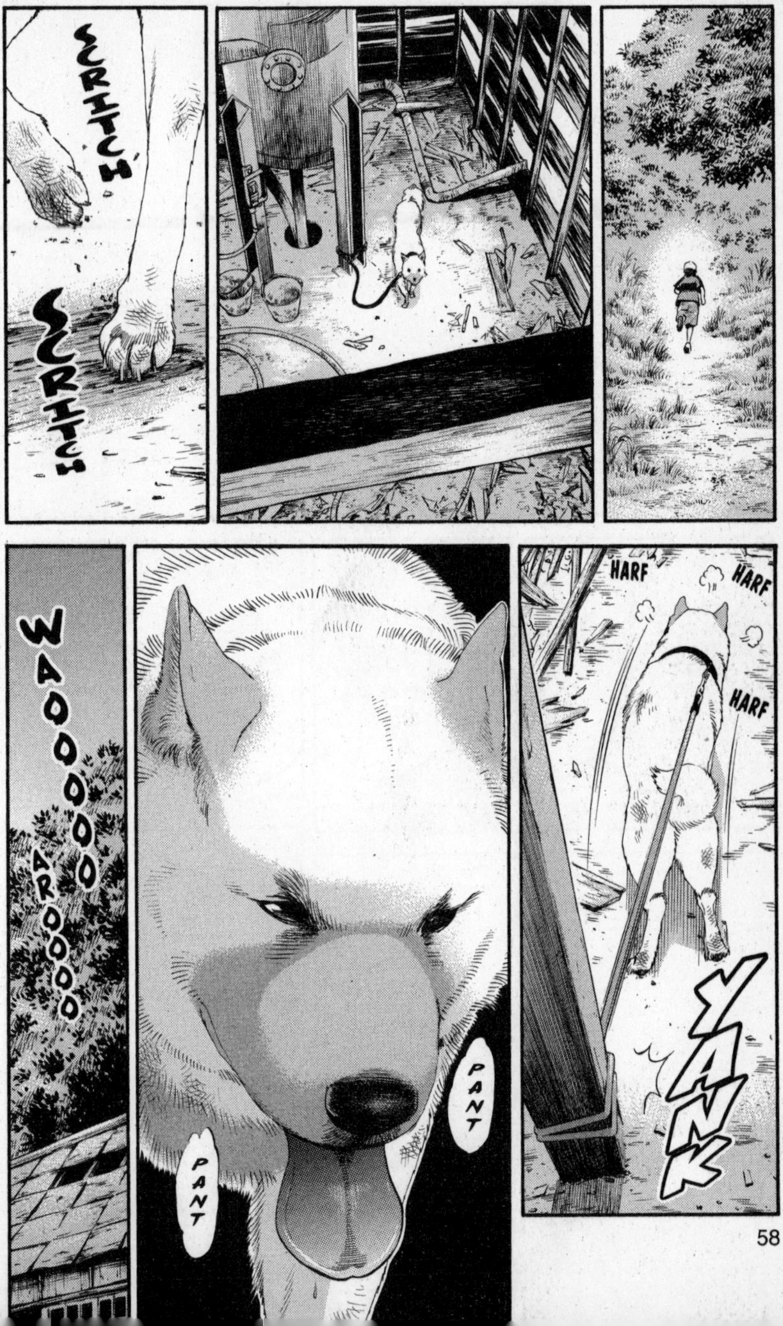
SCRITCH
SCRITCH
HARF
HARF
HARF
YANK
PANT
PANT
WAOOOOOO
AROOOO

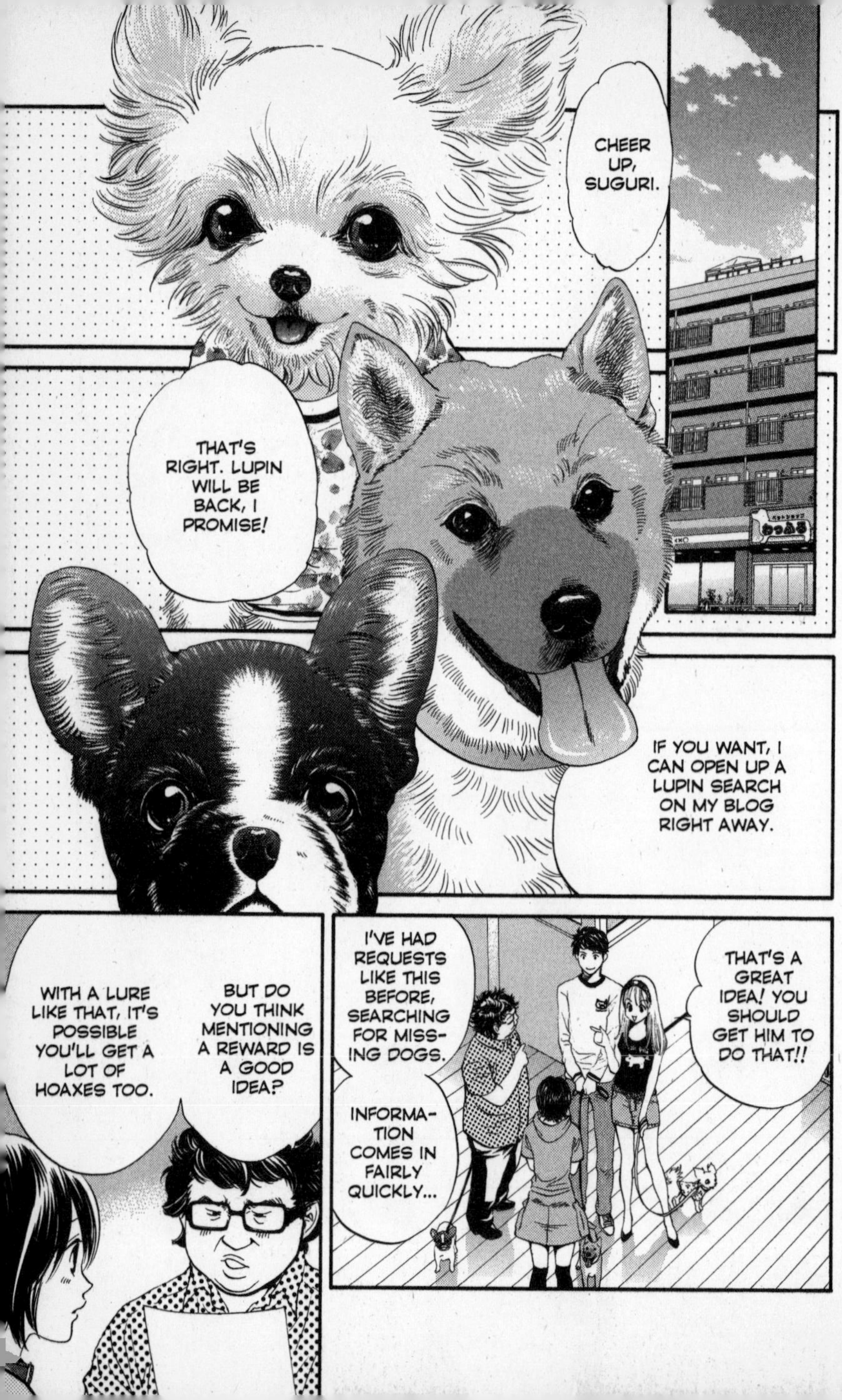
CHEER UP, SUGURI.
THAT'S RIGHT. LUPIN WILL BE BACK, I PROMISE!
IF YOU WANT, I CAN OPEN UP A LUPIN SEARCH ON MY BLOG RIGHT AWAY.
THAT'S A GREAT IDEA! YOU SHOULD GET HIM TO DO THAT!!
I'VE HAD REQUESTS LIKE THIS BEFORE, SEARCHING FOR MISSING DOGS.
INFORMATION COMES IN FAIRLY QUICKLY...
BUT DO YOU THINK MENTIONING A REWARD IS A GOOD IDEA?
WITH A LURE LIKE THAT, IT'S POSSIBLE YOU'LL GET A LOT OF HOAXES TOO.

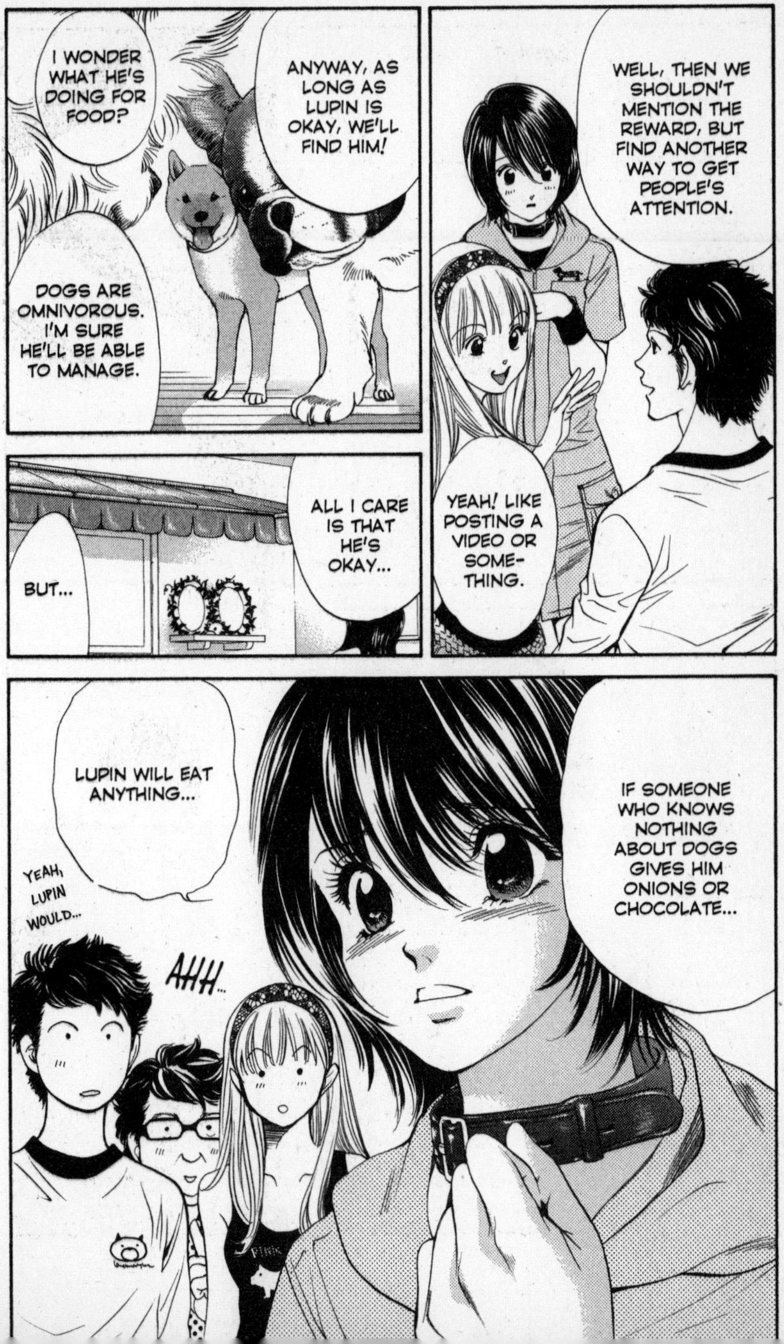
WELL, THEN WE SHOULDN'T MENTION THE REWARD, BUT FIND ANOTHER WAY TO GET PEOPLE'S ATTENTION.
YEAH! LIKE POSTING A VIDEO OR SOME-THING.
ANYWAY, AS LONG AS LUPIN IS OKAY, WE'LL FIND HIM!
I WONDER WHAT HE'S DOING FOR FOOD?
DOGS ARE OMNIVOROUS. I'M SURE HE'LL BE ABLE TO MANAGE.
ALL I CARE IS THAT HE'S OKAY...
BUT...
IF SOMEONE WHO KNOWS NOTHING ABOUT DOGS GIVES HIM ONIONS OR CHOCOLATE...
LUPIN WILL EAT ANYTHING...
YEAH, LUPIN WOULD...
AHH...

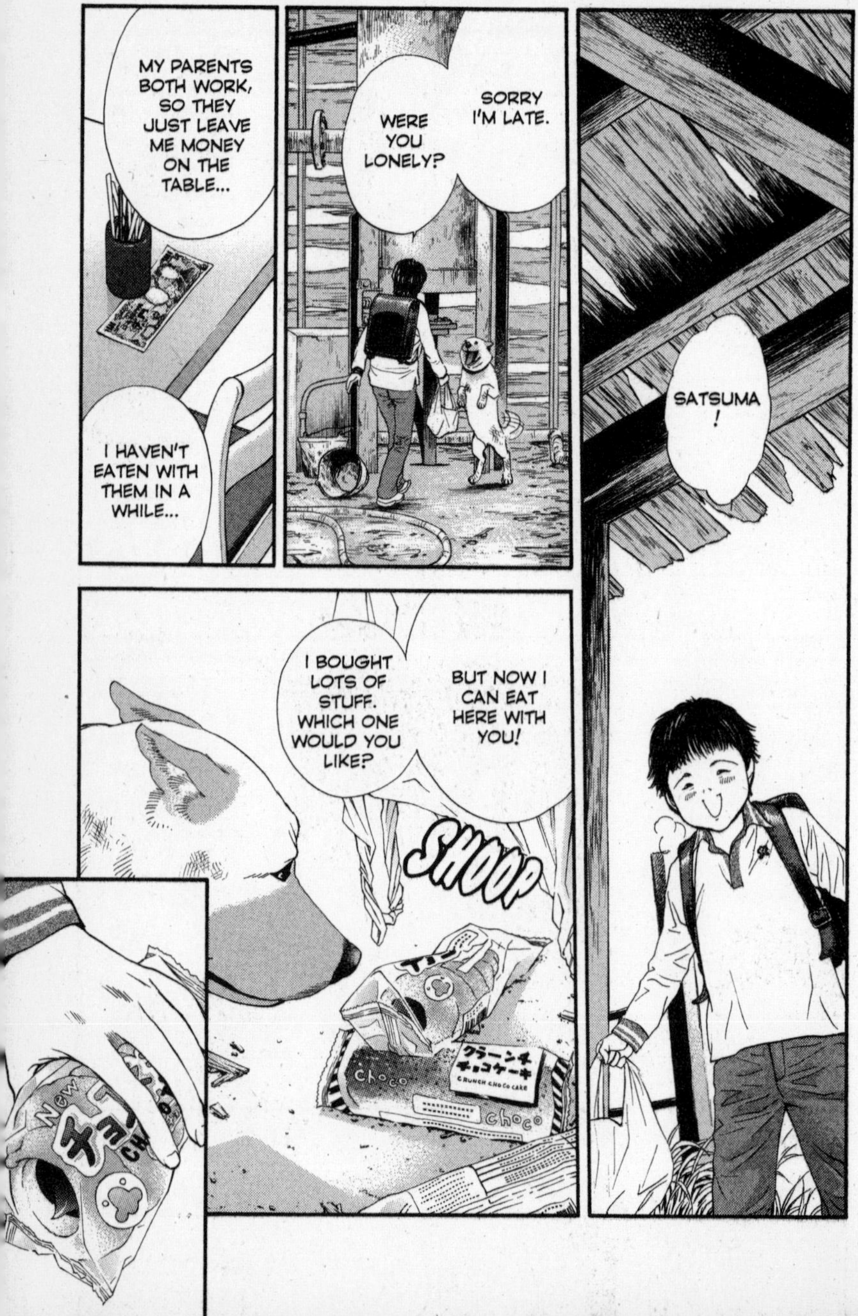
SATSUMA!
SORRY I'M LATE.
WERE YOU LONELY?
MY PARENTS BOTH WORK, SO THEY JUST LEAVE ME MONEY ON THE TABLE...
I HAVEN'T EATEN WITH THEM IN A WHILE...
BUT NOW I CAN EAT HERE WITH YOU!
I BOUGHT LOTS OF STUFF. WHICH ONE WOULD YOU LIKE?
SHOOP

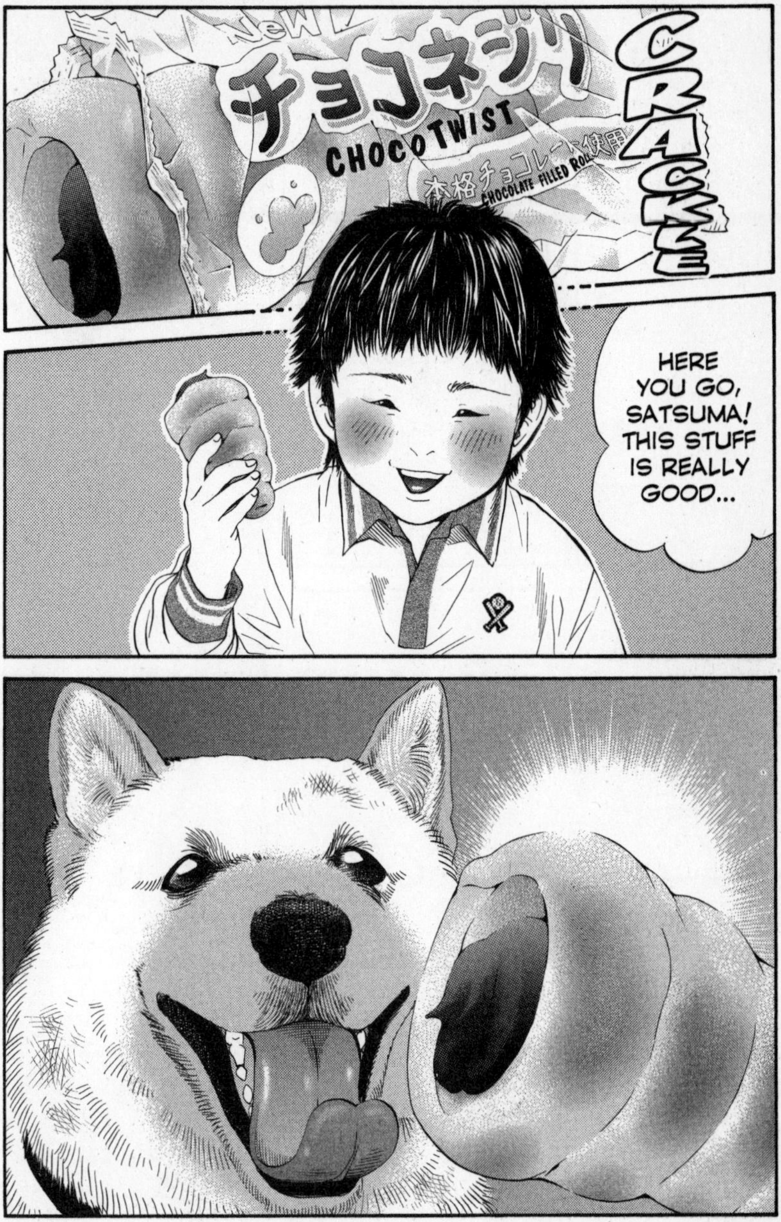
NEW!
チョコネジリ
CHOCO TWIST
本格チョコレート使用
CHOCOLATE FILLED ROLL
CRACKLE
HERE YOU GO, SATSUMA! THIS STUFF IS REALLY GOOD...

CHAPTER 79: LUPIN AND SATSUMA

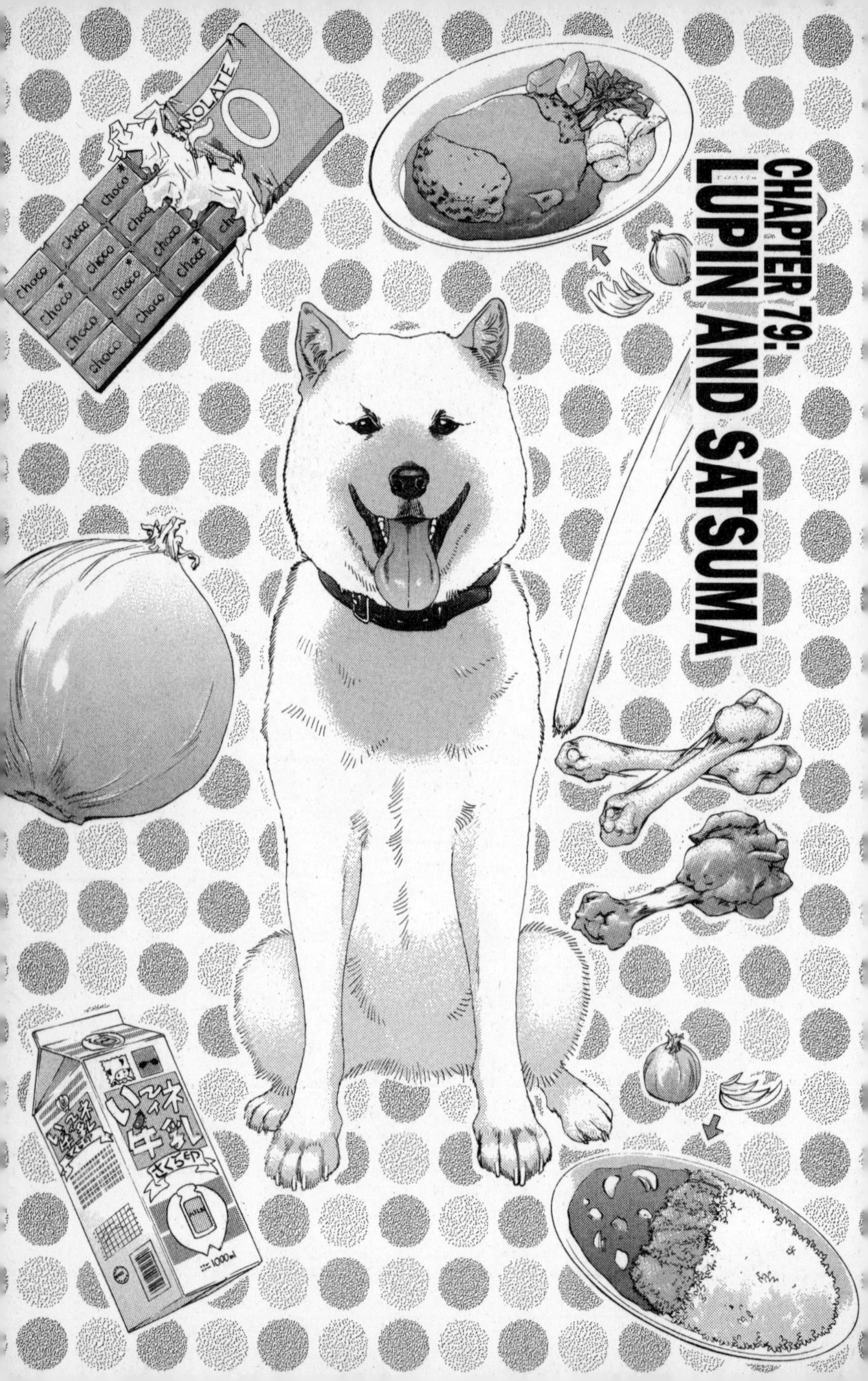
choco
1000ml

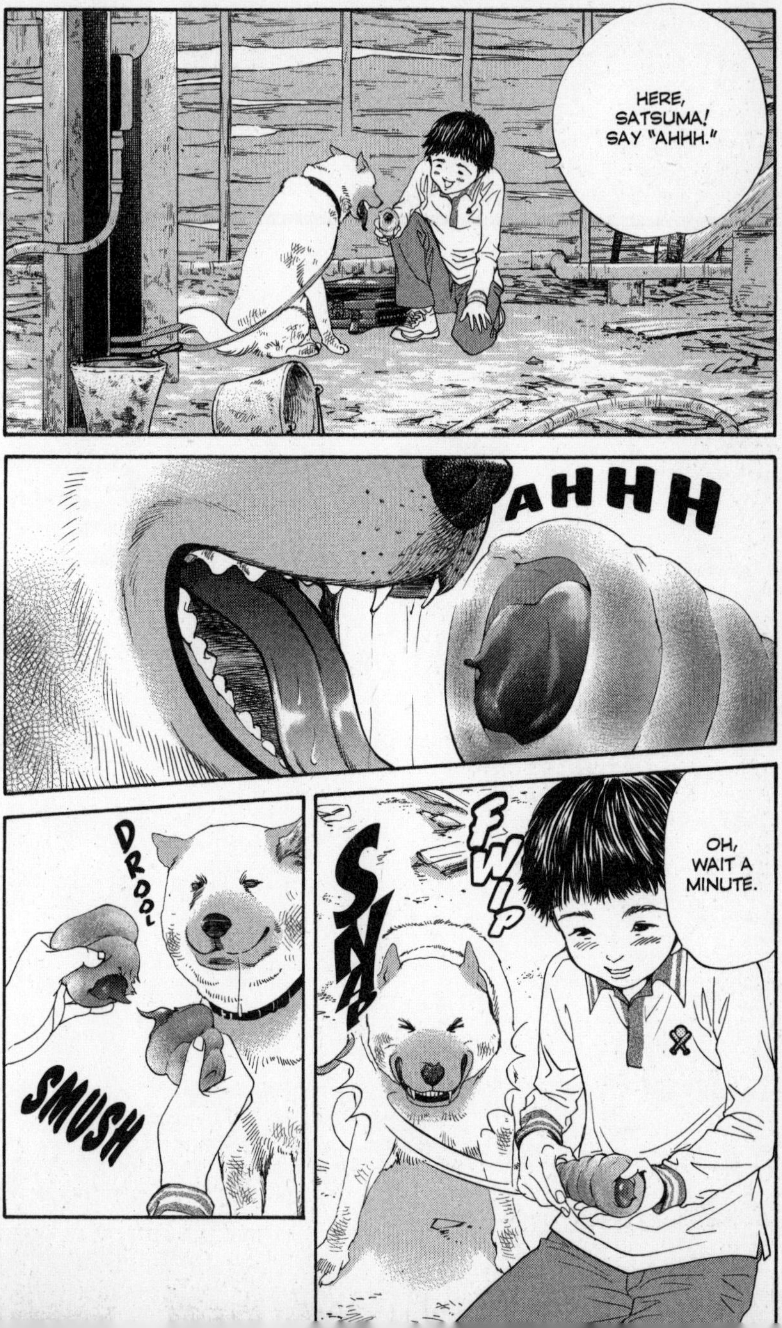
HERE, SATSUMA! SAY "AHHH."
AHHH
OH, WAIT A MINUTE.
FWIP
SNAP
DROOL
SMUSH

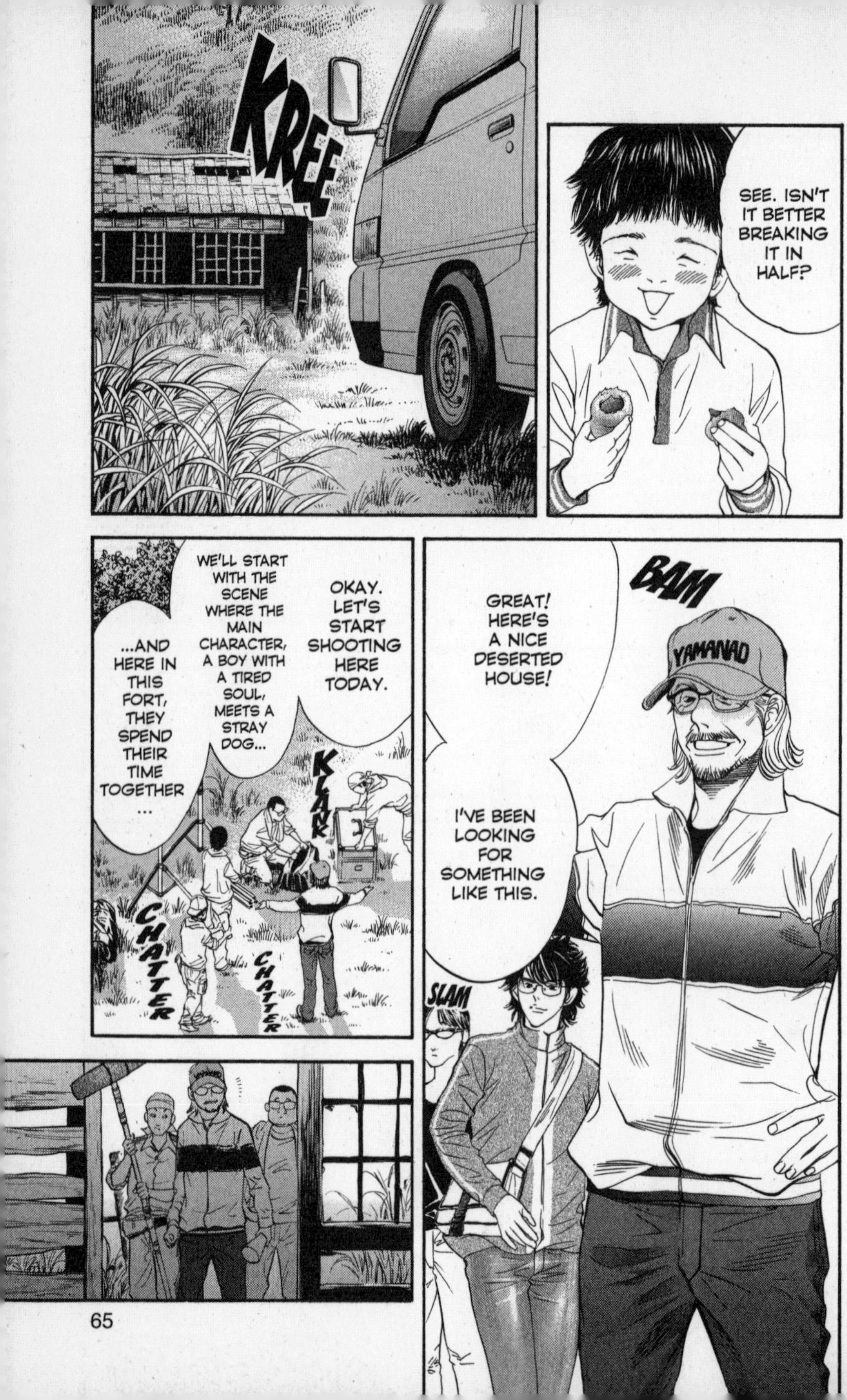
SEE. ISN'T IT BETTER BREAKING IT IN HALF?
KREE
BAM
GREAT! HERE'S A NICE DESERTED HOUSE!
I'VE BEEN LOOKING FOR SOMETHING LIKE THIS.
SLAM
OKAY. LET'S START SHOOTING HERE TODAY.
WE'LL START WITH THE SCENE WHERE THE MAIN CHARACTER, A BOY WITH A TIRED SOUL, MEETS A STRAY DOG...
...AND HERE IN THIS FORT, THEY SPEND THEIR TIME TOGETHER ...
KLANK
CHATTER
CHATTER

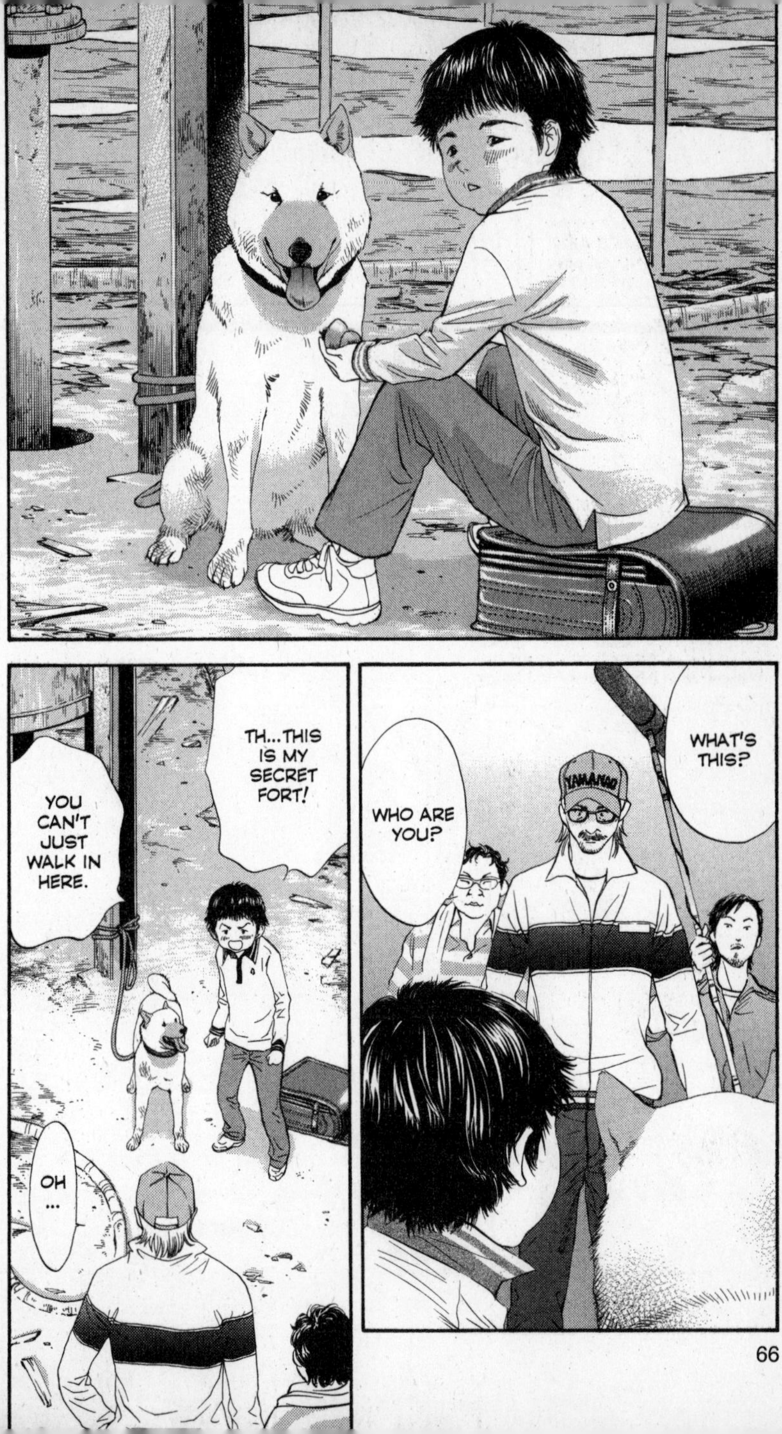
WHAT'S THIS?
WHO ARE YOU?
TH...THIS IS MY SECRET FORT!
YOU CAN'T JUST WALK IN HERE.
OH ...

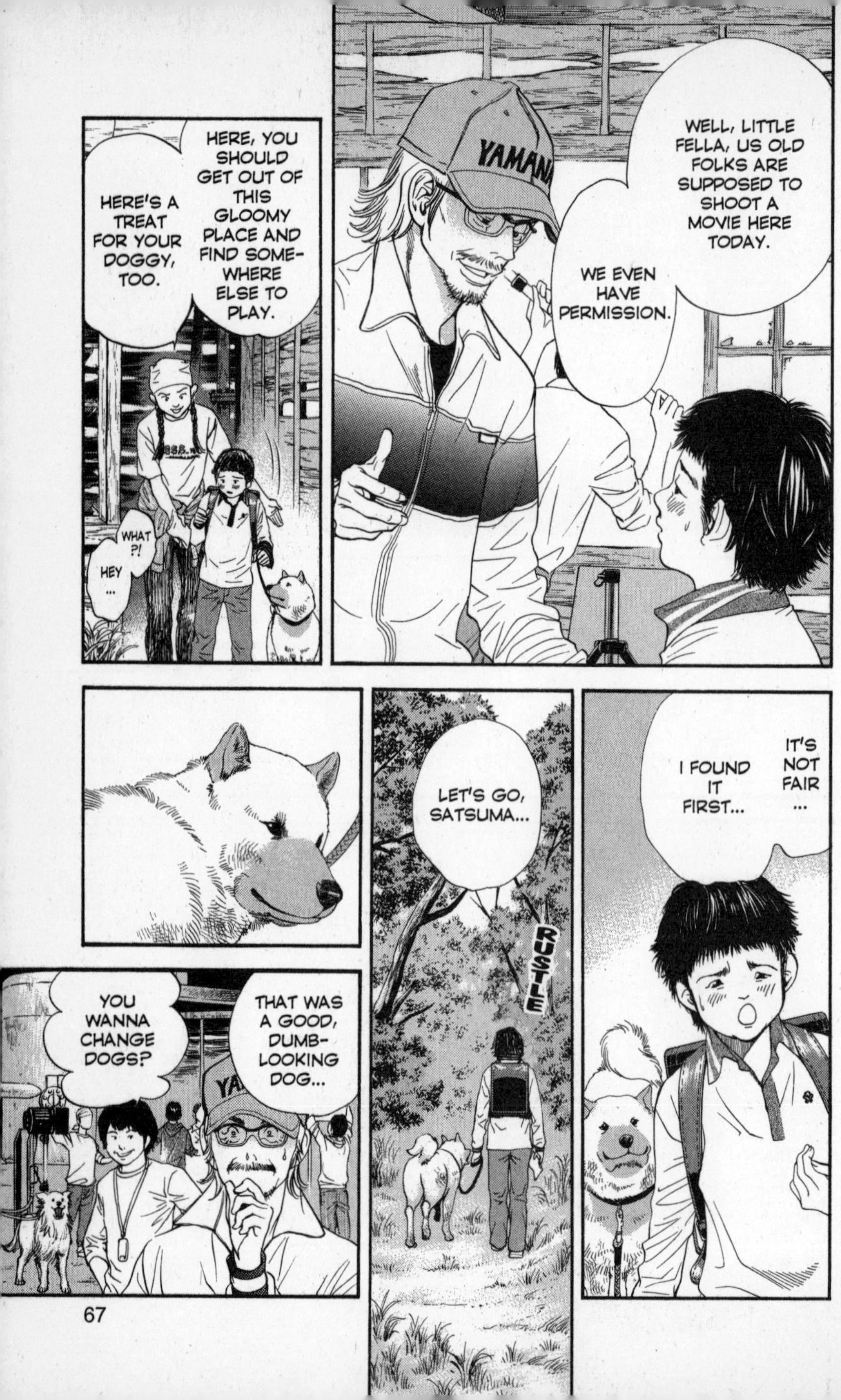
WELL, LITTLE FELLA, US OLD FOLKS ARE SUPPOSED TO SHOOT A MOVIE HERE TODAY.
WE EVEN HAVE PERMISSION.
YAMANA
HERE, YOU SHOULD GET OUT OF THIS GLOOMY PLACE AND FIND SOME-WHERE ELSE TO PLAY.
HERE'S A TREAT FOR YOUR DOGGY, TOO.
WHAT ?!
HEY ...
IT'S NOT FAIR ...
I FOUND IT FIRST...
LET'S GO, SATSUMA...
RUSTLE
THAT WAS A GOOD, DUMB-LOOKING DOG...
YOU WANNA CHANGE DOGS?

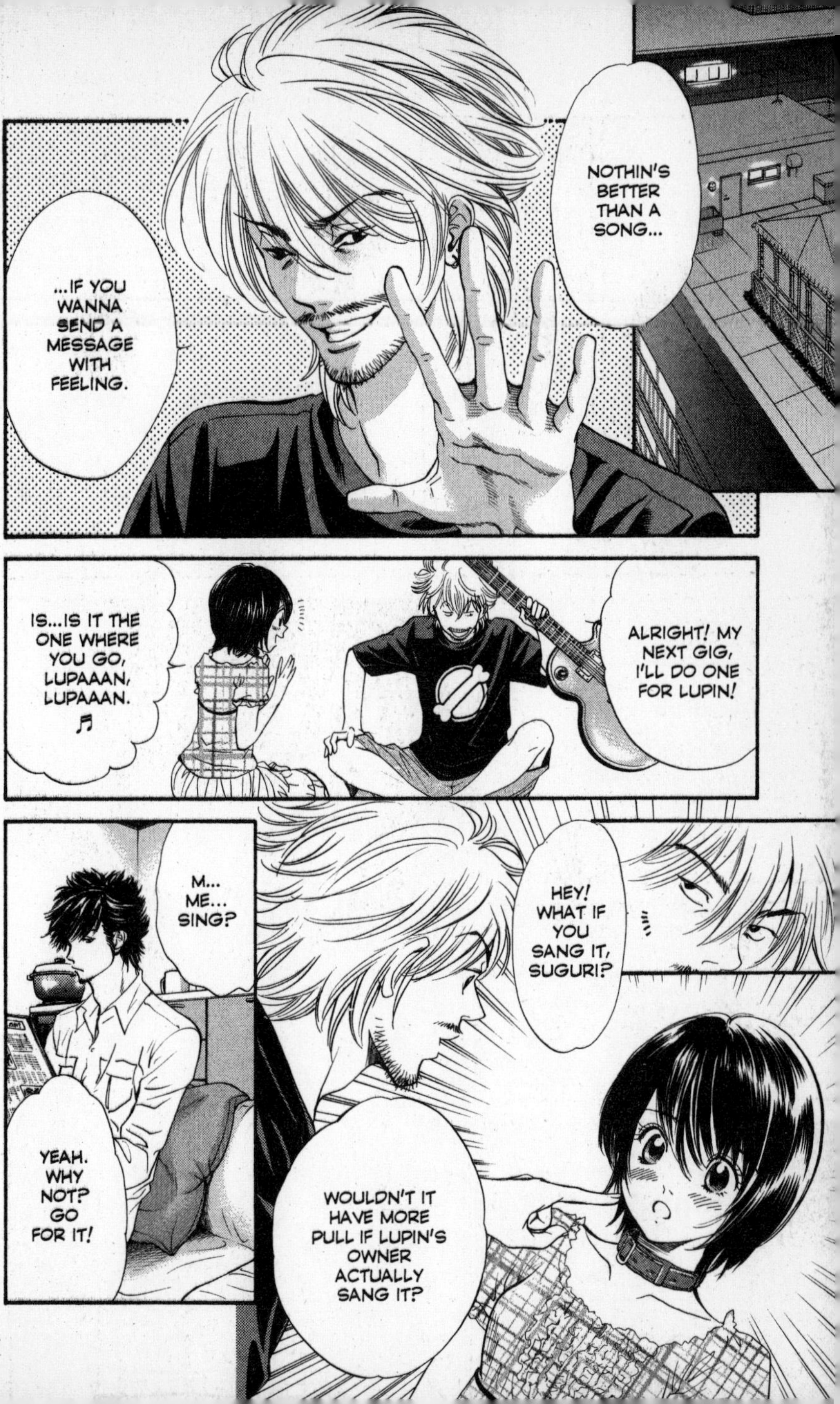
NOTHIN'S BETTER THAN A SONG...
...IF YOU WANNA SEND A MESSAGE WITH FEELING.
ALRIGHT! MY NEXT GIG, I'LL DO ONE FOR LUPIN!
IS...IS IT THE ONE WHERE YOU GO, LUPAAAN, LUPAAAN. ♬
HEY! WHAT IF YOU SANG IT, SUGURI?
WOULDN'T IT HAVE MORE PULL IF LUPIN'S OWNER ACTUALLY SANG IT?
M... ME... SING?
YEAH. WHY NOT? GO FOR IT!

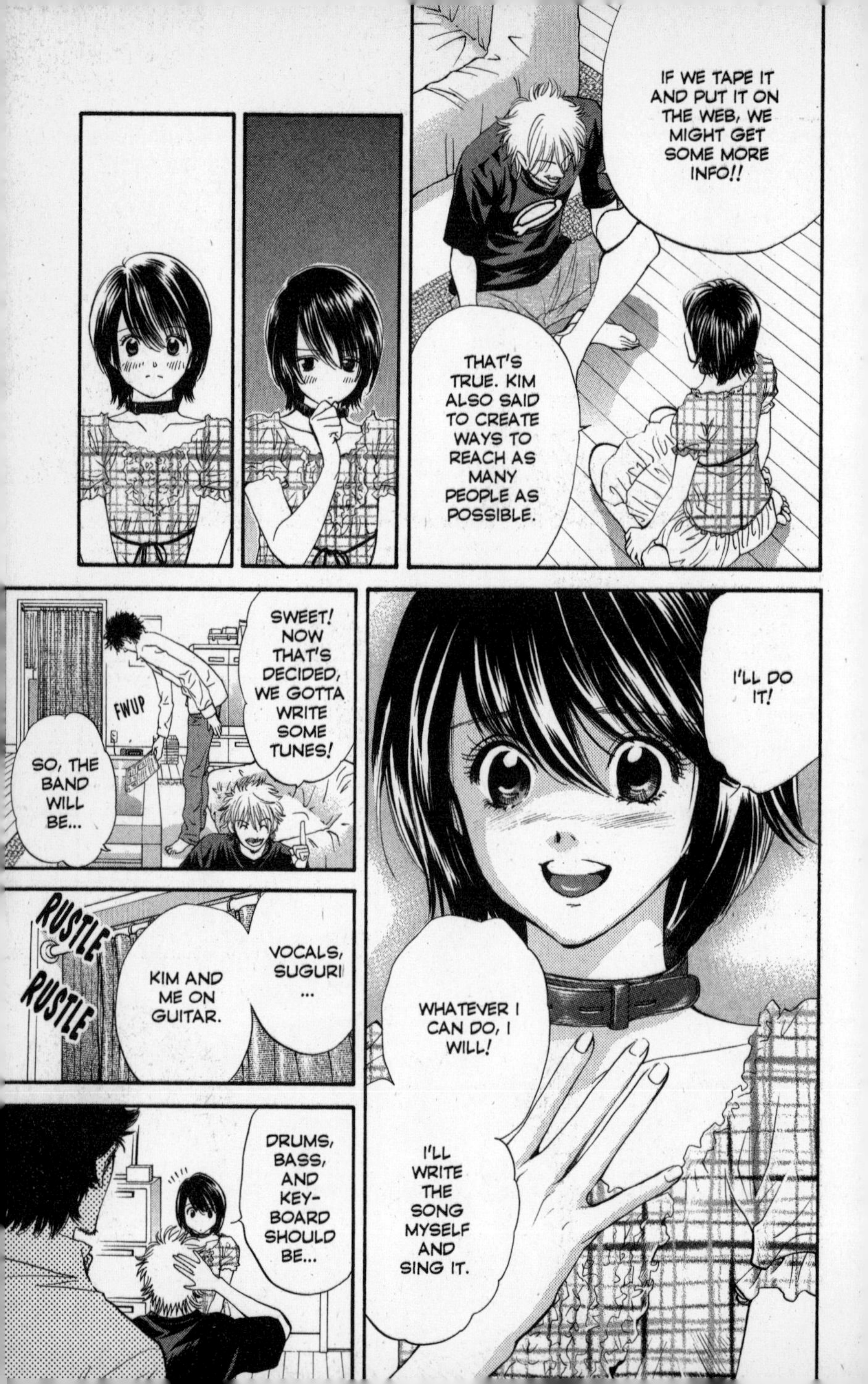
IF WE TAPE IT AND PUT IT ON THE WEB, WE MIGHT GET SOME MORE INFO!!
THAT'S TRUE. KIM ALSO SAID TO CREATE WAYS TO REACH AS MANY PEOPLE AS POSSIBLE.
I'LL DO IT!
WHATEVER I CAN DO, I WILL!
I'LL WRITE THE SONG MYSELF AND SING IT.
SWEET! NOW THAT'S DECIDED, WE GOTTA WRITE SOME TUNES!
FWUP
SO, THE BAND WILL BE...
RUSTLE RUSTLE
VOCALS, SUGURI ...
KIM AND ME ON GUITAR.
DRUMS, BASS, AND KEY-BOARD SHOULD BE...

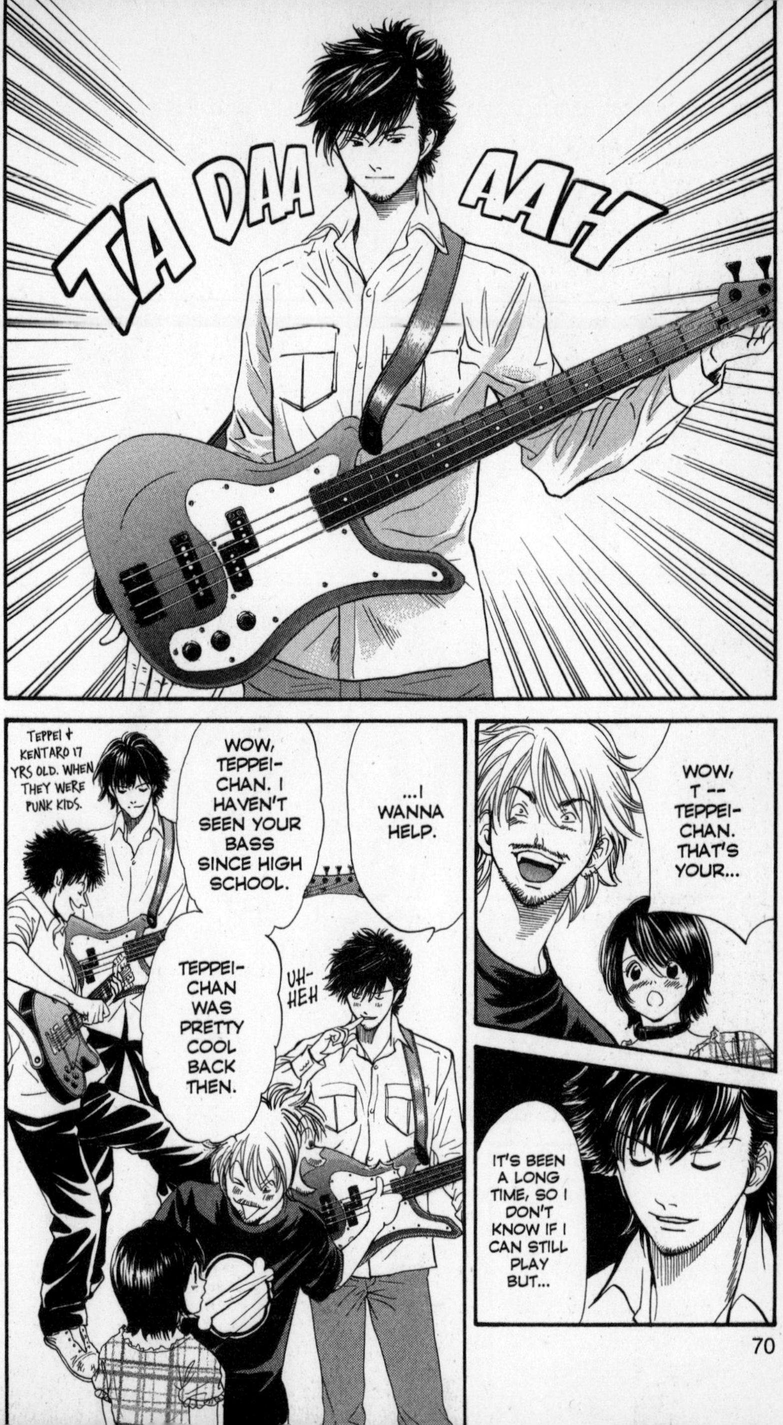
TA DAA AAH
WOW, T -- TEPPEI-CHAN. THAT'S YOUR...
IT'S BEEN A LONG TIME, SO I DON'T KNOW IF I CAN STILL PLAY BUT...
...I WANNA HELP.
WOW, TEPPEI-CHAN. I HAVEN'T SEEN YOUR BASS SINCE HIGH SCHOOL.
TEPPEI & KENTARO 17 YRS OLD. WHEN THEY WERE PUNK KIDS.
UH-HEH
TEPPEI-CHAN WAS PRETTY COOL BACK THEN.

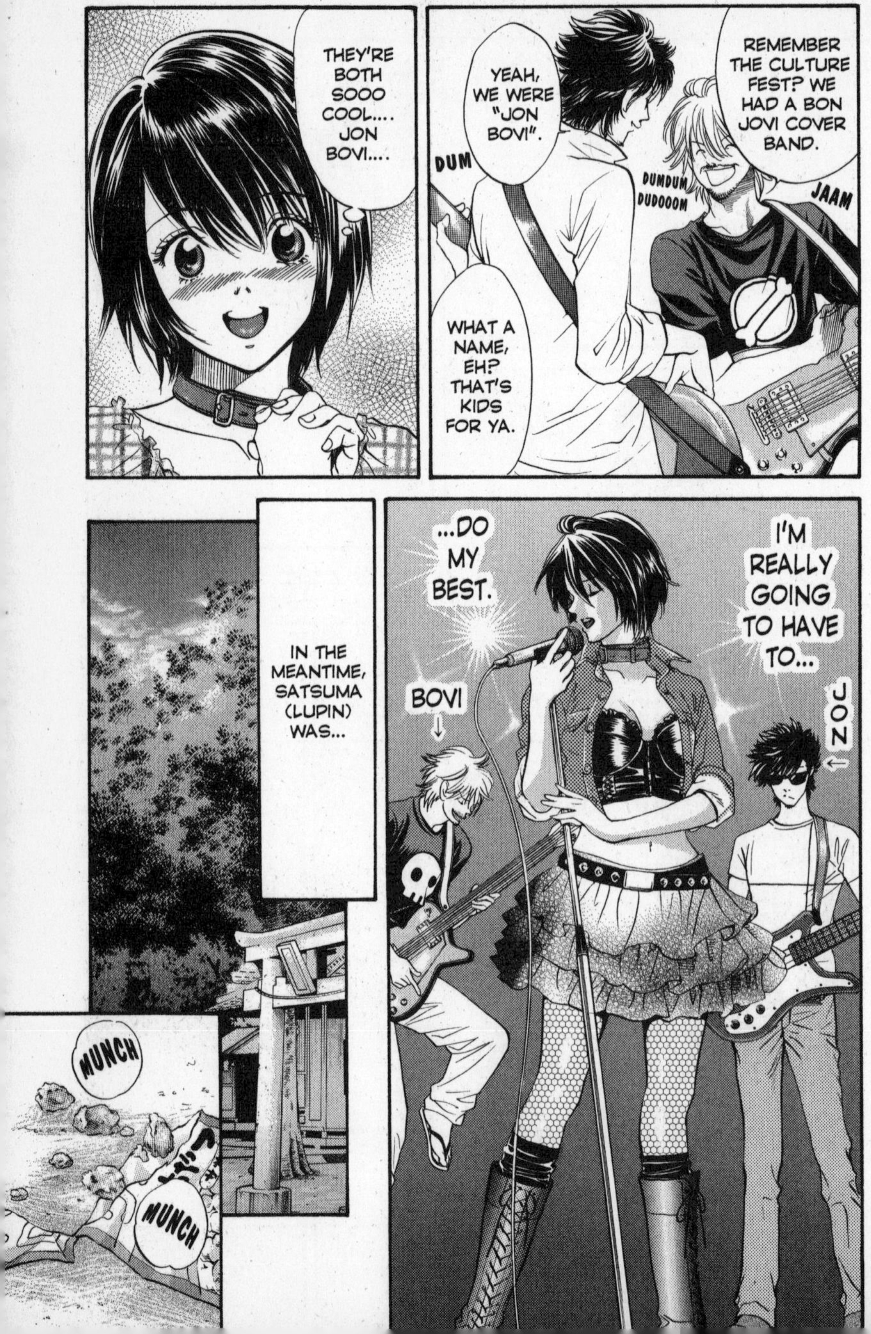
REMEMBER THE CULTURE FEST? WE HAD A BON JOVI COVER BAND.
JAAM
DUMDUM DUDOOOM
YEAH, WE WERE "JON BOVI".
DUM
WHAT A NAME, EH? THAT'S KIDS FOR YA.
THEY'RE BOTH SOOO COOL.... JON BOVI....
I'M REALLY GOING TO HAVE TO...
...DO MY BEST.
JON
BOVI
IN THE MEANTIME, SATSUMA (LUPIN) WAS...
MUNCH
MUNCH

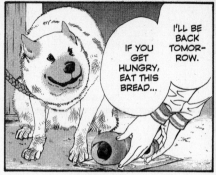

I'M SORRY SATSUMA... I GUESS THIS IS THE ONLY PLACE WE CAN HANG OUT AFTER ALL...
I'LL BE BACK TOMORROW.
IF YOU GET HUNGRY, EAT THIS BREAD...
BYE, SATSUMA
GNAW
GNAW
CHOMP

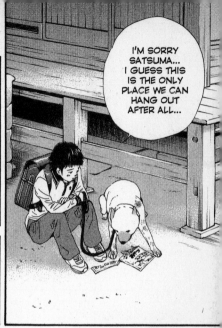

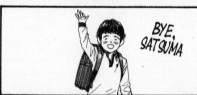

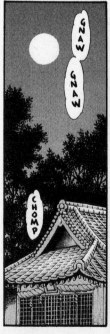

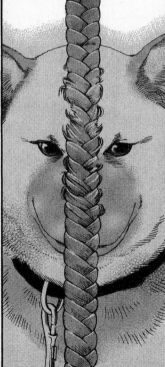

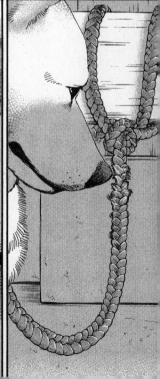

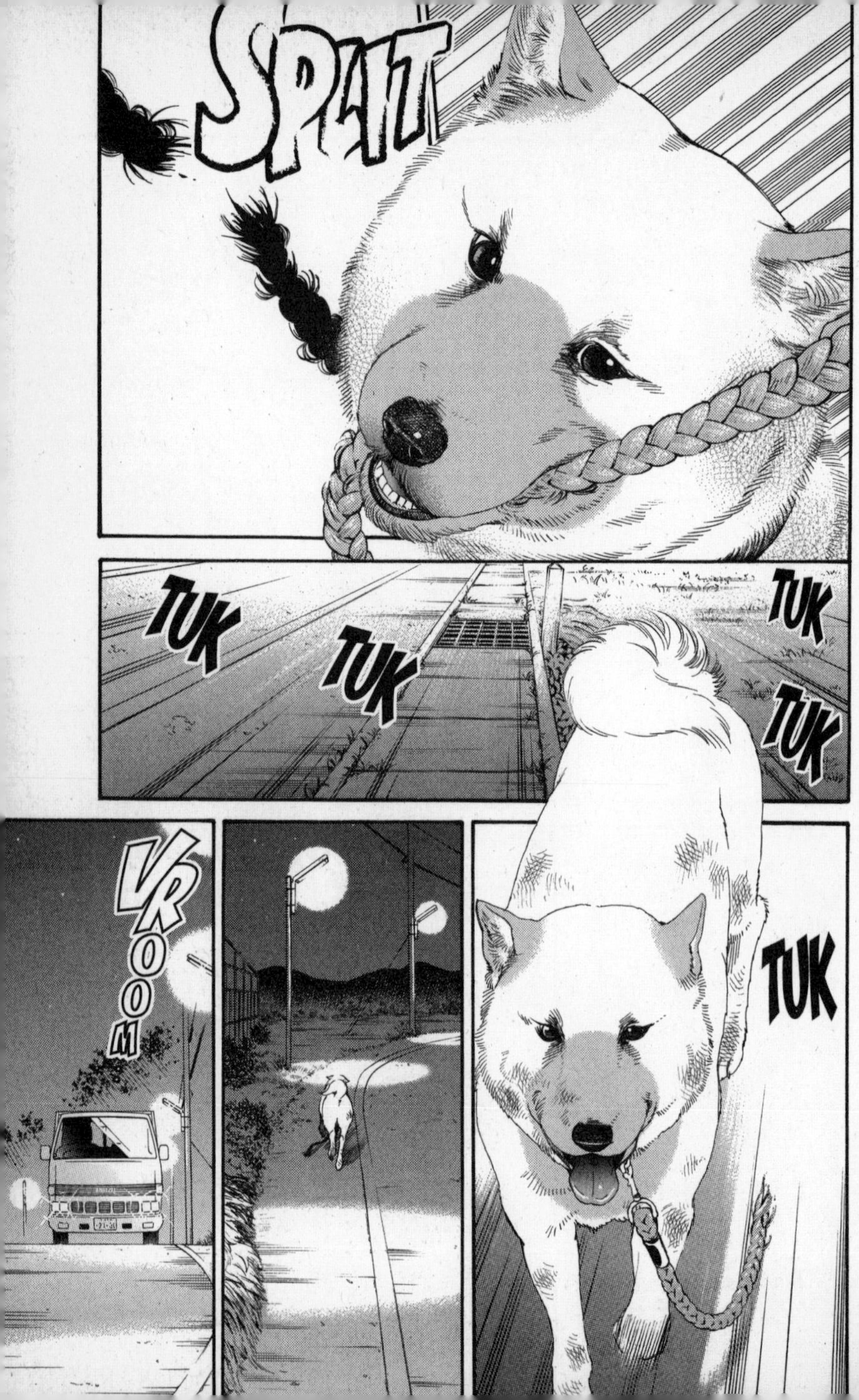
SPATT
TUK
TUK
TUK
TUK
TUK
VROOOM

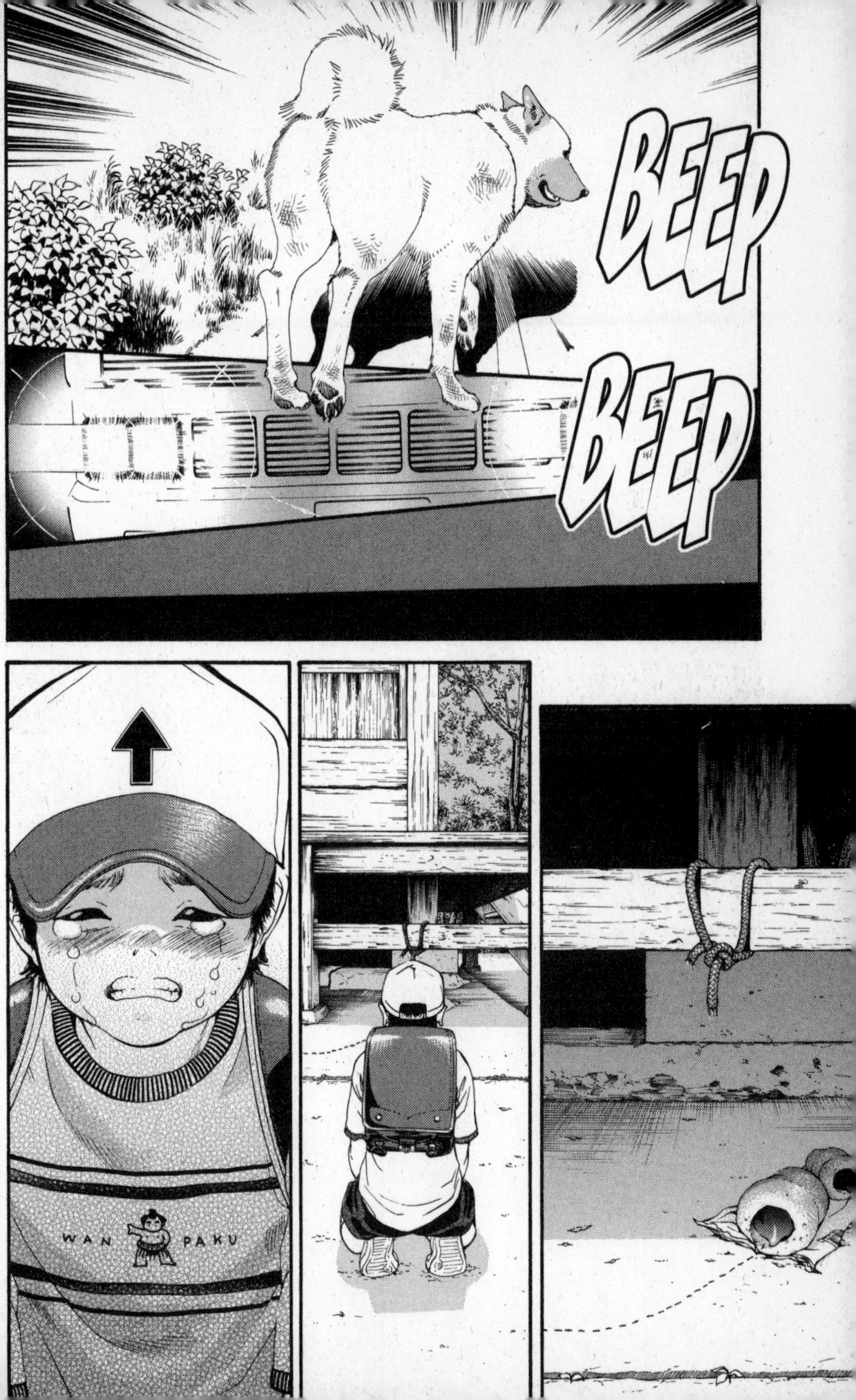
BEEP
BEEP
WAN PAKU

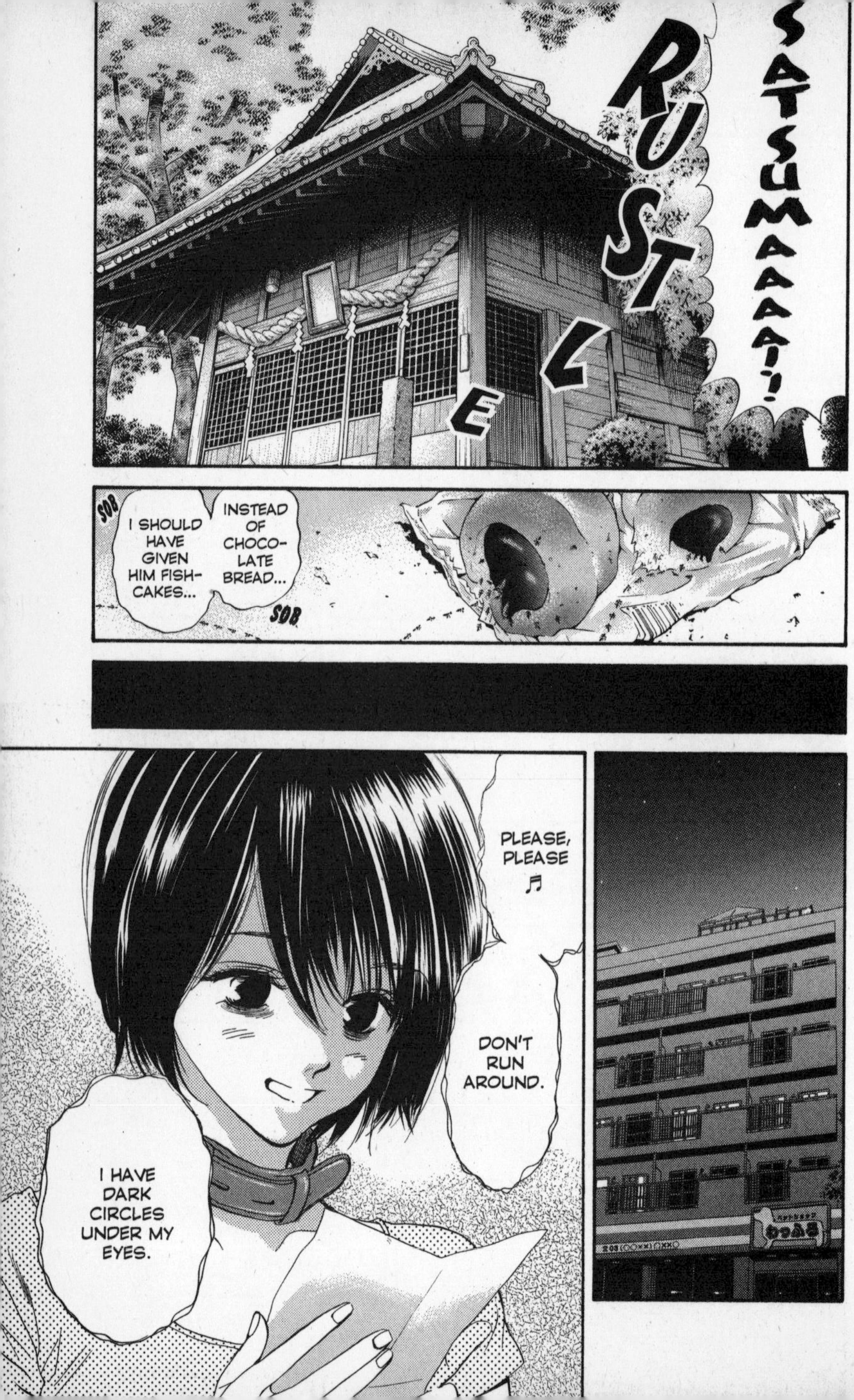
SATSUMAAAAA!!
RUSTLE
SOB
INSTEAD OF CHOCO-LATE BREAD...
I SHOULD HAVE GIVEN HIM FISH-CAKES...
SOB
PLEASE, PLEASE ♫
DON'T RUN AROUND.
I HAVE DARK CIRCLES UNDER MY EYES.

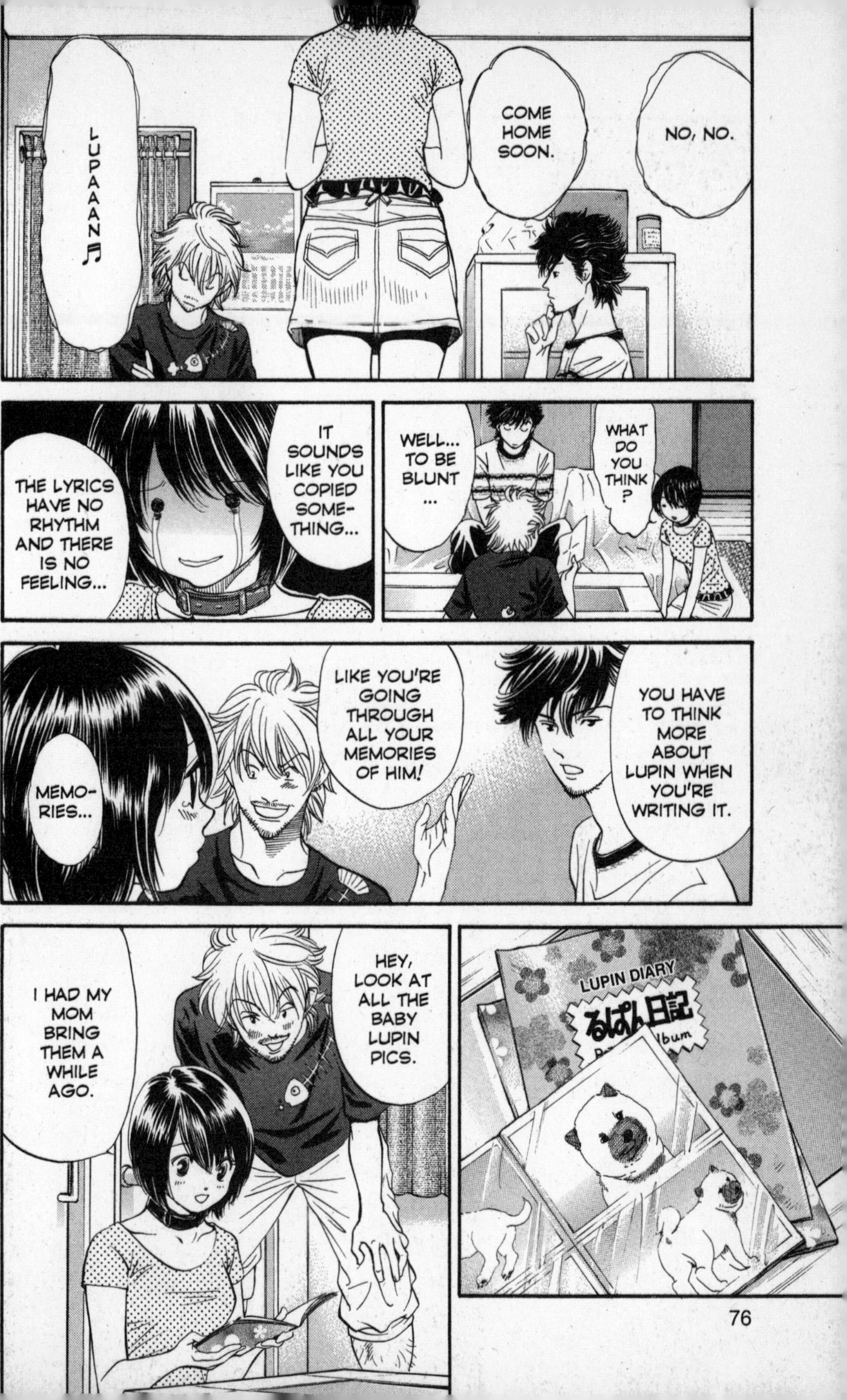
NO, NO.
COME HOME SOON.
LUPAAAAN♬
WHAT DO YOU THINK?
WELL... TO BE BLUNT...
IT SOUNDS LIKE YOU COPIED SOMETHING...
THE LYRICS HAVE NO RHYTHM AND THERE IS NO FEELING...
YOU HAVE TO THINK MORE ABOUT LUPIN WHEN YOU'RE WRITING IT.
LIKE YOU'RE GOING THROUGH ALL YOUR MEMORIES OF HIM!
MEMORIES...
LUPIN DIARY
るぱん日記
HEY, LOOK AT ALL THE BABY LUPIN PICS.
I HAD MY MOM BRING THEM A WHILE AGO.

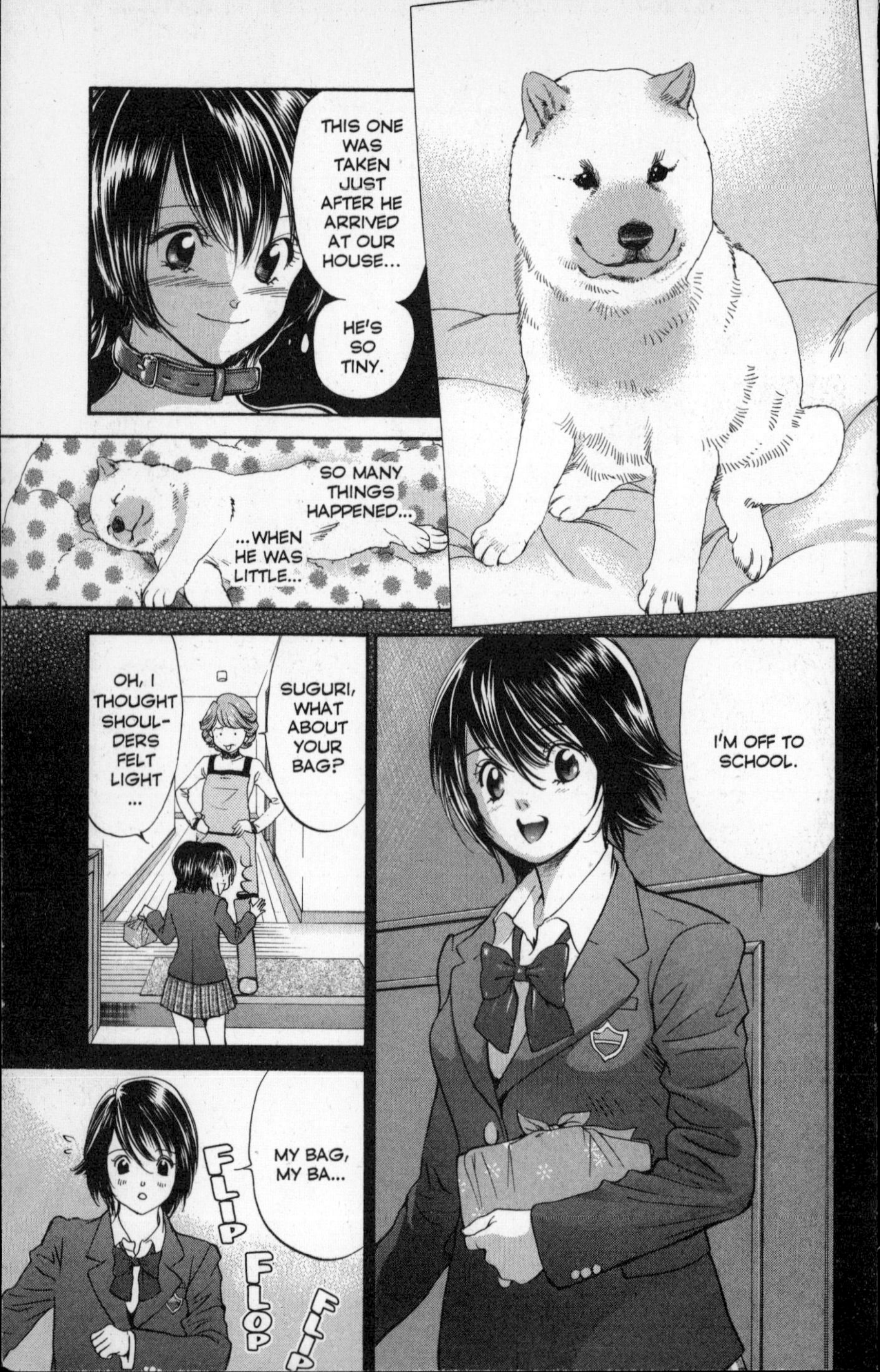
THIS ONE WAS TAKEN JUST AFTER HE ARRIVED AT OUR HOUSE...
HE'S SO TINY.
SO MANY THINGS HAPPENED...
...WHEN HE WAS LITTLE...
I'M OFF TO SCHOOL.
SUGURI, WHAT ABOUT YOUR BAG?
OH, I THOUGHT SHOUL-DERS FELT LIGHT ...
MY BAG, MY BA...
FLIP
FLOP
FLIP

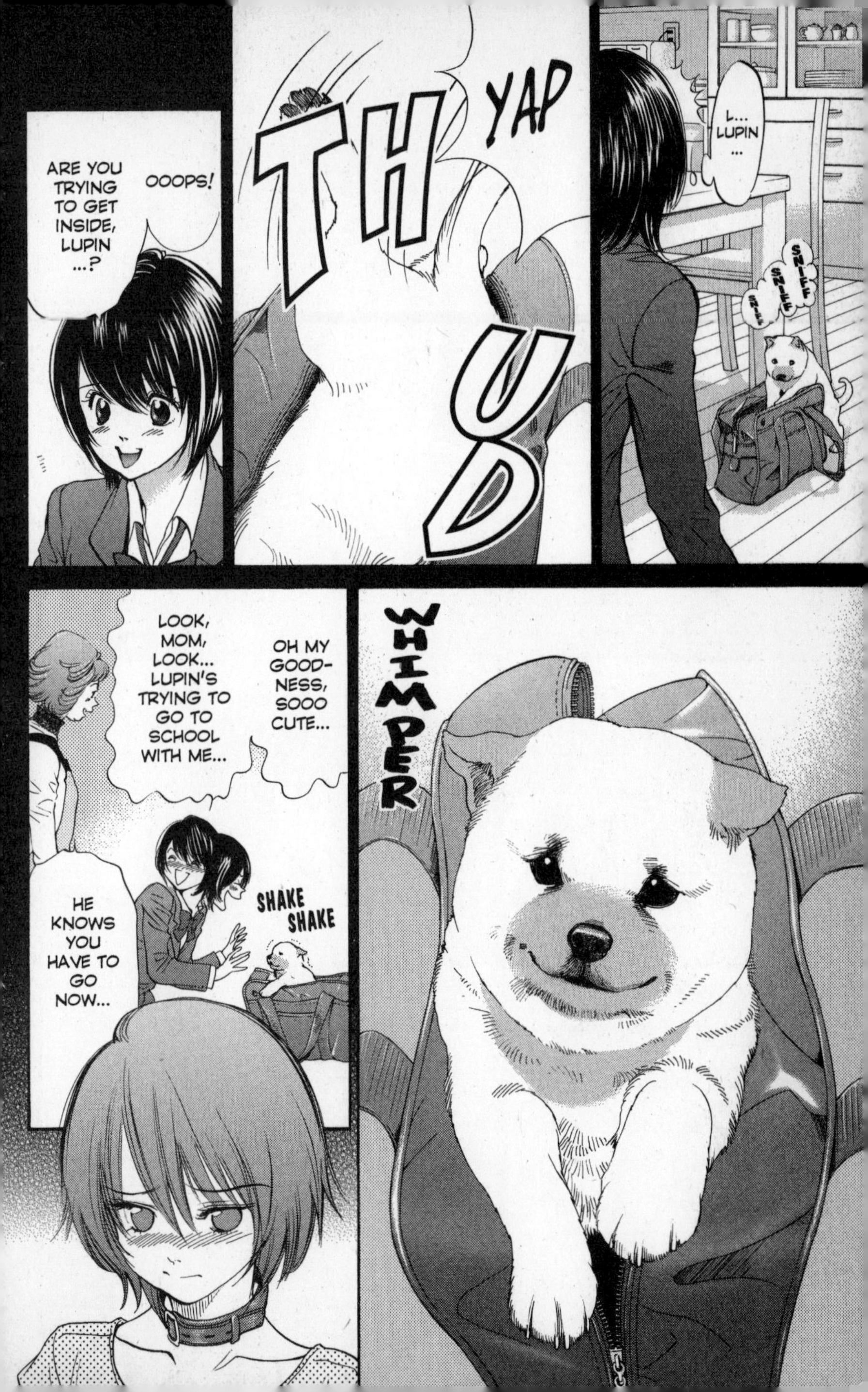
L... LUPIN ...
SNIFF SNIFF SNIFF
YAP
THUD
OOOPS!
ARE YOU TRYING TO GET INSIDE, LUPIN ...?
WHIMPER
OH MY GOODNESS, SOOO CUTE...
LOOK, MOM, LOOK... LUPIN'S TRYING TO GO TO SCHOOL WITH ME...
SHAKE SHAKE
HE KNOWS YOU HAVE TO GO NOW...

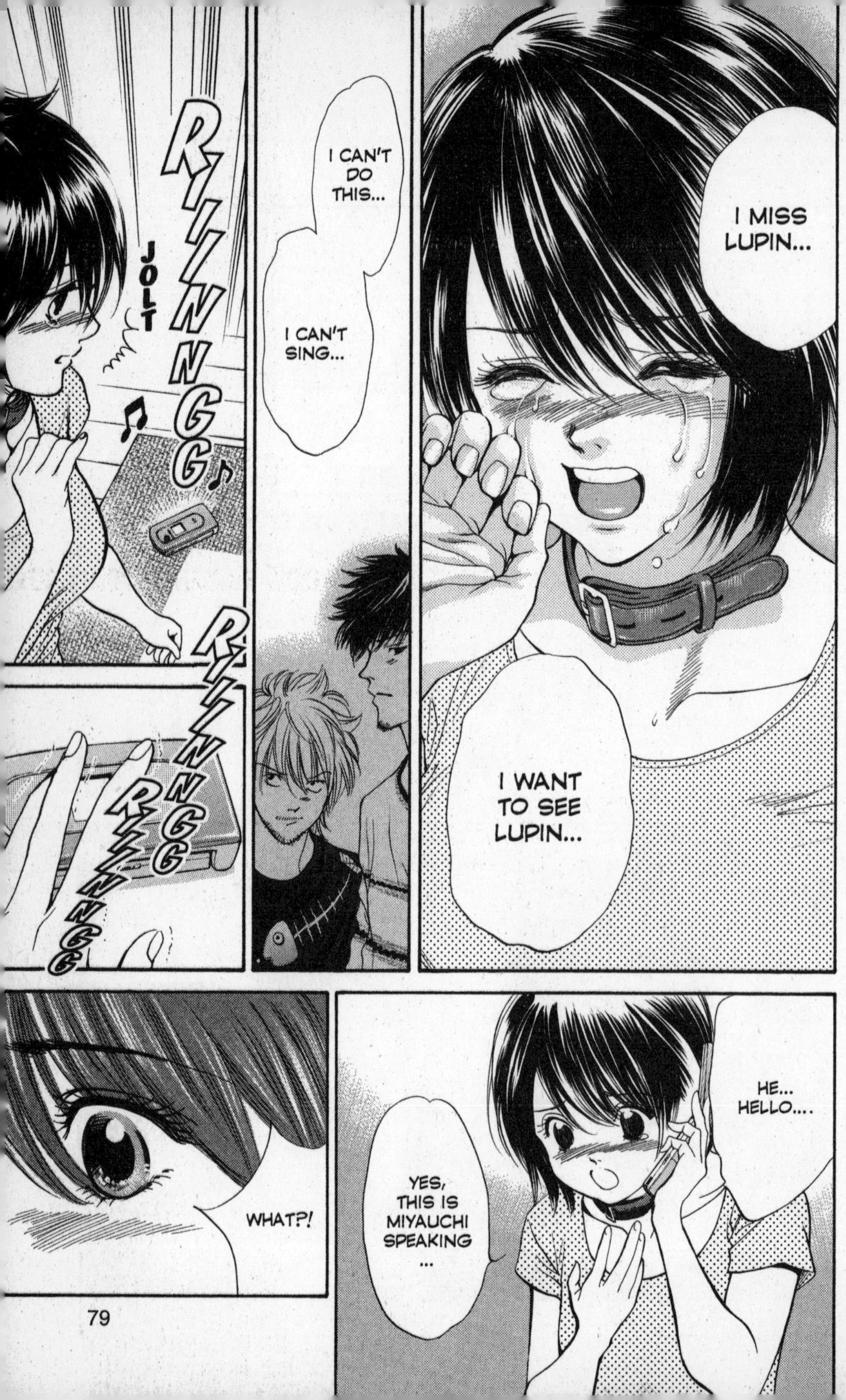
I MISS LUPIN...
I WANT TO SEE LUPIN...
I CAN'T DO THIS...
I CAN'T SING...
RIINNGG♪
JOLT
RIINNGG
RIINNGG
HE... HELLO....
YES, THIS IS MIYAUCHI SPEAKING ...
WHAT?!

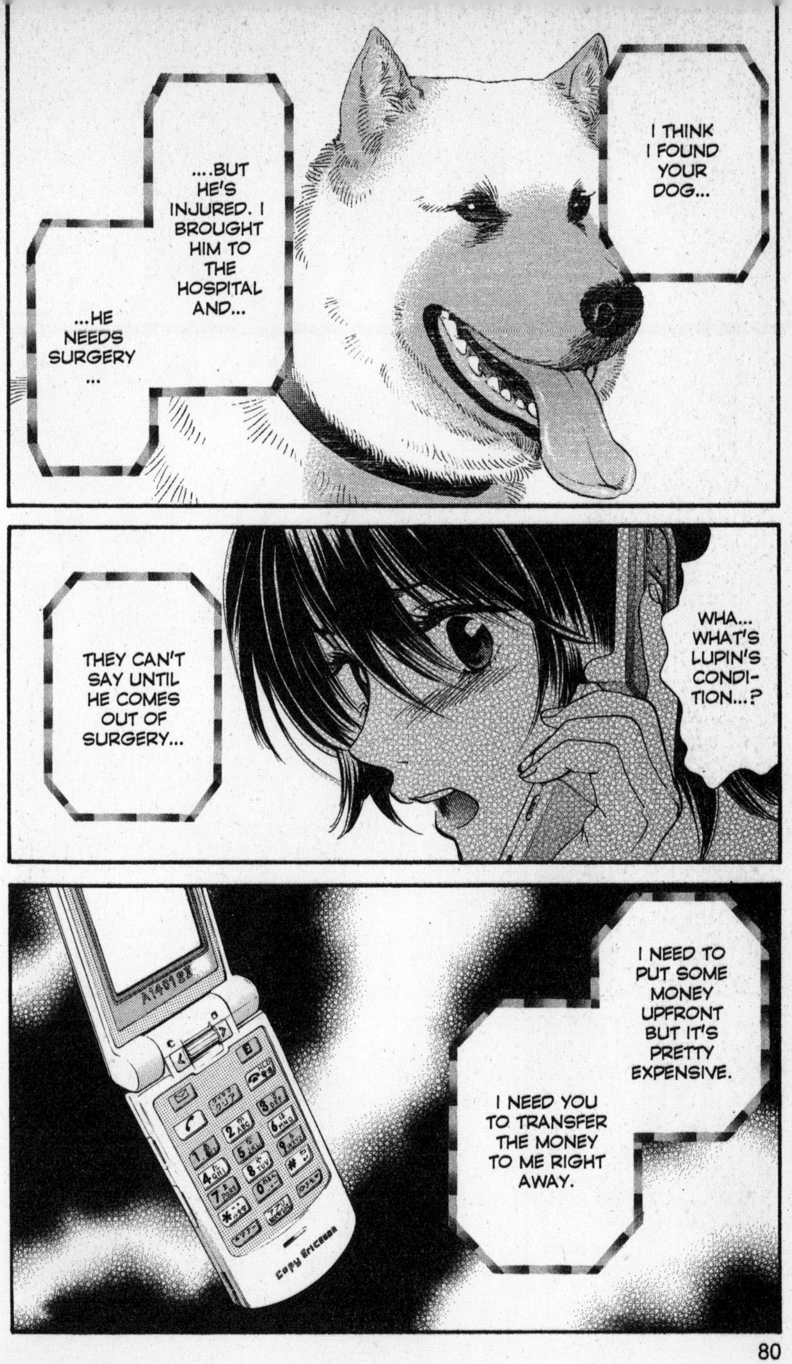
I THINK I FOUND YOUR DOG...
....BUT HE'S INJURED. I BROUGHT HIM TO THE HOSPITAL AND...
...HE NEEDS SURGERY ...
WHA... WHAT'S LUPIN'S CONDI- TION...?
THEY CAN'T SAY UNTIL HE COMES OUT OF SURGERY...
I NEED TO PUT SOME MONEY UPFRONT BUT IT'S PRETTY EXPENSIVE.
I NEED YOU TO TRANSFER THE MONEY TO ME RIGHT AWAY.

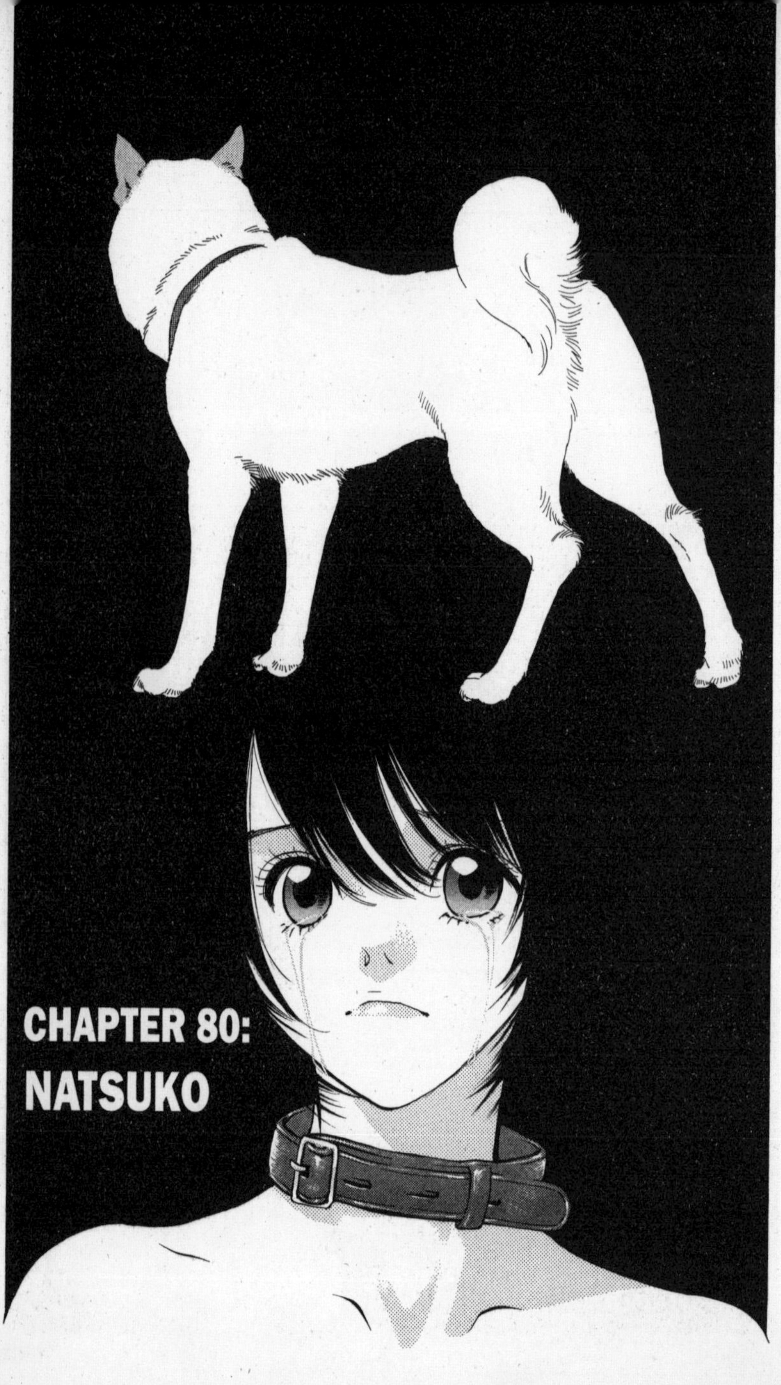
CHAPTER 80:
NATSUKO

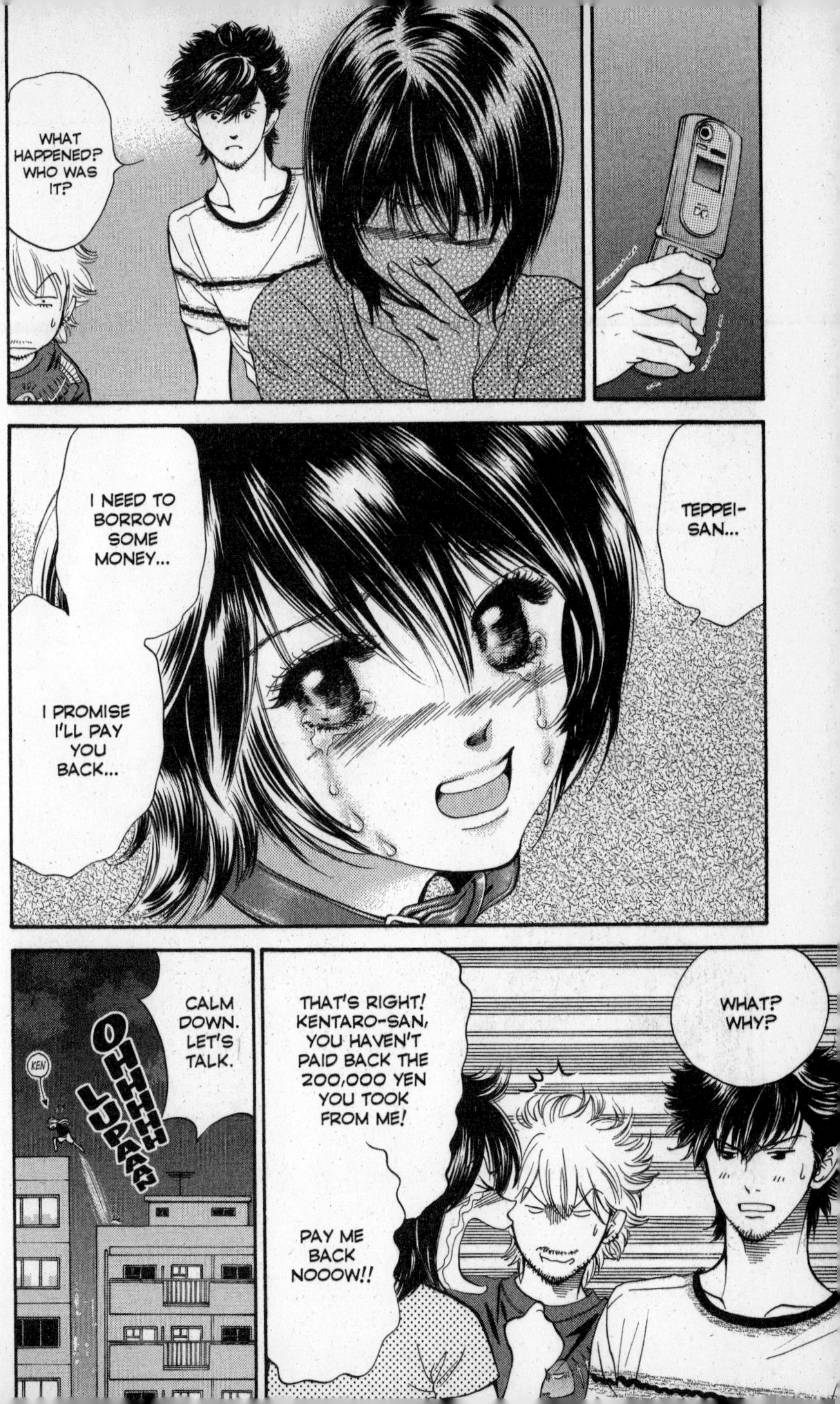
WHAT HAPPENED? WHO WAS IT?
TEPPEI-SAN...
I NEED TO BORROW SOME MONEY...
I PROMISE I'LL PAY YOU BACK...
WHAT? WHY?
THAT'S RIGHT! KENTARO-SAN, YOU HAVEN'T PAID BACK THE 200,000 YEN YOU TOOK FROM ME!
PAY ME BACK NOOOW!!
CALM DOWN. LET'S TALK.
OHHHHH LUPAAA☆
KEN

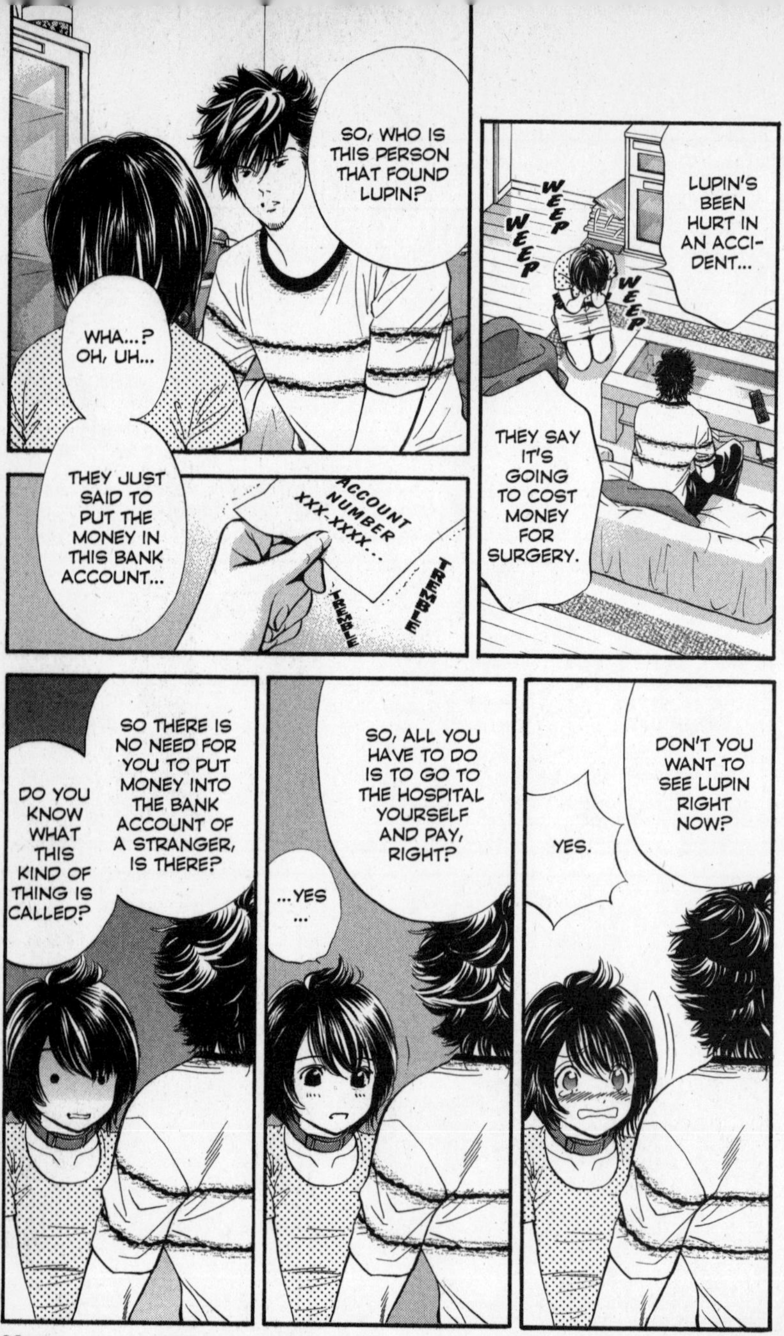
LUPIN'S BEEN HURT IN AN ACCI-DENT...
WEEP WEEP
WEEP
THEY SAY IT'S GOING TO COST MONEY FOR SURGERY.
SO, WHO IS THIS PERSON THAT FOUND LUPIN?
WHA...? OH, UH...
THEY JUST SAID TO PUT THE MONEY IN THIS BANK ACCOUNT...
ACCOUNT NUMBER XXX-XXXX...
TREMBLE
TREMBLE
DON'T YOU WANT TO SEE LUPIN RIGHT NOW?
YES.
SO, ALL YOU HAVE TO DO IS TO GO TO THE HOSPITAL YOURSELF AND PAY, RIGHT?
...YES ...
SO THERE IS NO NEED FOR YOU TO PUT MONEY INTO THE BANK ACCOUNT OF A STRANGER, IS THERE?
DO YOU KNOW WHAT THIS KIND OF THING IS CALLED?

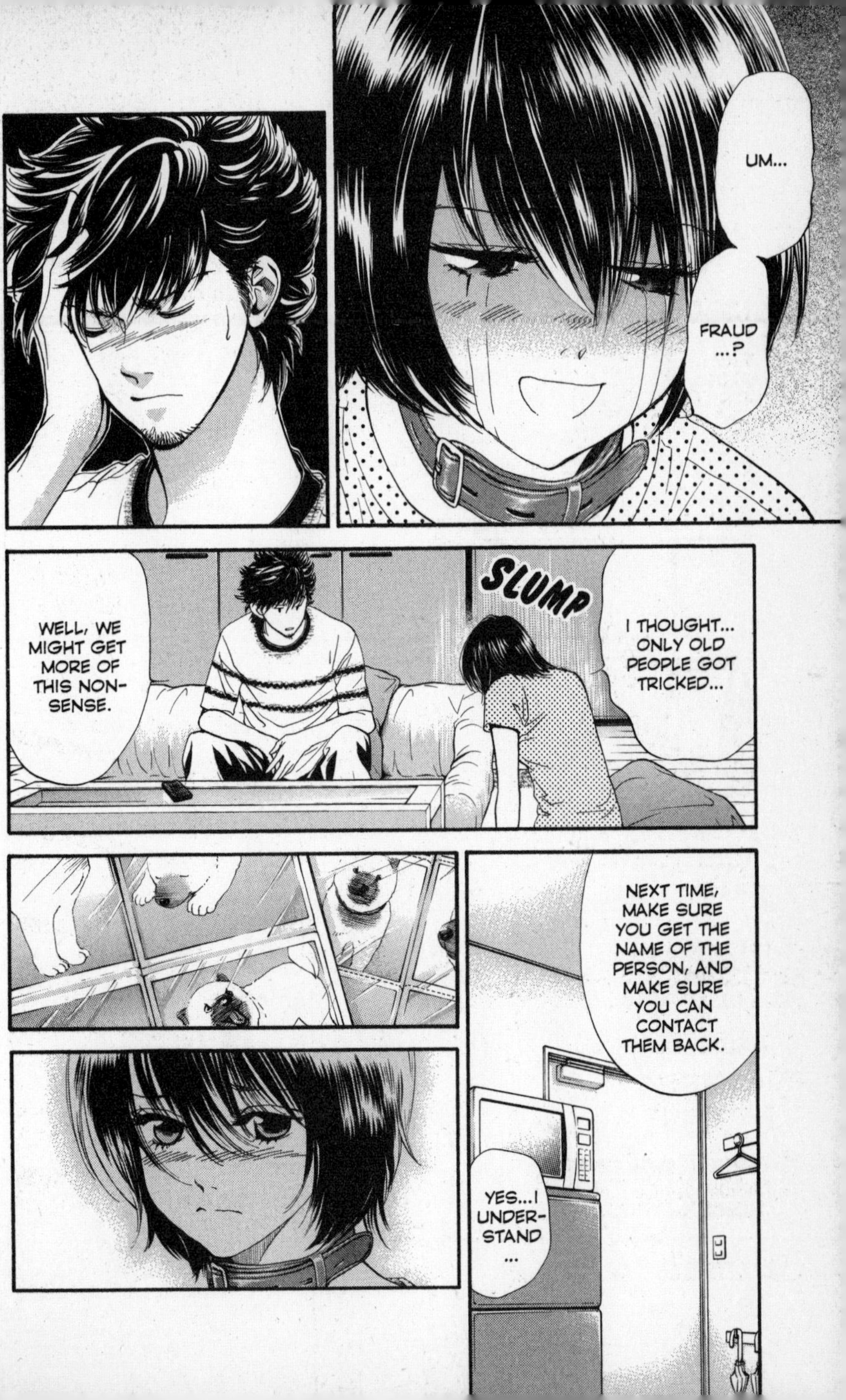
UM...
FRAUD ...?
I THOUGHT... ONLY OLD PEOPLE GOT TRICKED...
SLUMP
WELL, WE MIGHT GET MORE OF THIS NON-SENSE.
NEXT TIME, MAKE SURE YOU GET THE NAME OF THE PERSON, AND MAKE SURE YOU CAN CONTACT THEM BACK.
YES...I UNDER-STAND ...

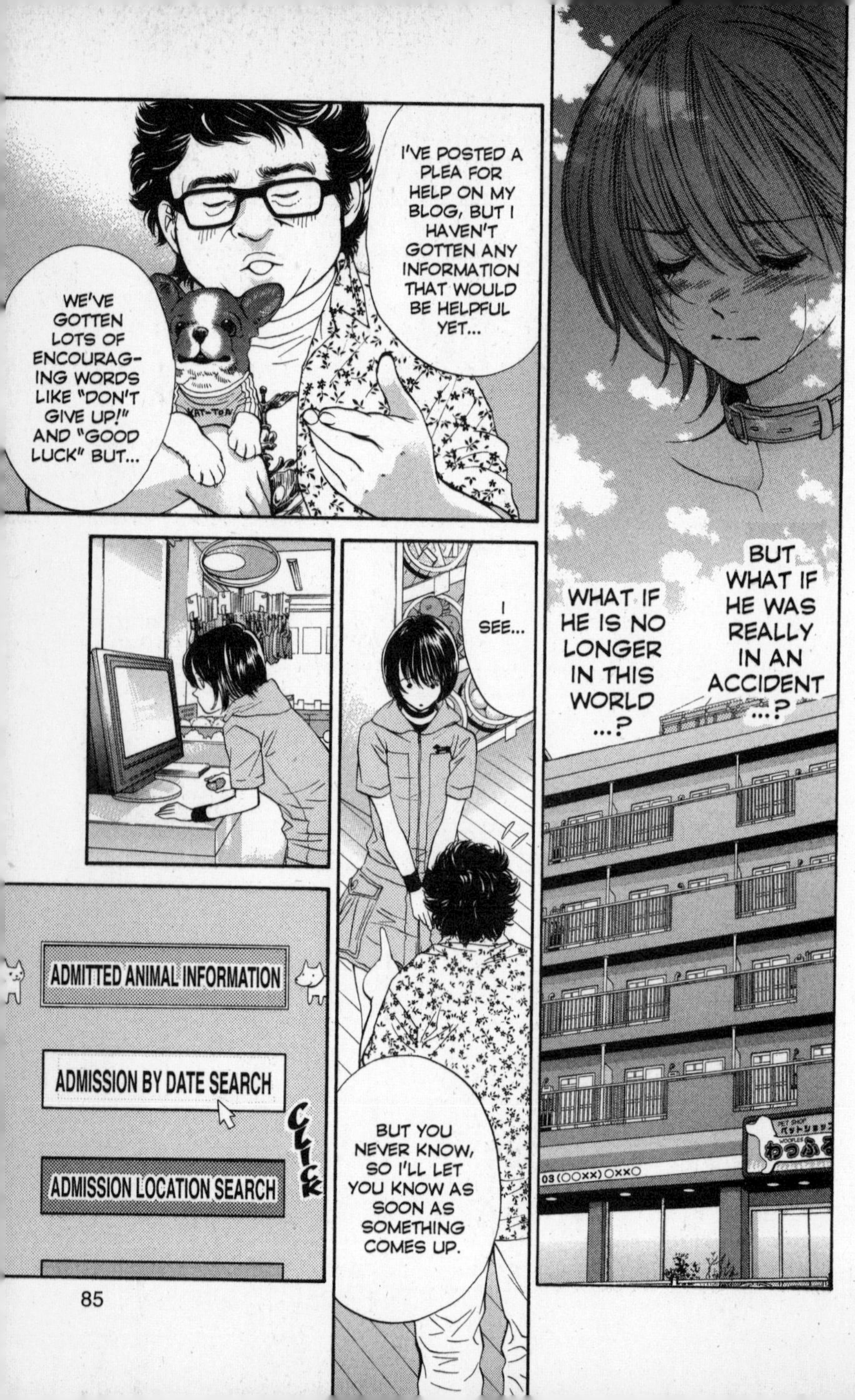
BUT WHAT IF HE WAS REALLY IN AN ACCIDENT ...?
WHAT IF HE IS NO LONGER IN THIS WORLD ...?
03 (○○xx) ○xx○
I'VE POSTED A PLEA FOR HELP ON MY BLOG, BUT I HAVEN'T GOTTEN ANY INFORMATION THAT WOULD BE HELPFUL YET...
WE'VE GOTTEN LOTS OF ENCOURAG-ING WORDS LIKE "DON'T GIVE UP!" AND "GOOD LUCK" BUT...
I SEE...
BUT YOU NEVER KNOW, SO I'LL LET YOU KNOW AS SOON AS SOMETHING COMES UP.
ADMITTED ANIMAL INFORMATION
ADMISSION BY DATE SEARCH
ADMISSION LOCATION SEARCH
CLICK

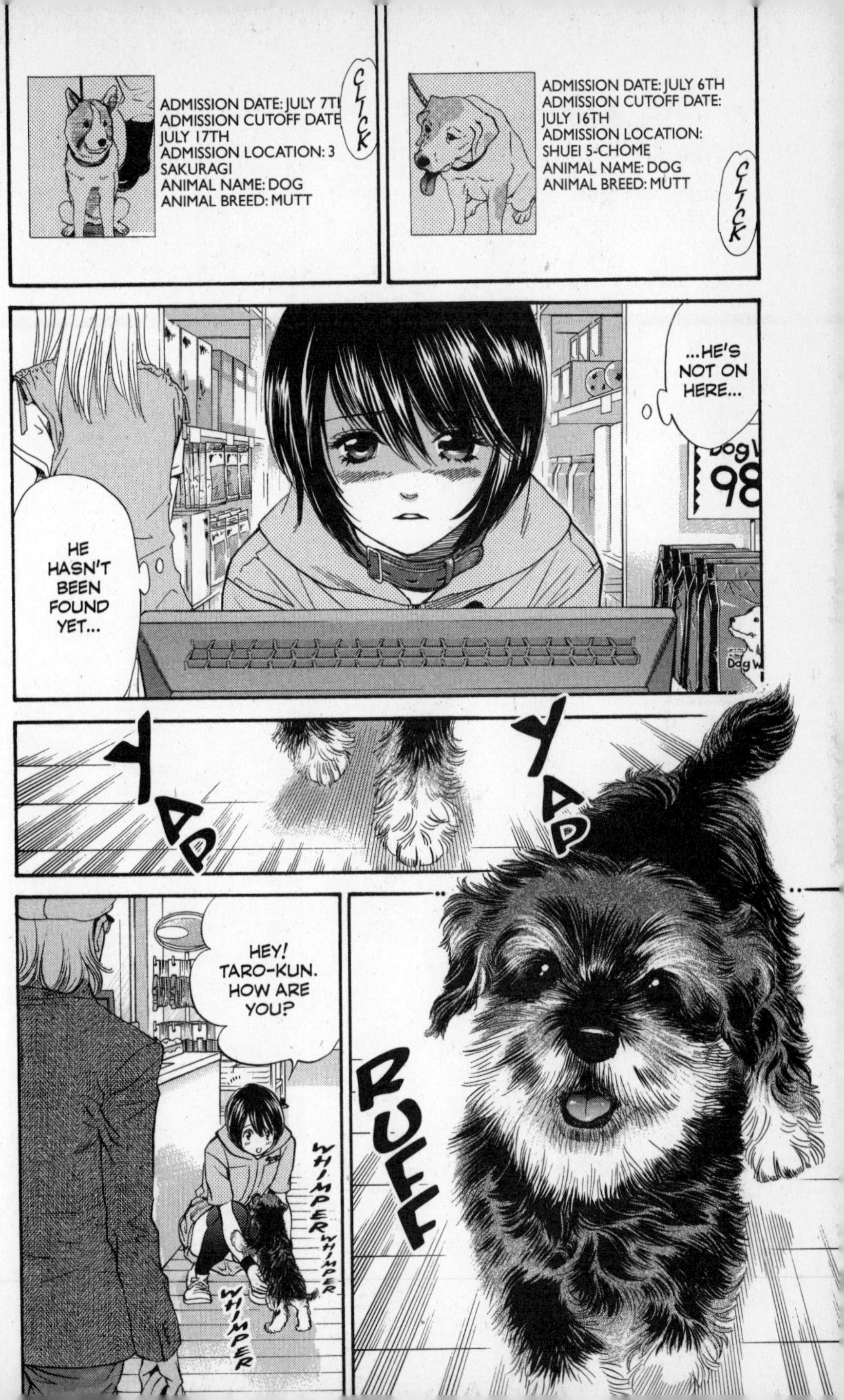
ADMISSION DATE: JULY 6TH
ADMISSION CUTOFF DATE: JULY 16TH
ADMISSION LOCATION: SHUEI 5-CHOME
ANIMAL NAME: DOG
ANIMAL BREED: MUTT
CLICK
CLICK
ADMISSION DATE: JULY 7T
ADMISSION CUTOFF DATE
JULY 17TH
ADMISSION LOCATION: 3 SAKURAGI
ANIMAL NAME: DOG
ANIMAL BREED: MUTT
...HE'S NOT ON HERE...
98
HE HASN'T BEEN FOUND YET...
YAP
YAP
RUFF
HEY! TARO-KUN. HOW ARE YOU?
WHIMPER
WHIMPER
WHIMPER

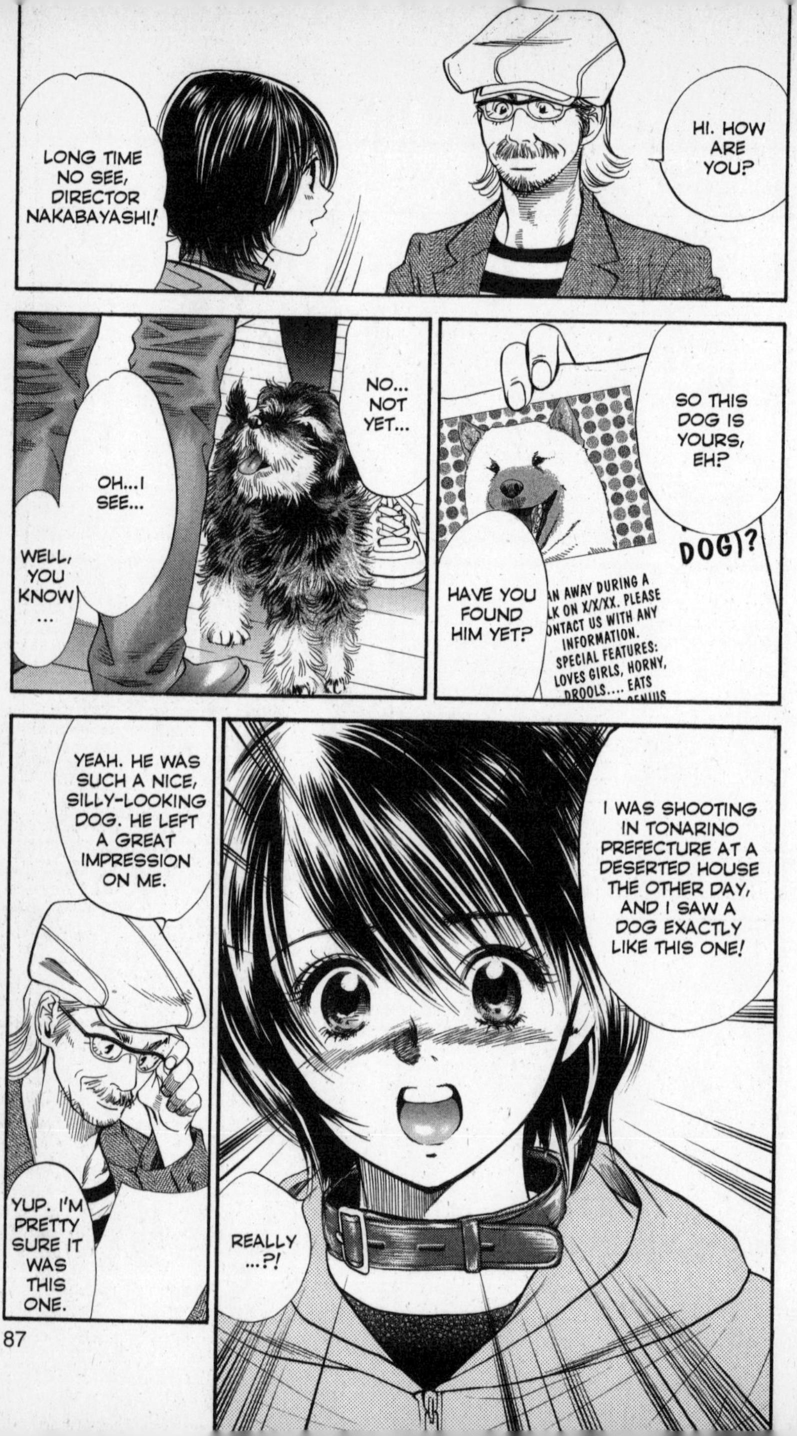
LONG TIME NO SEE, DIRECTOR NAKABAYASHI!
HI. HOW ARE YOU?
SO THIS DOG IS YOURS, EH?
DOG)?
AN AWAY DURING A
LK ON X/X/XX. PLEASE
ONTACT US WITH ANY
INFORMATION.
SPECIAL FEATURES:
LOVES GIRLS, HORNY, EATS
DROOLS....
HAVE YOU FOUND HIM YET?
NO... NOT YET...
OH...I SEE...
WELL, YOU KNOW ...
I WAS SHOOTING IN TONARINO PREFECTURE AT A DESERTED HOUSE THE OTHER DAY, AND I SAW A DOG EXACTLY LIKE THIS ONE!
REALLY ...?!
YEAH. HE WAS SUCH A NICE, SILLY-LOOKING DOG. HE LEFT A GREAT IMPRESSION ON ME.
YUP. I'M PRETTY SURE IT WAS THIS ONE.

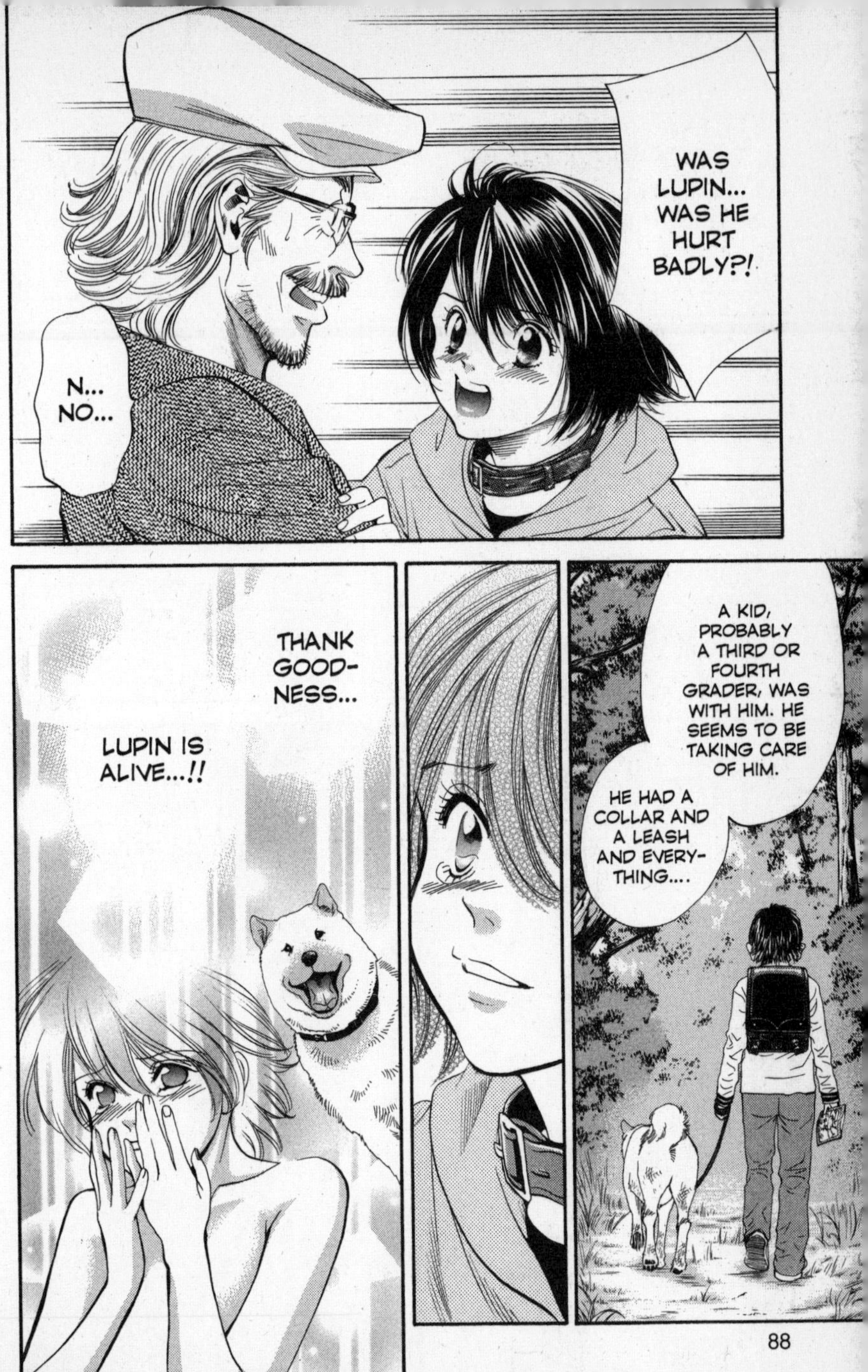
WAS LUPIN... WAS HE HURT BADLY?!
N... NO...
A KID, PROBABLY A THIRD OR FOURTH GRADER, WAS WITH HIM. HE SEEMS TO BE TAKING CARE OF HIM.
HE HAD A COLLAR AND A LEASH AND EVERY-THING....
THANK GOOD-NESS...
LUPIN IS ALIVE...!!

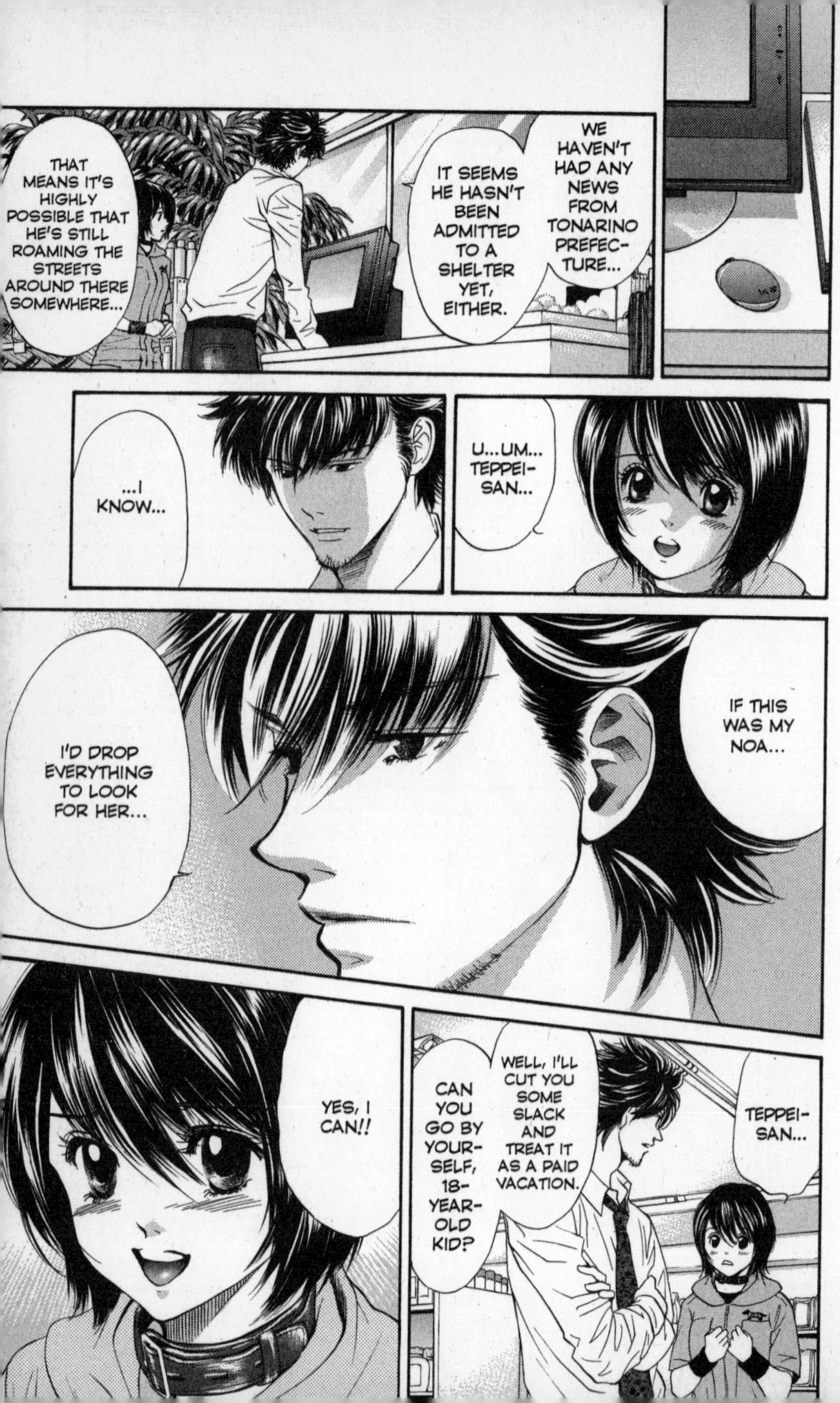
WE HAVEN'T HAD ANY NEWS FROM TONARINO PREFECTURE...
IT SEEMS HE HASN'T BEEN ADMITTED TO A SHELTER YET, EITHER.
THAT MEANS IT'S HIGHLY POSSIBLE THAT HE'S STILL ROAMING THE STREETS AROUND THERE SOMEWHERE...
U...UM... TEPPEI-SAN...
...I KNOW...
IF THIS WAS MY NOA...
I'D DROP EVERYTHING TO LOOK FOR HER...
TEPPEI-SAN...
WELL, I'LL CUT YOU SOME SLACK AND TREAT IT AS A PAID VACATION.
CAN YOU GO BY YOURSELF, 18-YEAR-OLD KID?
YES, I CAN!!

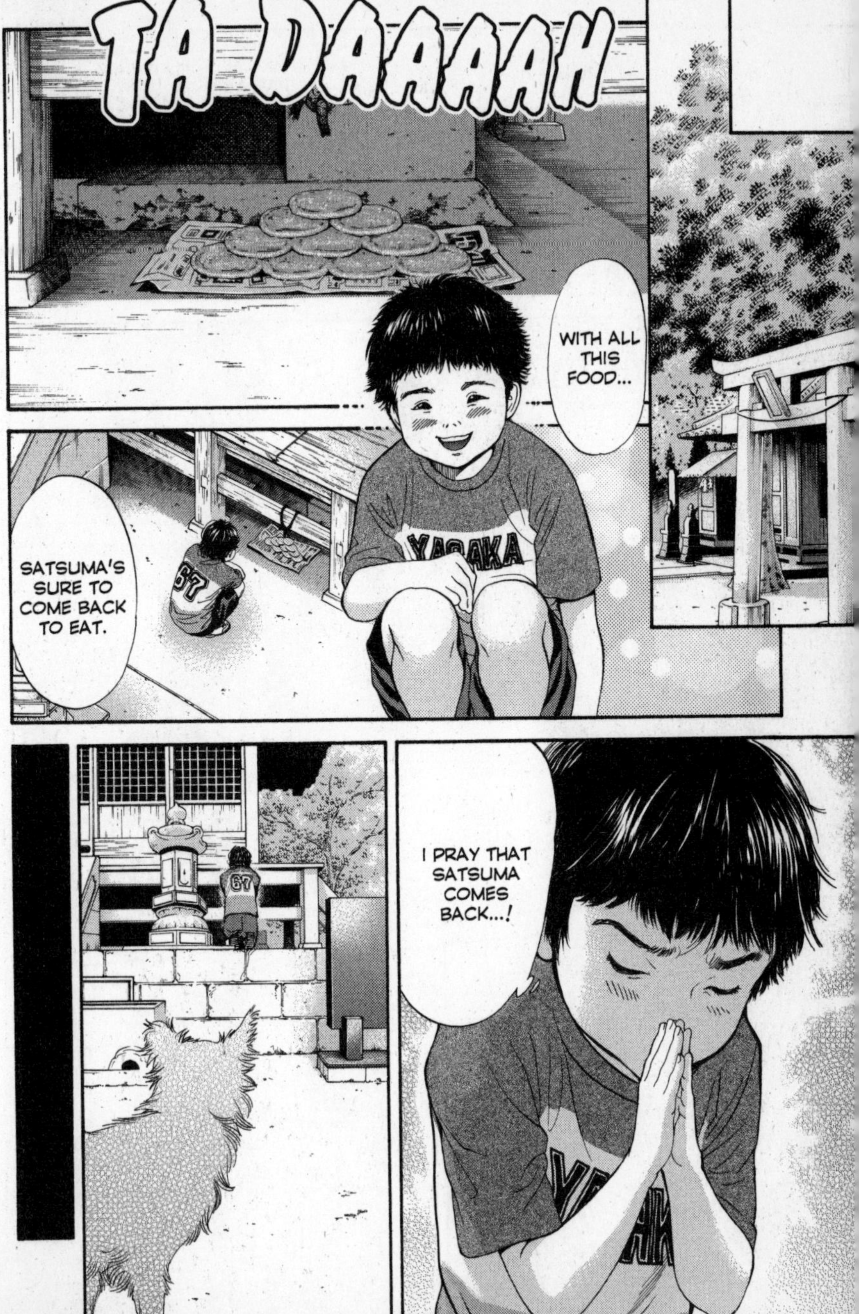
TA DAAAAH
WITH ALL THIS FOOD...
SATSUMA'S SURE TO COME BACK TO EAT.
I PRAY THAT SATSUMA COMES BACK...!

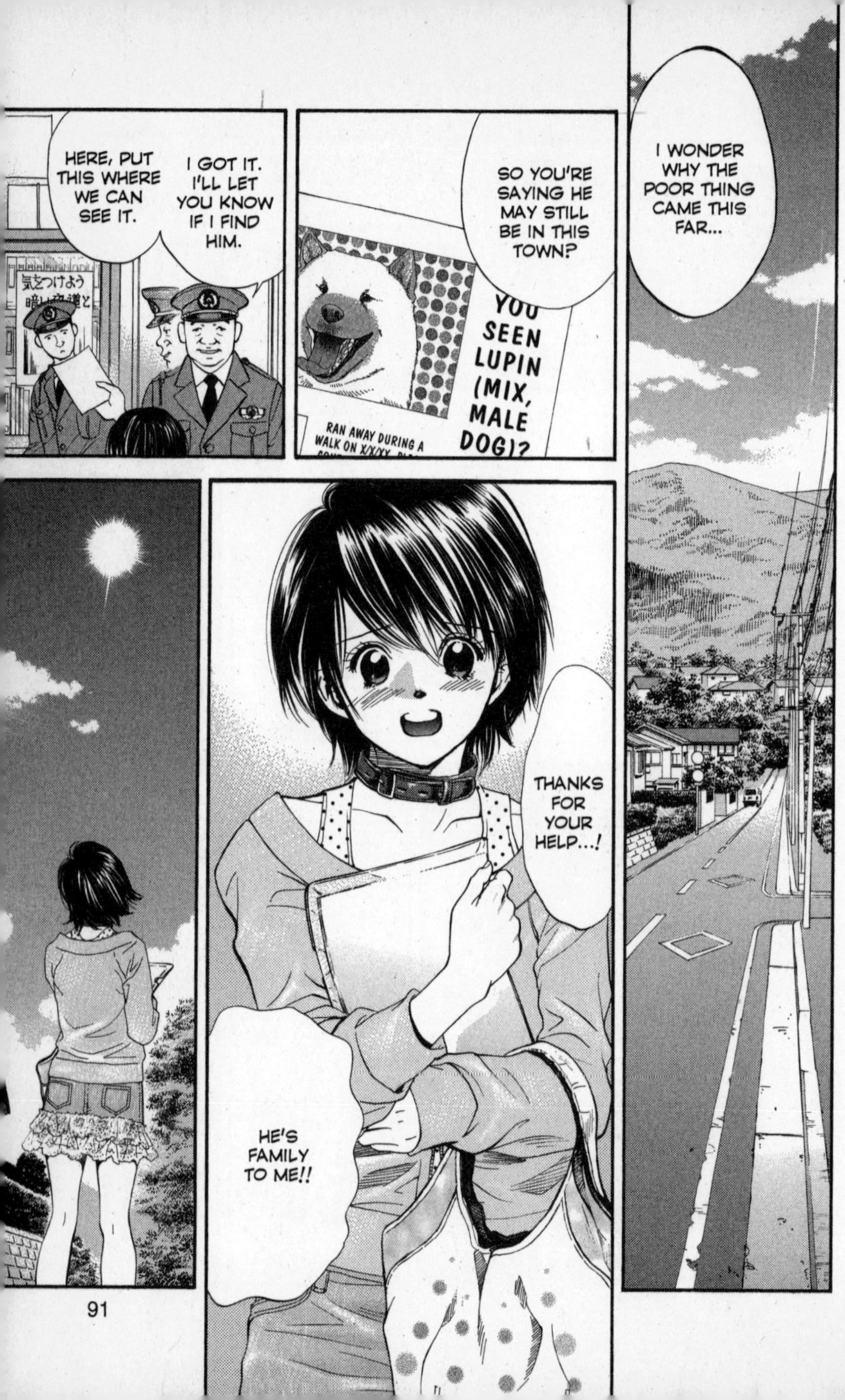
I WONDER WHY THE POOR THING CAME THIS FAR...
SO YOU'RE SAYING HE MAY STILL BE IN THIS TOWN?
YOU SEEN LUPIN (MIX, MALE DOG)?
RAN AWAY DURING A WALK ON X/X/XX.
I GOT IT. I'LL LET YOU KNOW IF I FIND HIM.
HERE, PUT THIS WHERE WE CAN SEE IT.
気をつけよう
THANKS FOR YOUR HELP...!
HE'S FAMILY TO ME!!

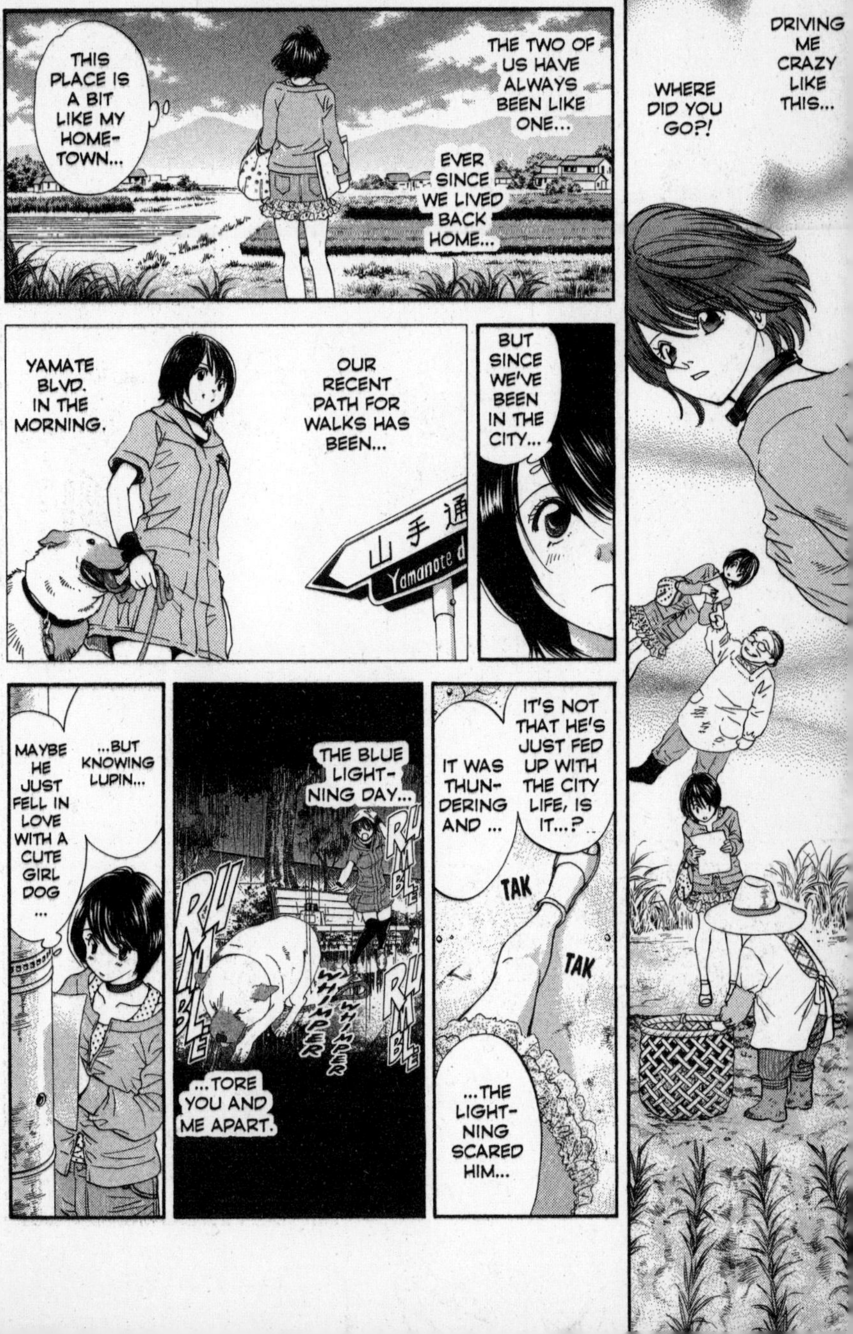
DRIVING ME CRAZY LIKE THIS...
WHERE DID YOU GO?!
THE TWO OF US HAVE ALWAYS BEEN LIKE ONE...
EVER SINCE WE LIVED BACK HOME...
THIS PLACE IS A BIT LIKE MY HOME-TOWN...
BUT SINCE WE'VE BEEN IN THE CITY...
山手通
Yamanote d
OUR RECENT PATH FOR WALKS HAS BEEN...
YAMATE BLVD. IN THE MORNING.
IT'S NOT THAT HE'S JUST FED UP WITH THE CITY LIFE, IS IT...?
IT WAS THUN-DERING AND ...
TAK
TAK
...THE LIGHT-NING SCARED HIM...
THE BLUE LIGHT-NING DAY...
RUMBLE
RUMBLE
RUMBLE
WHIMPER
WHIMPER
...TORE YOU AND ME APART.
...BUT KNOWING LUPIN...
MAYBE HE JUST FELL IN LOVE WITH A CUTE GIRL DOG ...

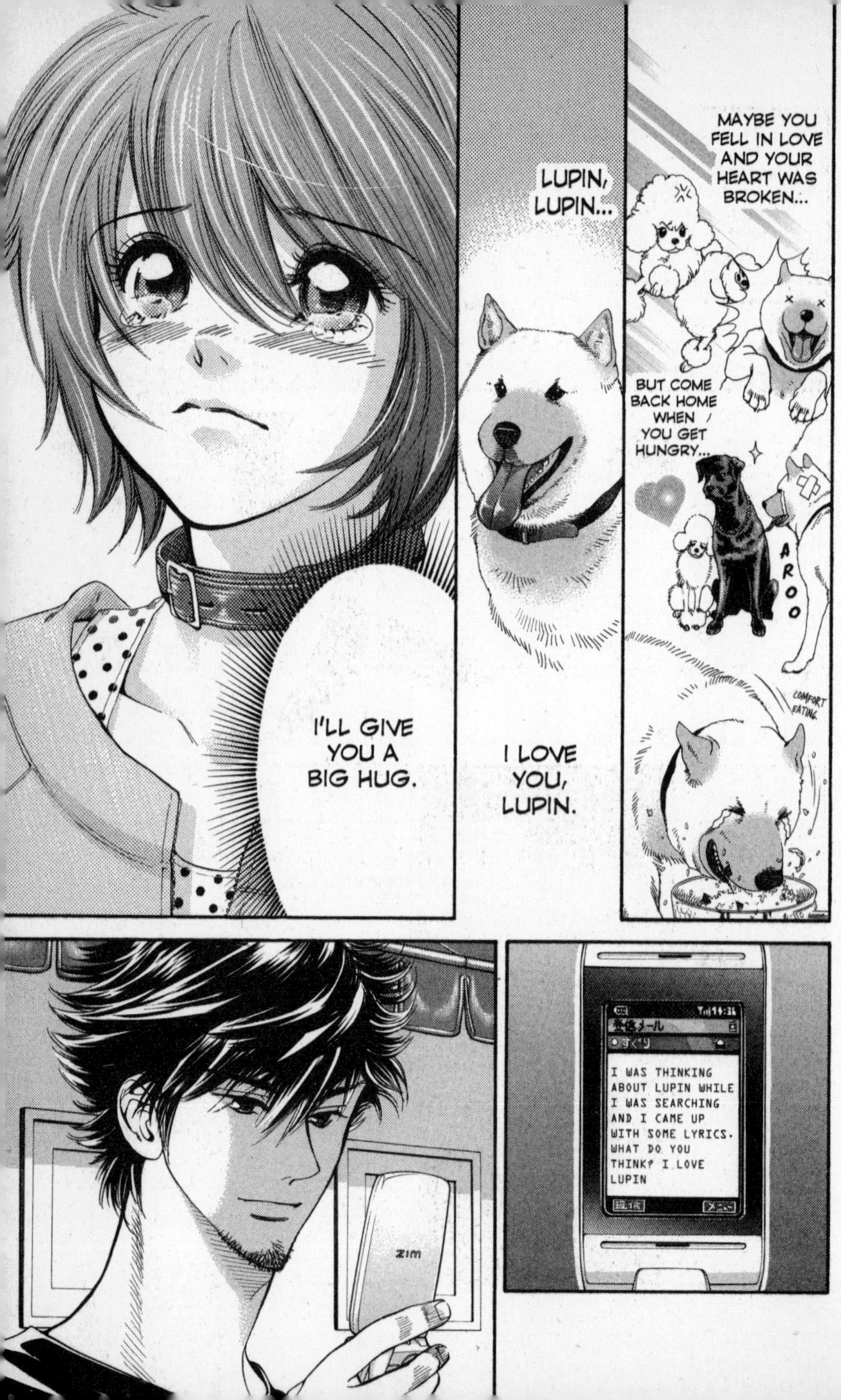
MAYBE YOU FELL IN LOVE AND YOUR HEART WAS BROKEN...
BUT COME BACK HOME WHEN YOU GET HUNGRY...
AROO
COMFORT EATING.
LUPIN, LUPIN...
I LOVE YOU, LUPIN.
I'LL GIVE YOU A BIG HUG.
I WAS THINKING ABOUT LUPIN WHILE I WAS SEARCHING AND I CAME UP WITH SOME LYRICS. WHAT DO YOU THINK? I LOVE LUPIN
ZIM

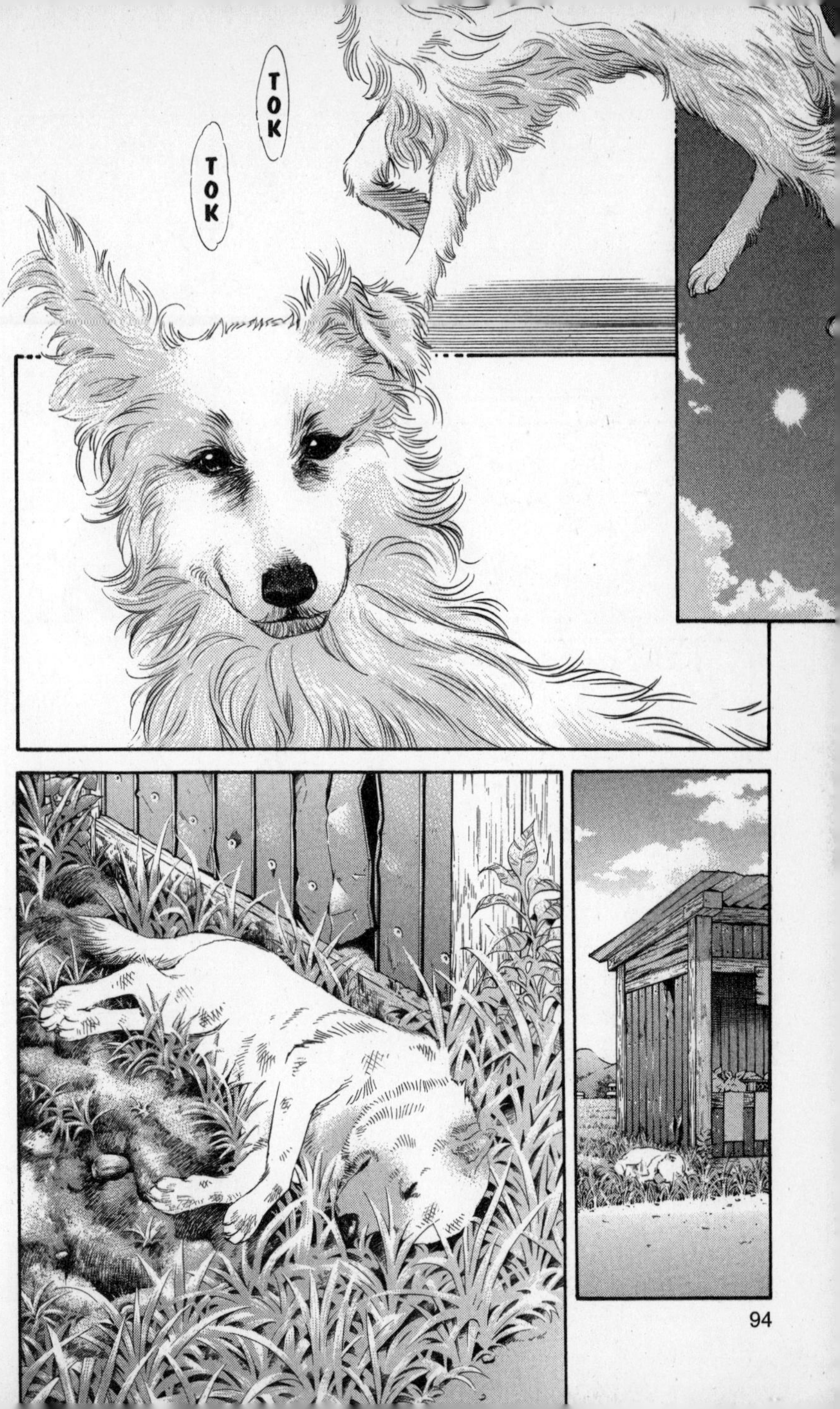
TOK
TOK

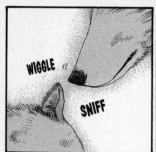

WIGGLE

SNIFF

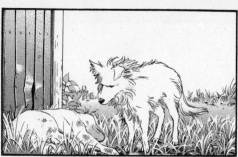

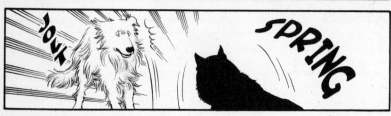

DOUK

SPRING

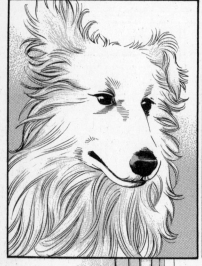

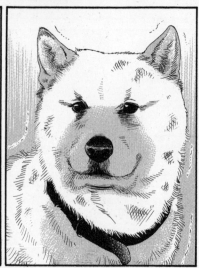

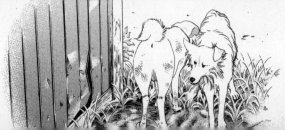

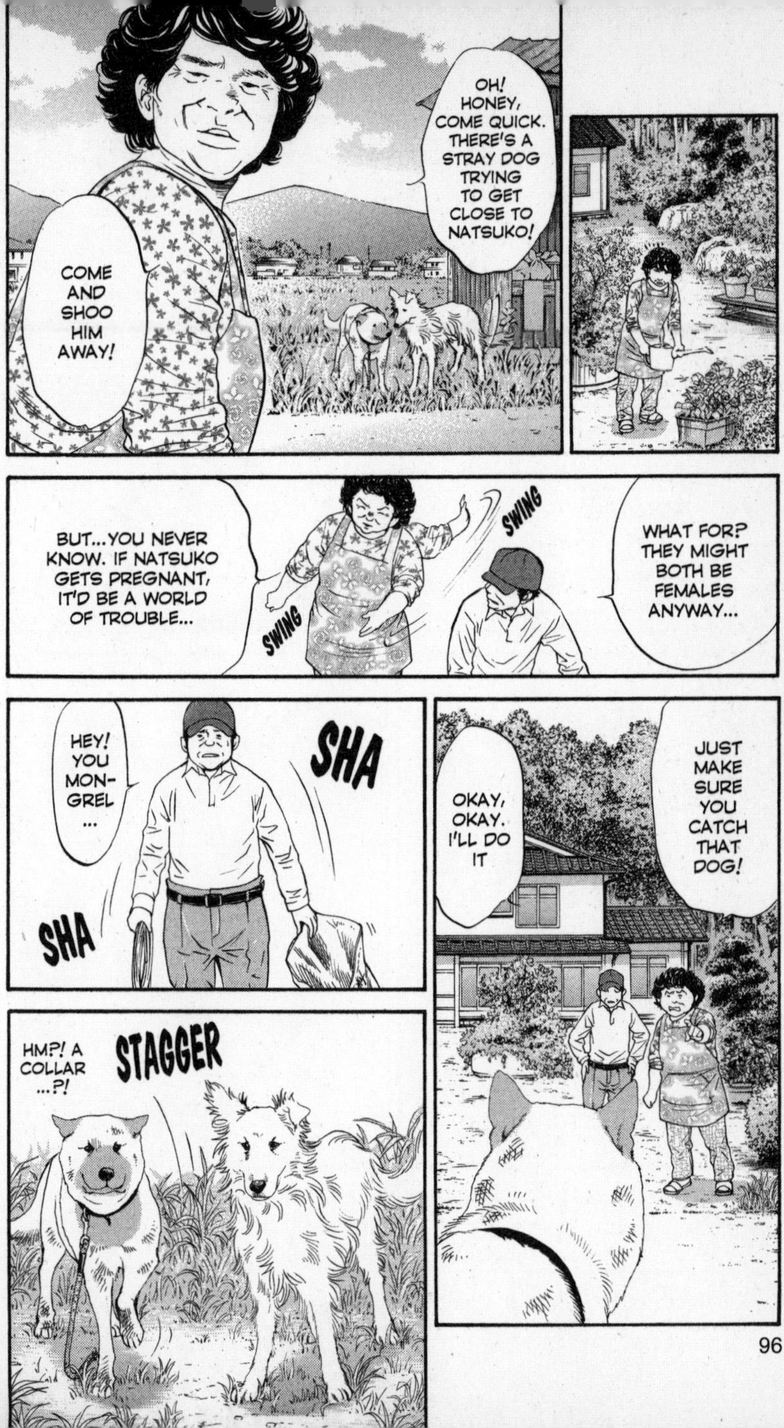
OH! HONEY, COME QUICK. THERE'S A STRAY DOG TRYING TO GET CLOSE TO NATSUKO!
COME AND SHOO HIM AWAY!
WHAT FOR? THEY MIGHT BOTH BE FEMALES ANYWAY...
SWING
BUT...YOU NEVER KNOW. IF NATSUKO GETS PREGNANT, IT'D BE A WORLD OF TROUBLE...
SWING
JUST MAKE SURE YOU CATCH THAT DOG!
OKAY, OKAY. I'LL DO IT
SHA
HEY! YOU MON-GREL ...
SHA
STAGGER
HM?! A COLLAR ...?!

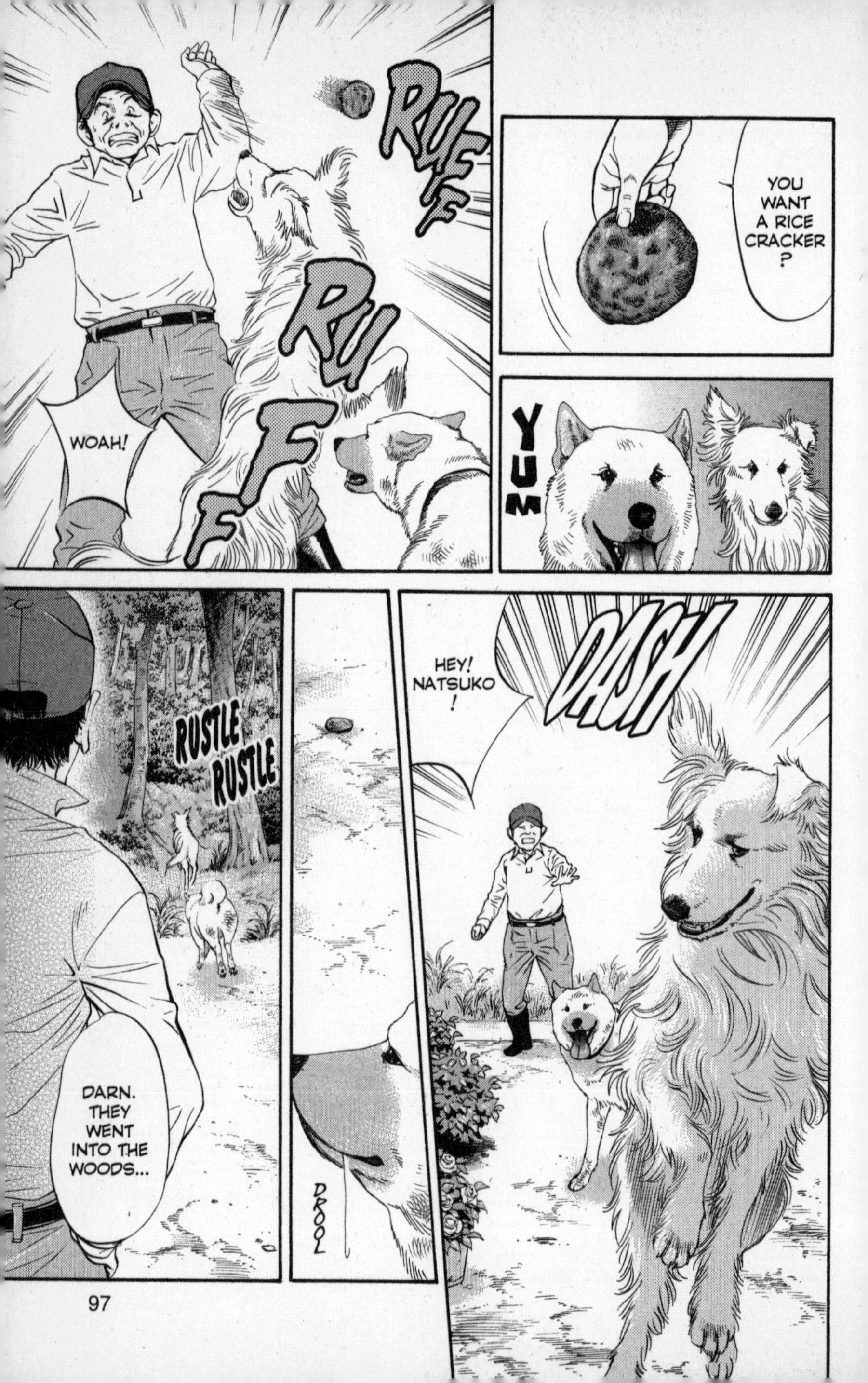
YOU WANT A RICE CRACKER?
YUM
RUFF
RUFF
WOAH!
DASH
HEY! NATSUKO!
DROOL
RUSTLE RUSTLE
DARN. THEY WENT INTO THE WOODS...

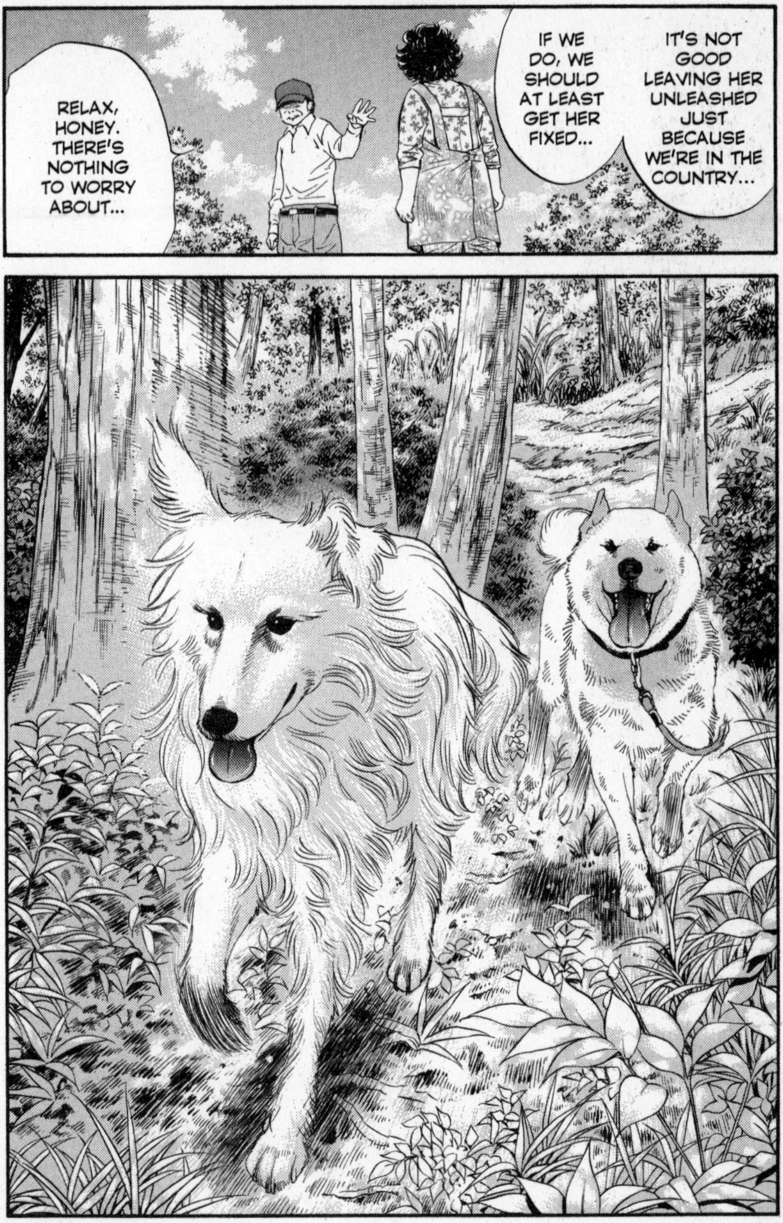
IT'S NOT GOOD LEAVING HER UNLEASHED JUST BECAUSE WE'RE IN THE COUNTRY...
IF WE DO, WE SHOULD AT LEAST GET HER FIXED...
RELAX, HONEY. THERE'S NOTHING TO WORRY ABOUT...

CHAPTER 81: PSG

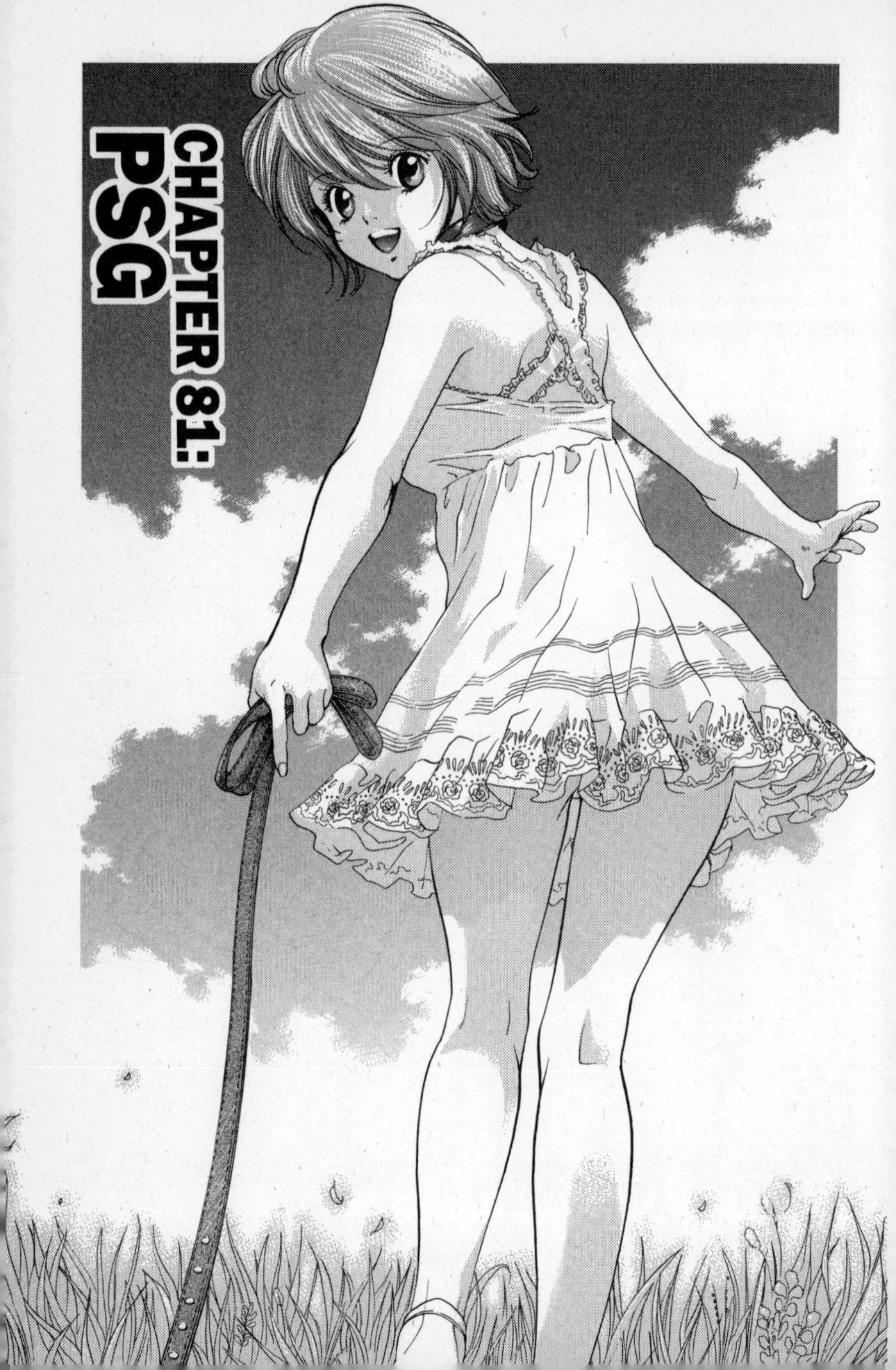

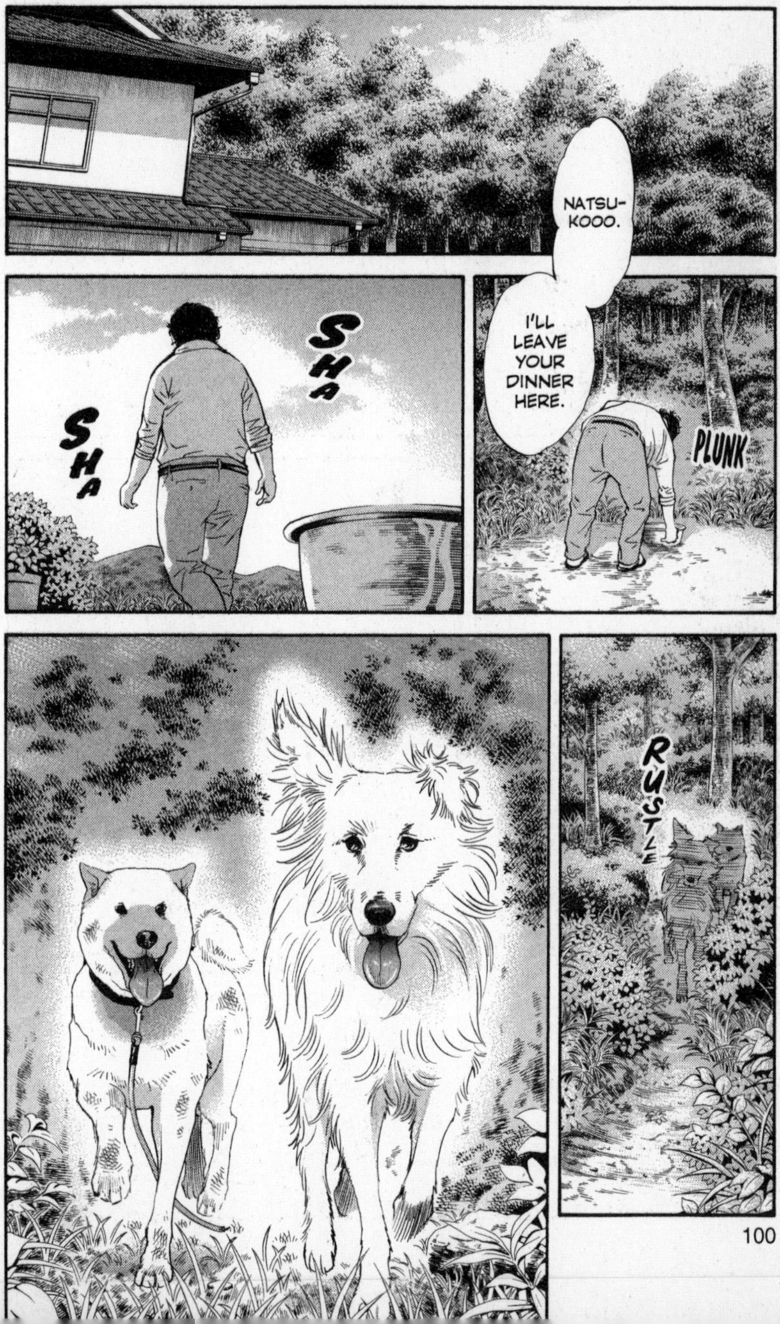
NATSU-KOOO.
I'LL LEAVE YOUR DINNER HERE.
PLUNK
SHA
SHA
RUSTLE

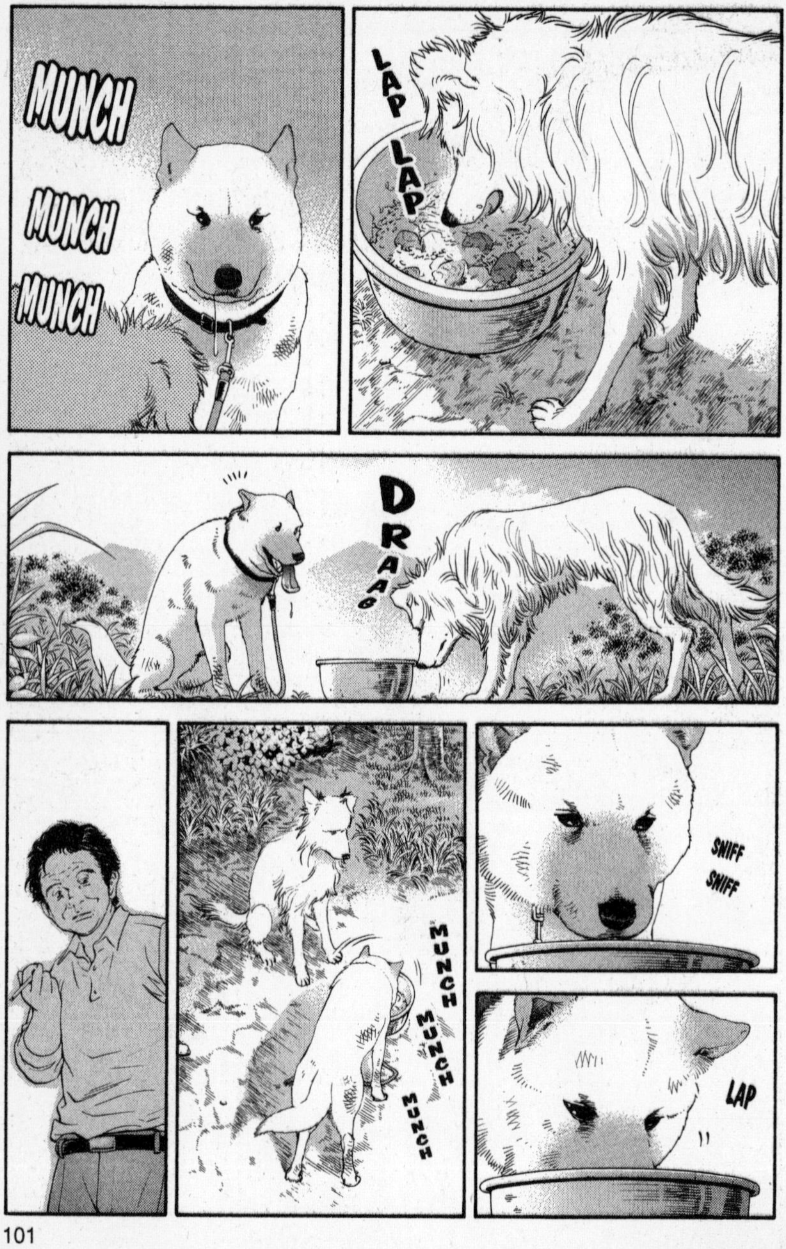
LAP LAP LAP
MUNCH
MUNCH
MUNCH
DRAAG
SNIFF SNIFF
LAP
MUNCH
MUNCH
MUNCH

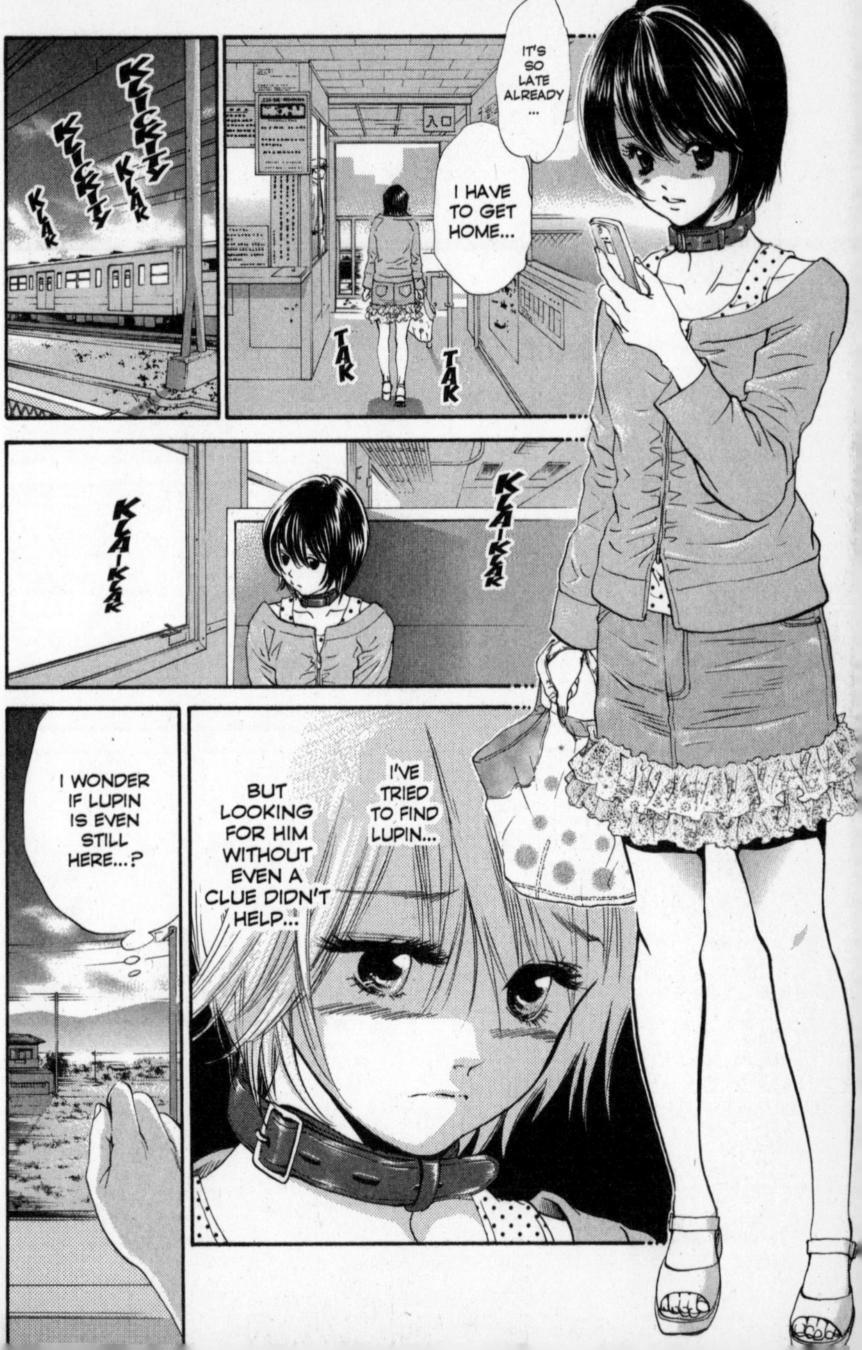
IT'S SO LATE ALREADY...
I HAVE TO GET HOME...
入口
TAK
TAK
KLICKITY KLAK
KLICKITY KLAK
KLAK KLAK
KLAK KLAK
I'VE TRIED TO FIND LUPIN...
BUT LOOKING FOR HIM WITHOUT EVEN A CLUE DIDN'T HELP...
I WONDER IF LUPIN IS EVEN STILL HERE...?

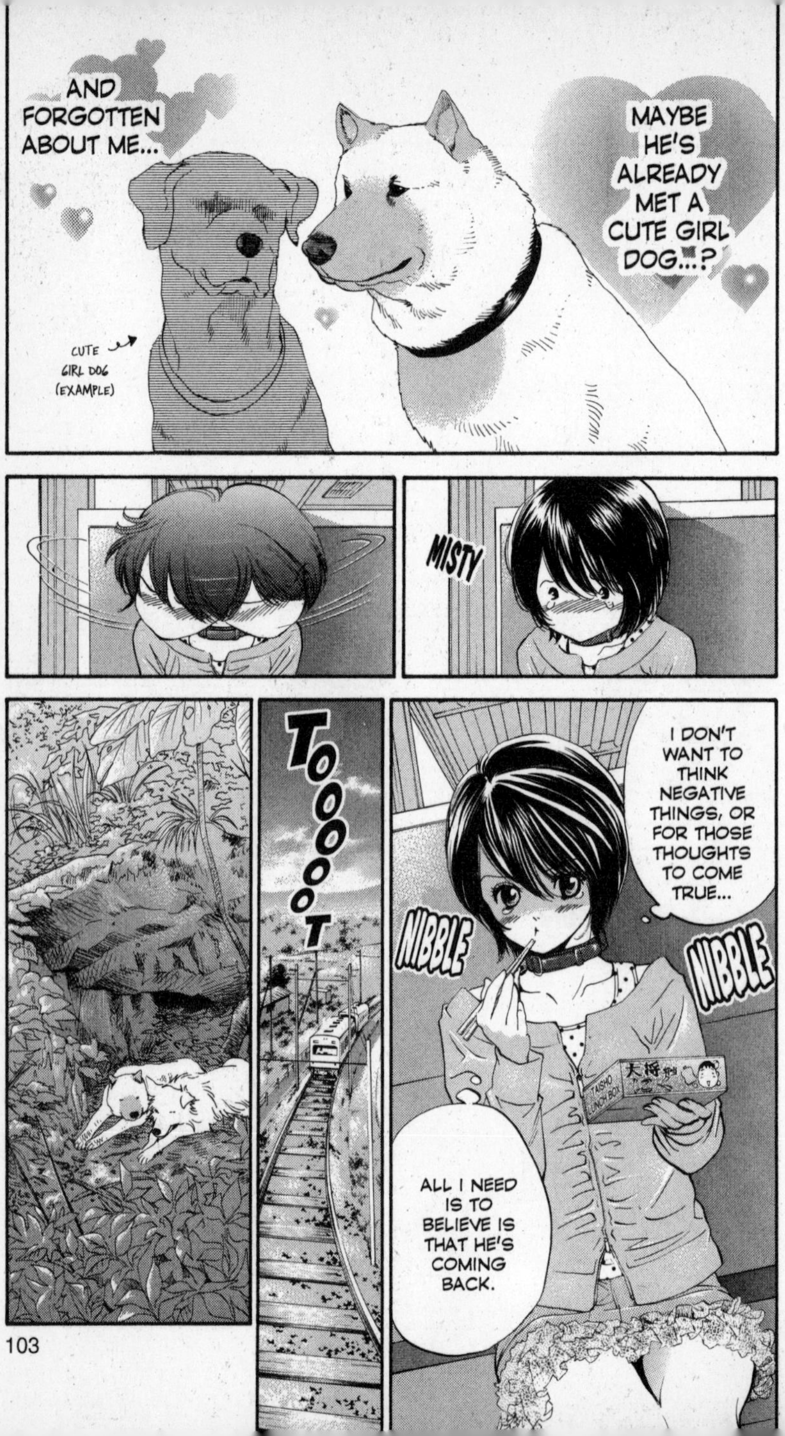
MAYBE HE'S ALREADY MET A CUTE GIRL DOG...?
AND FORGOTTEN ABOUT ME...
CUTE GIRL DOG (EXAMPLE)
MISTY
I DON'T WANT TO THINK NEGATIVE THINGS, OR FOR THOSE THOUGHTS TO COME TRUE...
NIBBLE
NIBBLE
TAISHO LUNCH BOX
ALL I NEED IS TO BELIEVE IS THAT HE'S COMING BACK.
TOOOOOT

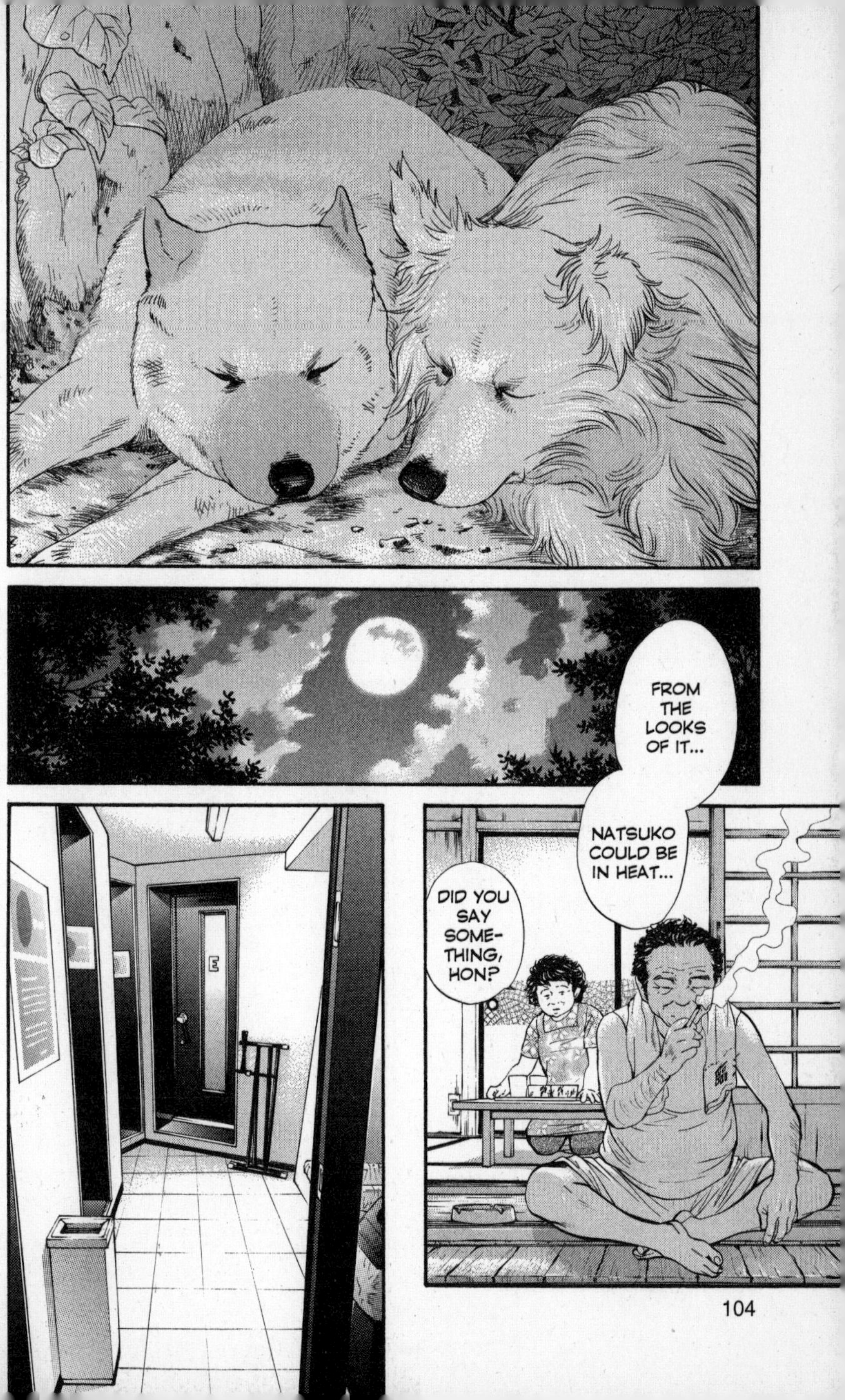
FROM THE LOOKS OF IT...
NATSUKO COULD BE IN HEAT...
DID YOU SAY SOME-THING, HON?

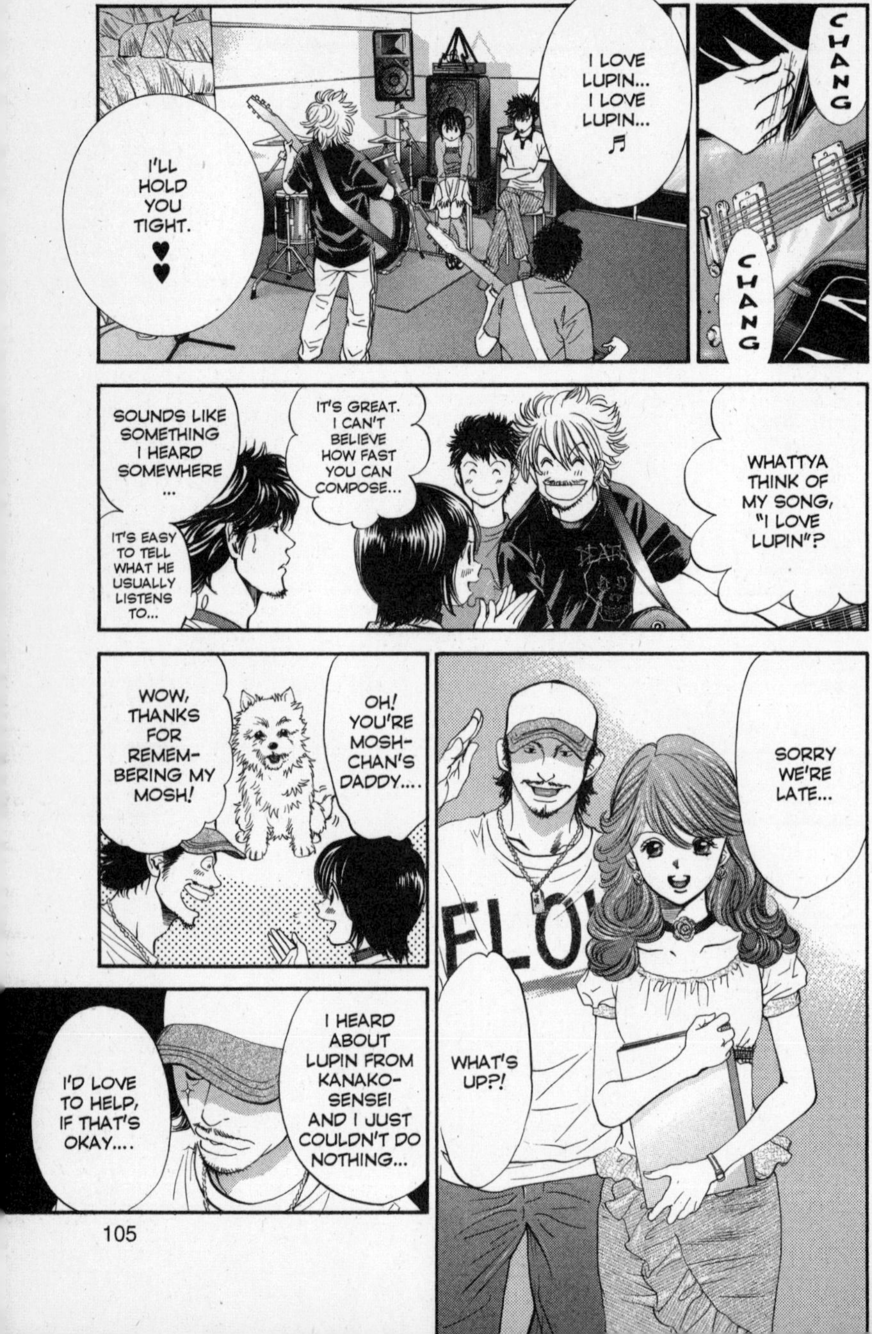

CHANG
CHANG
I LOVE LUPIN... I LOVE LUPIN... ♬
I'LL HOLD YOU TIGHT. ♥♥
WHATTYA THINK OF MY SONG, "I LOVE LUPIN"?
IT'S GREAT. I CAN'T BELIEVE HOW FAST YOU CAN COMPOSE...
SOUNDS LIKE SOMETHING I HEARD SOMEWHERE ...
IT'S EASY TO TELL WHAT HE USUALLY LISTENS TO...
SORRY WE'RE LATE...
WHAT'S UP?!
OH! YOU'RE MOSH-CHAN'S DADDY....
WOW, THANKS FOR REMEMBERING MY MOSH!
I HEARD ABOUT LUPIN FROM KANAKO-SENSEI AND I JUST COULDN'T DO NOTHING...
I'D LOVE TO HELP, IF THAT'S OKAY....

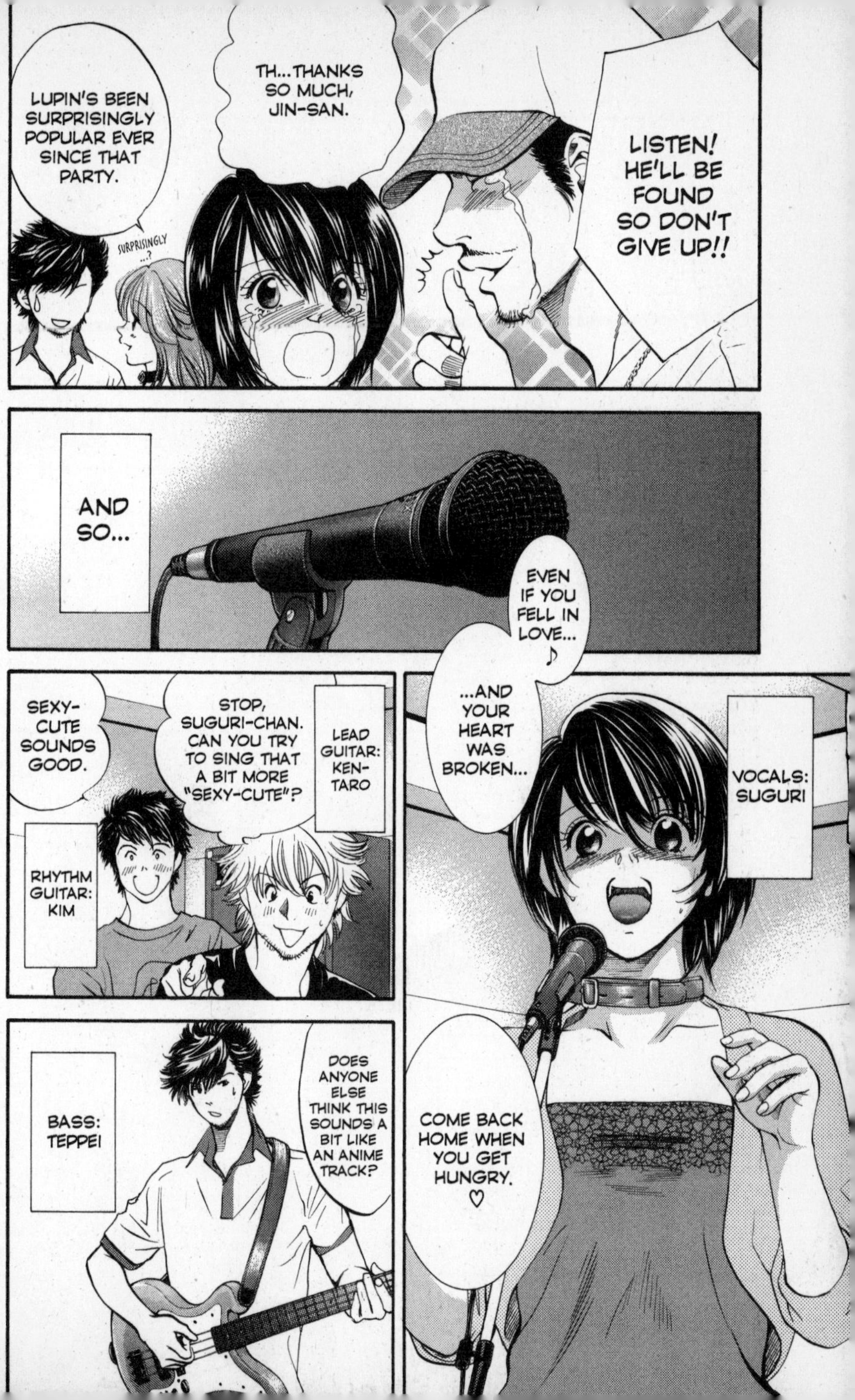
LISTEN! HE'LL BE FOUND SO DON'T GIVE UP!!
TH...THANKS SO MUCH, JIN-SAN.
LUPIN'S BEEN SURPRISINGLY POPULAR EVER SINCE THAT PARTY.
SURPRISINGLY ...?
AND SO...
EVEN IF YOU FELL IN LOVE... ♪
...AND YOUR HEART WAS BROKEN...
VOCALS: SUGURI
COME BACK HOME WHEN YOU GET HUNGRY. ♡
LEAD GUITAR: KEN-TARO
STOP, SUGURI-CHAN. CAN YOU TRY TO SING THAT A BIT MORE "SEXY-CUTE"?
SEXY-CUTE SOUNDS GOOD.
RHYTHM GUITAR: KIM
DOES ANYONE ELSE THINK THIS SOUNDS A BIT LIKE AN ANIME TRACK?
BASS: TEPPEI

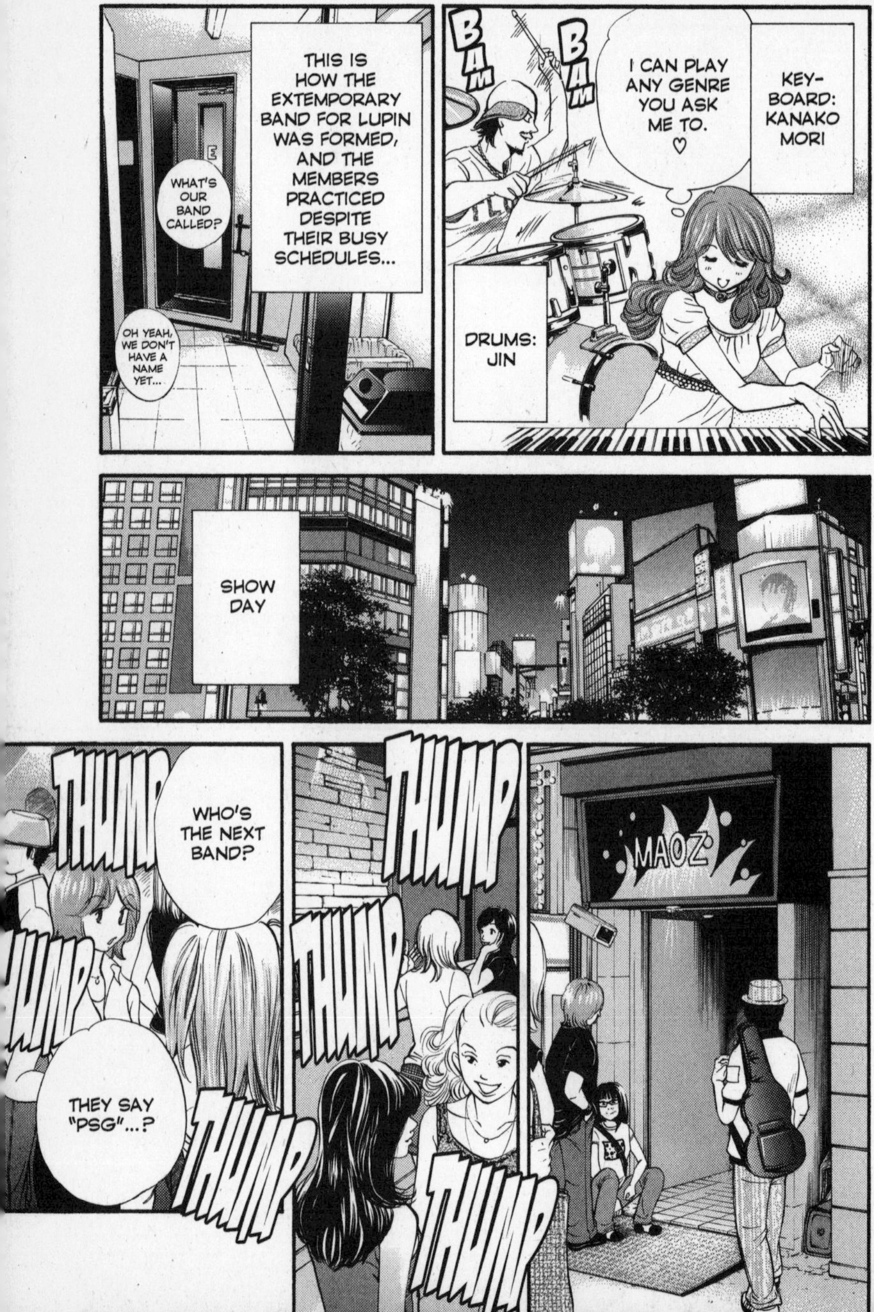
KEY-BOARD: KANAKO MORI
I CAN PLAY ANY GENRE YOU ASK ME TO. ♡
BAM
BAM
DRUMS: JIN
THIS IS HOW THE EXTEMPORARY BAND FOR LUPIN WAS FORMED, AND THE MEMBERS PRACTICED DESPITE THEIR BUSY SCHEDULES...
WHAT'S OUR BAND CALLED?
OH YEAH, WE DON'T HAVE A NAME YET...
SHOW DAY
MAOZ
THUMP
THUMP
THUMP
THUMP
WHO'S THE NEXT BAND?
THUMP
THUMP
THEY SAY "PSG"...?

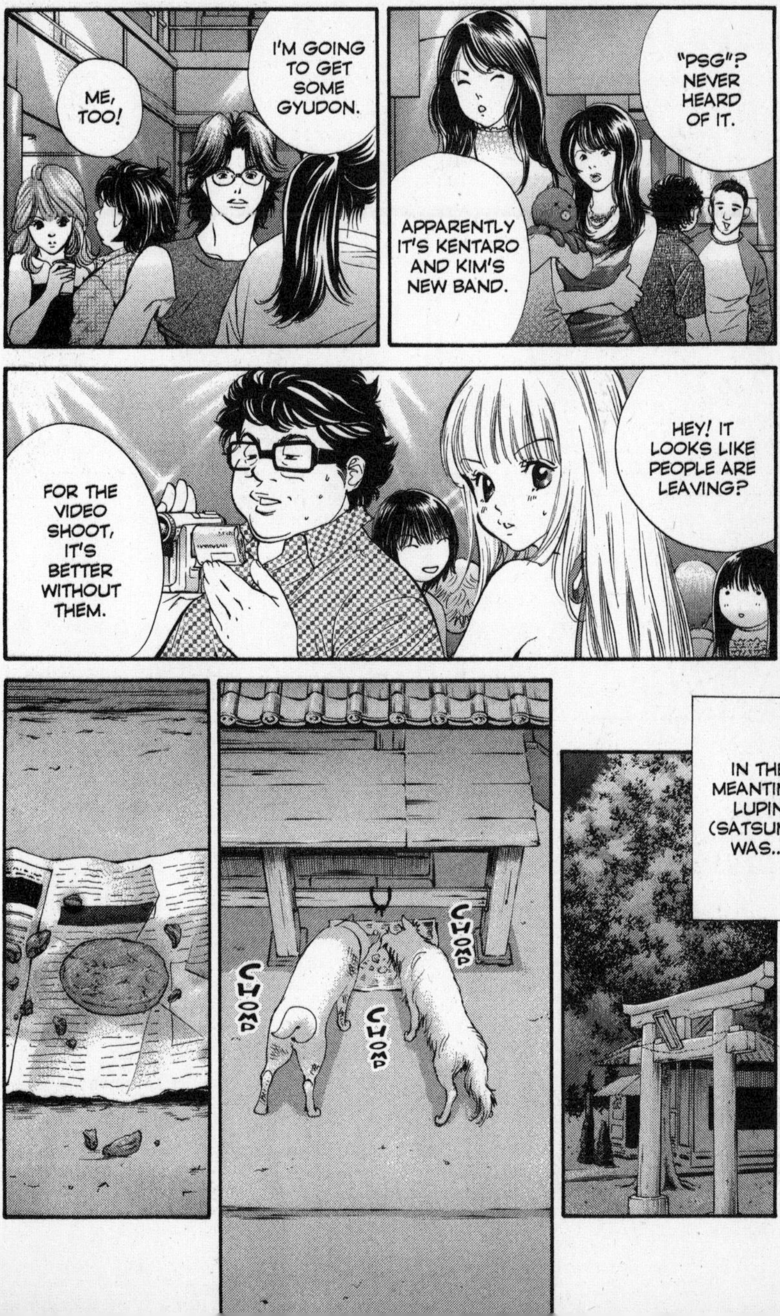
"PSG"? NEVER HEARD OF IT.
APPARENTLY IT'S KENTARO AND KIM'S NEW BAND.
I'M GOING TO GET SOME GYUDON.
ME, TOO!
HEY! IT LOOKS LIKE PEOPLE ARE LEAVING?
FOR THE VIDEO SHOOT, IT'S BETTER WITHOUT THEM.
IN THE MEANTIME, LUPIN (SATSUMA) WAS...
CHOMP
CHOMP
CHOMP

SLIDE
ONE...
TWO...
THREE...

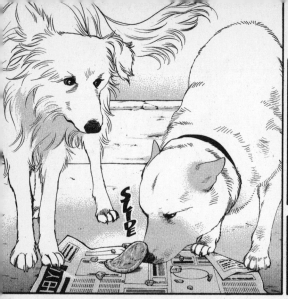

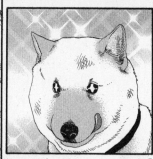

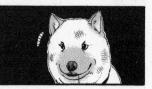

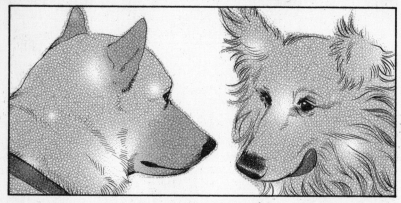

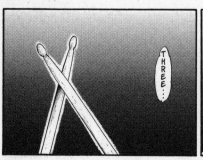

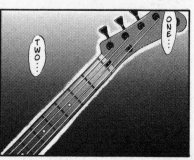

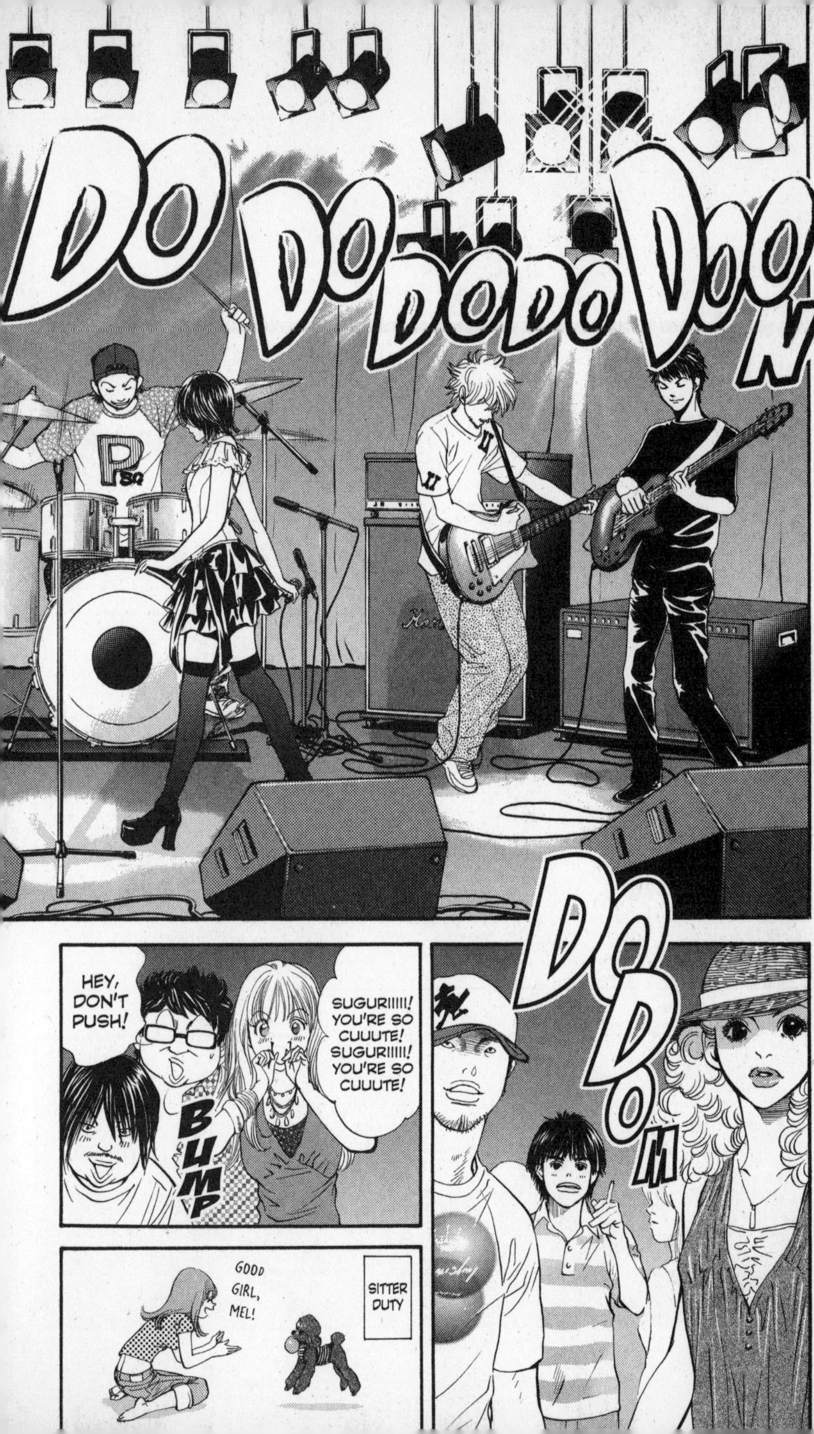
DO DO DODODO DOOON
DODODOM
SUGURIIIII! YOU'RE SO CUUUTE! SUGURIIIII! YOU'RE SO CUUUTE!
HEY, DON'T PUSH!
BUMP
SITTER DUTY
GOOD GIRL, MEL!

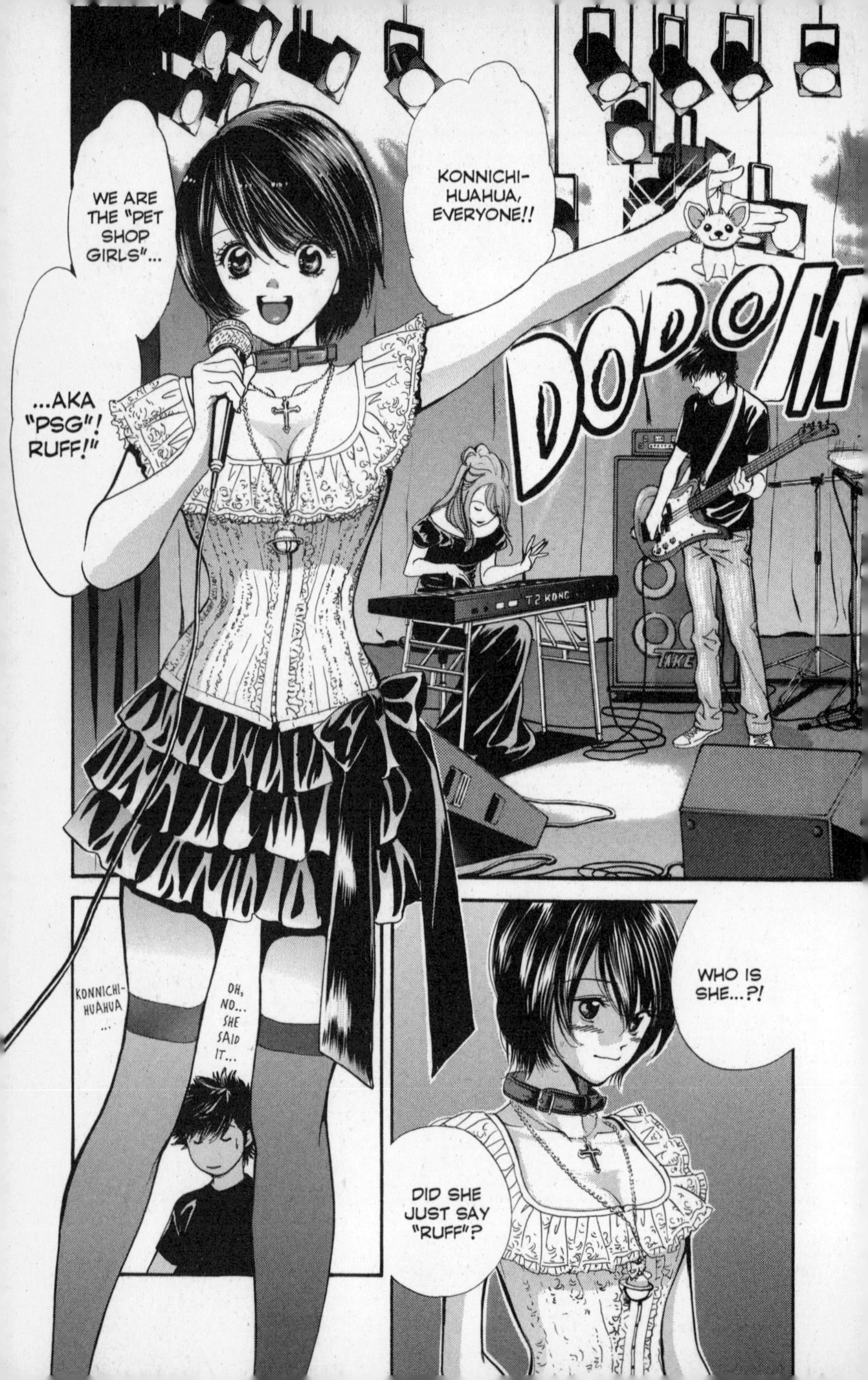
KONNICHI-HUAHUA, EVERYONE!!
DODOM
WE ARE THE "PET SHOP GIRLS"...
...AKA "PSG"! RUFF!"
WHO IS SHE...?!
DID SHE JUST SAY "RUFF"?
OH, NO... SHE SAID IT...
KONNICHI-HUAHUA...

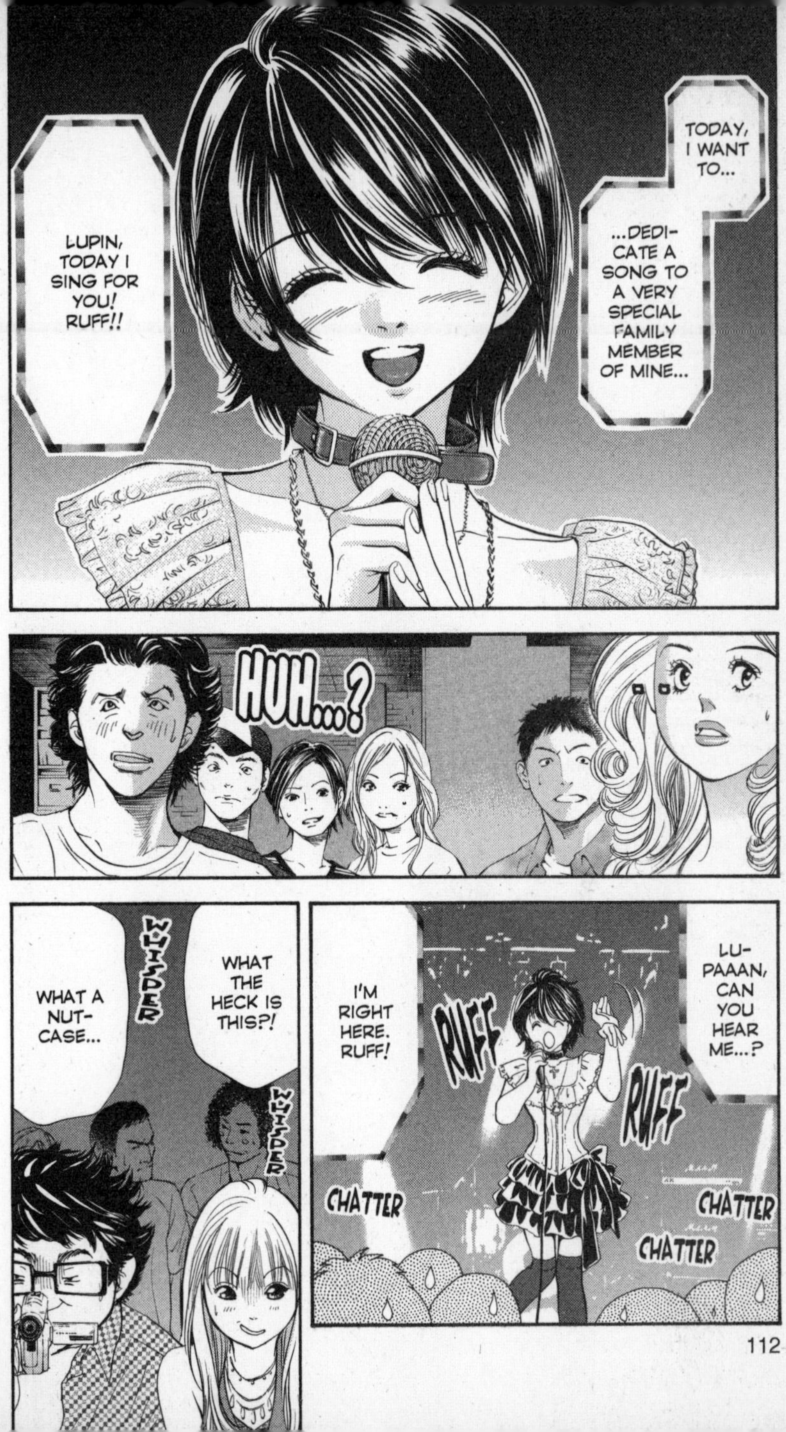
TODAY, I WANT TO...
...DEDICATE A SONG TO A VERY SPECIAL FAMILY MEMBER OF MINE...
LUPIN, TODAY I SING FOR YOU! RUFF!!
HUH...?
LU-PAAAN, CAN YOU HEAR ME...?
RUFF
RUFF
I'M RIGHT HERE. RUFF!
CHATTER
CHATTER
CHATTER
WHISPER
WHAT THE HECK IS THIS?!
WHAT A NUT-CASE...
WHISPER

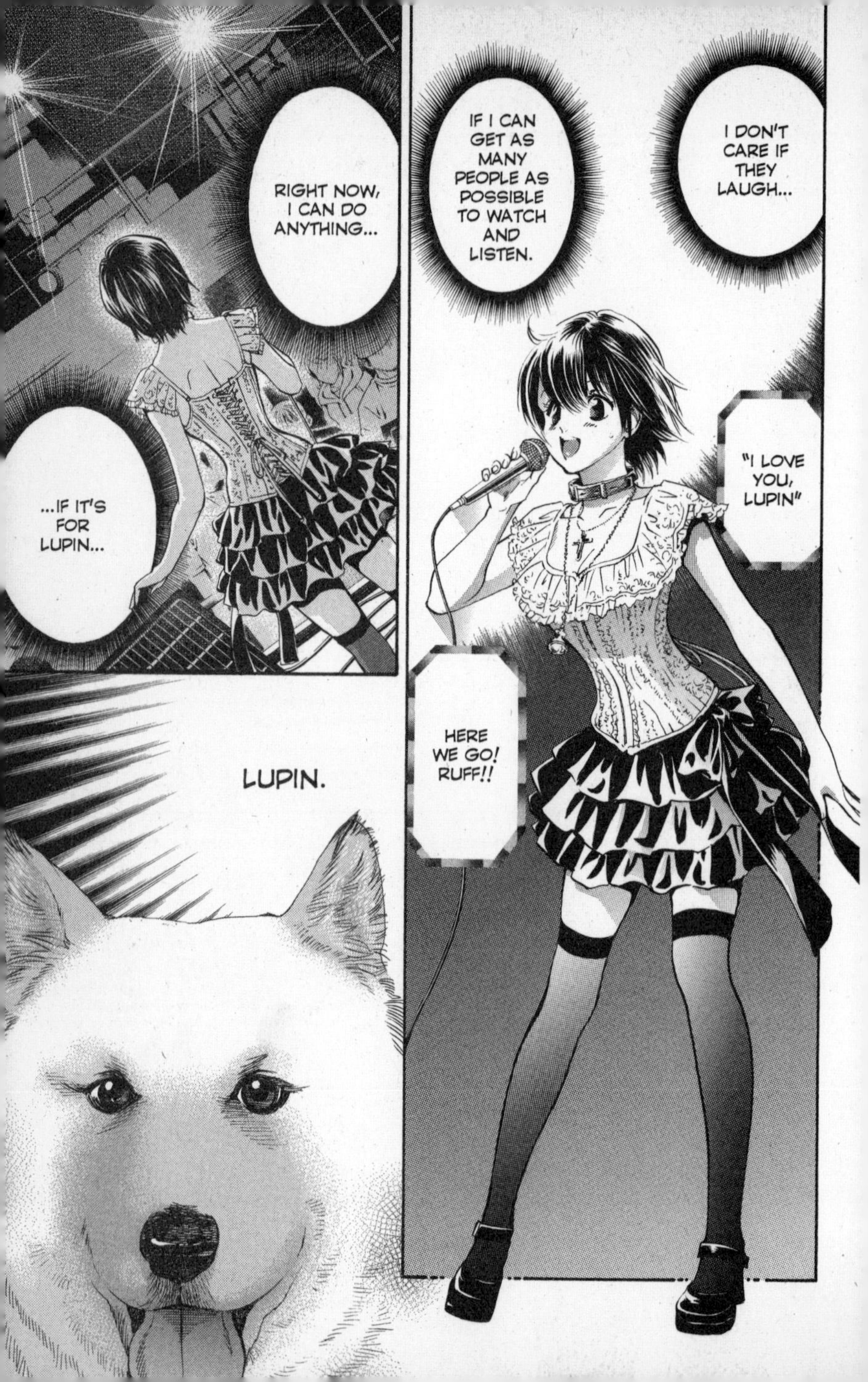
I DON'T CARE IF THEY LAUGH...
IF I CAN GET AS MANY PEOPLE AS POSSIBLE TO WATCH AND LISTEN.
"I LOVE YOU, LUPIN"
HERE WE GO! RUFF!!
RIGHT NOW, I CAN DO ANYTHING...
...IF IT'S FOR LUPIN...
LUPIN.

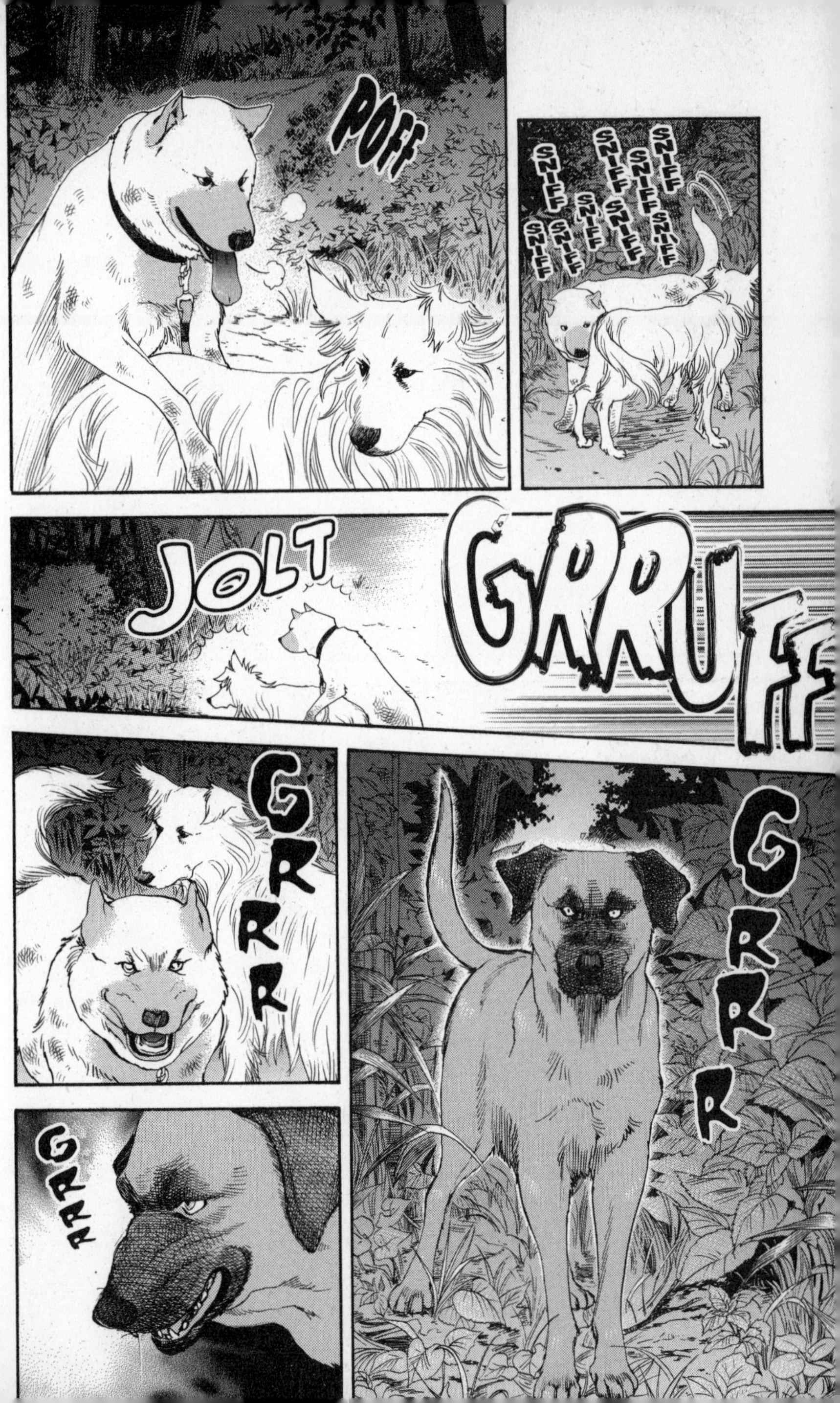
SNIFF SNIFF SNIFF SNIFF SNIFF SNIFF SNIFF SNIFF SNIFF
POFF
GRRUFF
JOLT
GRRRR
GRRR
GRRR

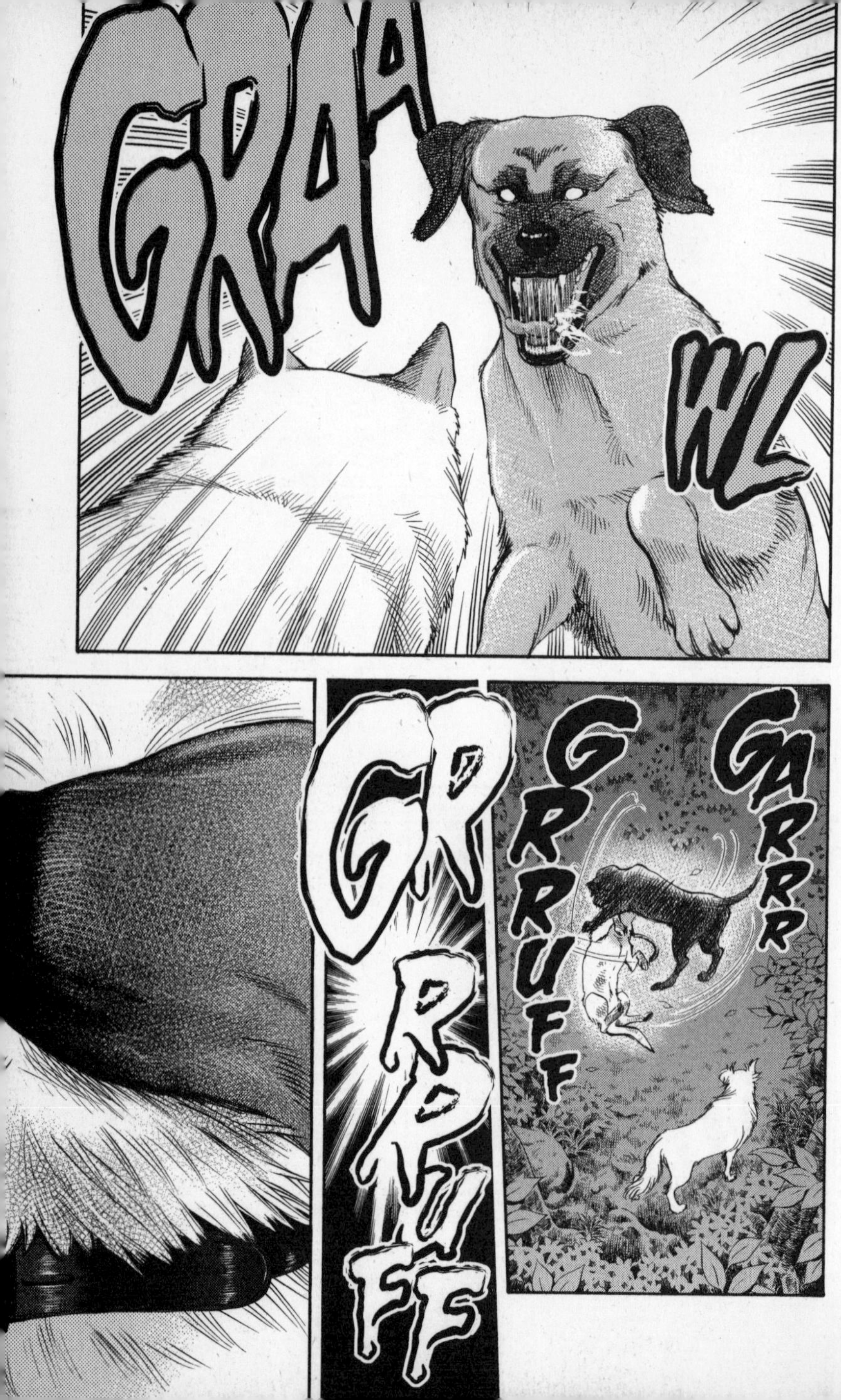
GRAA
WL
GARRR
GRRRUFF
GR
RRUFF

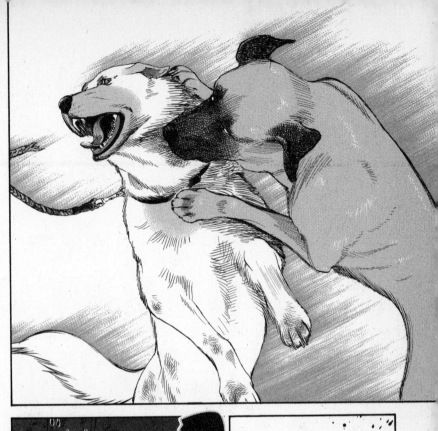

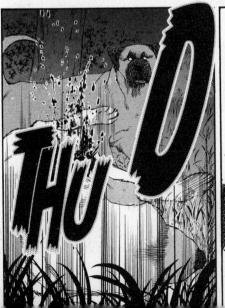

THUD

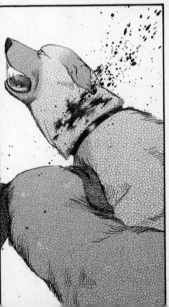

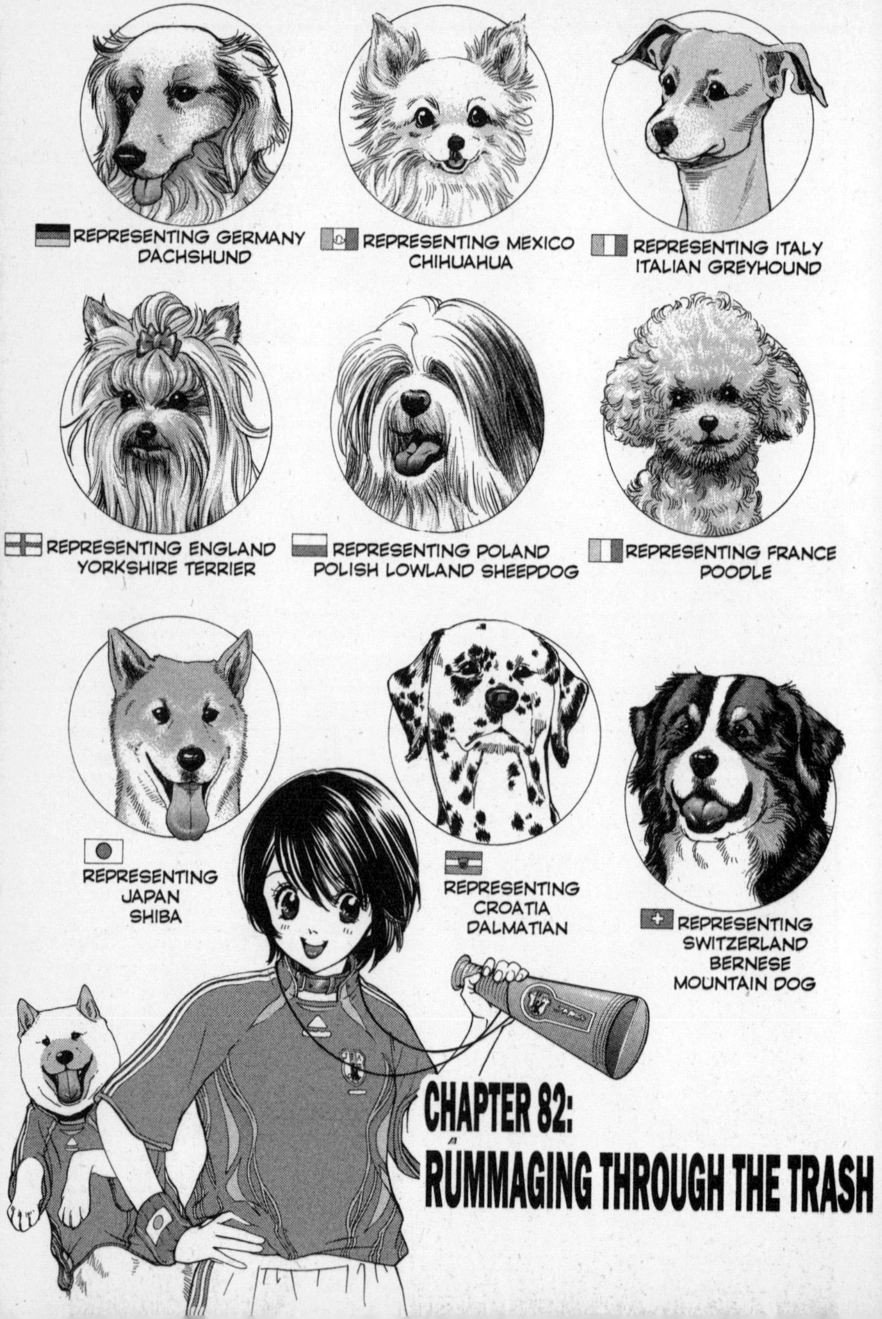
REPRESENTING ITALY
ITALIAN GREYHOUND
REPRESENTING MEXICO
CHIHUAHUA
REPRESENTING GERMANY
DACHSHUND
REPRESENTING FRANCE
POODLE
REPRESENTING POLAND
POLISH LOWLAND SHEEPDOG
REPRESENTING ENGLAND
YORKSHIRE TERRIER
REPRESENTING
SWITZERLAND
BERNESE
MOUNTAIN DOG
REPRESENTING
CROATIA
DALMATIAN
REPRESENTING
JAPAN
SHIBA

CHAPTER 82: RUMMAGING THROUGH THE TRASH

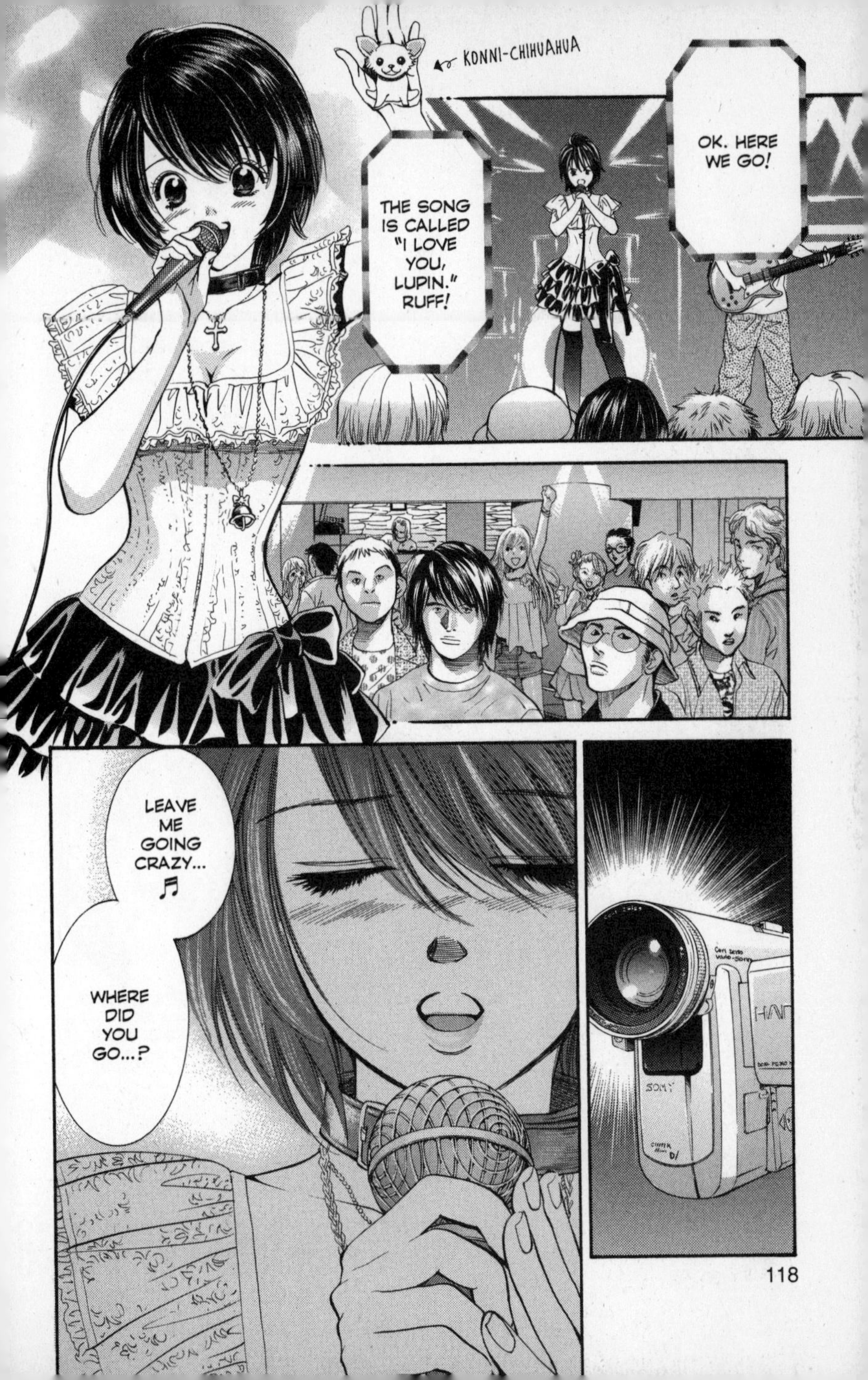
OK. HERE WE GO!
THE SONG IS CALLED "I LOVE YOU, LUPIN." RUFF!
KONNI-CHIHUAHUA
LEAVE ME GOING CRAZY... ♬
WHERE DID YOU GO...?

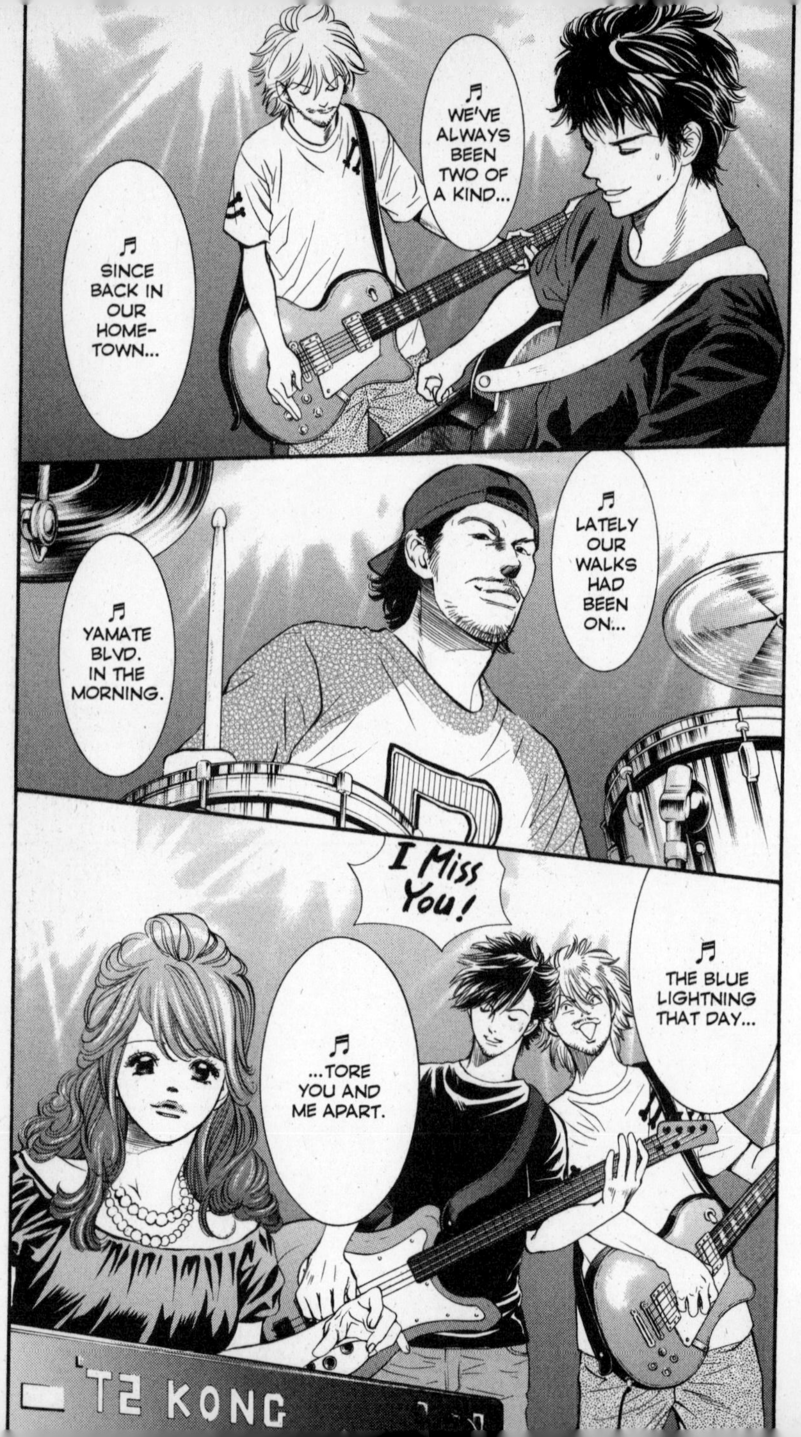
♬ WE'VE ALWAYS BEEN TWO OF A KIND...
♬ SINCE BACK IN OUR HOMETOWN...
♬ LATELY OUR WALKS HAD BEEN ON...
♬ YAMATE BLVD. IN THE MORNING.
I Miss You!
♬ THE BLUE LIGHTNING THAT DAY...
♬ ...TORE YOU AND ME APART.
T2 KONG

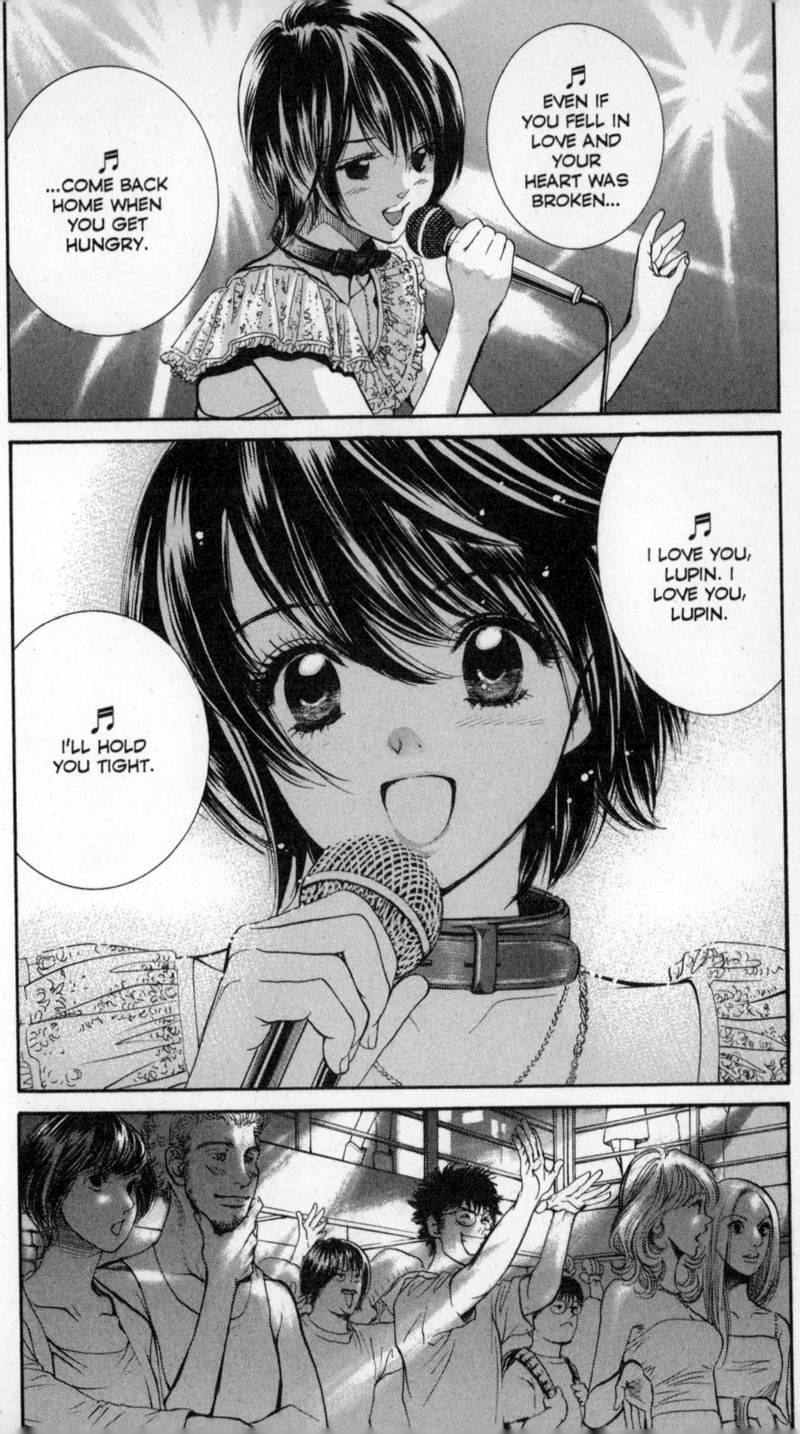
EVEN IF YOU FELL IN LOVE AND YOUR HEART WAS BROKEN...
...COME BACK HOME WHEN YOU GET HUNGRY.
I LOVE YOU, LUPIN. I LOVE YOU, LUPIN.
I'LL HOLD YOU TIGHT.

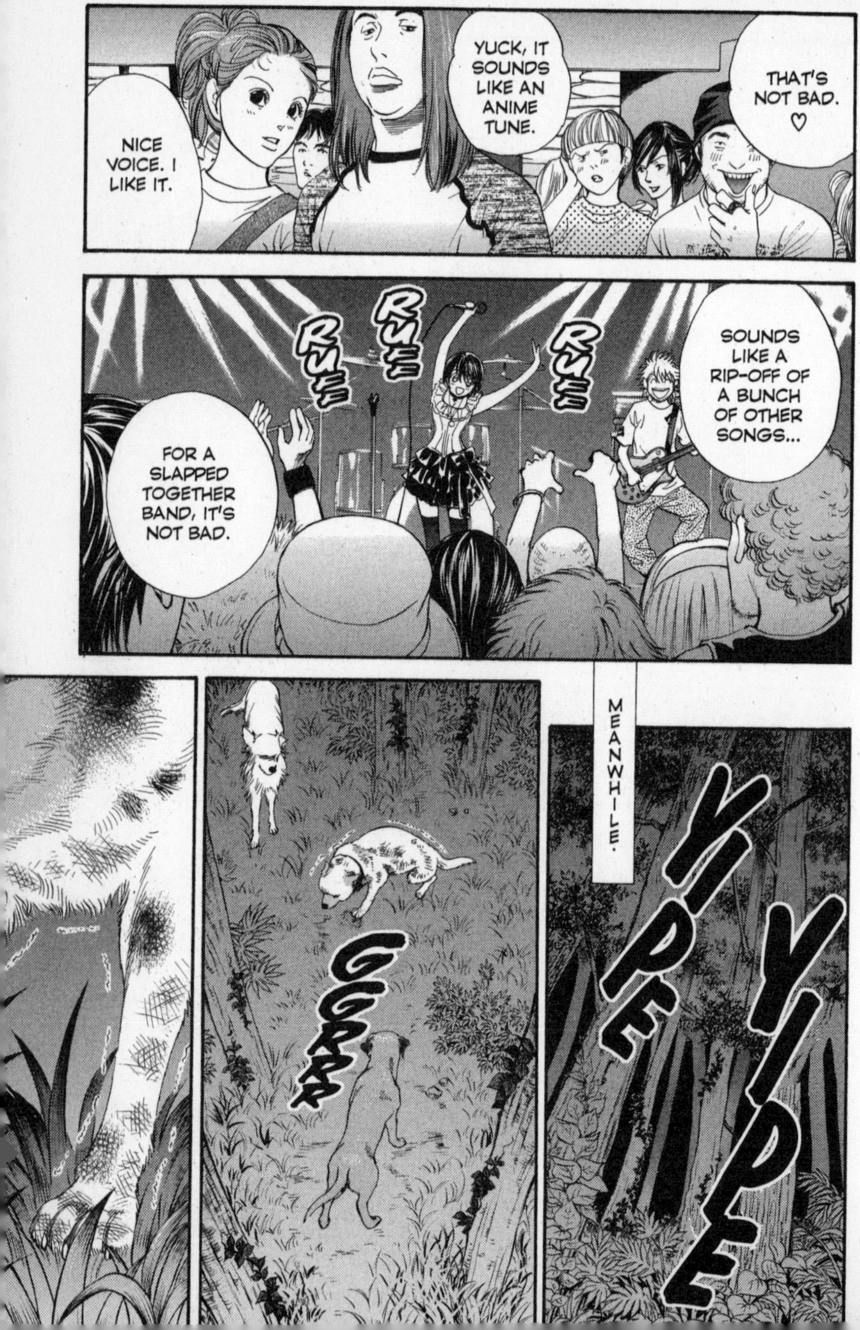
THAT'S NOT BAD. ♡
YUCK, IT SOUNDS LIKE AN ANIME TUNE.
NICE VOICE. I LIKE IT.
SOUNDS LIKE A RIP-OFF OF A BUNCH OF OTHER SONGS...
RUFF
RUFF
RUFF
FOR A SLAPPED TOGETHER BAND, IT'S NOT BAD.
MEANWHILE.
YIPE
YIPE
GGRRR

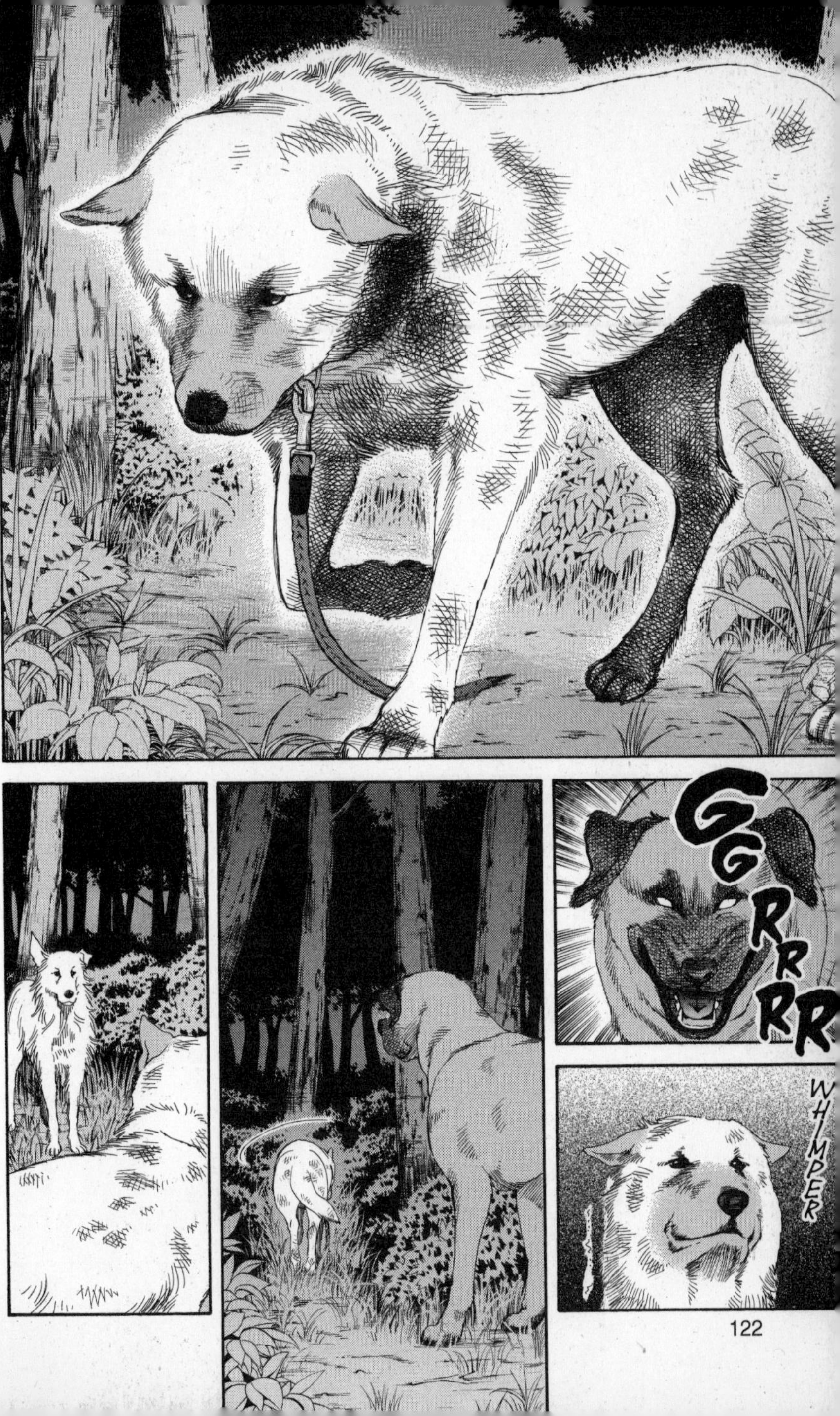
GRRRR
WHIMPER

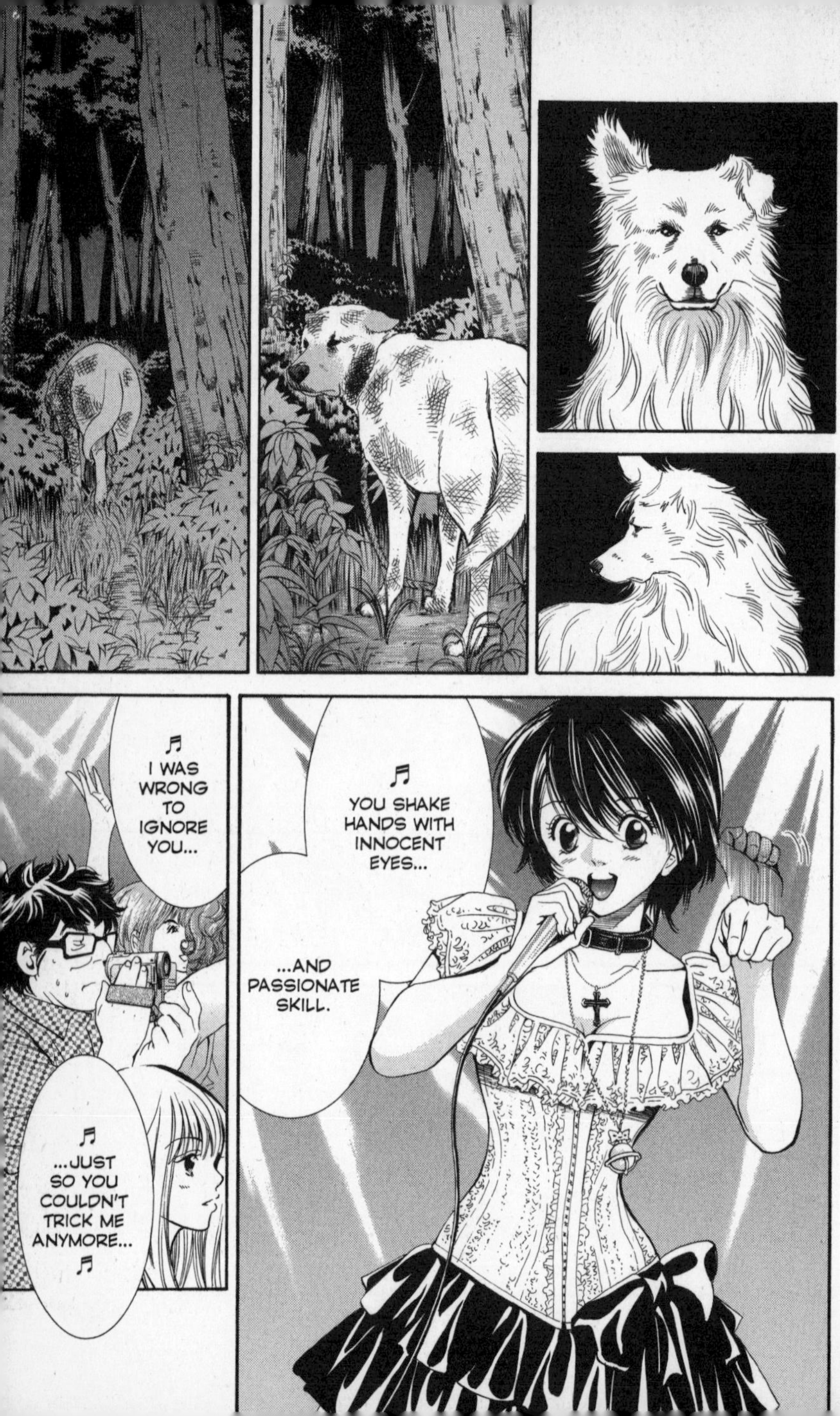
♬ YOU SHAKE HANDS WITH INNOCENT EYES...
...AND PASSIONATE SKILL.
♬ I WAS WRONG TO IGNORE YOU...
♬ ...JUST SO YOU COULDN'T TRICK ME ANYMORE... ♬

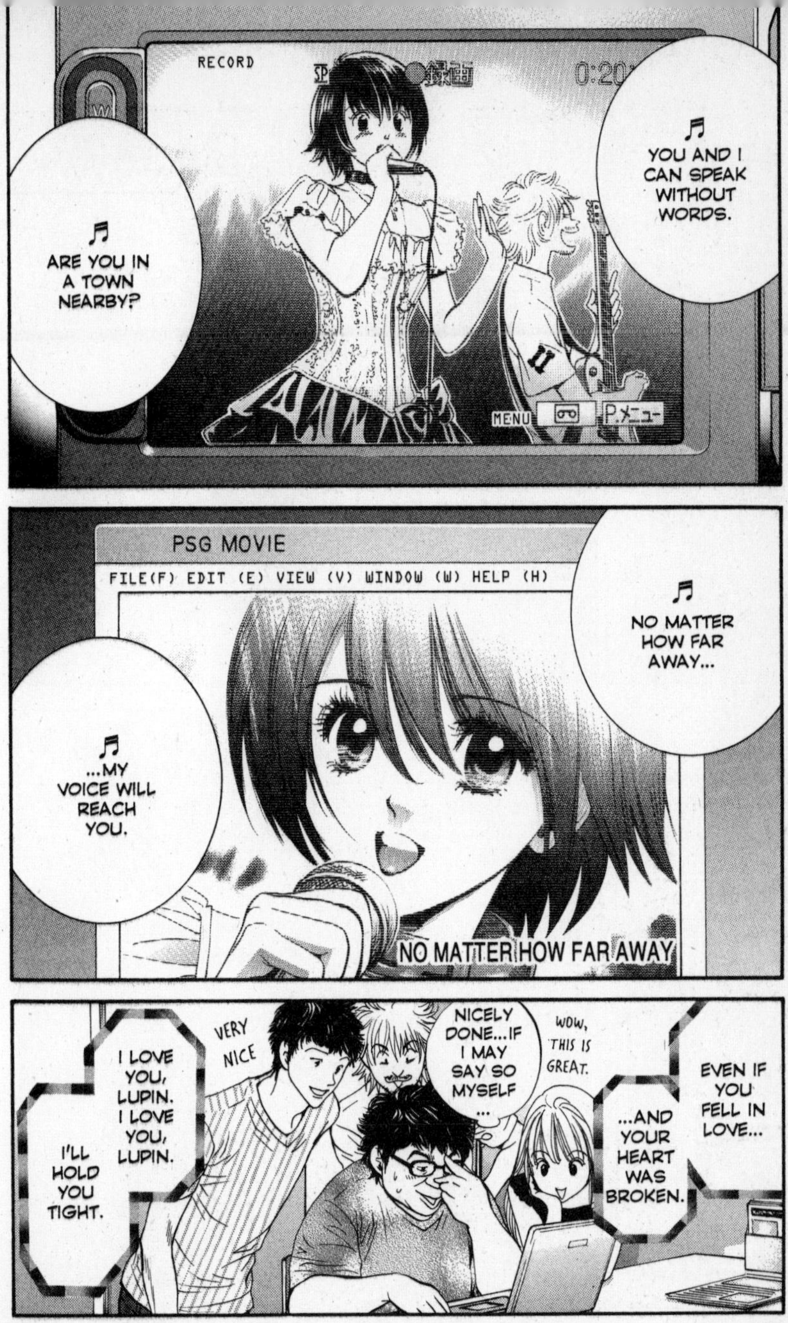
RECORD
SP
録画
0:20
YOU AND I CAN SPEAK WITHOUT WORDS.
ARE YOU IN A TOWN NEARBY?
MENU
P.メニュー
PSG MOVIE
FILE(F) EDIT (E) VIEW (V) WINDOW (W) HELP (H)
NO MATTER HOW FAR AWAY...
...MY VOICE WILL REACH YOU.
NO MATTER HOW FAR AWAY
EVEN IF YOU FELL IN LOVE...
...AND YOUR HEART WAS BROKEN.
WOW, THIS IS GREAT.
NICELY DONE...IF I MAY SAY SO MYSELF...
VERY NICE
I LOVE YOU, LUPIN. I LOVE YOU, LUPIN.
I'LL HOLD YOU TIGHT.

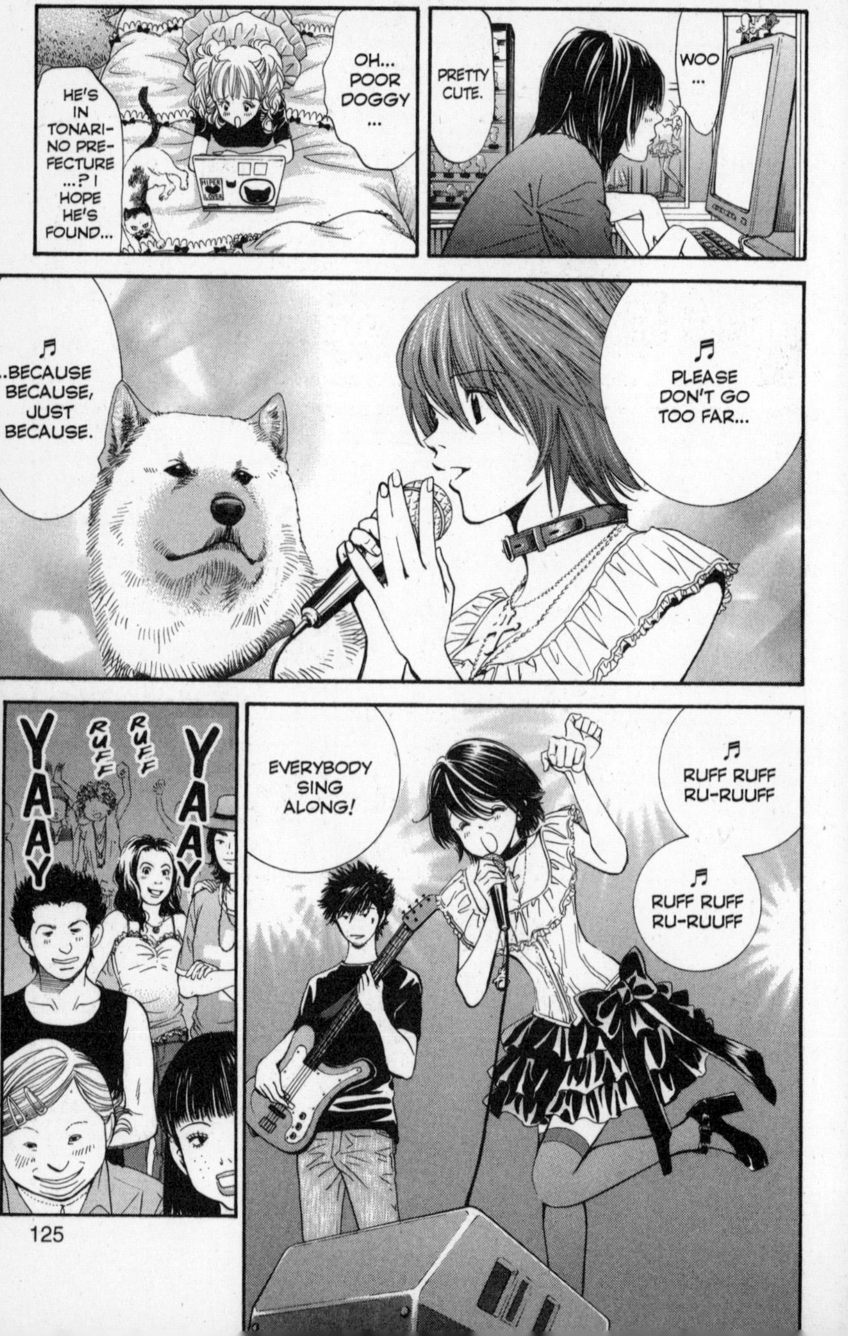
WOO ...
PRETTY CUTE.
OH... POOR DOGGY ...
HE'S IN TONARI-NO PRE-FECTURE ...? I HOPE HE'S FOUND...
♬ PLEASE DON'T GO TOO FAR...
♬ ...BECAUSE BECAUSE, JUST BECAUSE.
♬ RUFF RUFF RU-RUUFF
♬ RUFF RUFF RU-RUUFF
EVERYBODY SING ALONG!
YAAY
RUFF RUFF
YAAY

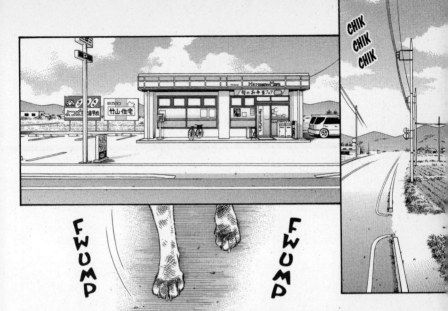

CHIK
CHIK
CHIK

FWUMP

FWUMP

WHOA?!

RUSTLE

RUSTLE

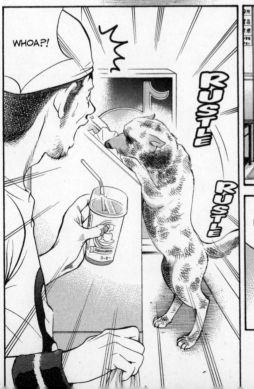

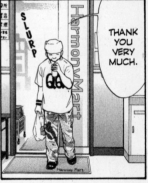

SLURP

THANK
YOU
VERY
MUCH.

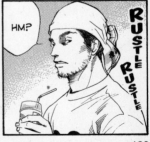

HM?

RUSTLE

RUSTLE

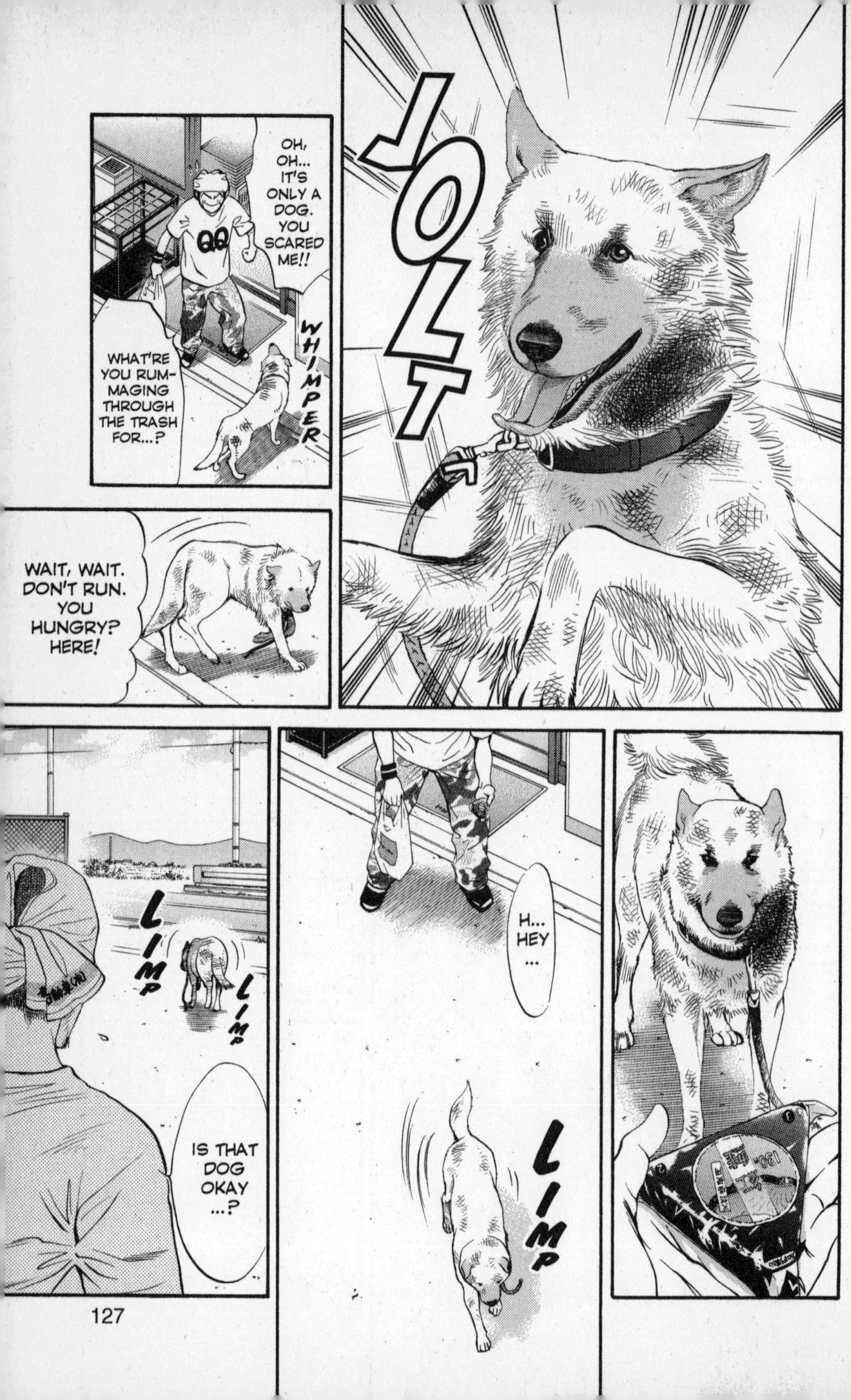
JOLT
OH, OH... IT'S ONLY A DOG. YOU SCARED ME!!
WHIMPER
WHAT'RE YOU RUMMAGING THROUGH THE TRASH FOR...?
WAIT, WAIT. DON'T RUN. YOU HUNGRY? HERE!
H... HEY ...
LIMP
LIMP
LIMP
IS THAT DOG OKAY ...?

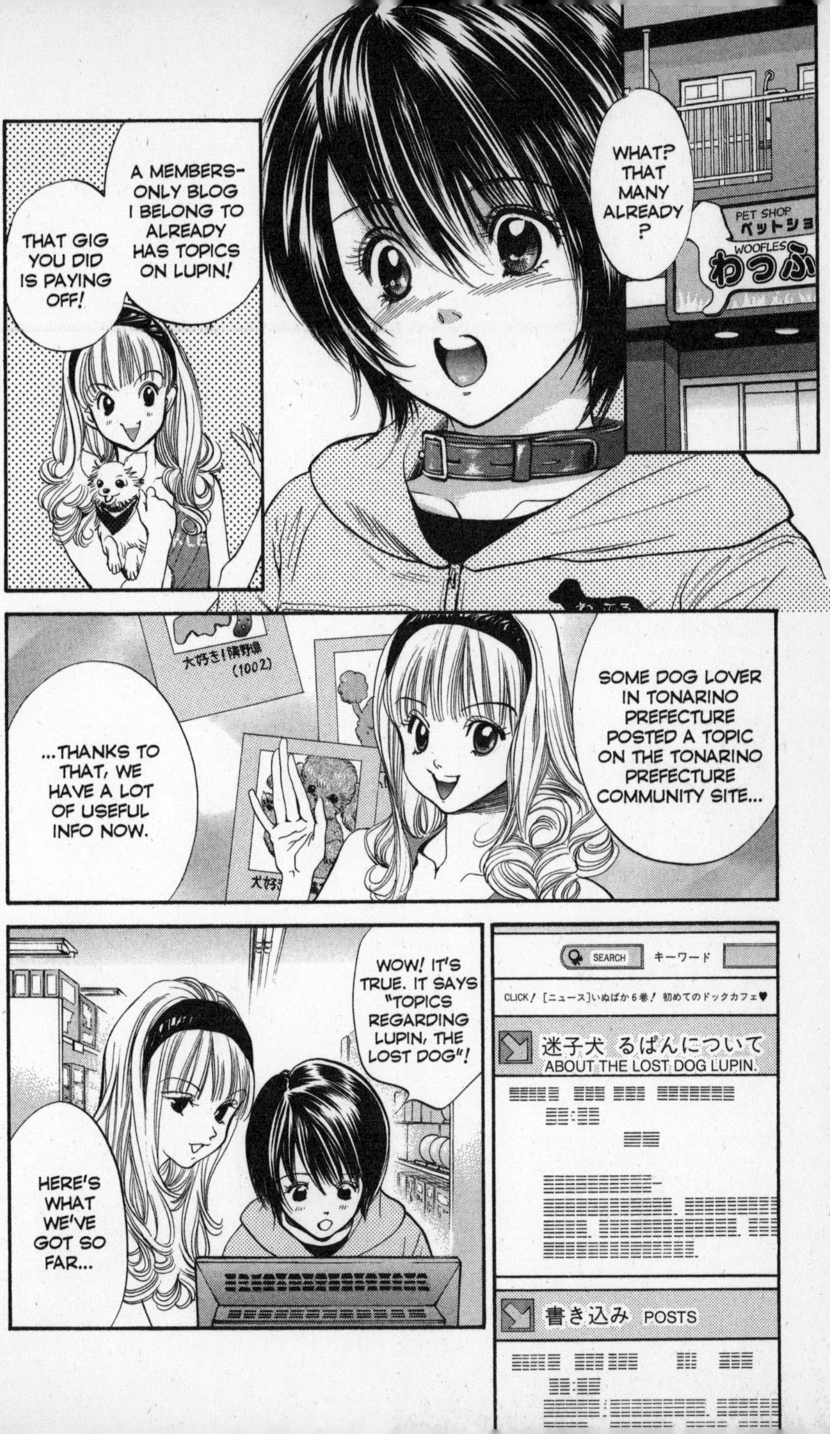

WHAT? THAT MANY ALREADY?
PET SHOP ペットショ
WOOFLES わつふ
A MEMBERS-ONLY BLOG I BELONG TO ALREADY HAS TOPICS ON LUPIN!
THAT GIG YOU DID IS PAYING OFF!
SOME DOG LOVER IN TONARINO PREFECTURE POSTED A TOPIC ON THE TONARINO PREFECTURE COMMUNITY SITE...
大好き!隣野県
(1002)
...THANKS TO THAT, WE HAVE A LOT OF USEFUL INFO NOW.
SEARCH
キーワード
CLICK! [ニュース]いぬばか6巻! 初めてのドックカフェ♥
迷子犬 るぱんについて
ABOUT THE LOST DOG LUPIN.
書き込み POSTS
WOW! IT'S TRUE. IT SAYS "TOPICS REGARDING LUPIN, THE LOST DOG"!
HERE'S WHAT WE'VE GOT SO FAR...

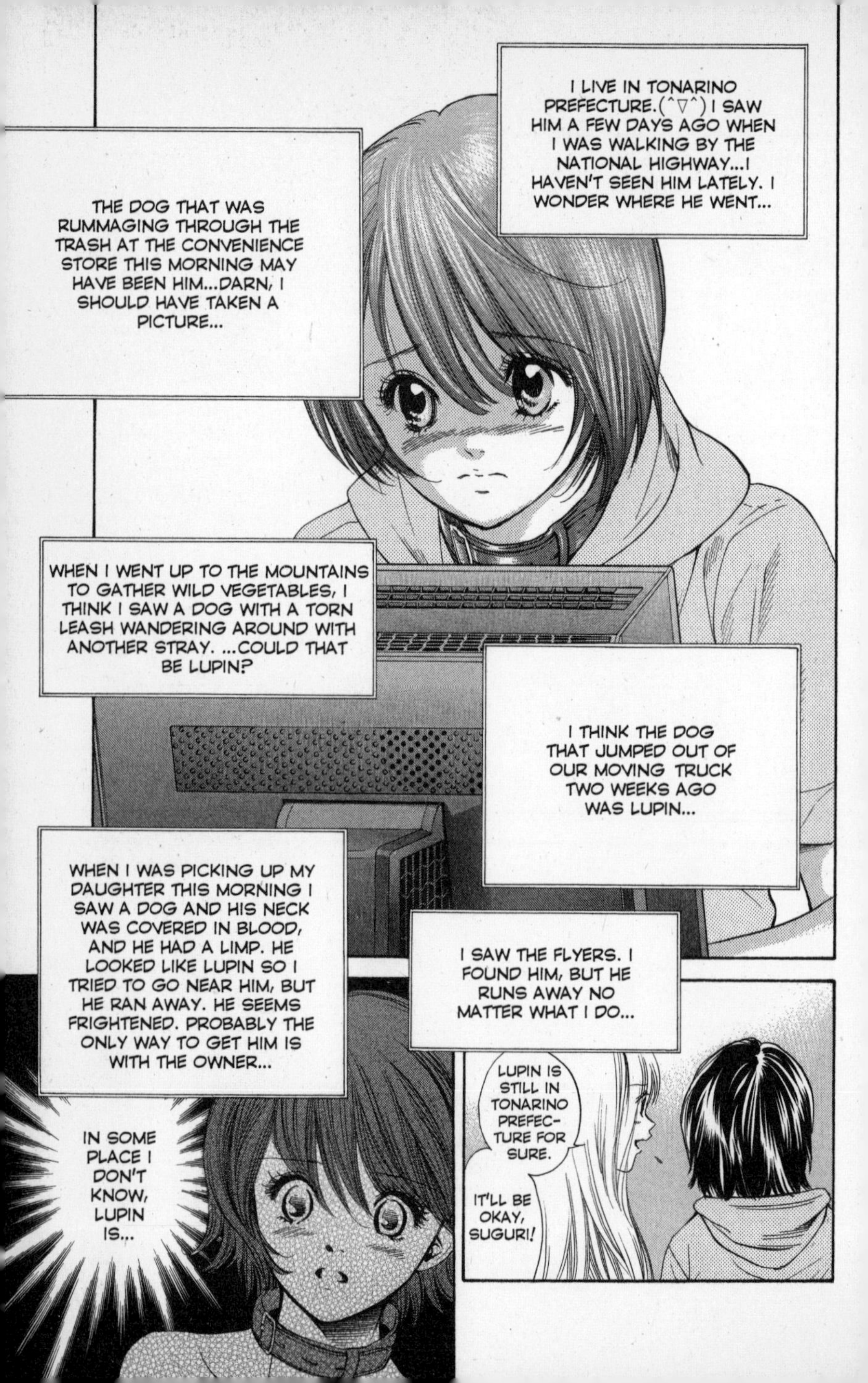
I LIVE IN TONARINO PREFECTURE.(^▽^) I SAW HIM A FEW DAYS AGO WHEN I WAS WALKING BY THE NATIONAL HIGHWAY...I HAVEN'T SEEN HIM LATELY. I WONDER WHERE HE WENT...
THE DOG THAT WAS RUMMAGING THROUGH THE TRASH AT THE CONVENIENCE STORE THIS MORNING MAY HAVE BEEN HIM...DARN, I SHOULD HAVE TAKEN A PICTURE...
WHEN I WENT UP TO THE MOUNTAINS TO GATHER WILD VEGETABLES, I THINK I SAW A DOG WITH A TORN LEASH WANDERING AROUND WITH ANOTHER STRAY. ...COULD THAT BE LUPIN?
I THINK THE DOG THAT JUMPED OUT OF OUR MOVING TRUCK TWO WEEKS AGO WAS LUPIN...
I SAW THE FLYERS. I FOUND HIM, BUT HE RUNS AWAY NO MATTER WHAT I DO...
WHEN I WAS PICKING UP MY DAUGHTER THIS MORNING I SAW A DOG AND HIS NECK WAS COVERED IN BLOOD, AND HE HAD A LIMP. HE LOOKED LIKE LUPIN SO I TRIED TO GO NEAR HIM, BUT HE RAN AWAY. HE SEEMS FRIGHTENED. PROBABLY THE ONLY WAY TO GET HIM IS WITH THE OWNER...
LUPIN IS STILL IN TONARINO PREFECTURE FOR SURE.
IT'LL BE OKAY, SUGURI!
IN SOME PLACE I DON'T KNOW, LUPIN IS...

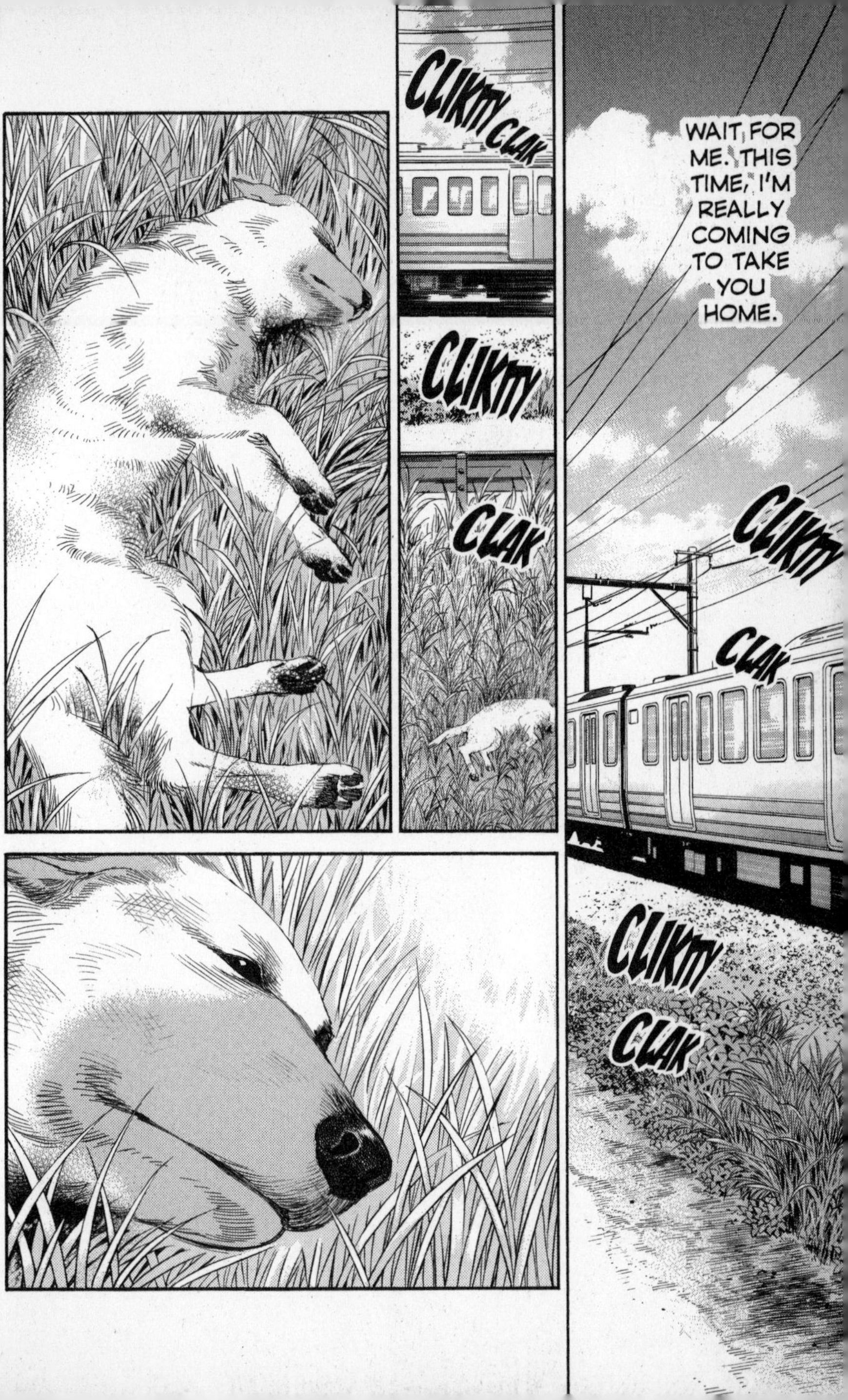
WAIT FOR ME. THIS TIME, I'M REALLY COMING TO TAKE YOU HOME.
CLIKITTY
CLAK
CLIKITTY
CLAK
CLIKITTY CLAK
CLIKITTY
CLAK

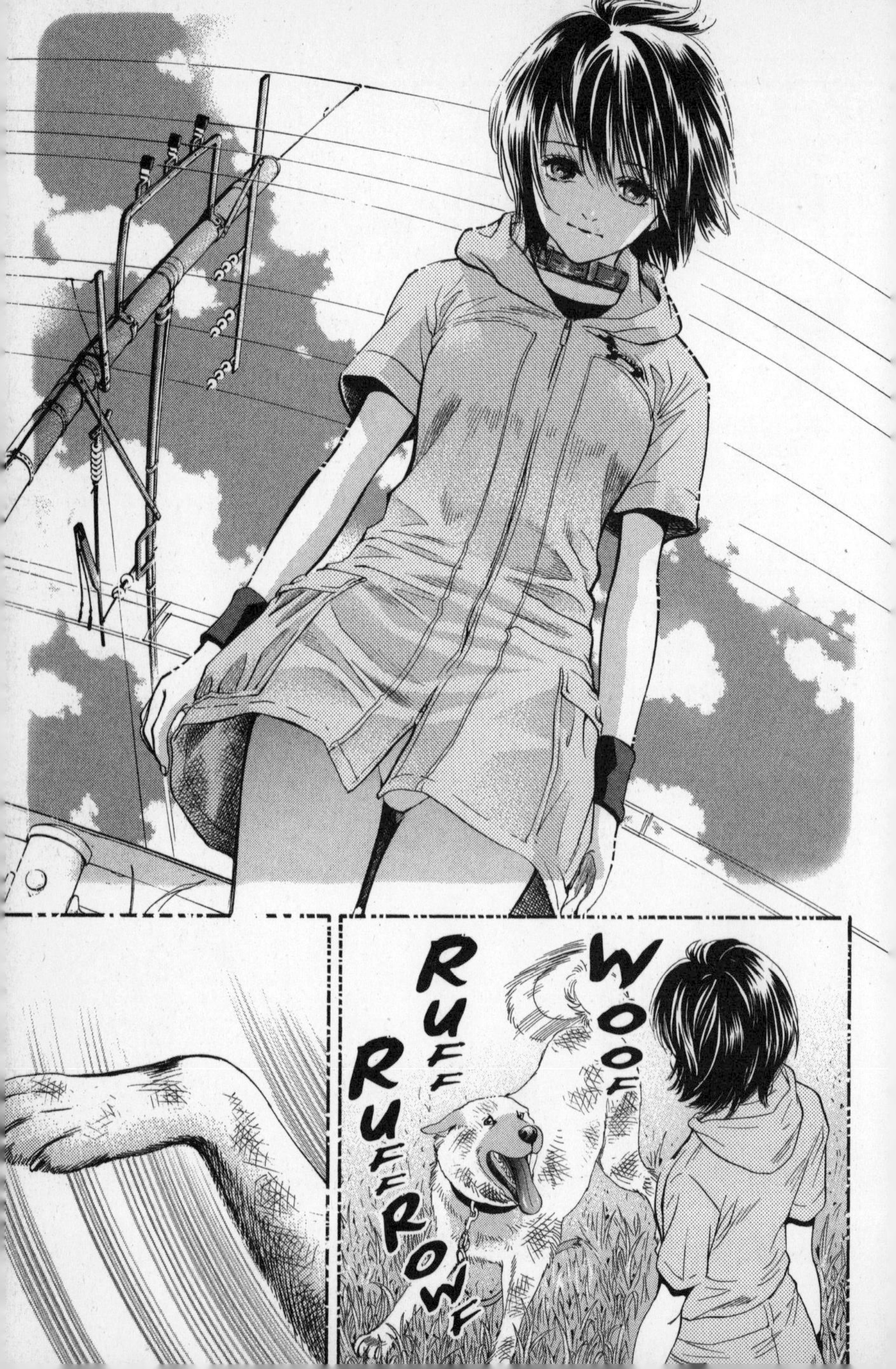
WOOF
RUFF
RUFFROWF

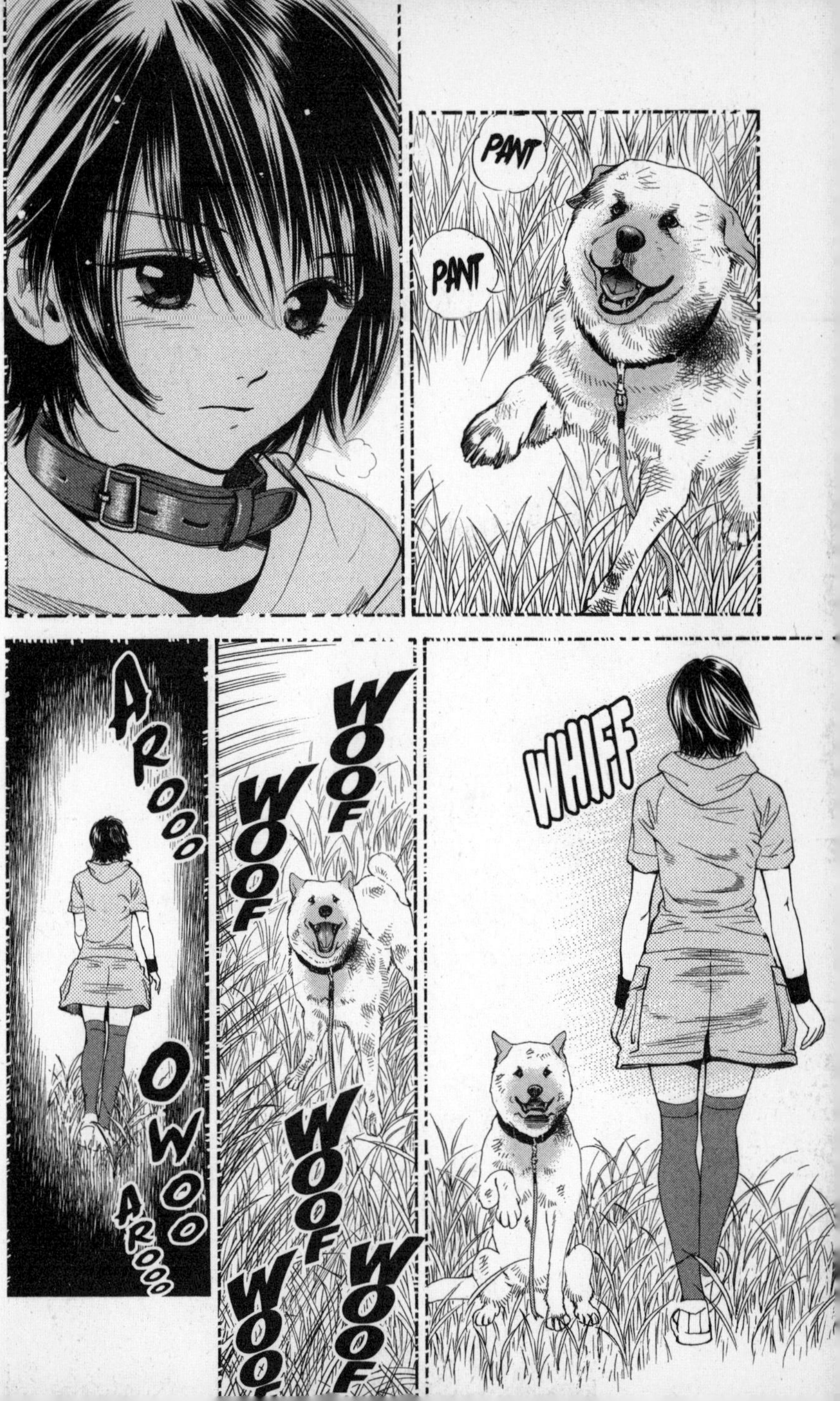
PANT
PANT
WHIFF
WOOF
WOOF
WOOF
WOOF
AROOO
OWOO
AROOO

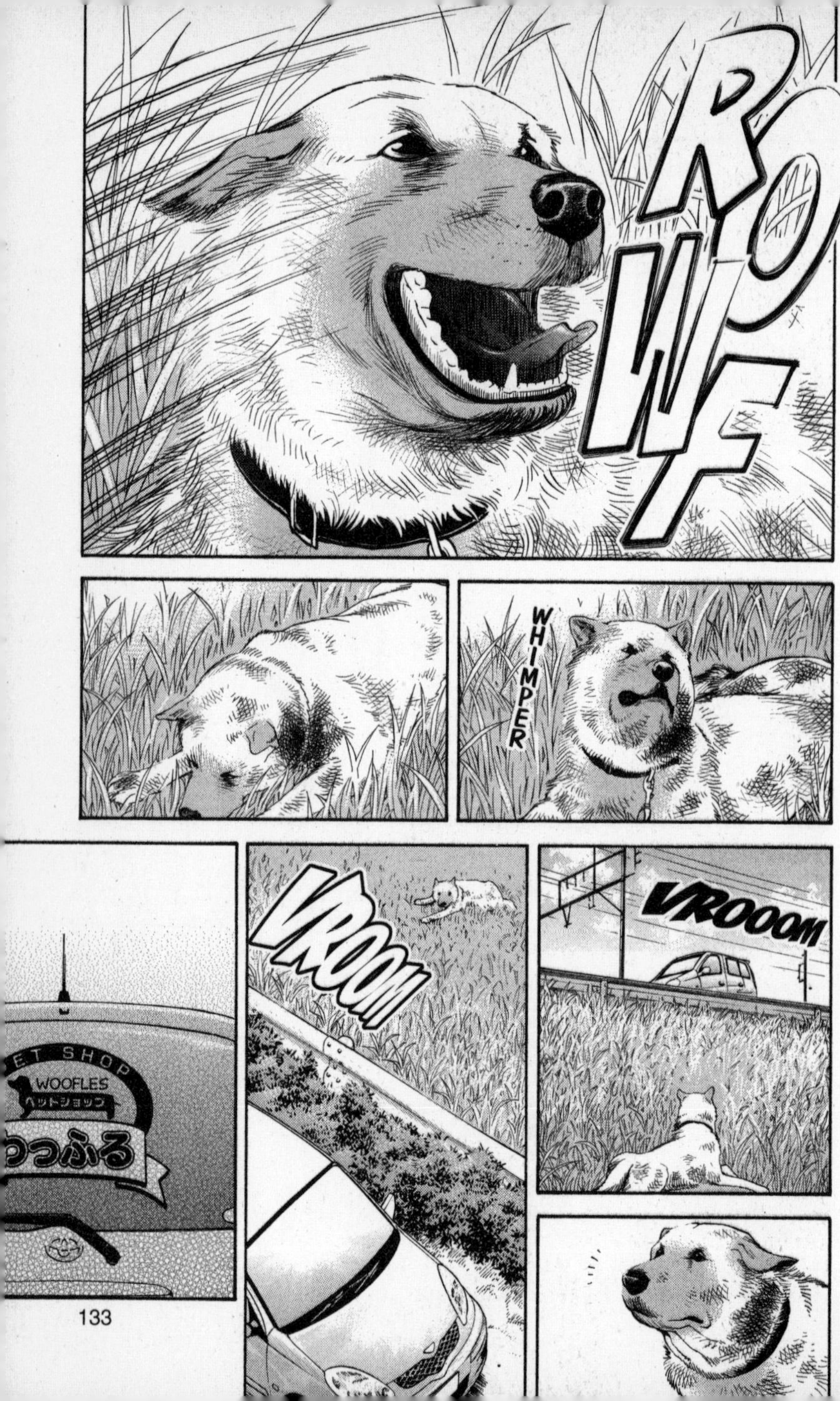

ROWF
WHIMPER
VROOOM
VROOM
PET SHOP
WOOFLES
ペットショップ
わっふる

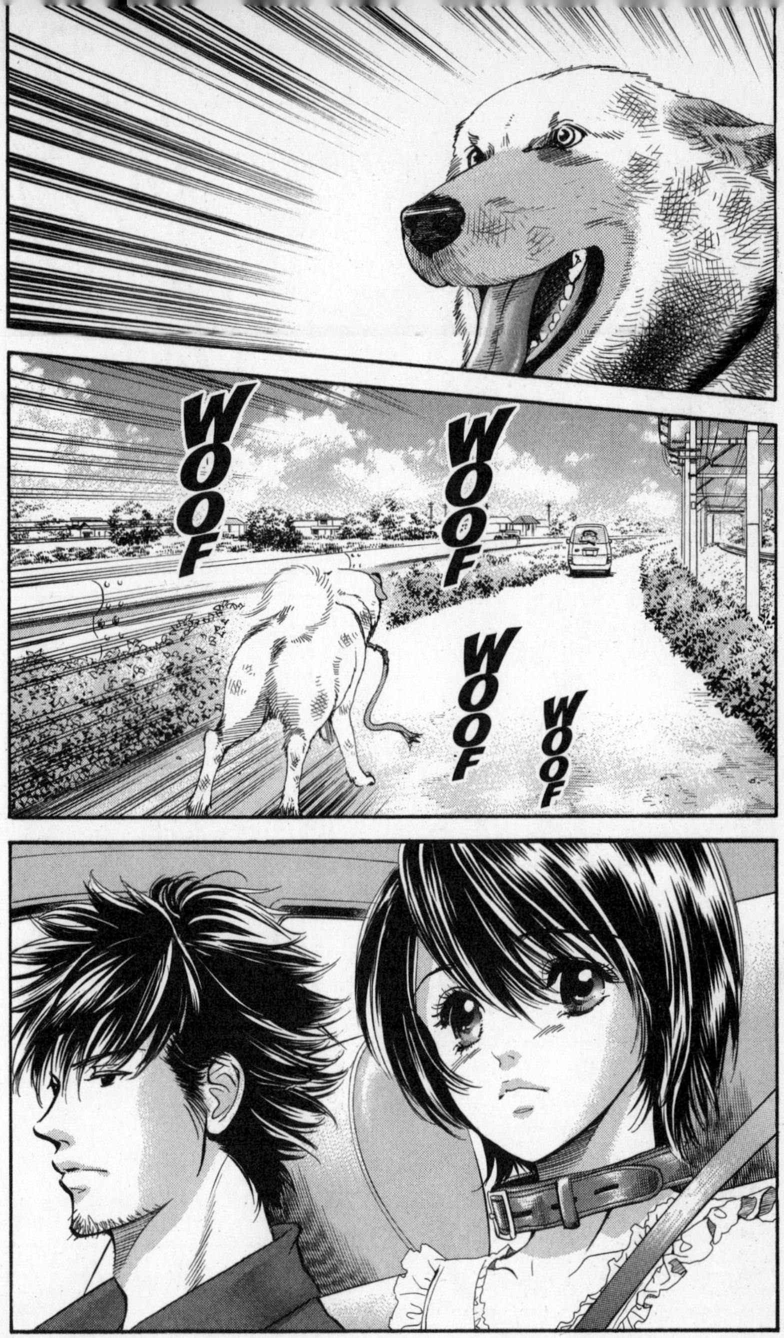
WOOF
WOOF
WOOF
WOOF

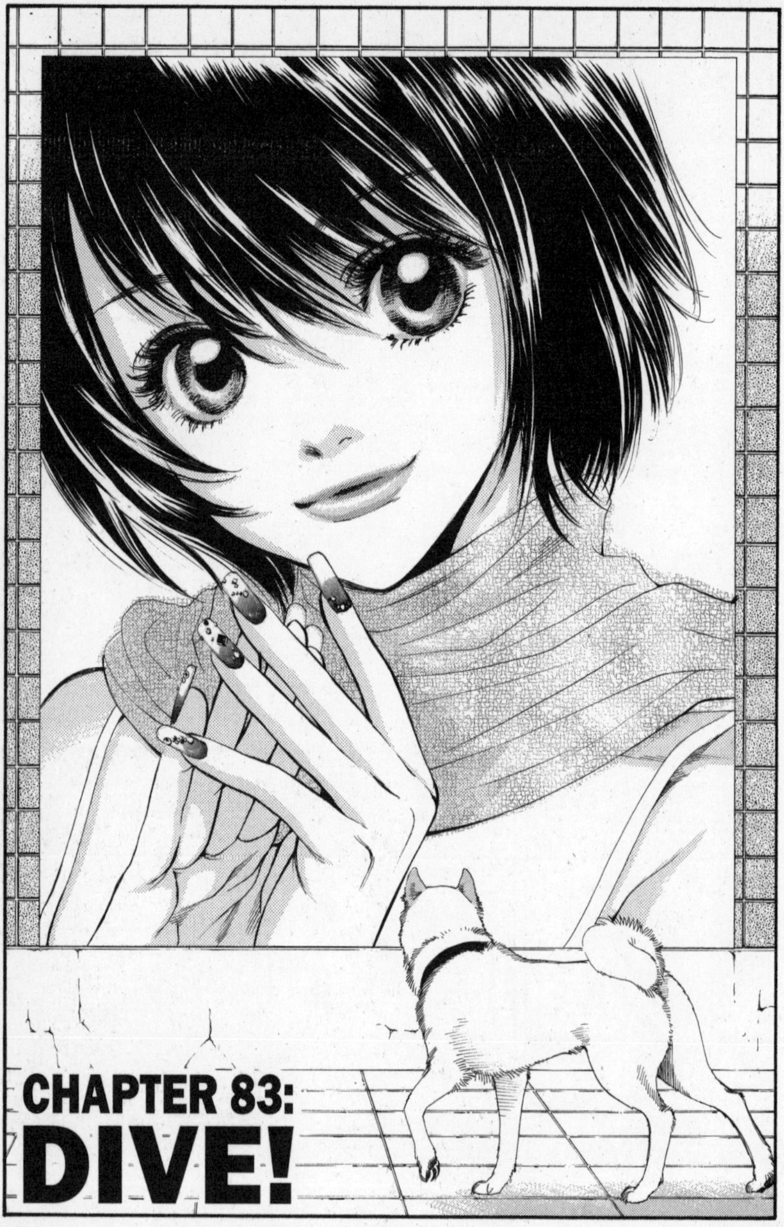
CHAPTER 83:
DIVE!

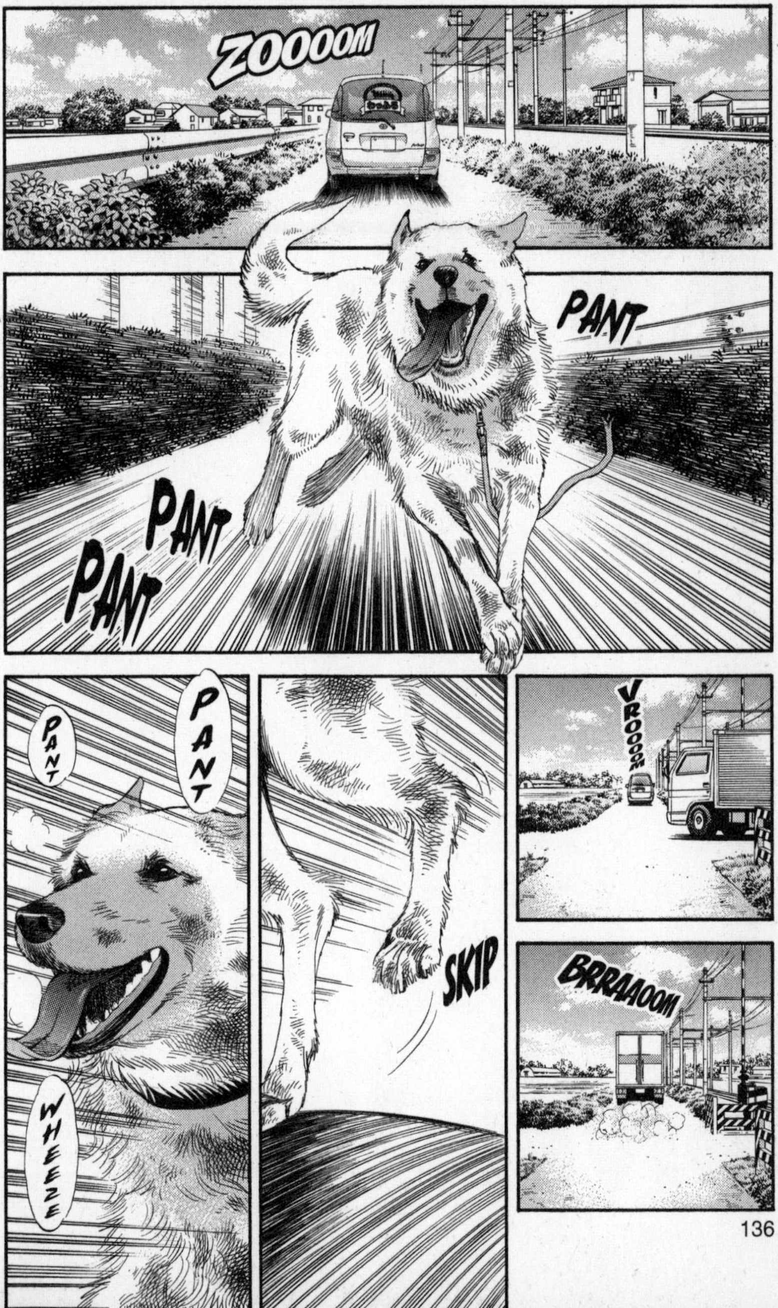
ZOOOOM
PANT
PANT
PANT
VROOOOM
BRRAAOOM
SKIP
PANT
PANT
WHEEZE

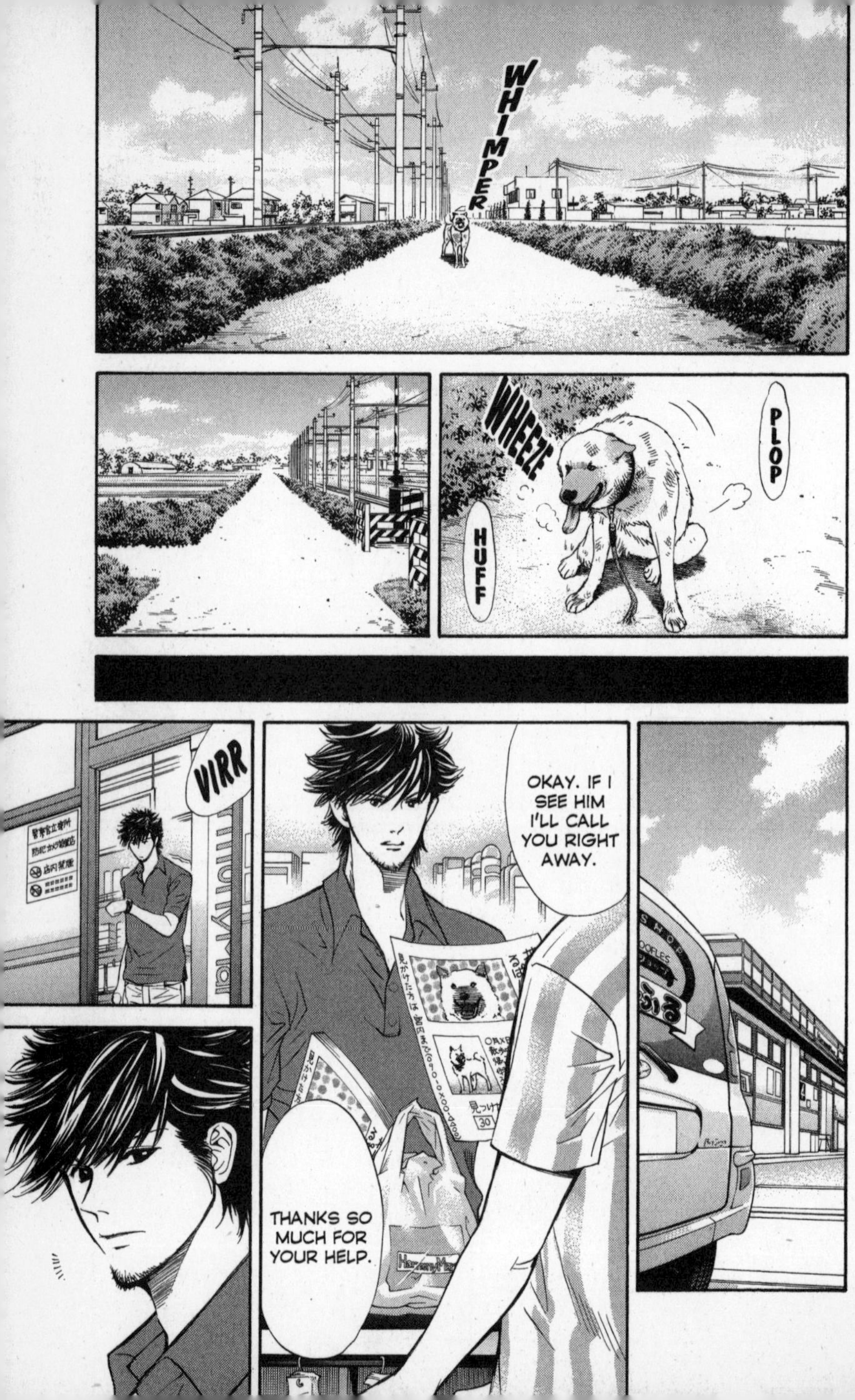
WHIMPER
PLOP
WHEEZE
HUFF
OKAY. IF I SEE HIM I'LL CALL YOU RIGHT AWAY.
THANKS SO MUCH FOR YOUR HELP.
VIRR

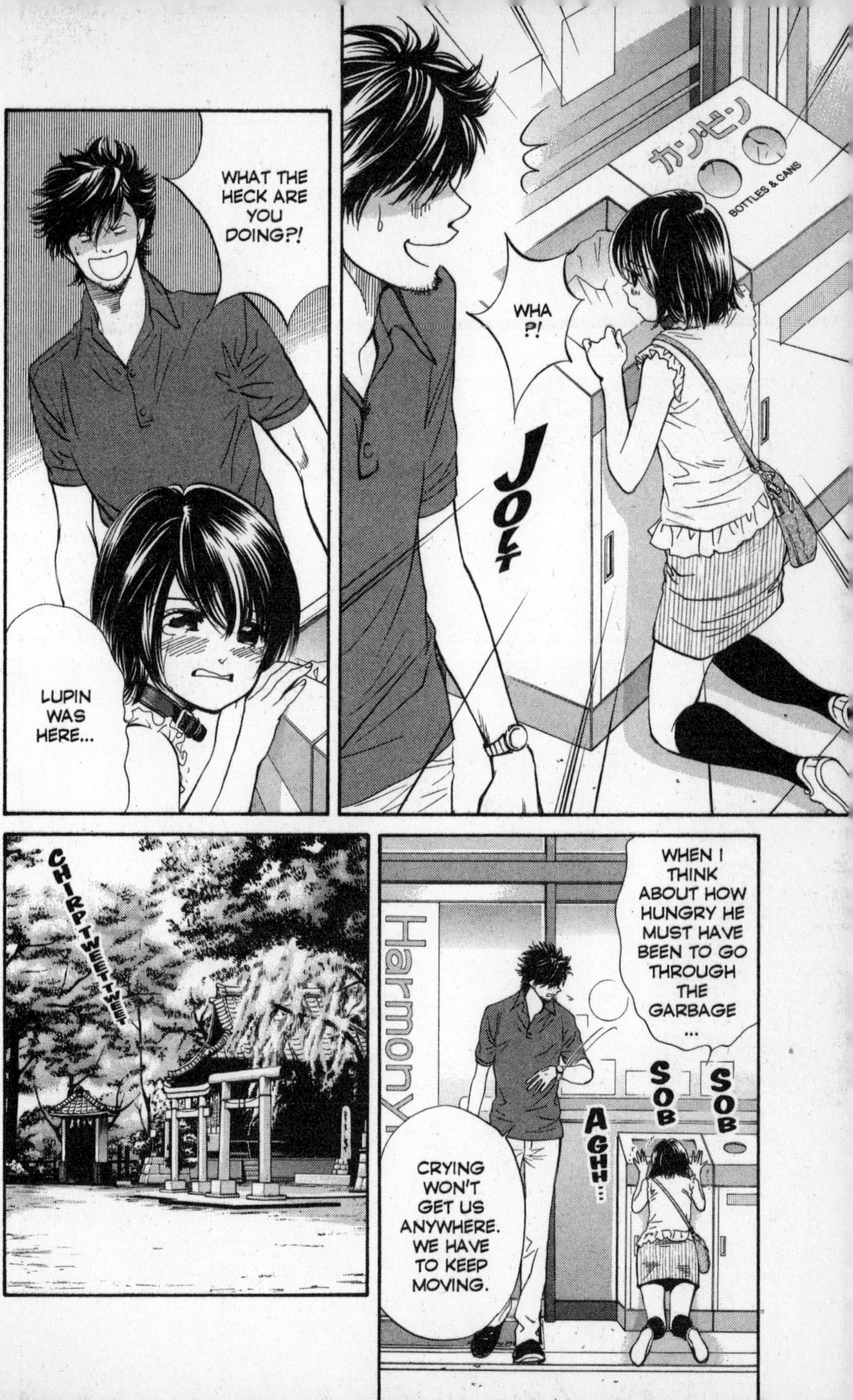
カン・ビン
BOTTLES & CANS
WHA?!
JOLT
WHAT THE HECK ARE YOU DOING?!
LUPIN WAS HERE...
WHEN I THINK ABOUT HOW HUNGRY HE MUST HAVE BEEN TO GO THROUGH THE GARBAGE ...
SOB SOB
AGHH...
Harmony
CRYING WON'T GET US ANYWHERE. WE HAVE TO KEEP MOVING.
CHIRP TWEET TWEET

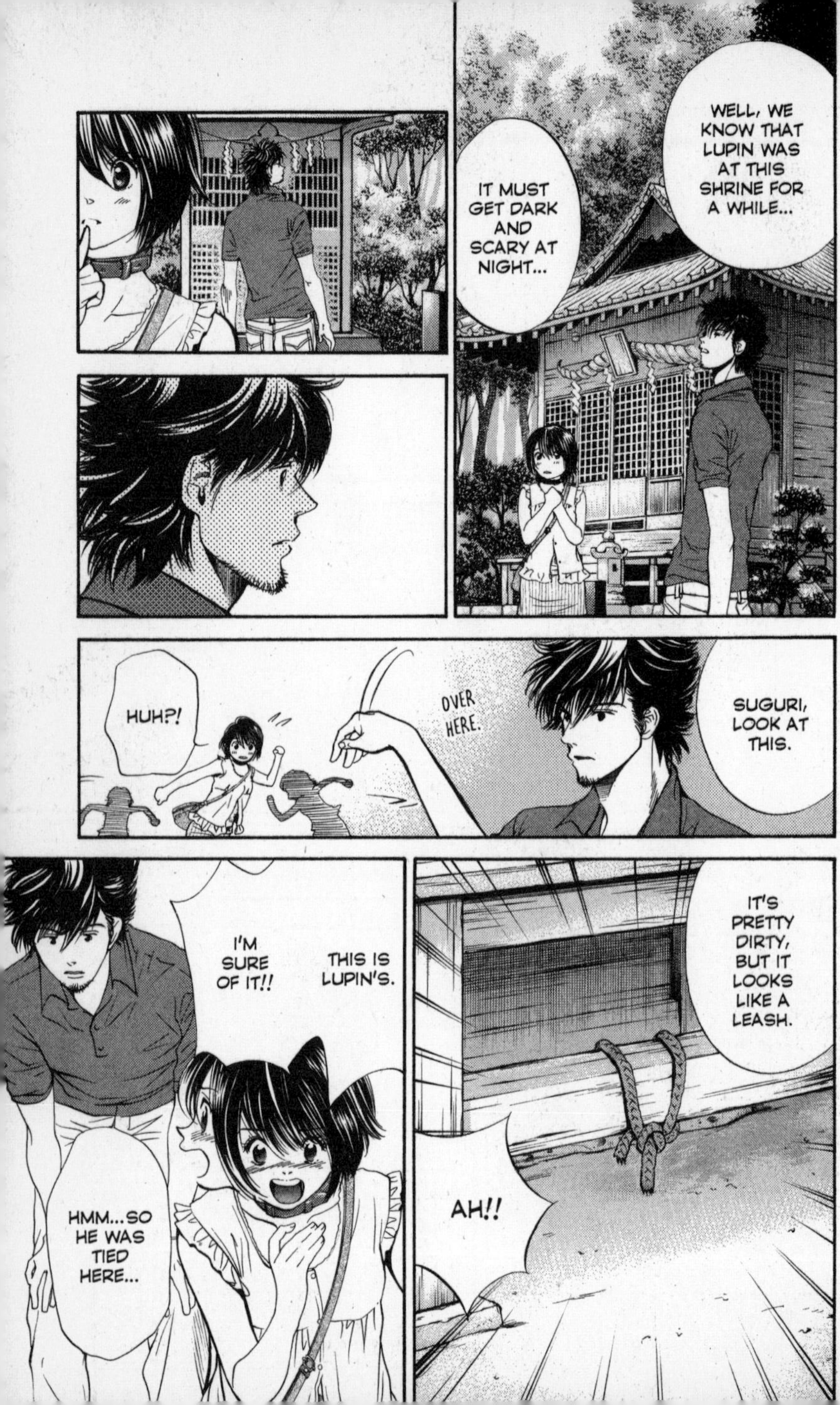
WELL, WE KNOW THAT LUPIN WAS AT THIS SHRINE FOR A WHILE...
IT MUST GET DARK AND SCARY AT NIGHT...
SUGURI, LOOK AT THIS.
OVER HERE.
HUH?!
IT'S PRETTY DIRTY, BUT IT LOOKS LIKE A LEASH.
AH!!
THIS IS LUPIN'S.
I'M SURE OF IT!!
HMM...SO HE WAS TIED HERE...

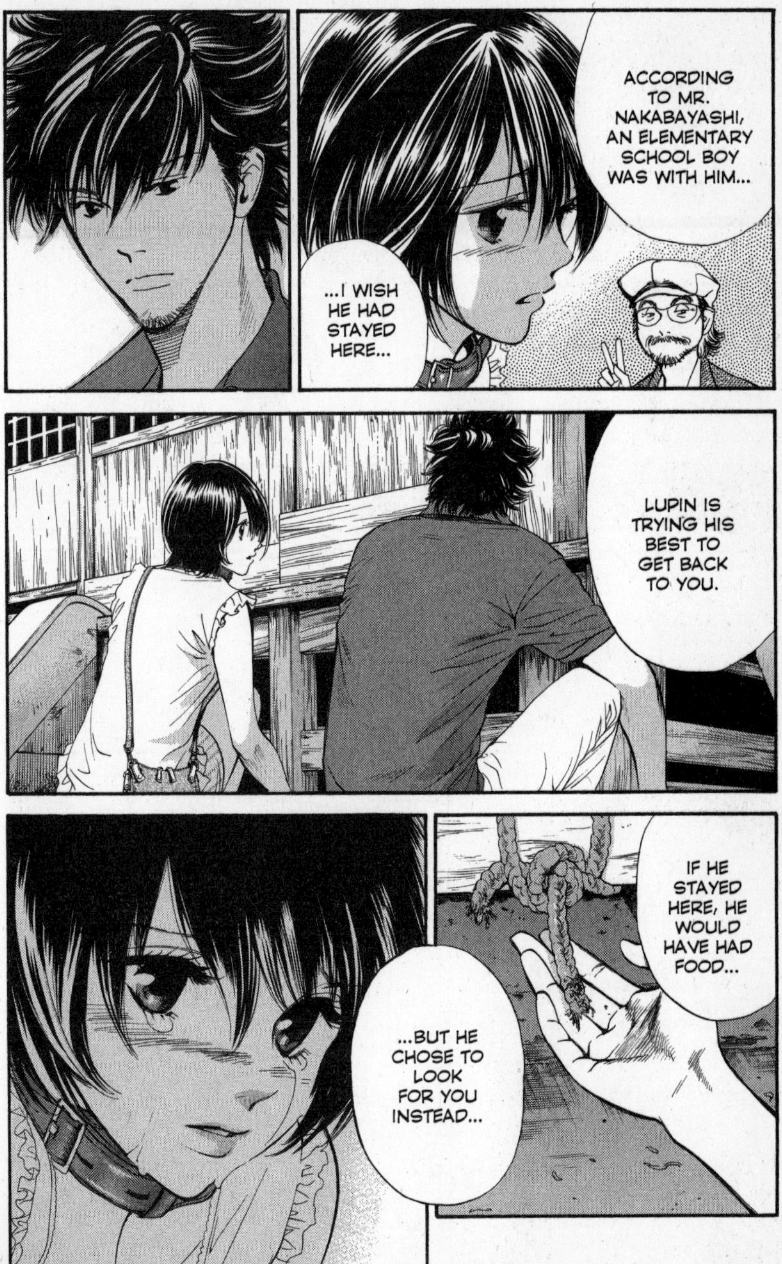
ACCORDING TO MR. NAKABAYASHI, AN ELEMENTARY SCHOOL BOY WAS WITH HIM...
...I WISH HE HAD STAYED HERE...
LUPIN IS TRYING HIS BEST TO GET BACK TO YOU.
IF HE STAYED HERE, HE WOULD HAVE HAD FOOD...
...BUT HE CHOSE TO LOOK FOR YOU INSTEAD...

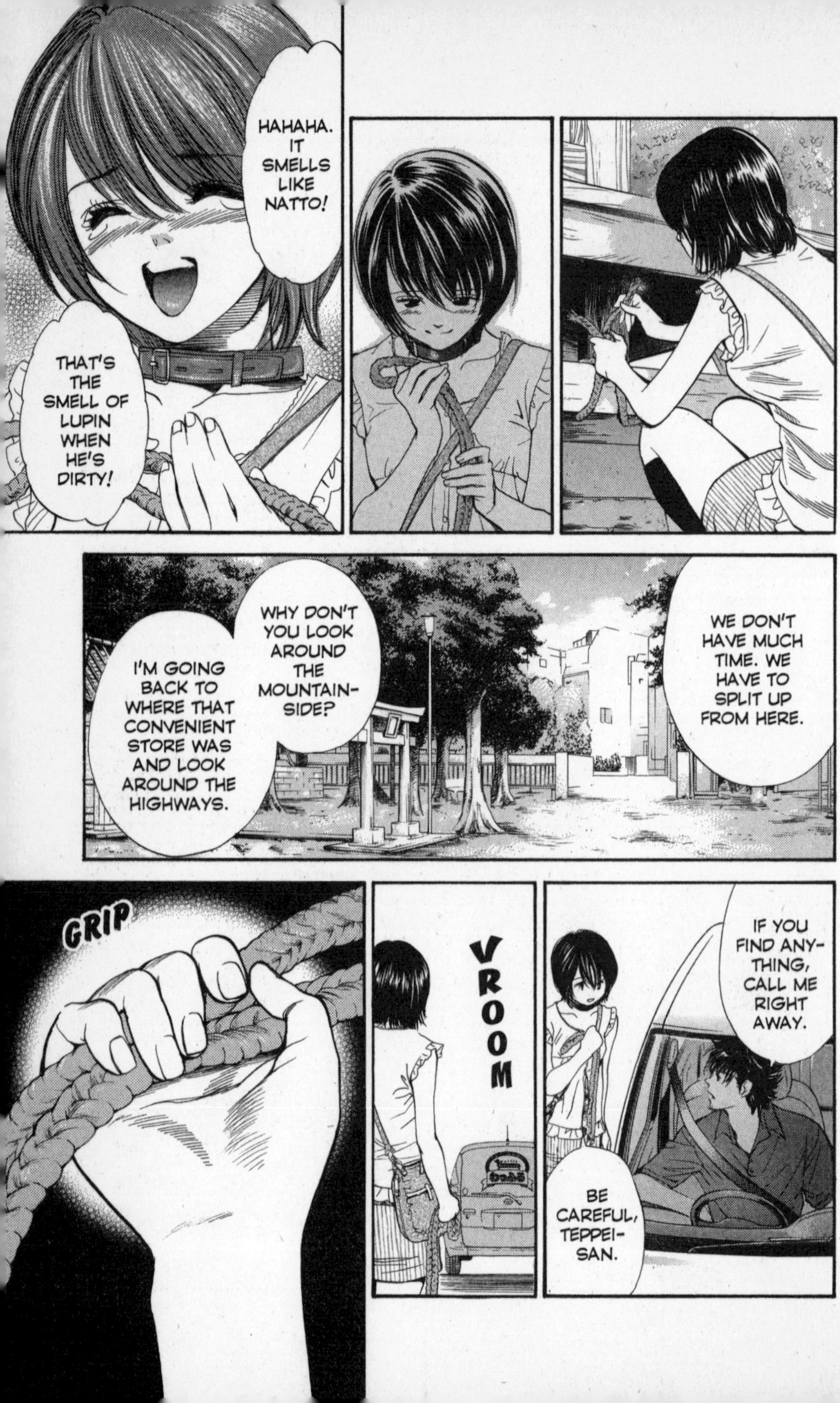
HAHAHA. IT SMELLS LIKE NATTO!
THAT'S THE SMELL OF LUPIN WHEN HE'S DIRTY!
WE DON'T HAVE MUCH TIME. WE HAVE TO SPLIT UP FROM HERE.
WHY DON'T YOU LOOK AROUND THE MOUNTAIN-SIDE?
I'M GOING BACK TO WHERE THAT CONVENIENT STORE WAS AND LOOK AROUND THE HIGHWAYS.
IF YOU FIND ANY-THING, CALL ME RIGHT AWAY.
BE CAREFUL, TEPPEI-SAN.
VROOM
GRIP

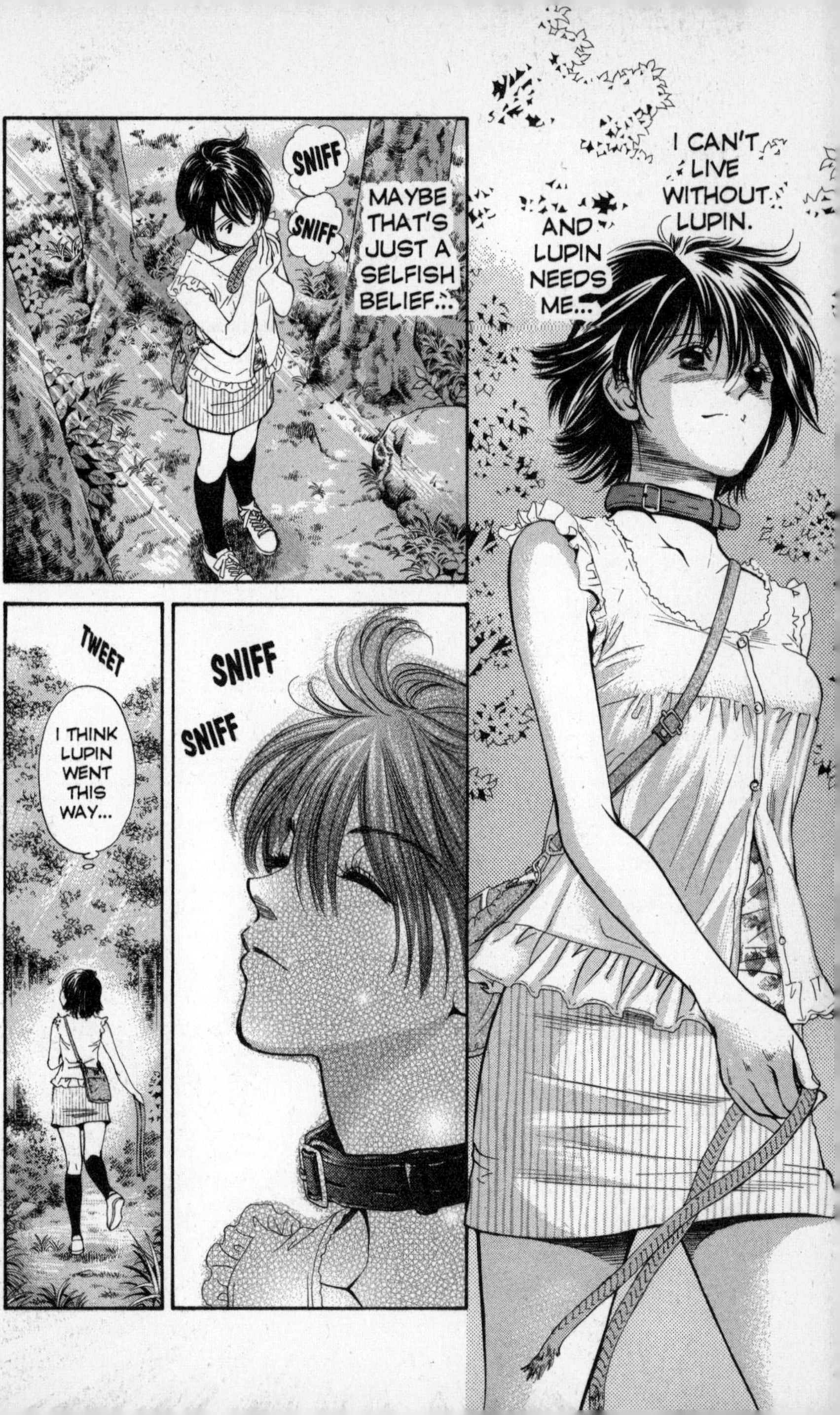
I CAN'T LIVE WITHOUT LUPIN.
AND LUPIN NEEDS ME...
MAYBE THAT'S JUST A SELFISH BELIEF...
SNIFF
SNIFF
SNIFF
SNIFF
TWEET
I THINK LUPIN WENT THIS WAY...

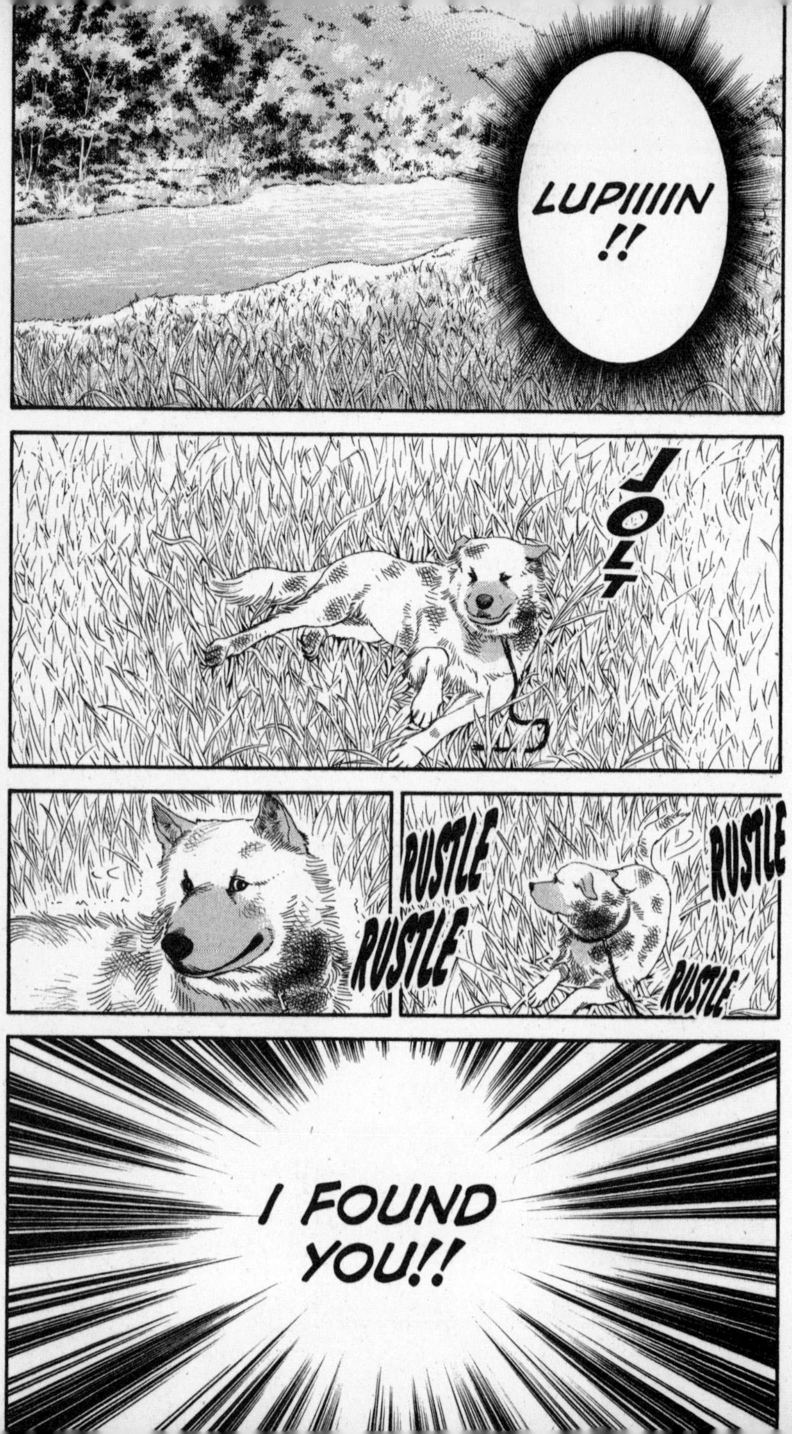
LUPIIIIN !!
JOLT
RUSTLE
RUSTLE
RUSTLE
RUSTLE
I FOUND YOU!!

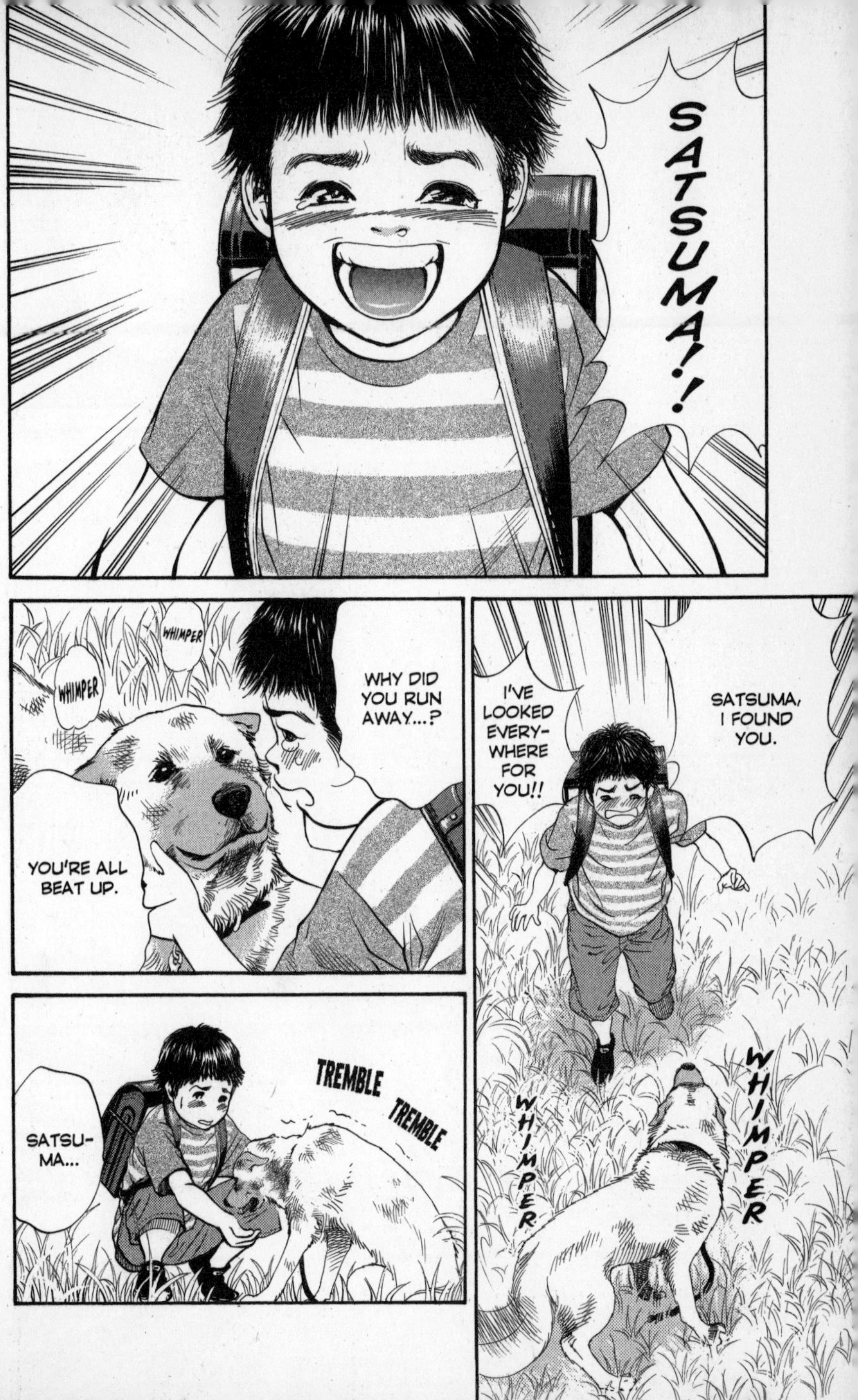
SATSUMA!!
SATSUMA, I FOUND YOU.
I'VE LOOKED EVERY-WHERE FOR YOU!!
WHIMPER
WHIMPER
WHY DID YOU RUN AWAY...?
WHIMPER
WHIMPER
YOU'RE ALL BEAT UP.
TREMBLE
TREMBLE
SATSU-MA...

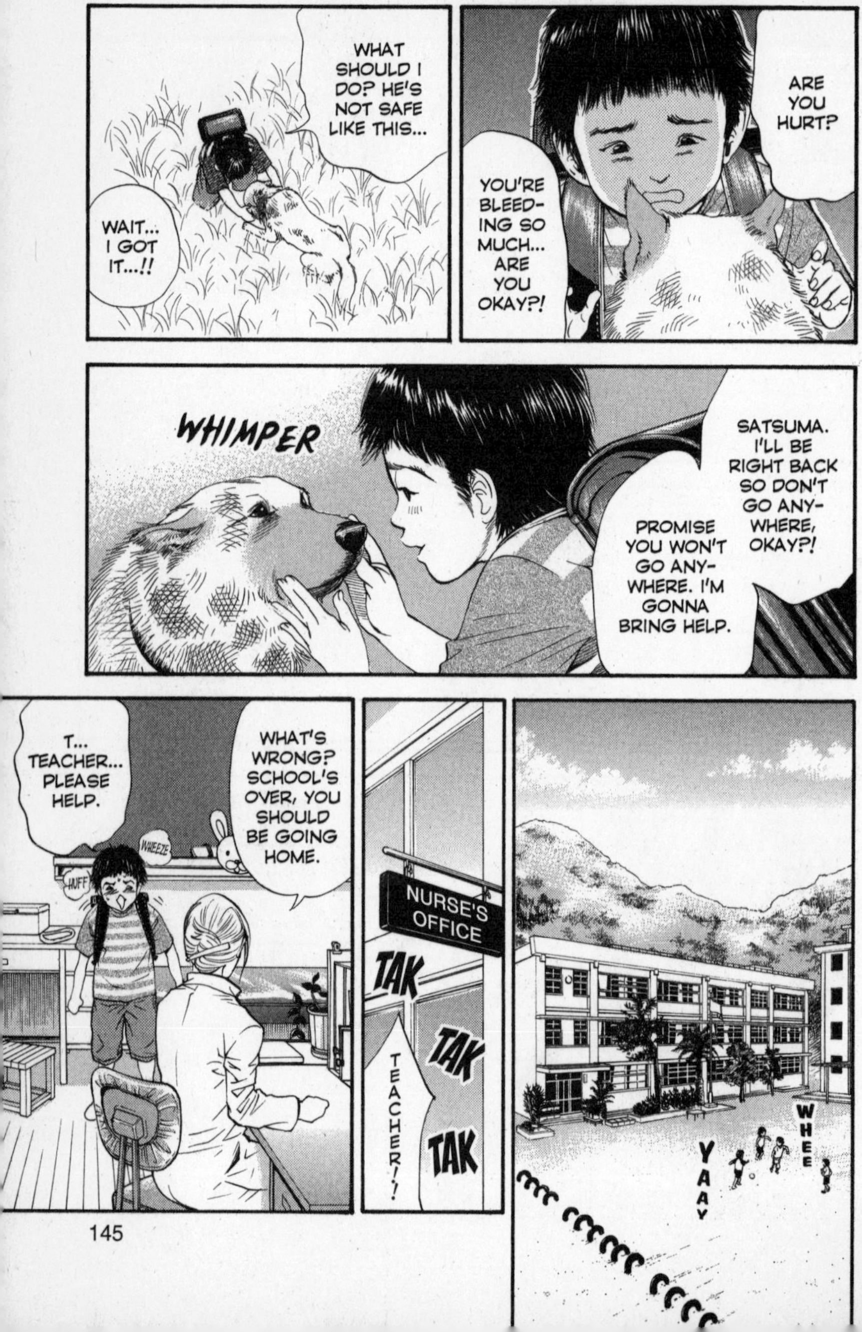
ARE YOU HURT?
YOU'RE BLEEDING SO MUCH... ARE YOU OKAY?!
WHAT SHOULD I DO? HE'S NOT SAFE LIKE THIS...
WAIT... I GOT IT...!!
SATSUMA. I'LL BE RIGHT BACK SO DON'T GO ANYWHERE, OKAY?!
PROMISE YOU WON'T GO ANYWHERE. I'M GONNA BRING HELP.
WHIMPER
WHEE
YAAY
NURSE'S OFFICE
TAK
TAK
TAK
TEACHER!!
WHAT'S WRONG? SCHOOL'S OVER, YOU SHOULD BE GOING HOME.
T... TEACHER... PLEASE HELP.
WHEEZE
HUFF

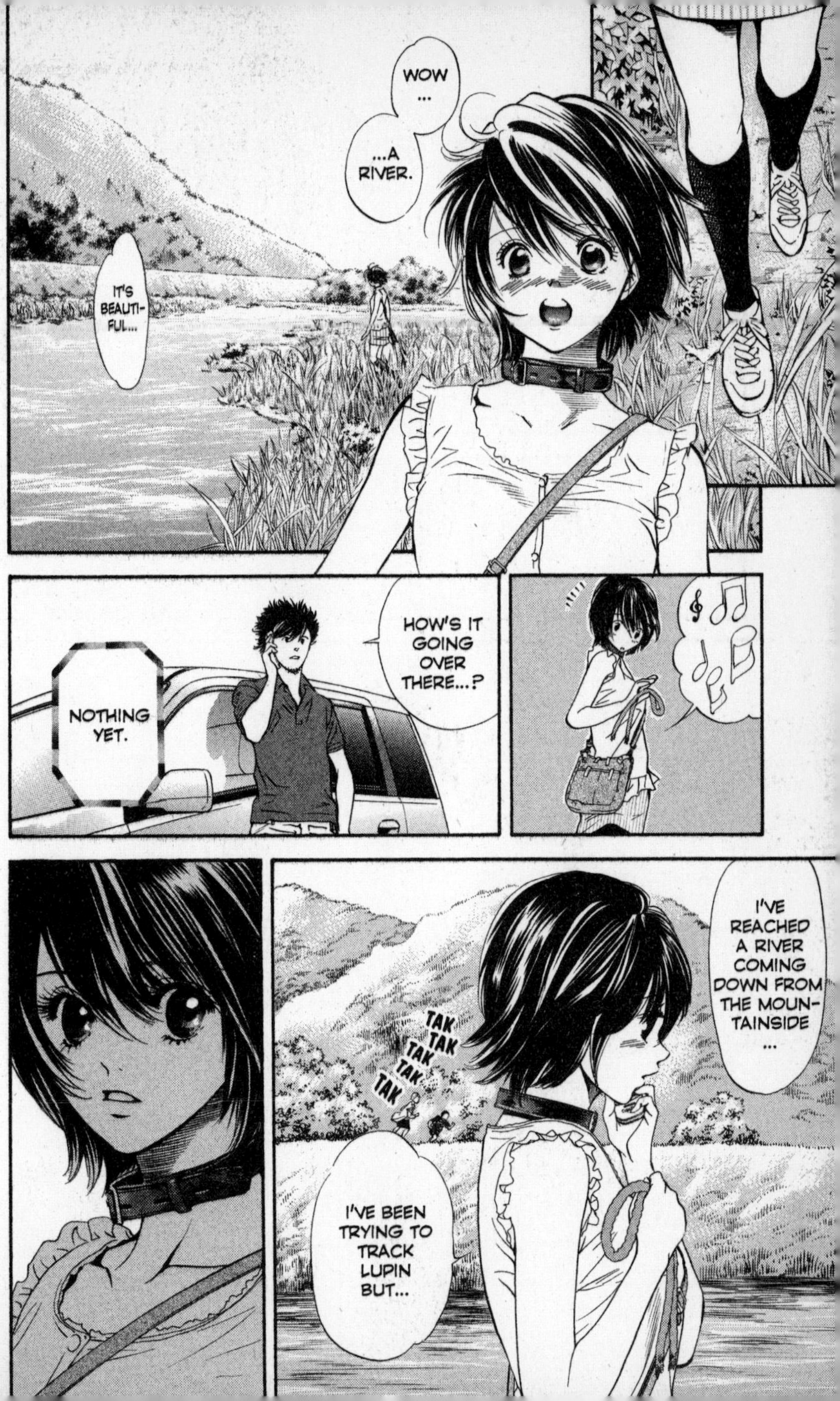
WOW ...
...A RIVER.
IT'S BEAUTI-FUL...
HOW'S IT GOING OVER THERE...?
NOTHING YET.
I'VE REACHED A RIVER COMING DOWN FROM THE MOUN-TAINSIDE ...
TAK TAK TAK TAK TAK
I'VE BEEN TRYING TO TRACK LUPIN BUT...

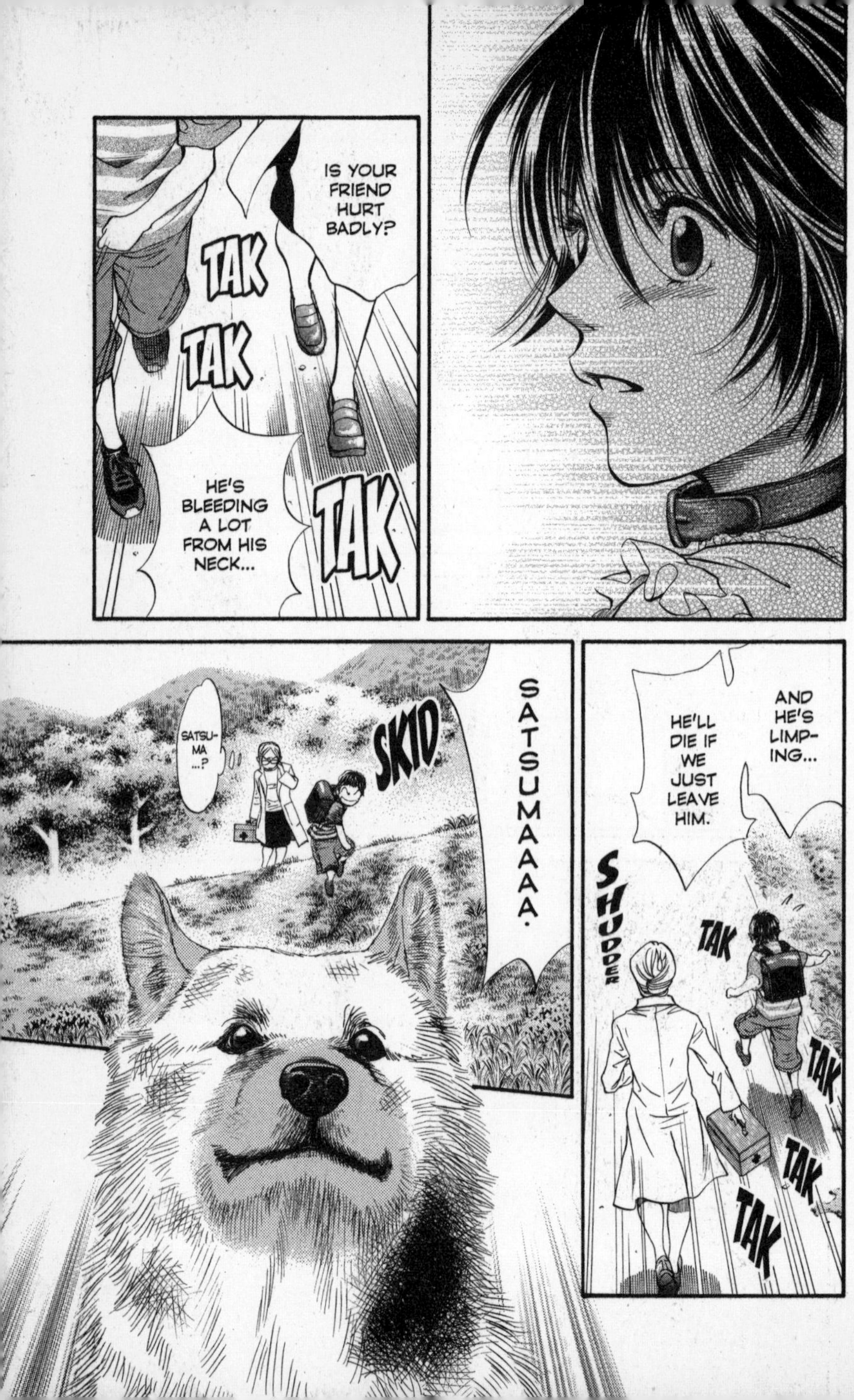
IS YOUR FRIEND HURT BADLY?
TAK
TAK
HE'S BLEEDING A LOT FROM HIS NECK...
TAK
AND HE'S LIMPING...
HE'LL DIE IF WE JUST LEAVE HIM.
SHUDDER
TAK
TAK
TAK
TAK
SATSUMAAAAA.
SKID
SATSUMA ...?

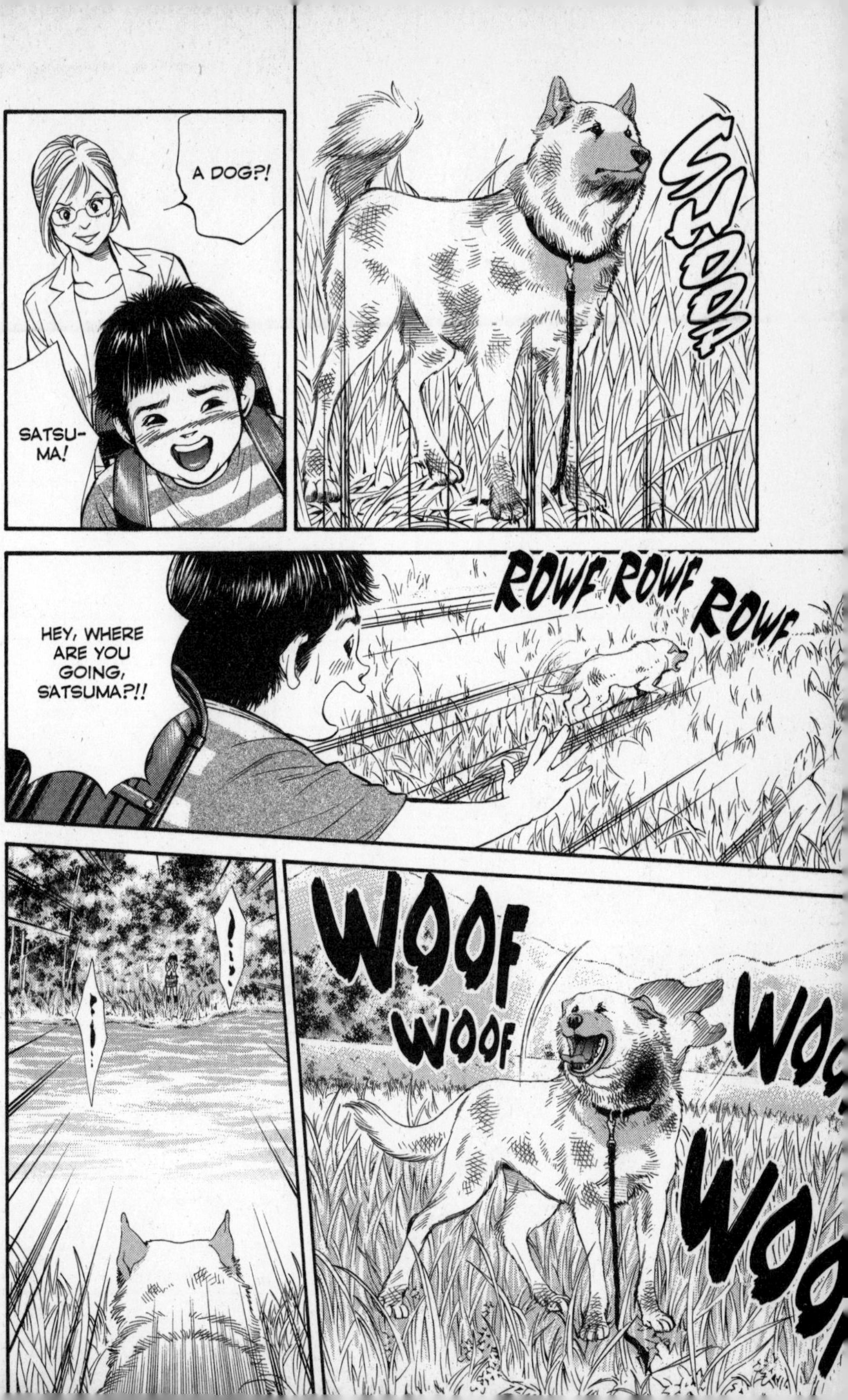
SHOOP
A DOG?!
SATSU-MA!
ROWF ROWF ROWF
HEY, WHERE ARE YOU GOING, SATSUMA?!!
WOOF WOOF

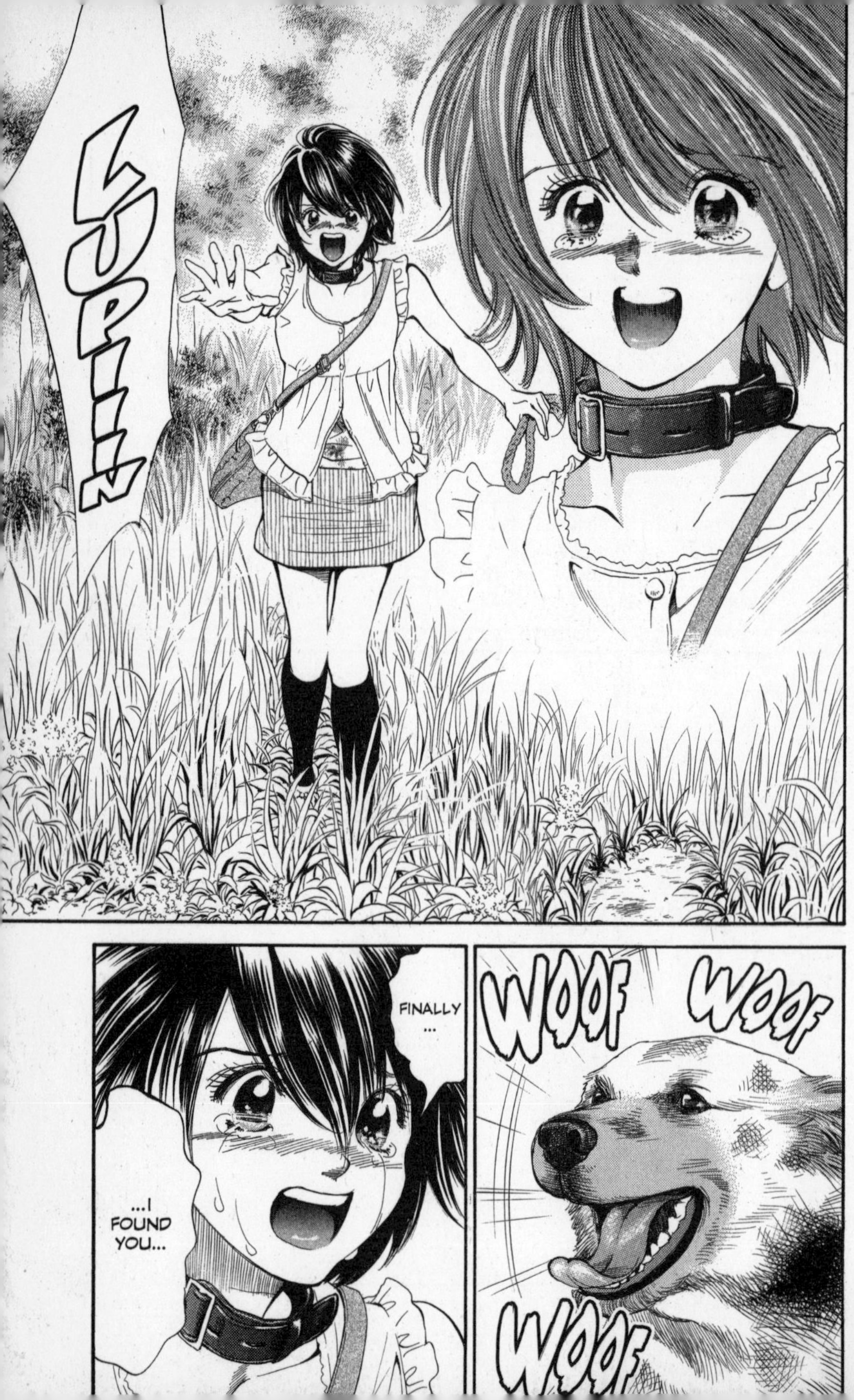
LUPIIIN
WOOF WOOF
WOOF
FINALLY ...
...I FOUND YOU...

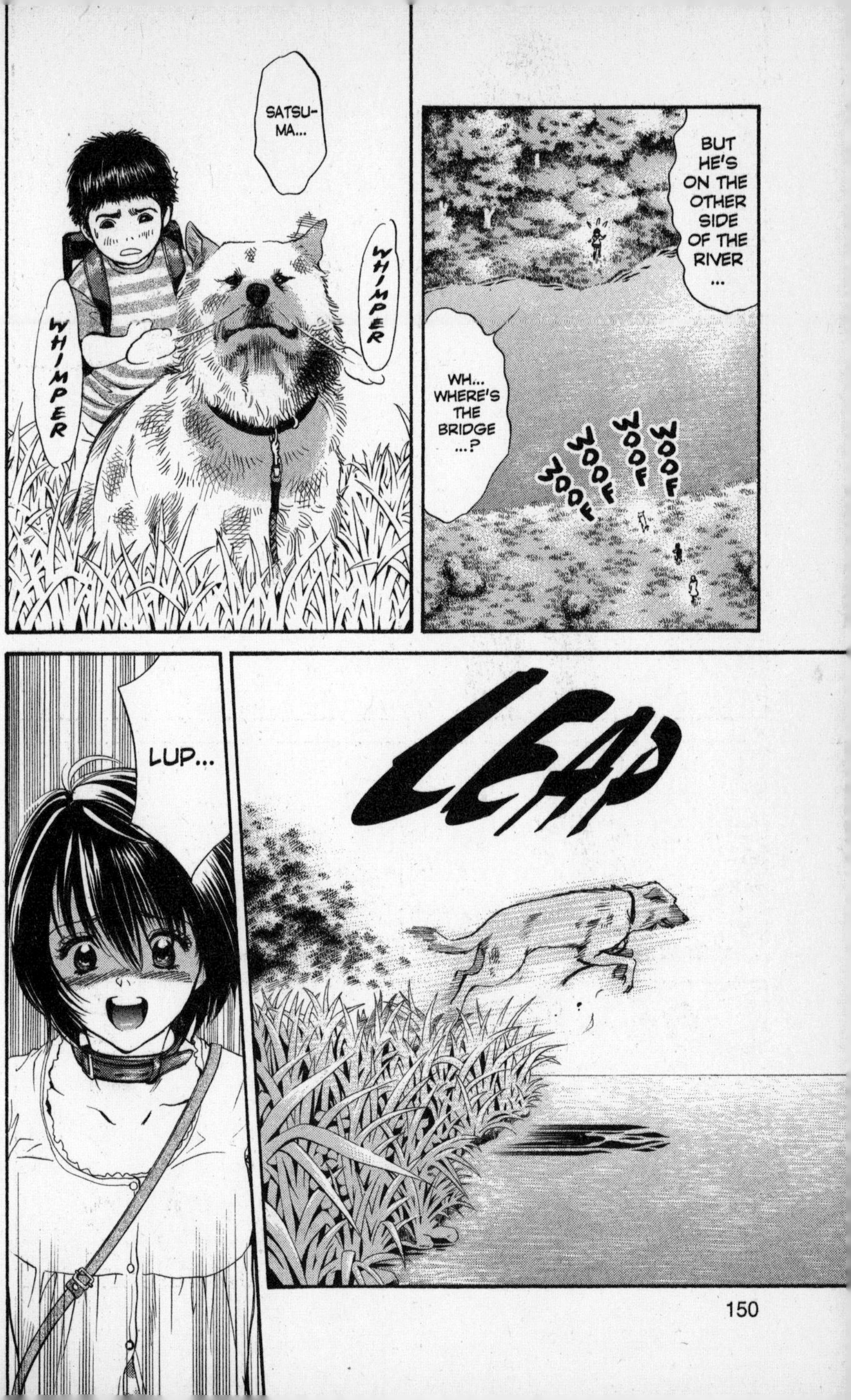
BUT HE'S ON THE OTHER SIDE OF THE RIVER ...
WH... WHERE'S THE BRIDGE ...?
WOOF WOOF
WOOF WOOF
SATSU-MA...
WHIMPER
WHIMPER
LEAP
LUP...

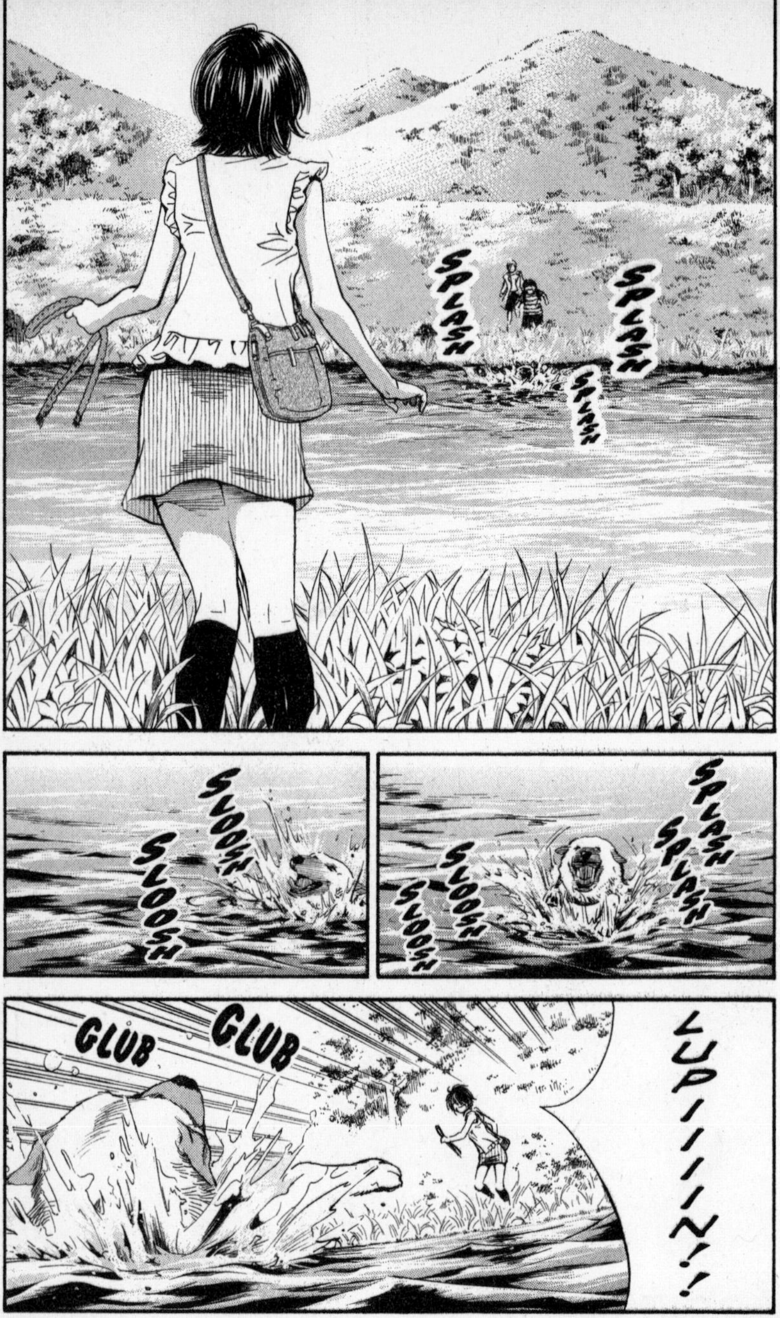
SPLASH
SPLASH
SPLASH
SPLASH
SPLASH
SLOOSH
SLOOSH
SLOOSH
SLOOSH
LUPIIIIIN!!
GLUB
GLUB

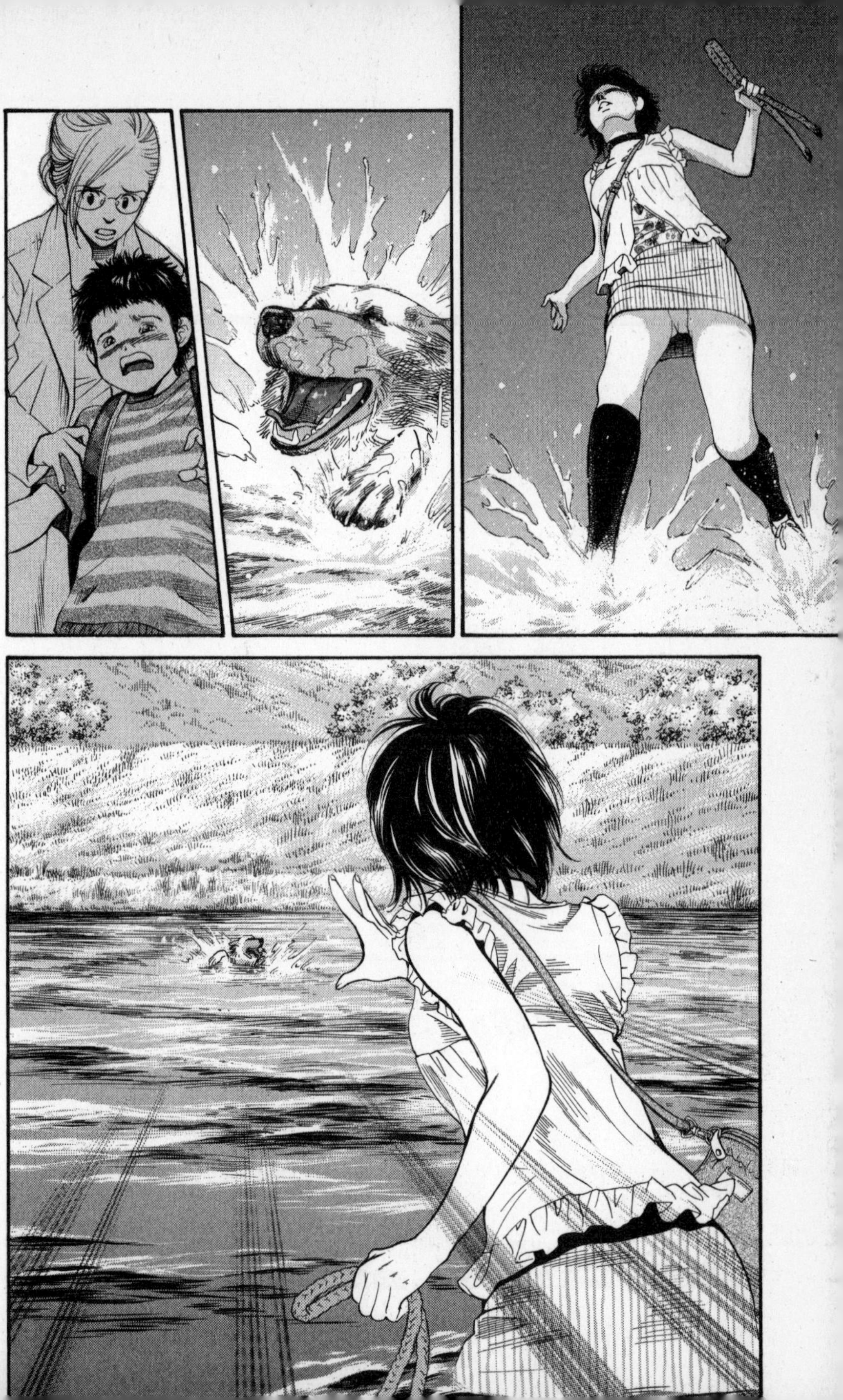

CHAPTER 84: LET'S GO HOME

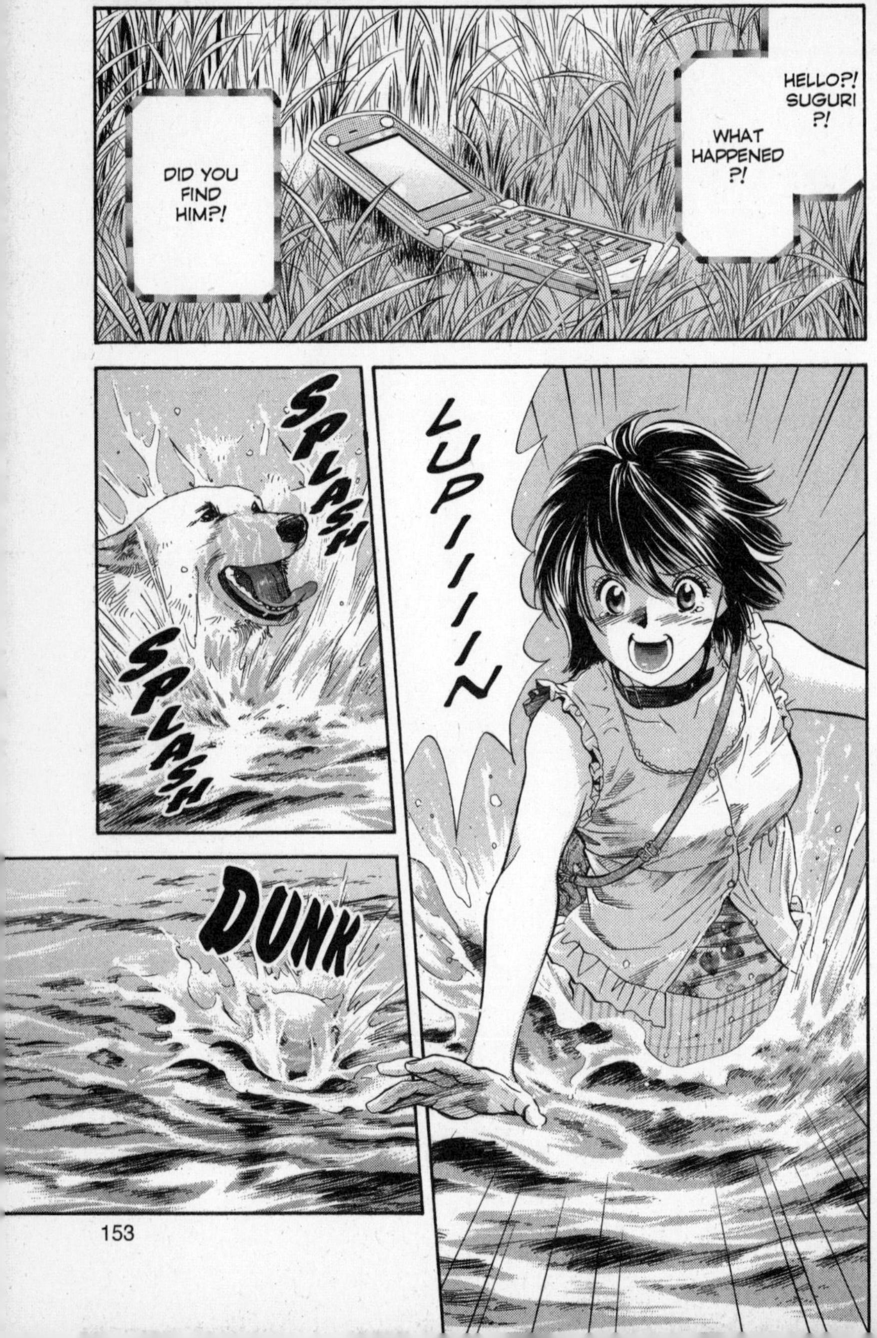
HELLO?! SUGURI ?!
WHAT HAPPENED ?!
DID YOU FIND HIM?!
LUPIIIIIN
SPLASH
SPLASH
DUNK

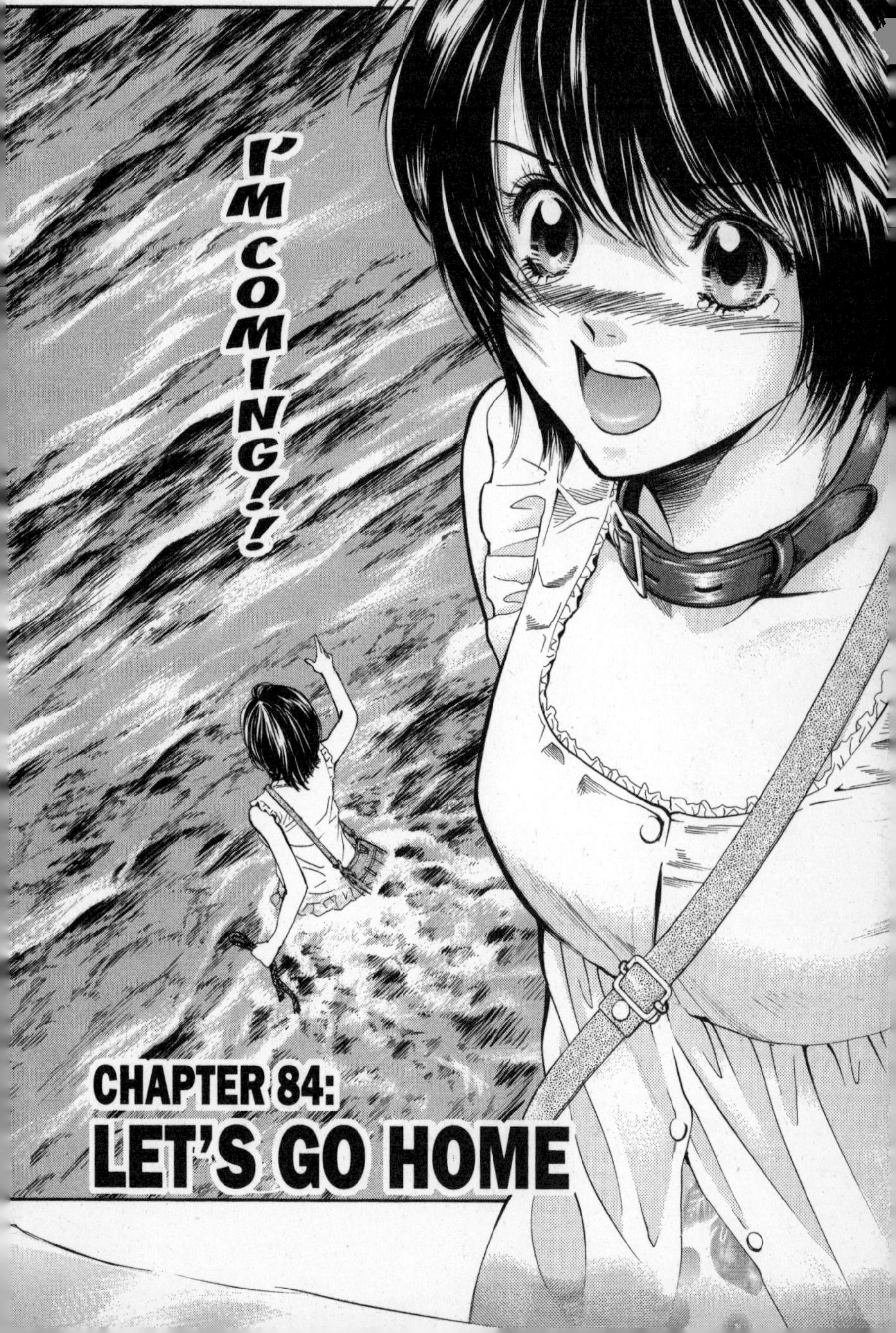
I'M COMING!!
CHAPTER 84:
LET'S GO HOME

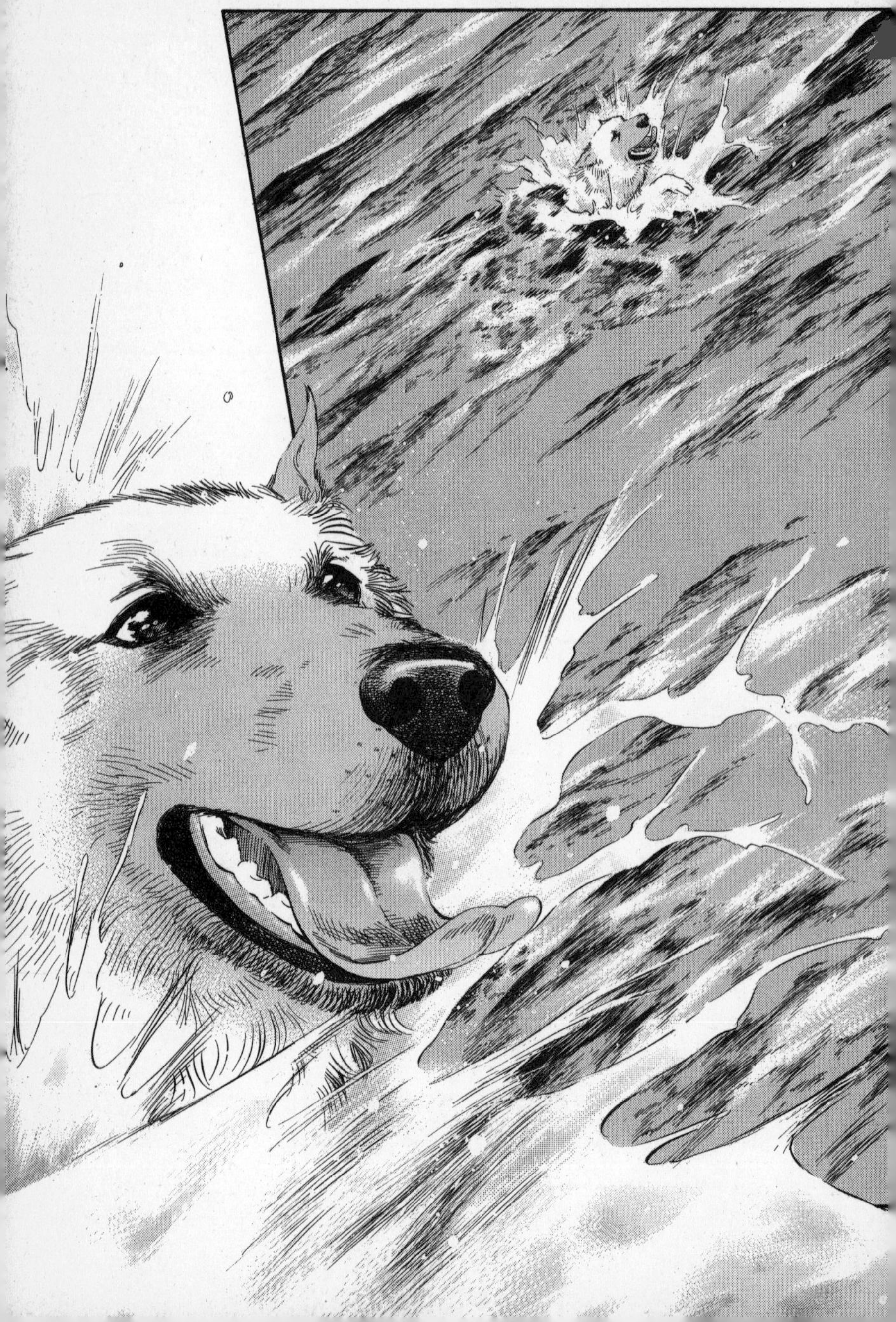

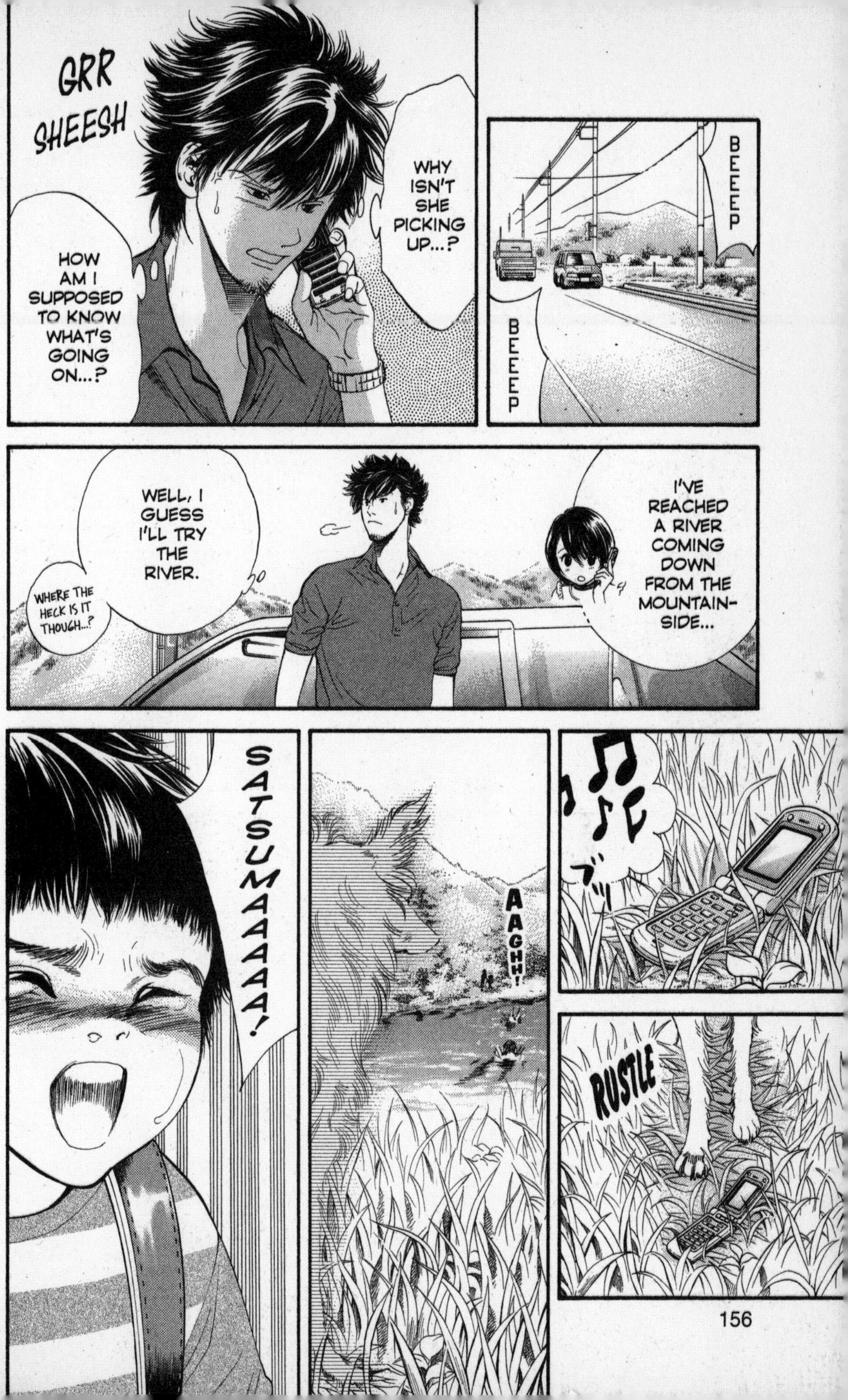

BEEEP
BEEEP
WHY ISN'T SHE PICKING UP...?
GRR
SHEESH
HOW AM I SUPPOSED TO KNOW WHAT'S GOING ON...?
I'VE REACHED A RIVER COMING DOWN FROM THE MOUNTAIN-SIDE...
WELL, I GUESS I'LL TRY THE RIVER.
WHERE THE HECK IS IT THOUGH...?
RUSTLE
AAGH!
SATSUMAAAAAAA!

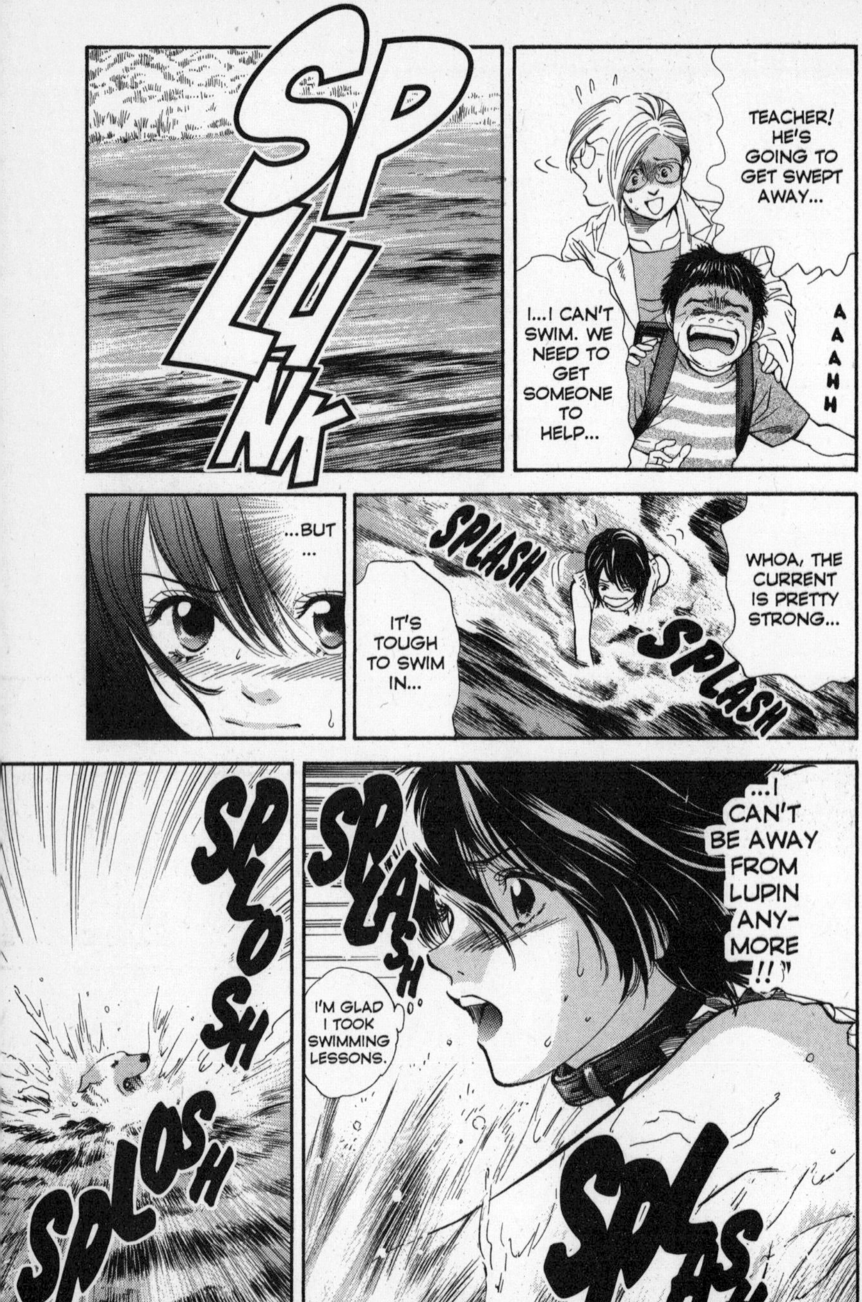
TEACHER! HE'S GOING TO GET SWEPT AWAY...
AAAHH
I...I CAN'T SWIM. WE NEED TO GET SOMEONE TO HELP...
SPLUNK
SPLASH
WHOA, THE CURRENT IS PRETTY STRONG...
SPLASH
IT'S TOUGH TO SWIM IN...
...BUT ...
...I CAN'T BE AWAY FROM LUPIN ANYMORE!!
SPLASH
I'M GLAD I TOOK SWIMMING LESSONS.
SPLASH
SPLOSH
SPLOSH

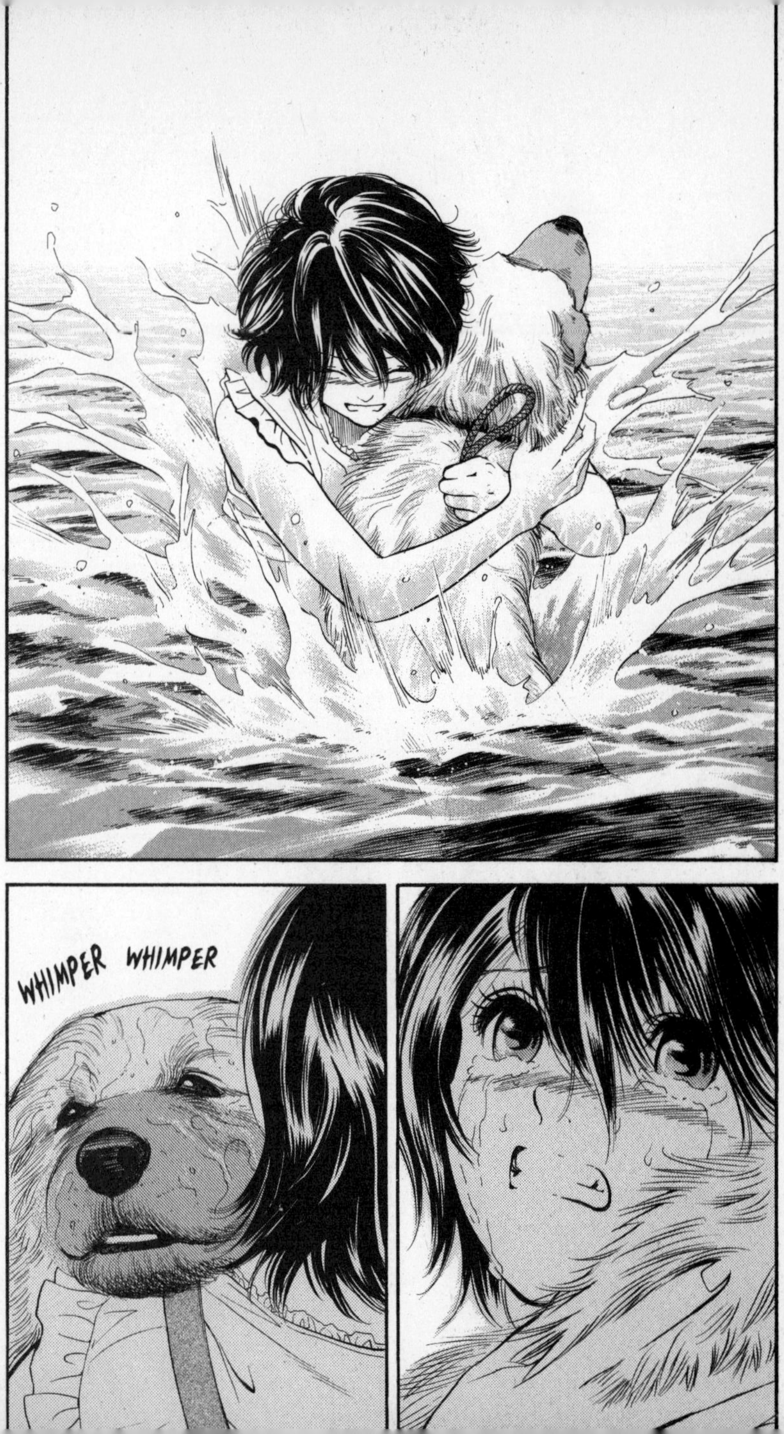
WHIMPER WHIMPER

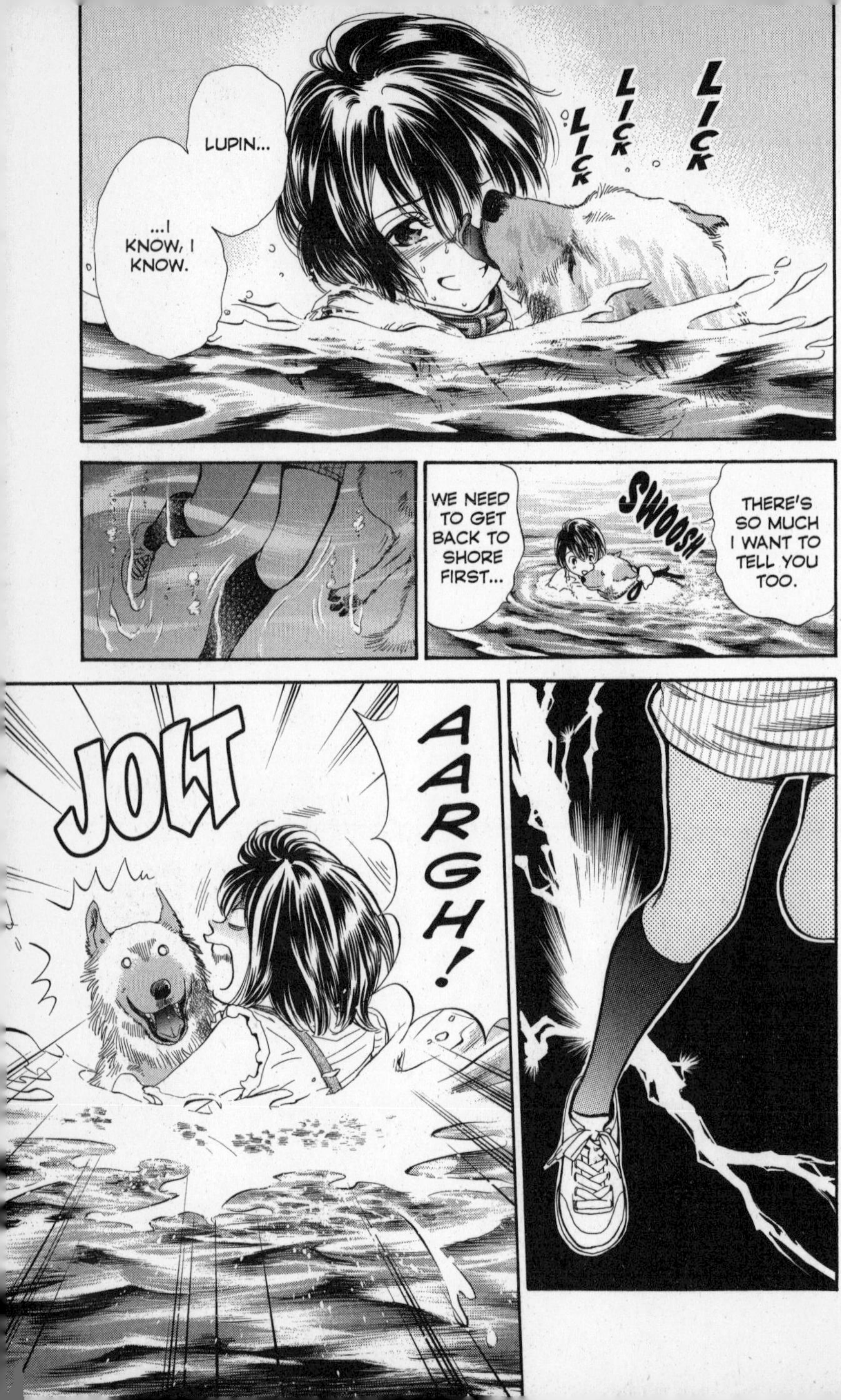
LICK
LICK
LICK
LUPIN...
...I KNOW, I KNOW.
THERE'S SO MUCH I WANT TO TELL YOU TOO.
SWOOSH
WE NEED TO GET BACK TO SHORE FIRST...
AARGH!
JOLT

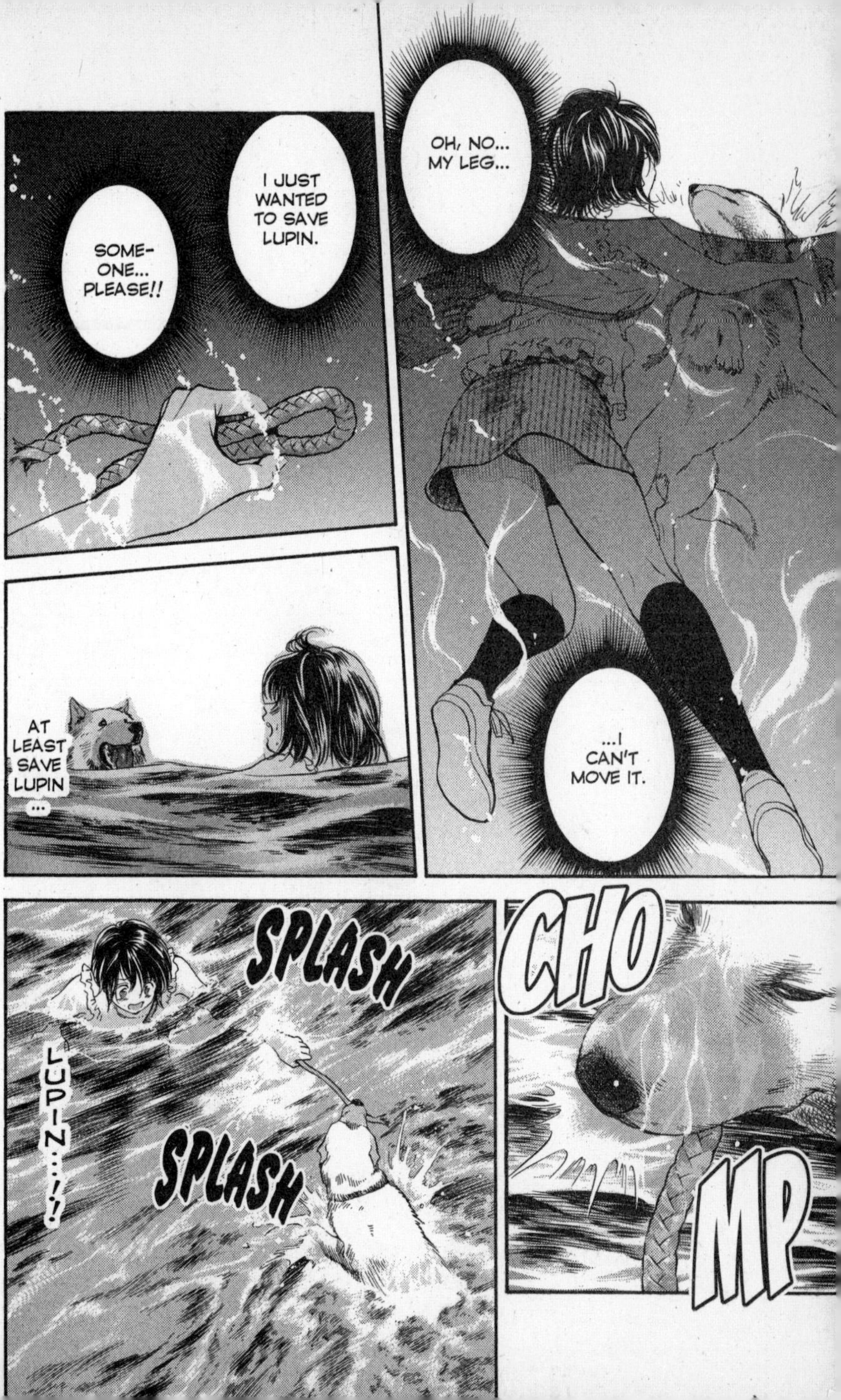
OH, NO... MY LEG...
...I CAN'T MOVE IT.
I JUST WANTED TO SAVE LUPIN.
SOME-ONE... PLEASE!!
AT LEAST SAVE LUPIN...
CHOMP
SPLASH
SPLASH
LUPIN...!!

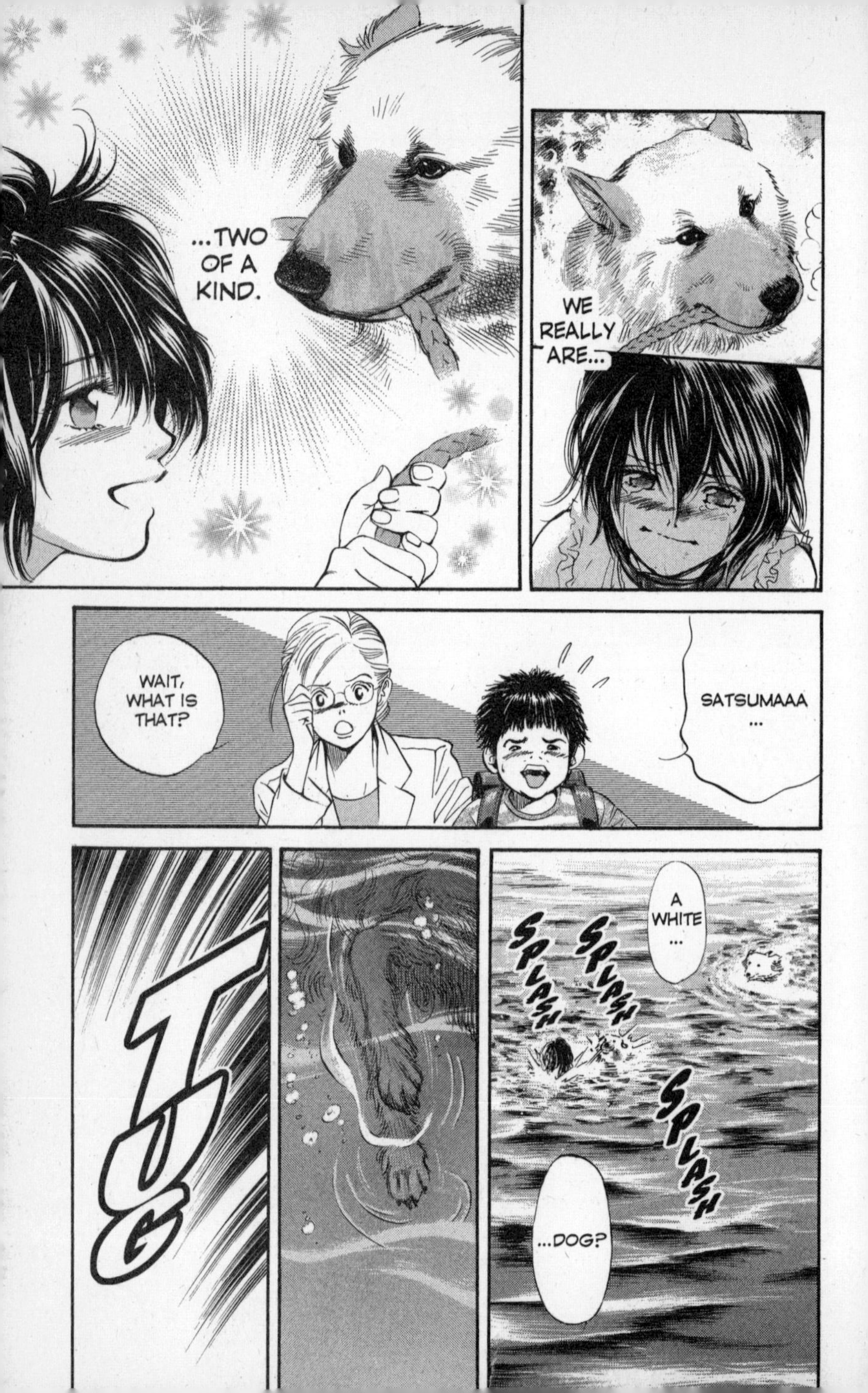
WE REALLY ARE...
...TWO OF A KIND.
SATSUMAAA ...
WAIT, WHAT IS THAT?
A WHITE ...
SPLASH
SPLASH
SPLASH
...DOG?
TUG

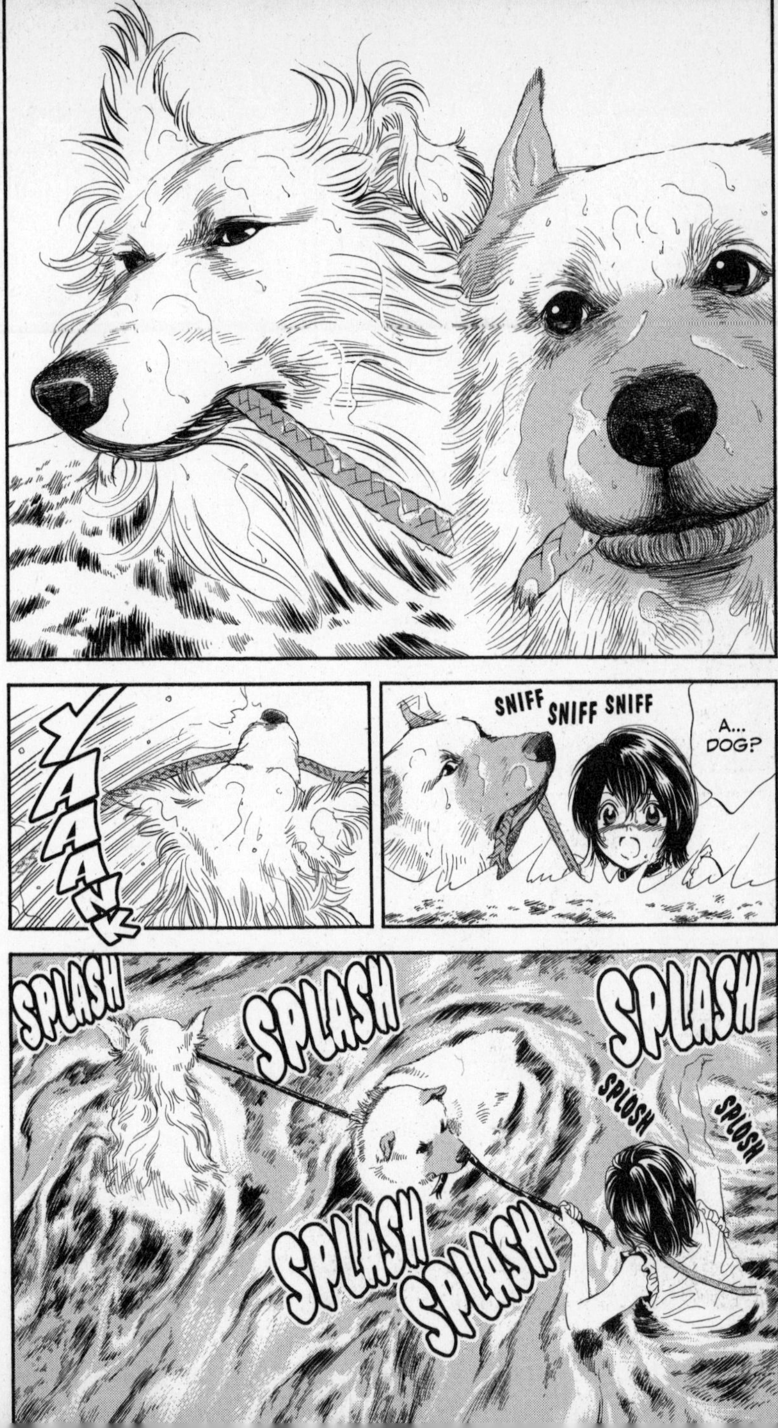
SNIFF SNIFF SNIFF
A... DOG?
YAAAANK
SPLASH
SPLOSH
SPLOSH
SPLASH
SPLASH
SPLASH
SPLASH

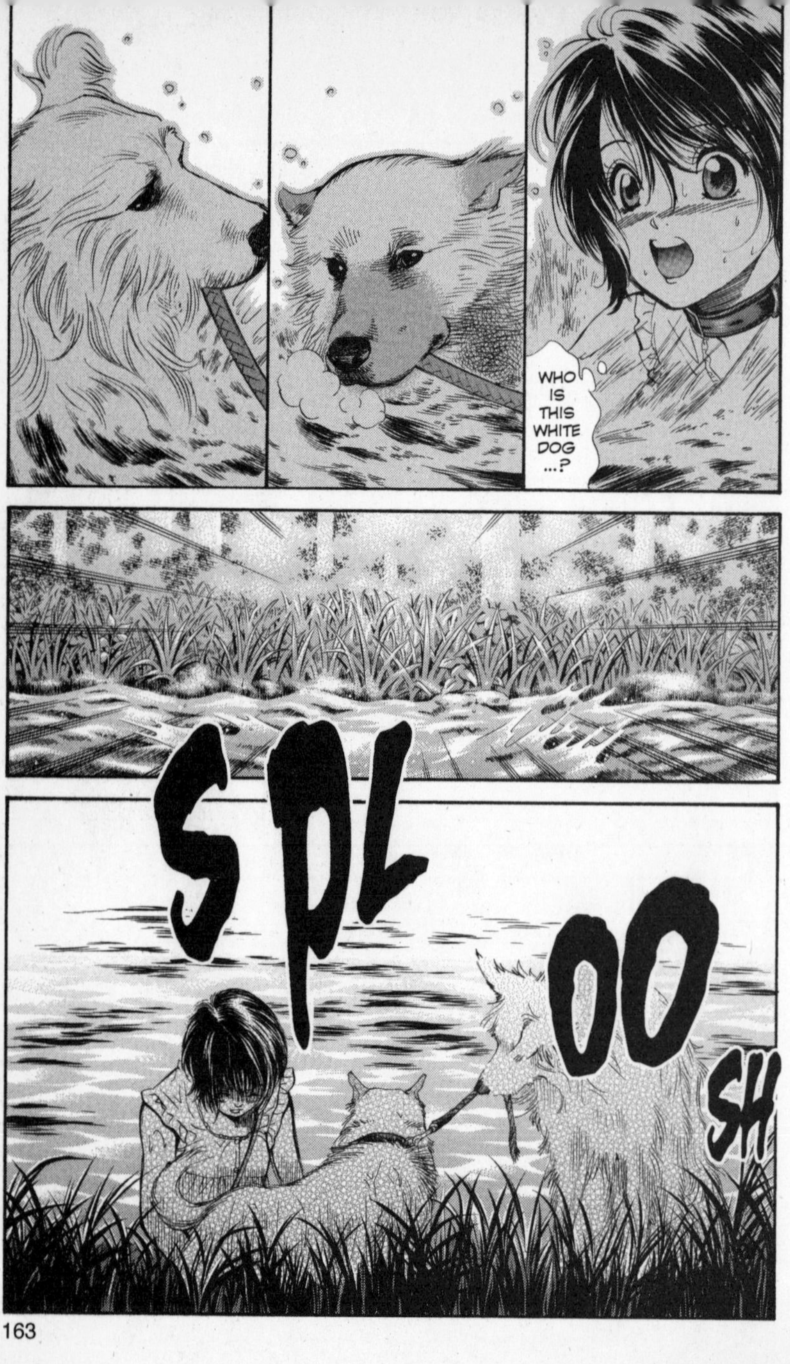
WHO IS THIS WHITE DOG ...?
SPLOOSH

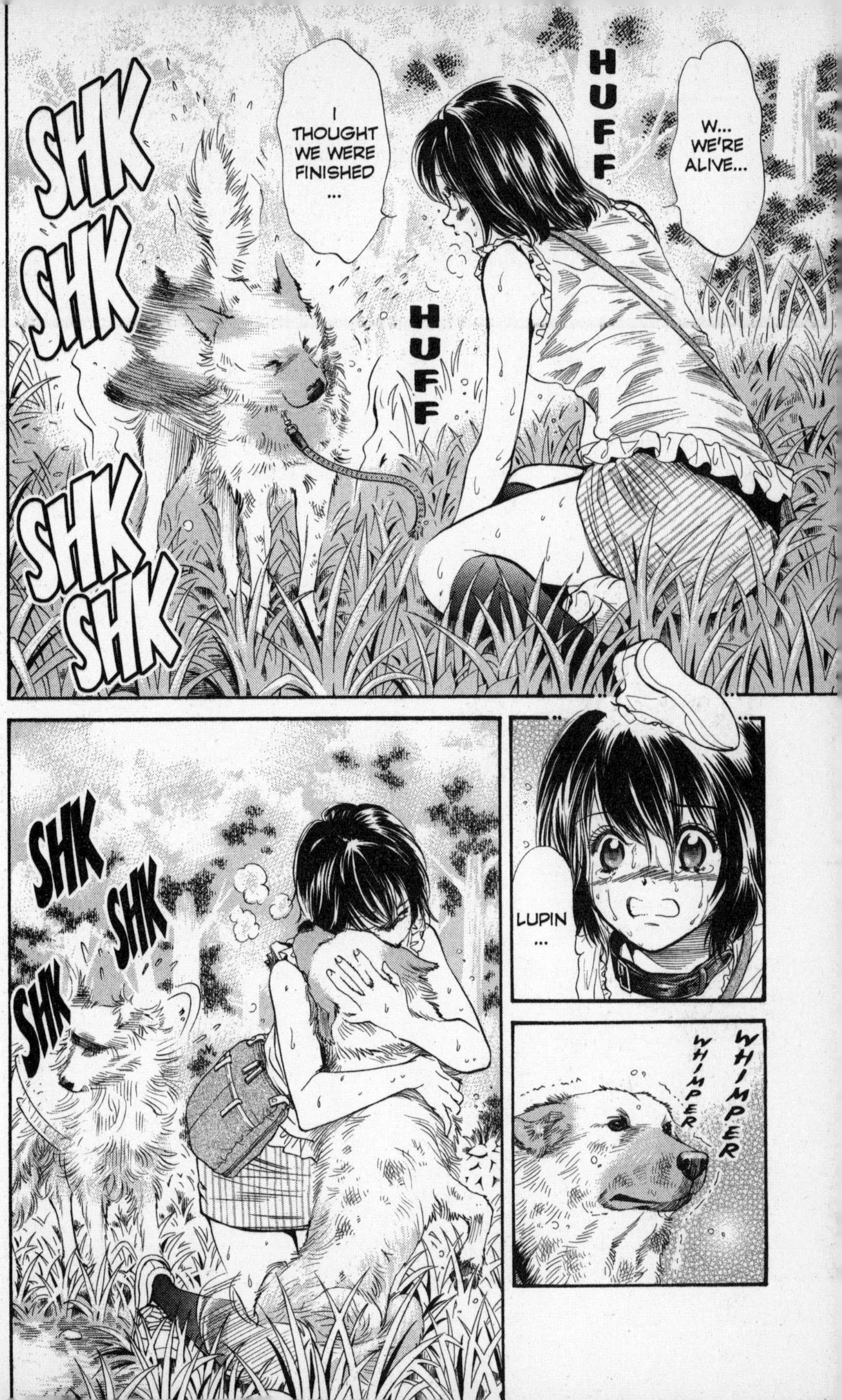
W... WE'RE ALIVE...
HUFF
I THOUGHT WE WERE FINISHED ...
HUFF
SHK SHK
SHK SHK
LUPIN ...
WHIMPER
WHIMPER
SHK
SHK
SHK

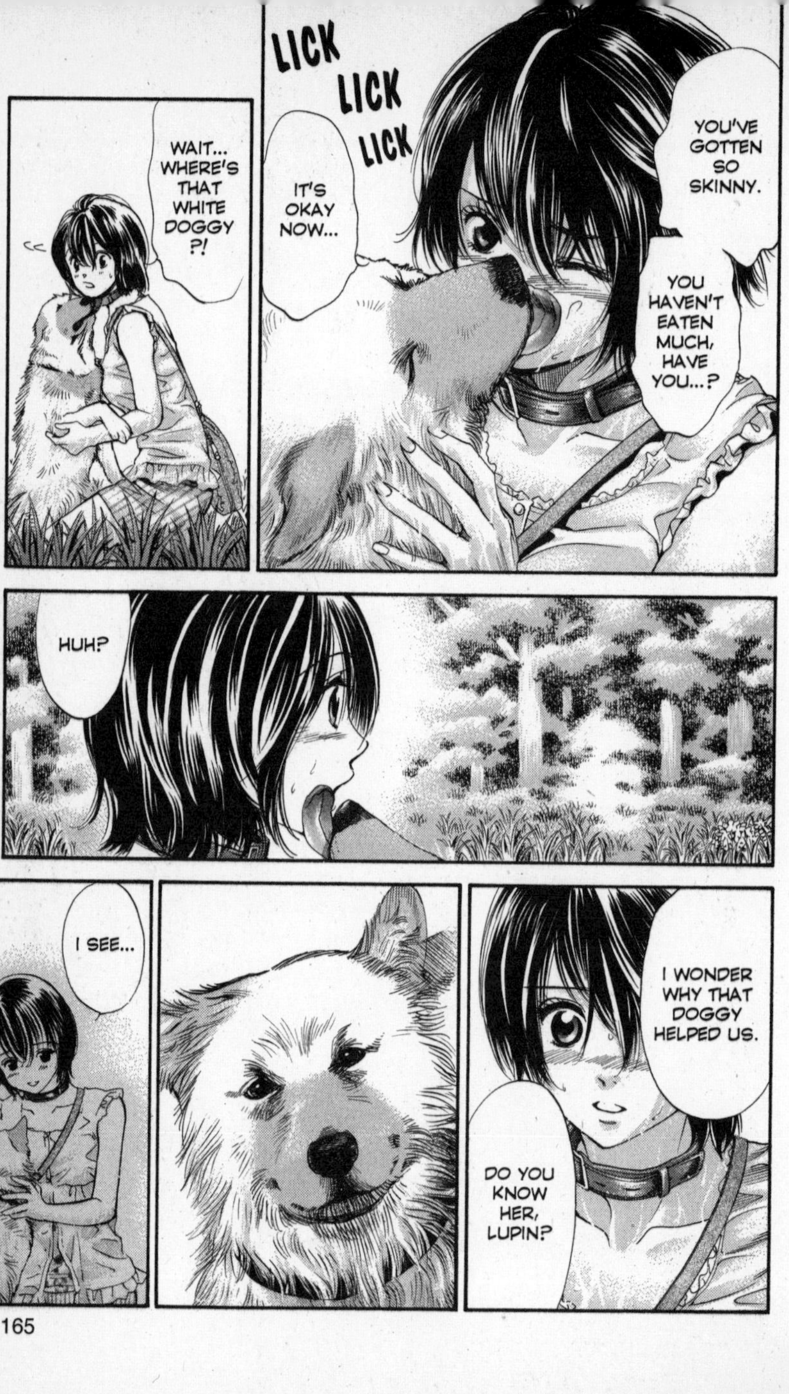
LICK LICK LICK
IT'S OKAY NOW...
YOU'VE GOTTEN SO SKINNY.
YOU HAVEN'T EATEN MUCH, HAVE YOU...?
WAIT... WHERE'S THAT WHITE DOGGY?!
HUH?
I WONDER WHY THAT DOGGY HELPED US.
DO YOU KNOW HER, LUPIN?
I SEE...

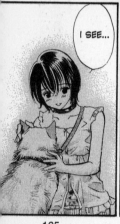

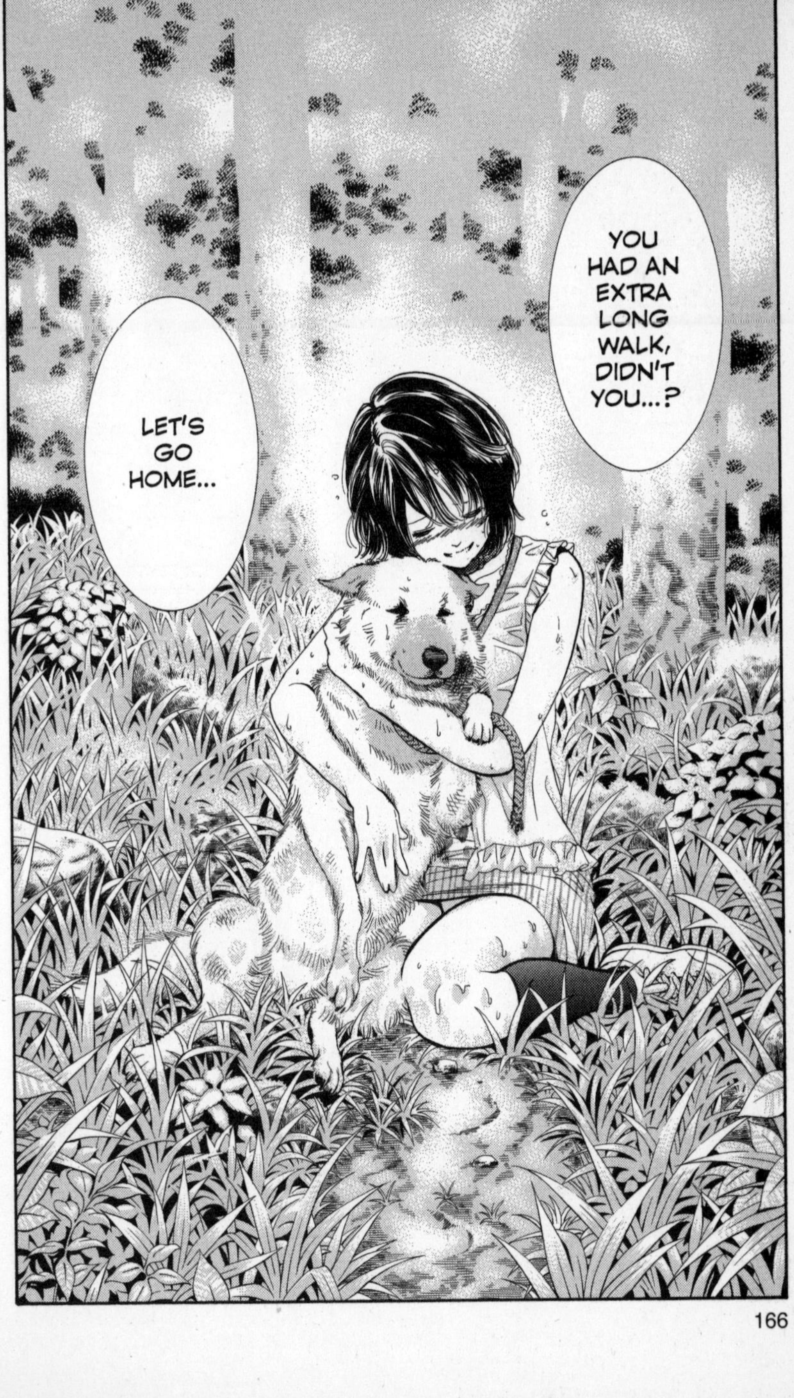
YOU HAD AN EXTRA LONG WALK, DIDN'T YOU...?
LET'S GO HOME...

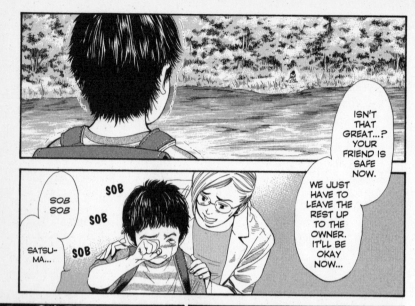

ISN'T THAT GREAT...? YOUR FRIEND IS SAFE NOW.

WE JUST HAVE TO LEAVE THE REST UP TO THE OWNER. IT'LL BE OKAY NOW...

SOB SOB

SOB

SOB

SATSU-MA...

SOB

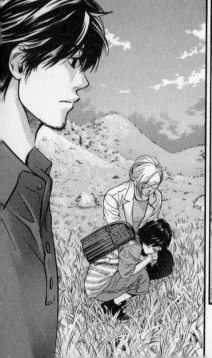

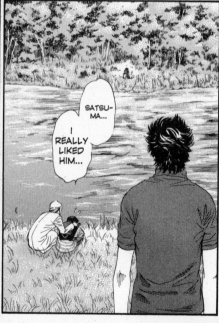

SATSU-MA...

I REALLY LIKED HIM...

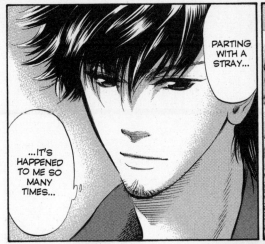

WHAAAH ... SATSU-MA...
PARTING WITH A STRAY...
...IT'S HAPPENED TO ME SO MANY TIMES...
OH, MY PHONE...
HELLO?
OH, TEPPEI-SAN, I JUST...

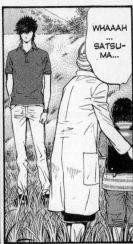

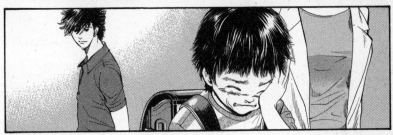

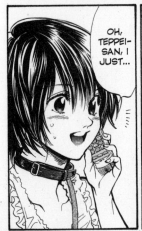

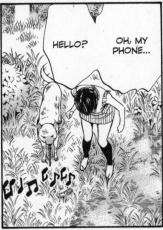

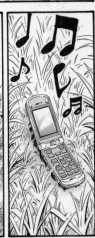

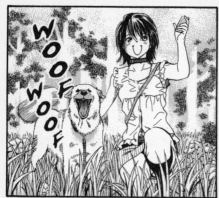

WOOF
WOOF

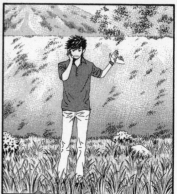

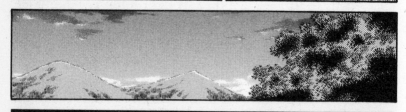

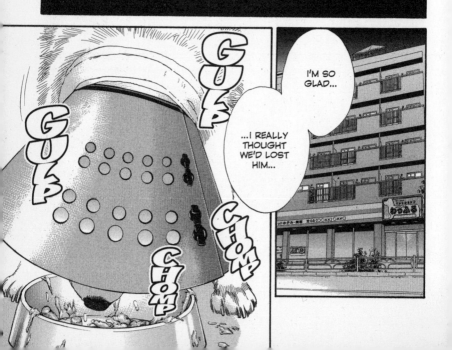

I'M SO
GLAD...

...I REALLY
THOUGHT
WE'D LOST
HIM...

GULP

GULP

CHOMP

CHOMP

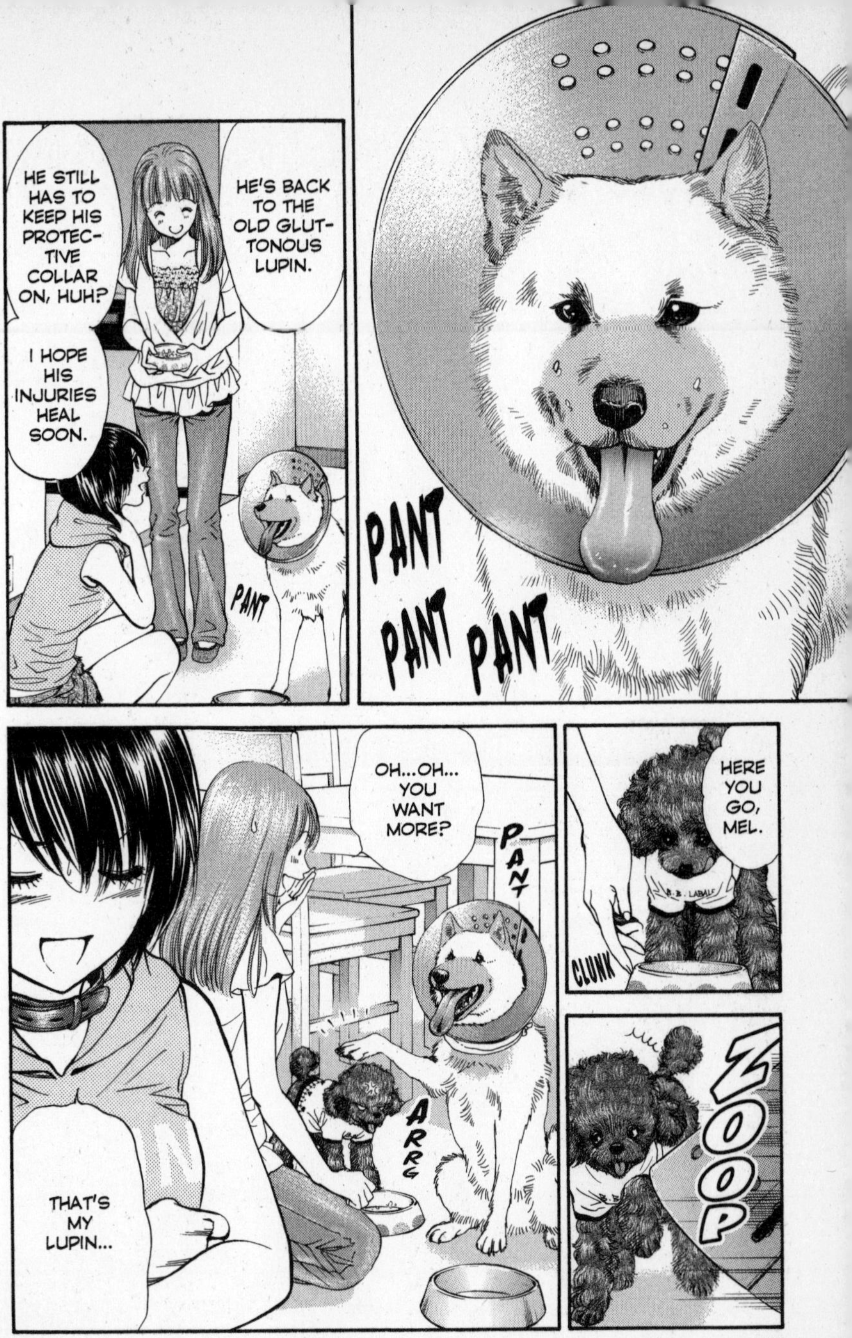
PANT
PANT
PANT
HE'S BACK TO THE OLD GLUT-TONOUS LUPIN.
HE STILL HAS TO KEEP HIS PROTEC-TIVE COLLAR ON, HUH?
I HOPE HIS INJURIES HEAL SOON.
PANT
HERE YOU GO, MEL.
CLUNK
ZOOP
OH...OH... YOU WANT MORE?
PANT
ARRG
THAT'S MY LUPIN...

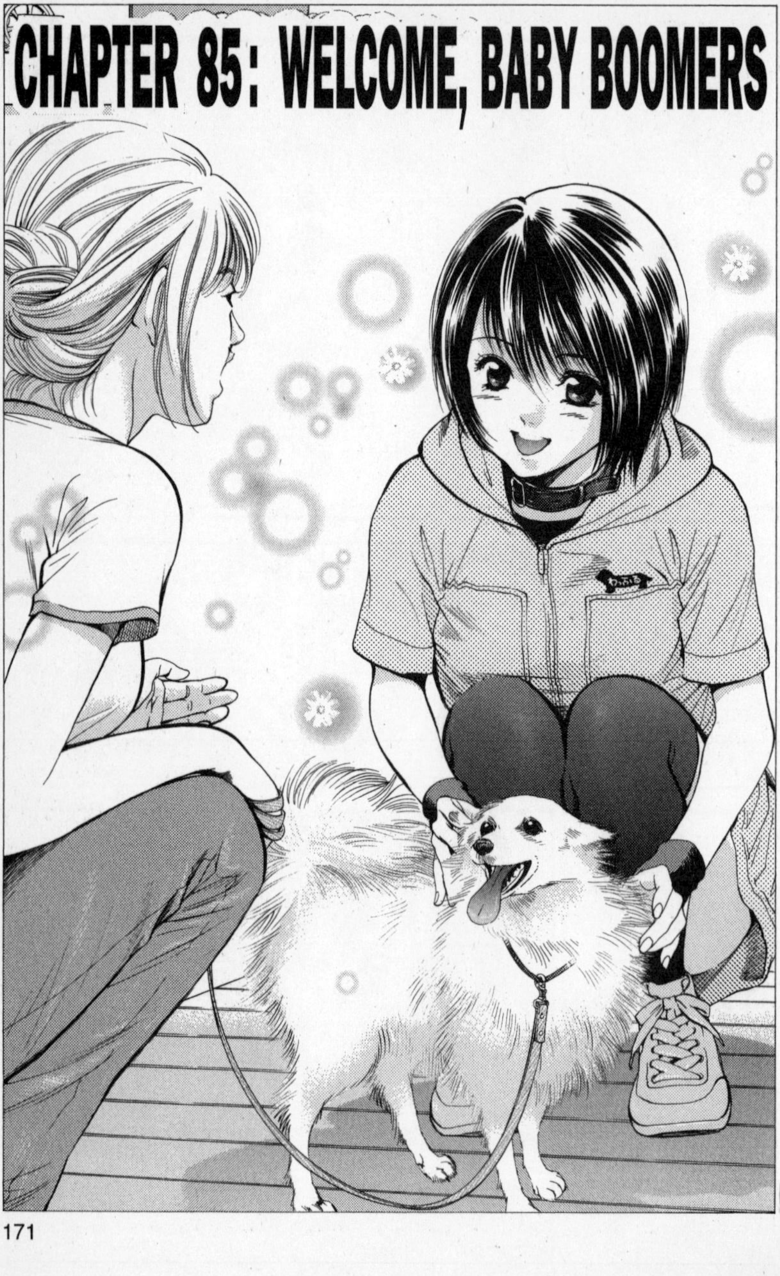
CHAPTER 85: WELCOME, BABY BOOMERS

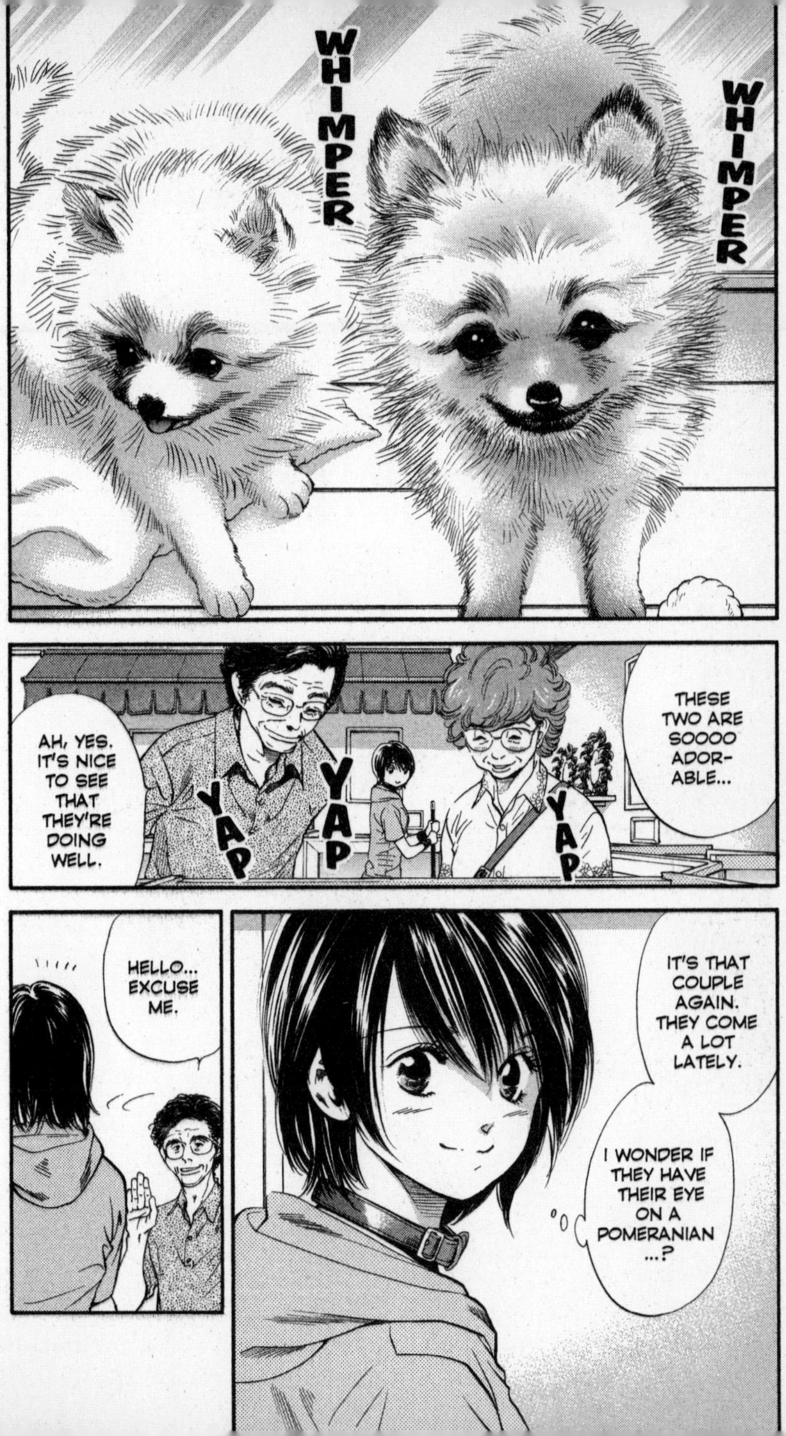
WHIMPER
WHIMPER
THESE TWO ARE SOOOO ADOR-ABLE...
YAP
YAP
YAP
AH, YES. IT'S NICE TO SEE THAT THEY'RE DOING WELL.
IT'S THAT COUPLE AGAIN. THEY COME A LOT LATELY.
I WONDER IF THEY HAVE THEIR EYE ON A POMERANIAN ...?
HELLO... EXCUSE ME.

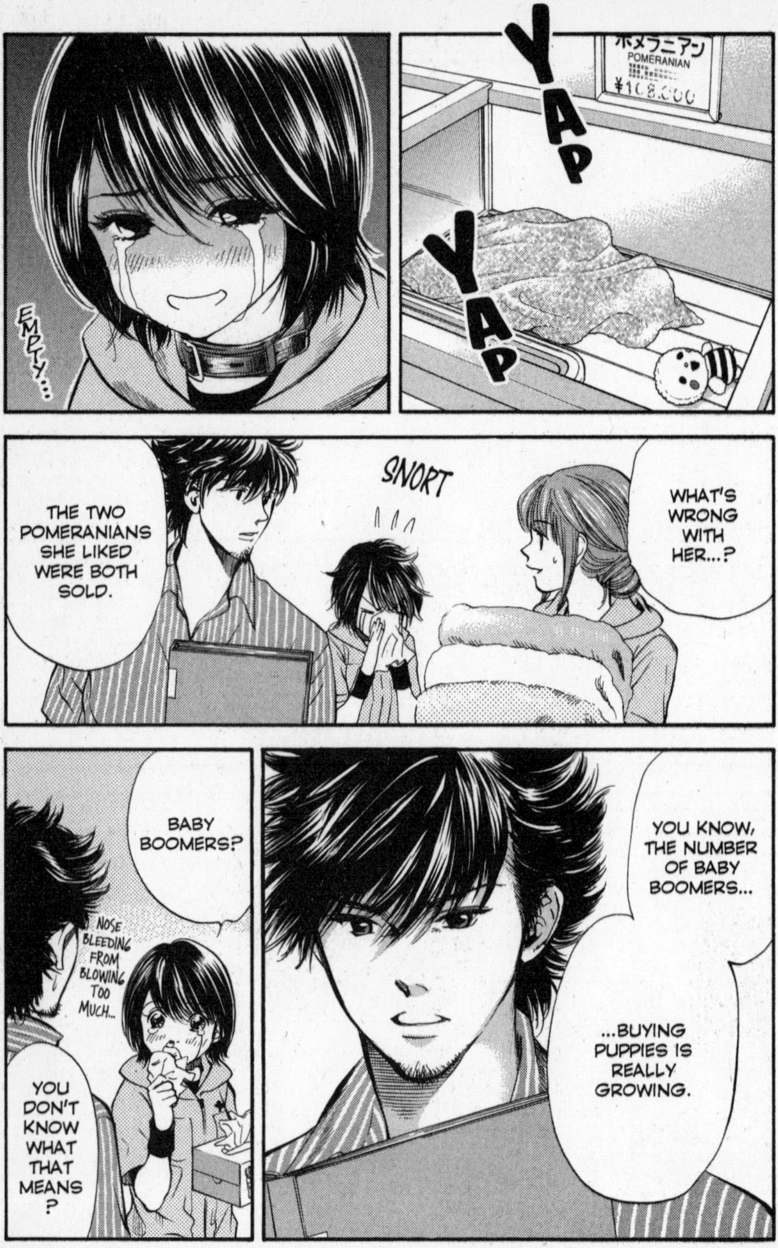
YAP
YAP
ポメラニアン
POMERANIAN
EMPTY...
WHAT'S WRONG WITH HER...?
SNORT
THE TWO POMERANIANS SHE LIKED WERE BOTH SOLD.
YOU KNOW, THE NUMBER OF BABY BOOMERS...
...BUYING PUPPIES IS REALLY GROWING.
BABY BOOMERS?
NOSE BLEEDING FROM BLOWING TOO MUCH...
YOU DON'T KNOW WHAT THAT MEANS?

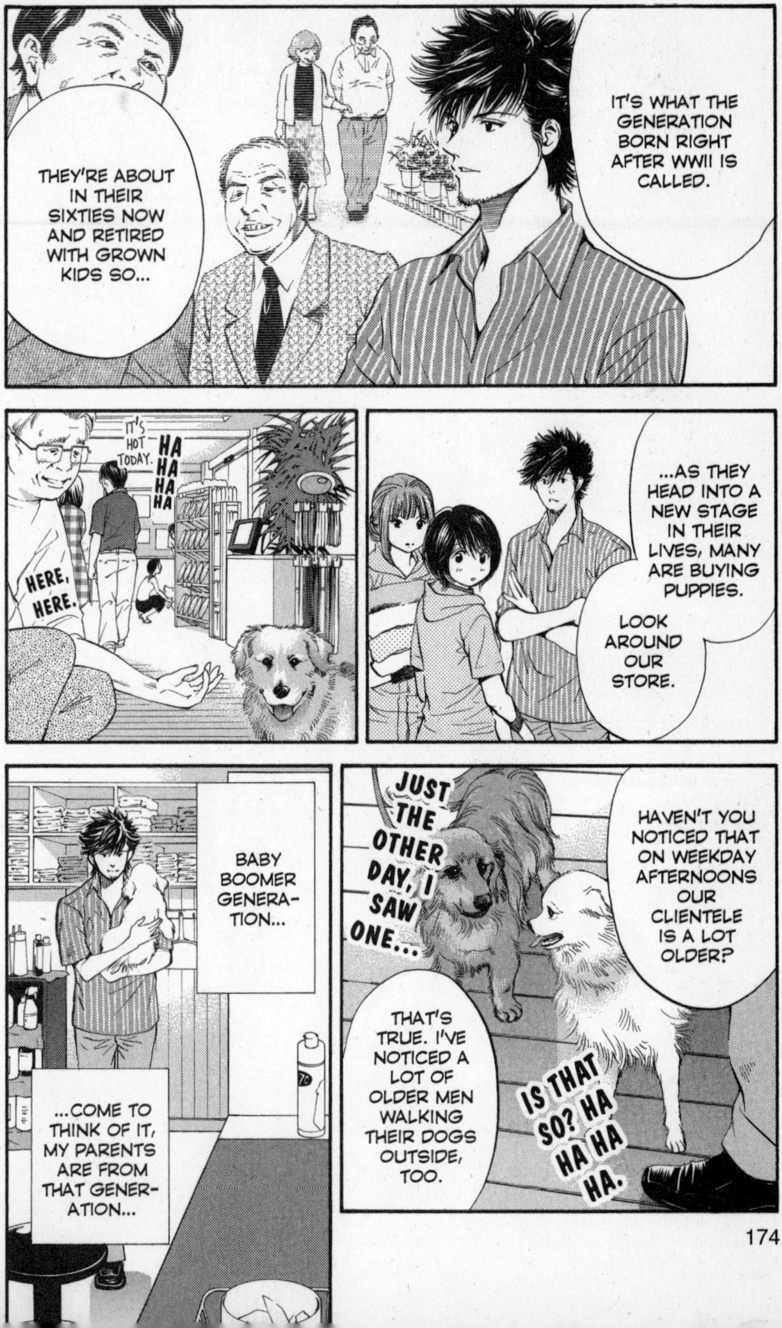
IT'S WHAT THE GENERATION BORN RIGHT AFTER WWII IS CALLED.
THEY'RE ABOUT IN THEIR SIXTIES NOW AND RETIRED WITH GROWN KIDS SO...
...AS THEY HEAD INTO A NEW STAGE IN THEIR LIVES, MANY ARE BUYING PUPPIES.
LOOK AROUND OUR STORE.
IT'S HOT TODAY.
HA HA HA HA HA
HERE, HERE.
HAVEN'T YOU NOTICED THAT ON WEEKDAY AFTERNOONS OUR CLIENTELE IS A LOT OLDER?
JUST THE OTHER DAY, I SAW ONE...
THAT'S TRUE. I'VE NOTICED A LOT OF OLDER MEN WALKING THEIR DOGS OUTSIDE, TOO.
IS THAT SO? HA HA HA HA.
BABY BOOMER GENERA-TION...
...COME TO THINK OF IT, MY PARENTS ARE FROM THAT GENER-ATION...

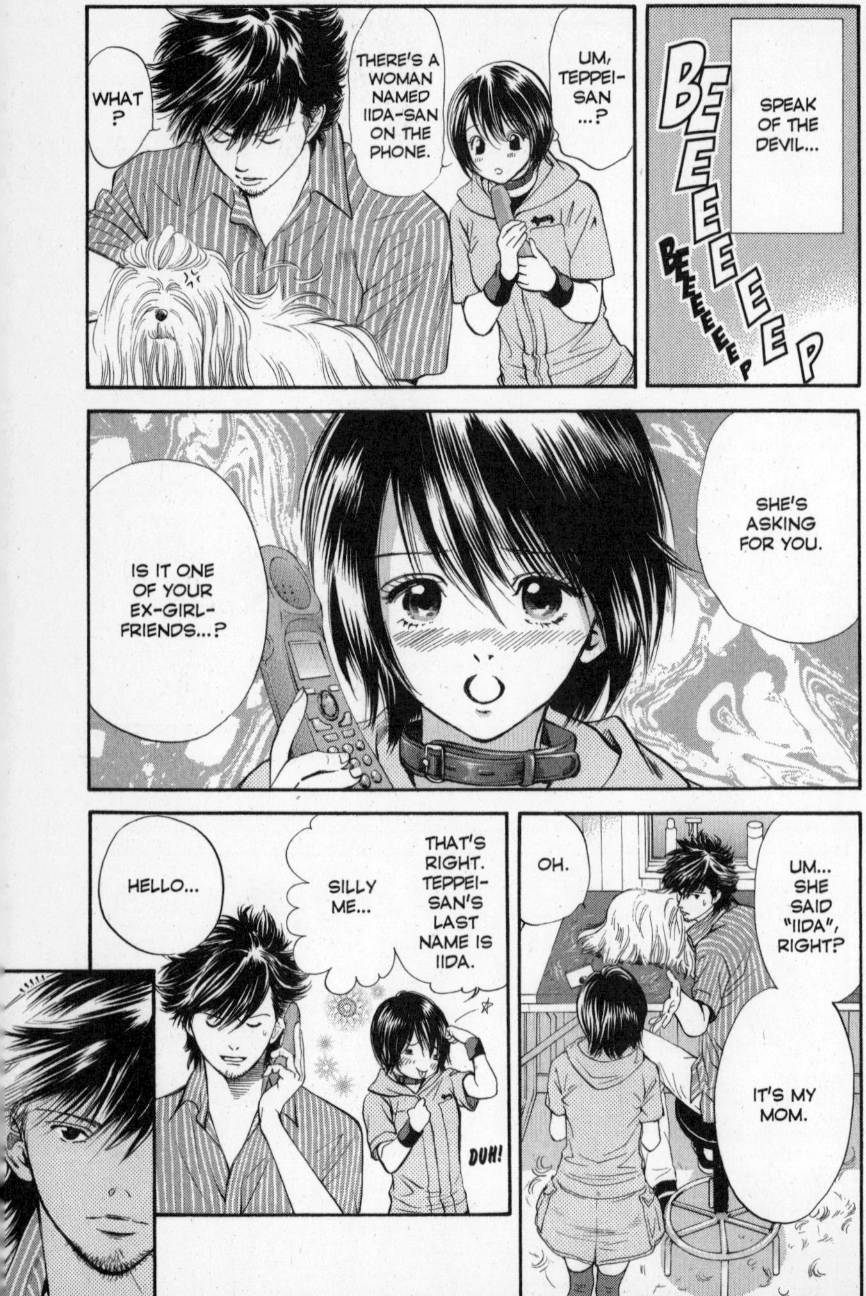
BEEEEEEP
BEEEEEEEP
SPEAK OF THE DEVIL...
UM, TEPPEI-SAN ...?
THERE'S A WOMAN NAMED IIDA-SAN ON THE PHONE.
WHAT?
SHE'S ASKING FOR YOU.
IS IT ONE OF YOUR EX-GIRL-FRIENDS...?
UM... SHE SAID "IIDA", RIGHT?
OH.
IT'S MY MOM.
THAT'S RIGHT. TEPPEI-SAN'S LAST NAME IS IIDA.
SILLY ME...
DUH!
HELLO...

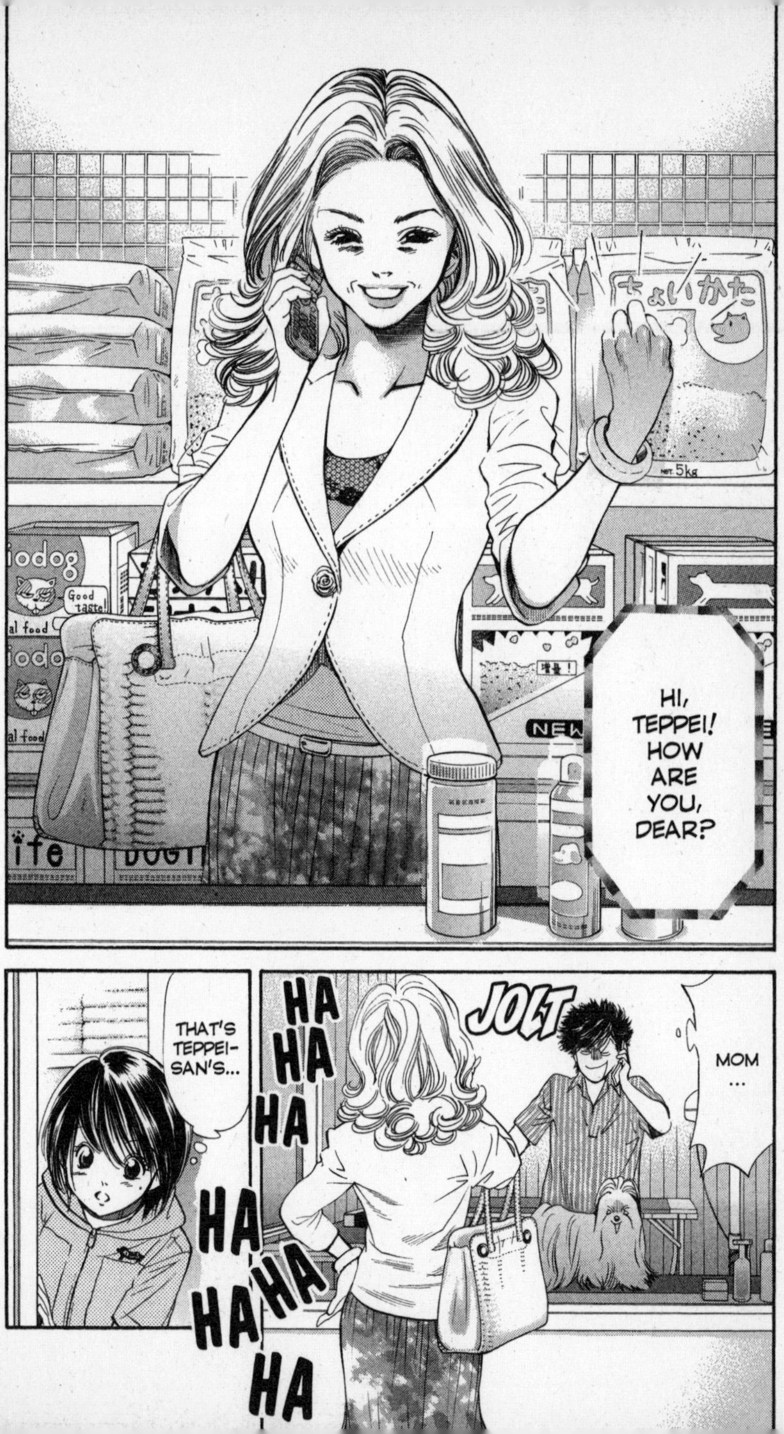
HI, TEPPEI! HOW ARE YOU, DEAR?
MOM ...
JOLT
HA HA HA HA
HA HA HA HA HA
THAT'S TEPPEI-SAN'S...

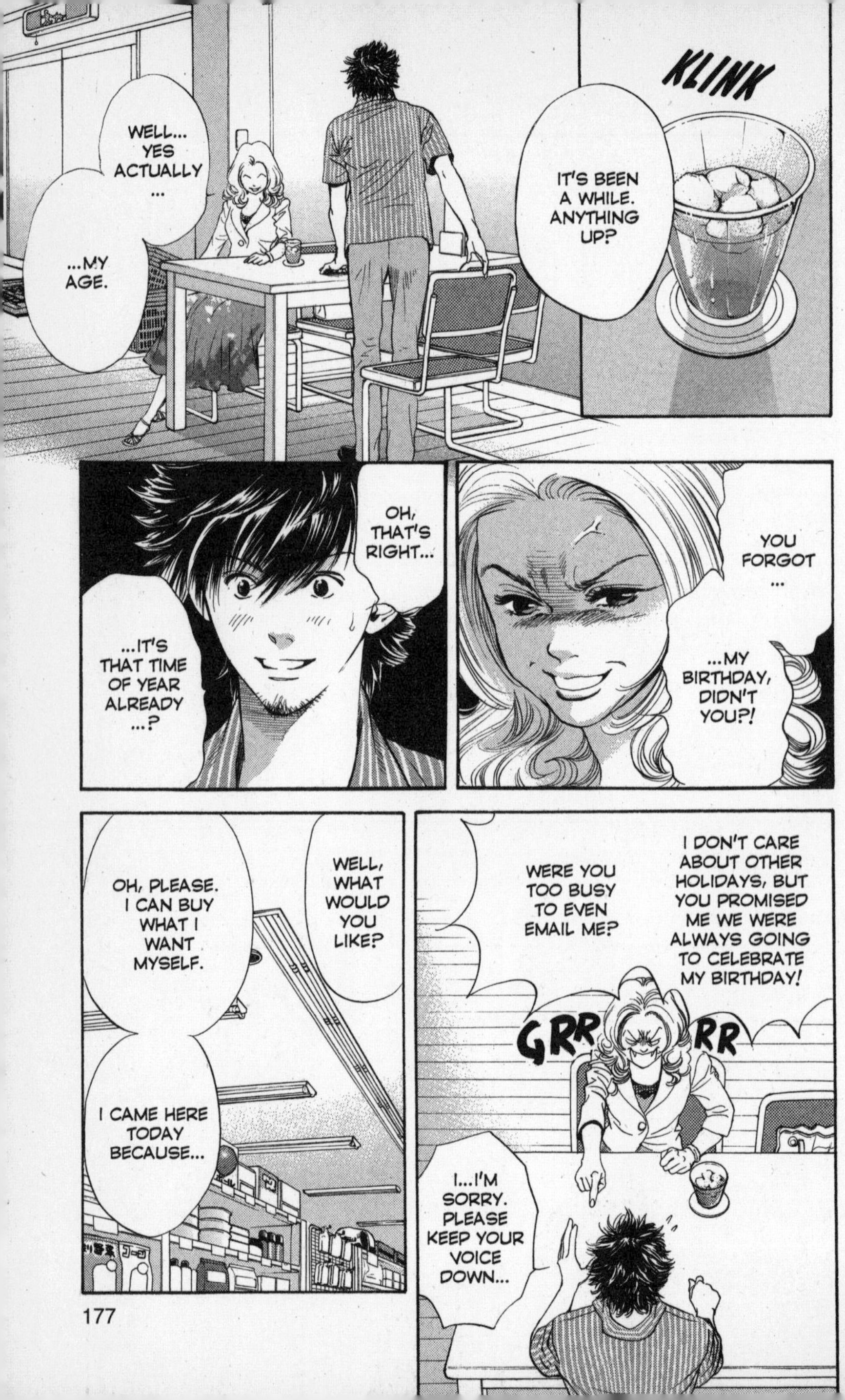
KLINK
IT'S BEEN A WHILE. ANYTHING UP?
WELL... YES ACTUALLY ...
...MY AGE.
YOU FORGOT ...
...MY BIRTHDAY, DIDN'T YOU?!
OH, THAT'S RIGHT...
...IT'S THAT TIME OF YEAR ALREADY ...?
I DON'T CARE ABOUT OTHER HOLIDAYS, BUT YOU PROMISED ME WE WERE ALWAYS GOING TO CELEBRATE MY BIRTHDAY!
WERE YOU TOO BUSY TO EVEN EMAIL ME?
GRR RR
I...I'M SORRY. PLEASE KEEP YOUR VOICE DOWN...
WELL, WHAT WOULD YOU LIKE?
OH, PLEASE. I CAN BUY WHAT I WANT MYSELF.
I CAME HERE TODAY BECAUSE...

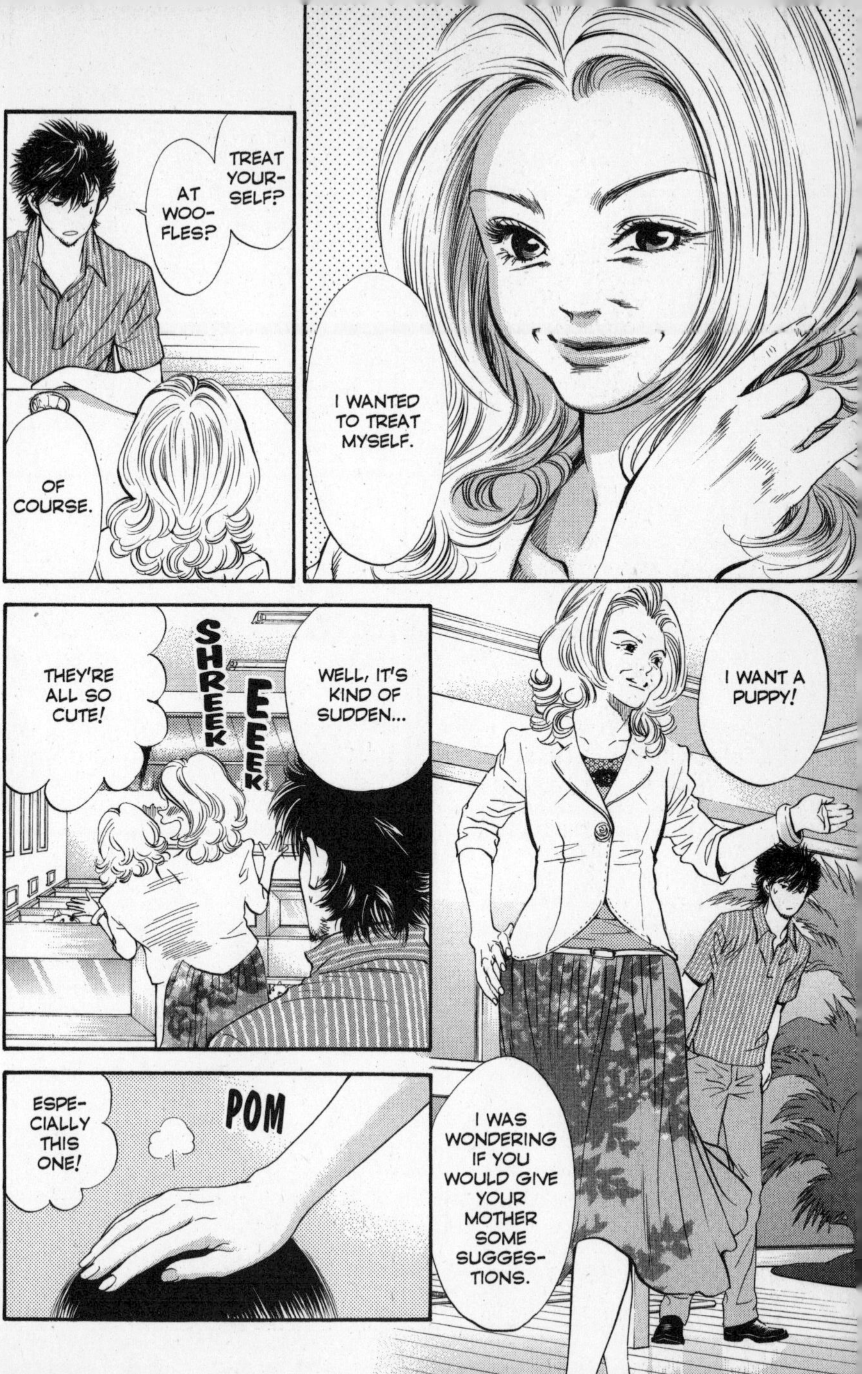
I WANTED TO TREAT MYSELF.
TREAT YOUR-SELF?
AT WOO-FLES?
OF COURSE.
I WANT A PUPPY!
I WAS WONDERING IF YOU WOULD GIVE YOUR MOTHER SOME SUGGES-TIONS.
WELL, IT'S KIND OF SUDDEN...
SHREEK
EEEEK
THEY'RE ALL SO CUTE!
POM
ESPE-CIALLY THIS ONE!

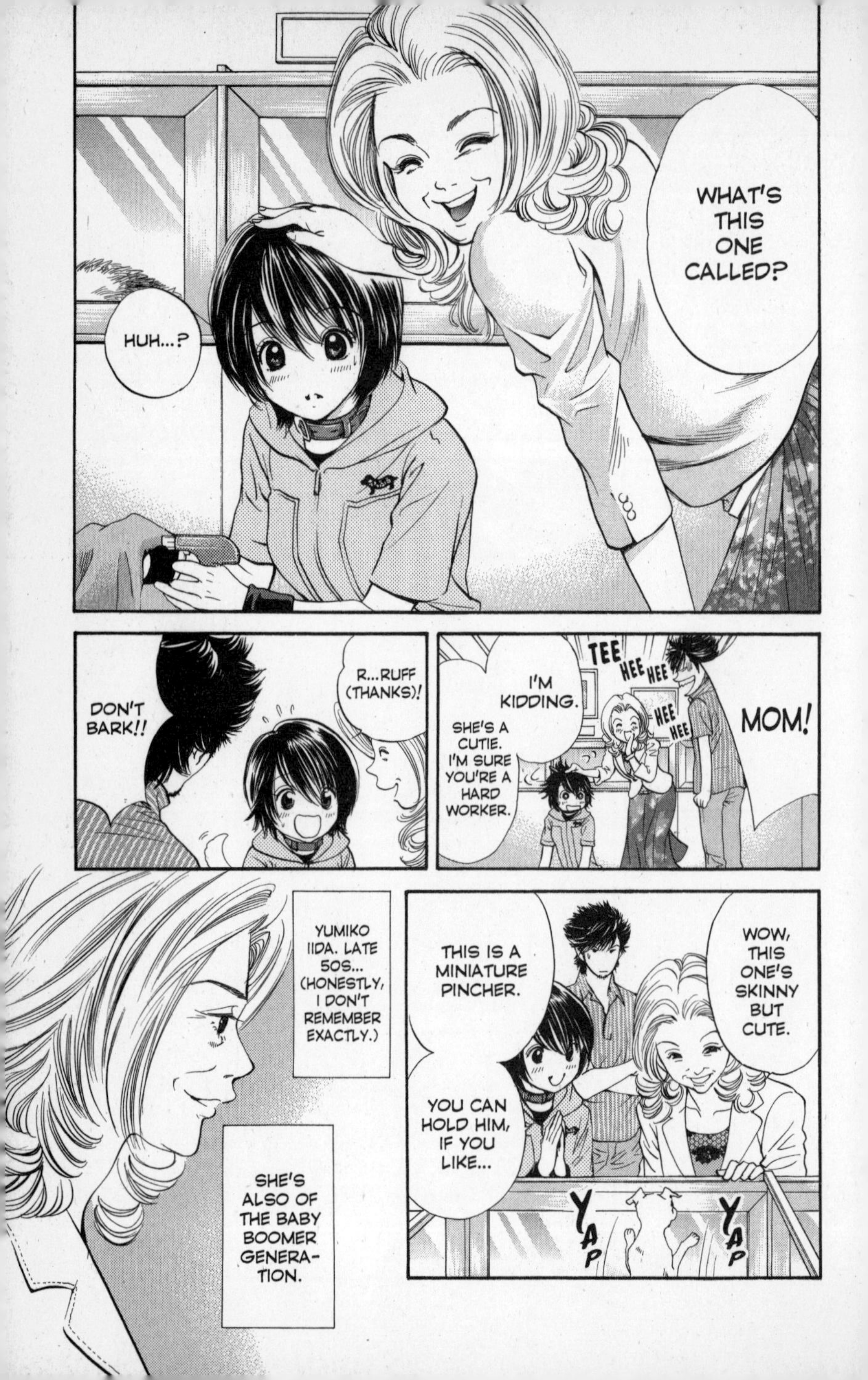
WHAT'S THIS ONE CALLED?
HUH...?
MOM!
TEE HEE HEE HEE HEE
I'M KIDDING.
SHE'S A CUTIE. I'M SURE YOU'RE A HARD WORKER.
R...RUFF (THANKS)!
DON'T BARK!!
WOW, THIS ONE'S SKINNY BUT CUTE.
THIS IS A MINIATURE PINCHER.
YOU CAN HOLD HIM, IF YOU LIKE...
YAP YAP
YUMIKO IIDA. LATE 50S... (HONESTLY, I DON'T REMEMBER EXACTLY.)
SHE'S ALSO OF THE BABY BOOMER GENERA-TION.

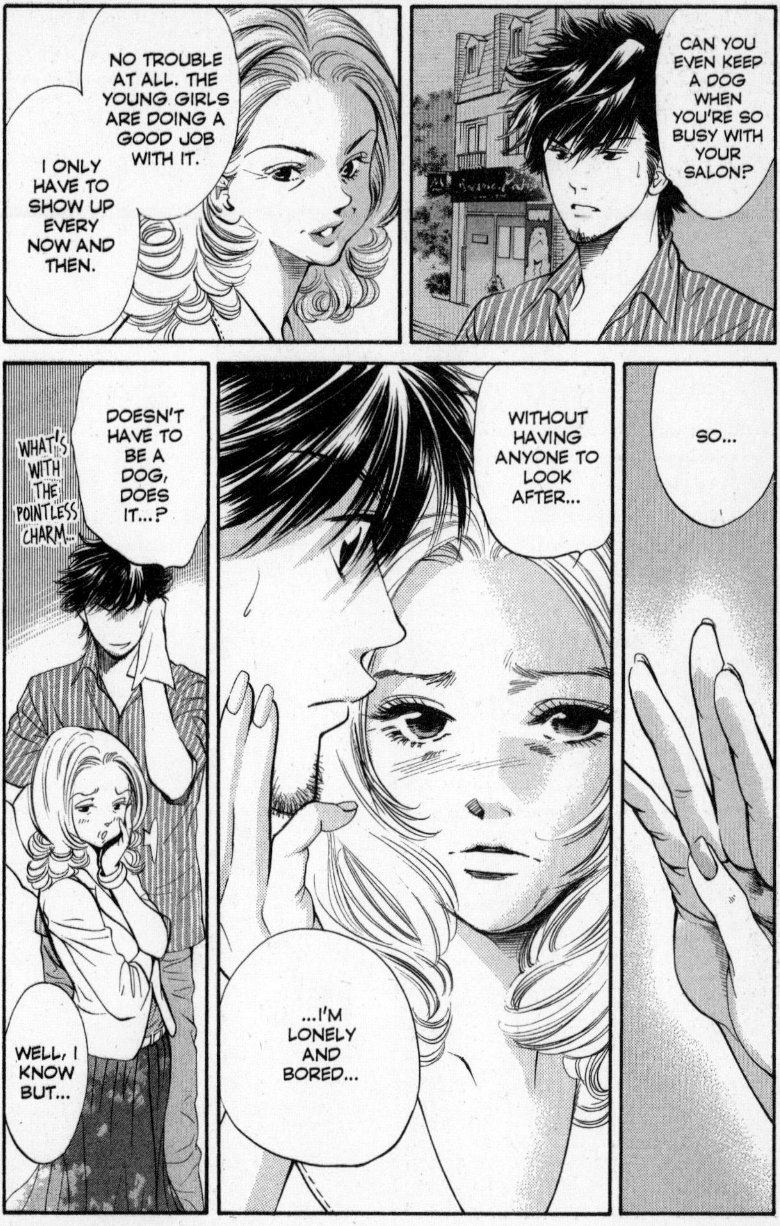
CAN YOU EVEN KEEP A DOG WHEN YOU'RE SO BUSY WITH YOUR SALON?
NO TROUBLE AT ALL. THE YOUNG GIRLS ARE DOING A GOOD JOB WITH IT.
I ONLY HAVE TO SHOW UP EVERY NOW AND THEN.
SO...
WITHOUT HAVING ANYONE TO LOOK AFTER...
...I'M LONELY AND BORED...
DOESN'T HAVE TO BE A DOG, DOES IT...?
WHAT'S WITH THE POINTLESS CHARM...
WELL, I KNOW BUT...

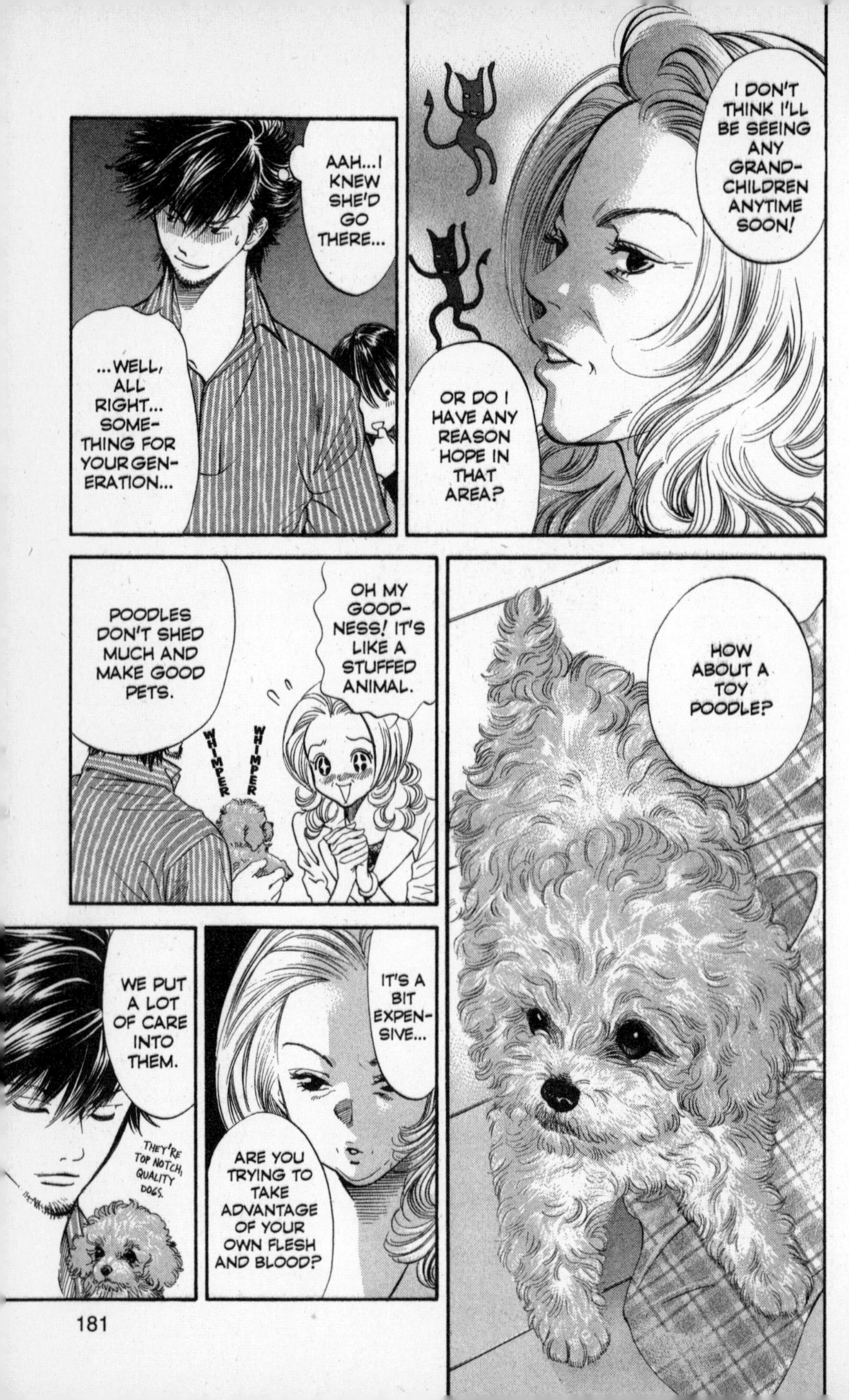
I DON'T THINK I'LL BE SEEING ANY GRAND-CHILDREN ANYTIME SOON!
OR DO I HAVE ANY REASON HOPE IN THAT AREA?
AAH...I KNEW SHE'D GO THERE...
...WELL, ALL RIGHT... SOME-THING FOR YOUR GEN-ERATION...
HOW ABOUT A TOY POODLE?
OH MY GOOD-NESS! IT'S LIKE A STUFFED ANIMAL.
POODLES DON'T SHED MUCH AND MAKE GOOD PETS.
WHIMPER
WHIMPER
IT'S A BIT EXPEN-SIVE...
ARE YOU TRYING TO TAKE ADVANTAGE OF YOUR OWN FLESH AND BLOOD?
WE PUT A LOT OF CARE INTO THEM.
THEY'RE TOP NOTCH, QUALITY DOGS.

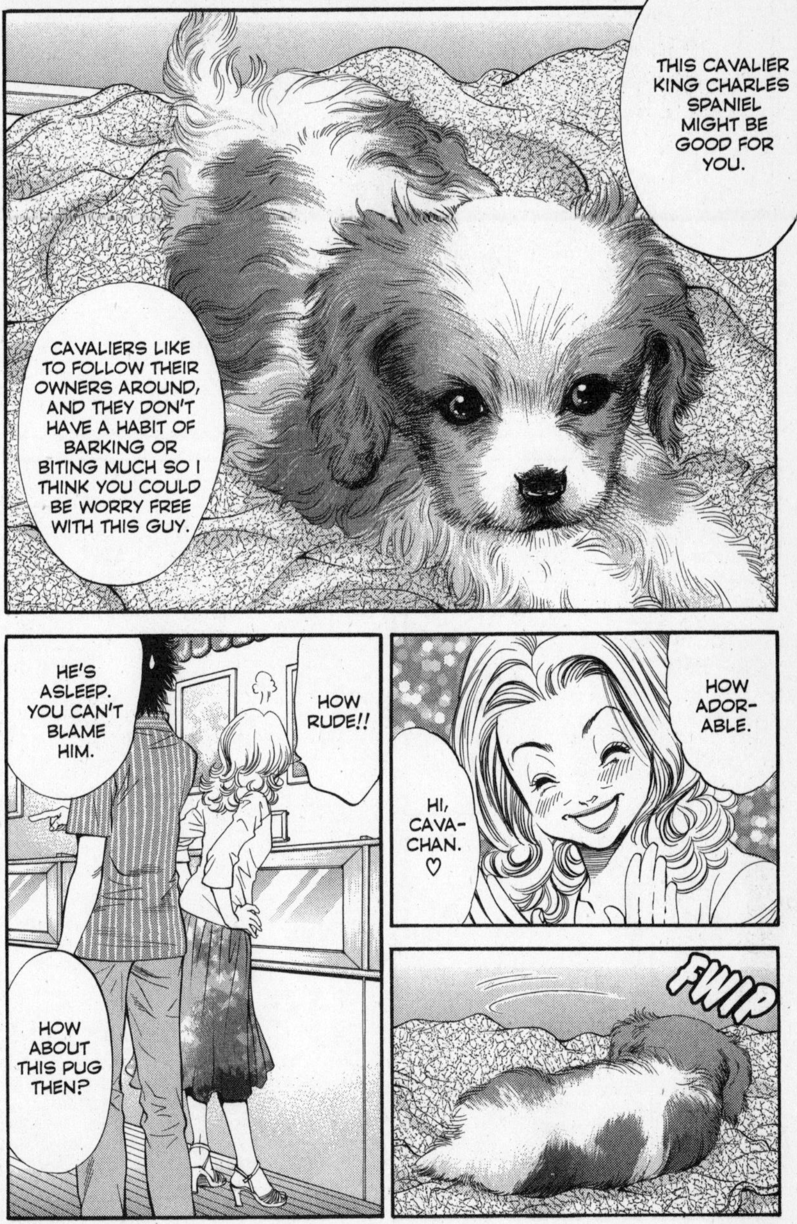
THIS CAVALIER KING CHARLES SPANIEL MIGHT BE GOOD FOR YOU.
CAVALIERS LIKE TO FOLLOW THEIR OWNERS AROUND, AND THEY DON'T HAVE A HABIT OF BARKING OR BITING MUCH SO I THINK YOU COULD BE WORRY FREE WITH THIS GUY.
HOW ADOR-ABLE.
HI, CAVA-CHAN. ♡
FWIP
HOW RUDE!!
HE'S ASLEEP. YOU CAN'T BLAME HIM.
HOW ABOUT THIS PUG THEN?

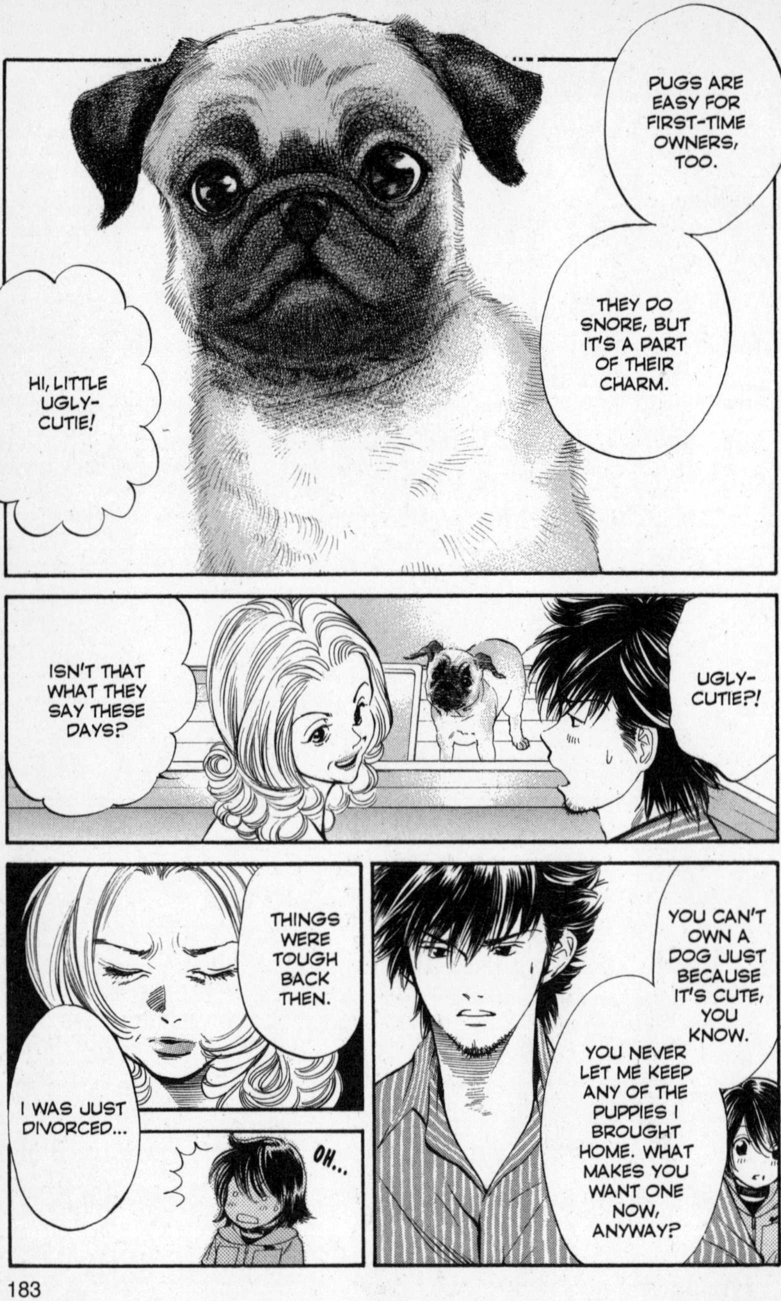
PUGS ARE EASY FOR FIRST-TIME OWNERS, TOO.
THEY DO SNORE, BUT IT'S A PART OF THEIR CHARM.
HI, LITTLE UGLY-CUTIE!
UGLY-CUTIE?!
ISN'T THAT WHAT THEY SAY THESE DAYS?
YOU CAN'T OWN A DOG JUST BECAUSE IT'S CUTE, YOU KNOW.
YOU NEVER LET ME KEEP ANY OF THE PUPPIES I BROUGHT HOME. WHAT MAKES YOU WANT ONE NOW, ANYWAY?
THINGS WERE TOUGH BACK THEN.
I WAS JUST DIVORCED...
OH...

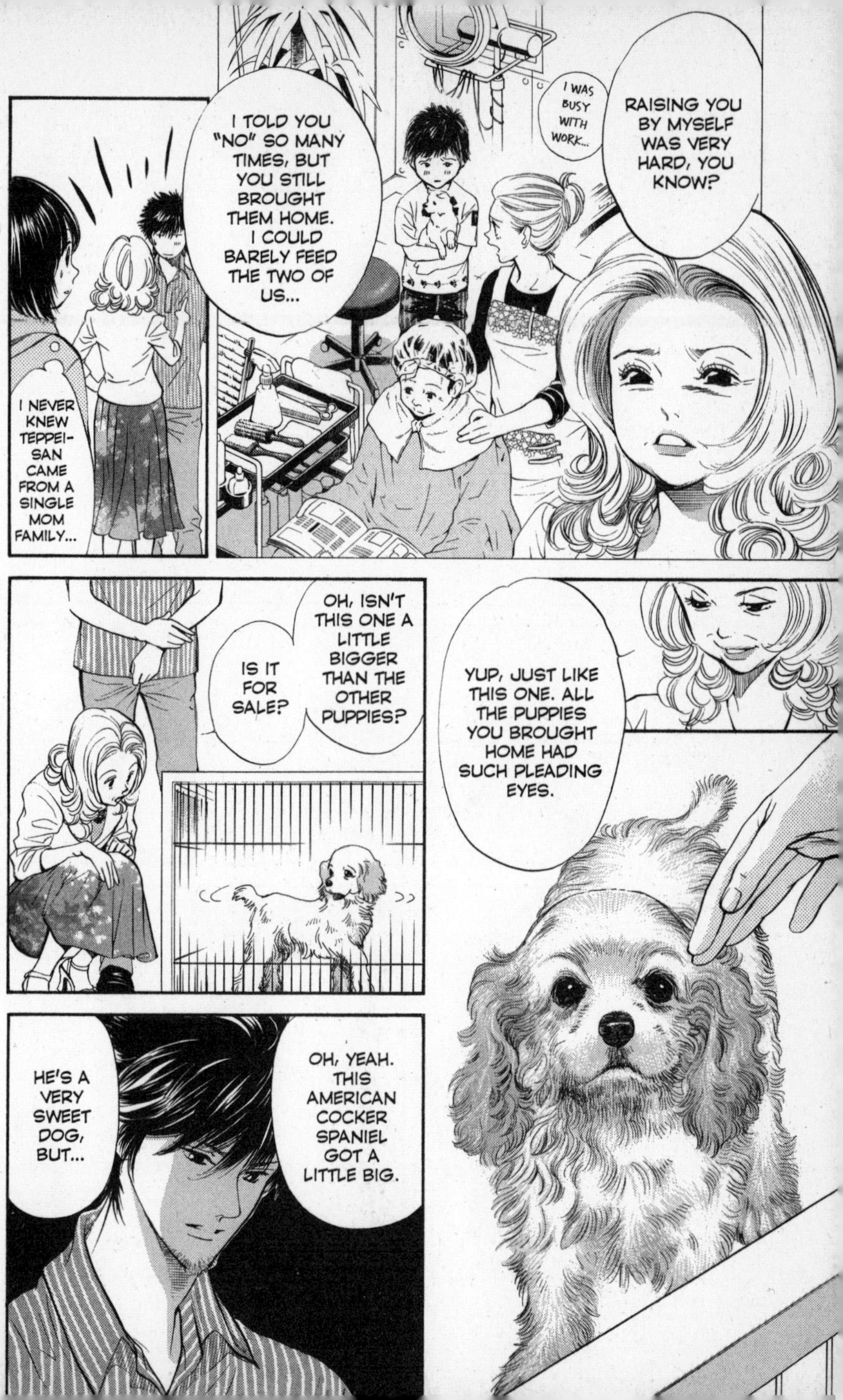
RAISING YOU BY MYSELF WAS VERY HARD, YOU KNOW?
I WAS BUSY WITH WORK...
I TOLD YOU "NO" SO MANY TIMES, BUT YOU STILL BROUGHT THEM HOME. I COULD BARELY FEED THE TWO OF US...
I NEVER KNEW TEPPEI-SAN CAME FROM A SINGLE MOM FAMILY...
YUP, JUST LIKE THIS ONE. ALL THE PUPPIES YOU BROUGHT HOME HAD SUCH PLEADING EYES.
OH, ISN'T THIS ONE A LITTLE BIGGER THAN THE OTHER PUPPIES?
IS IT FOR SALE?
OH, YEAH. THIS AMERICAN COCKER SPANIEL GOT A LITTLE BIG.
HE'S A VERY SWEET DOG, BUT...

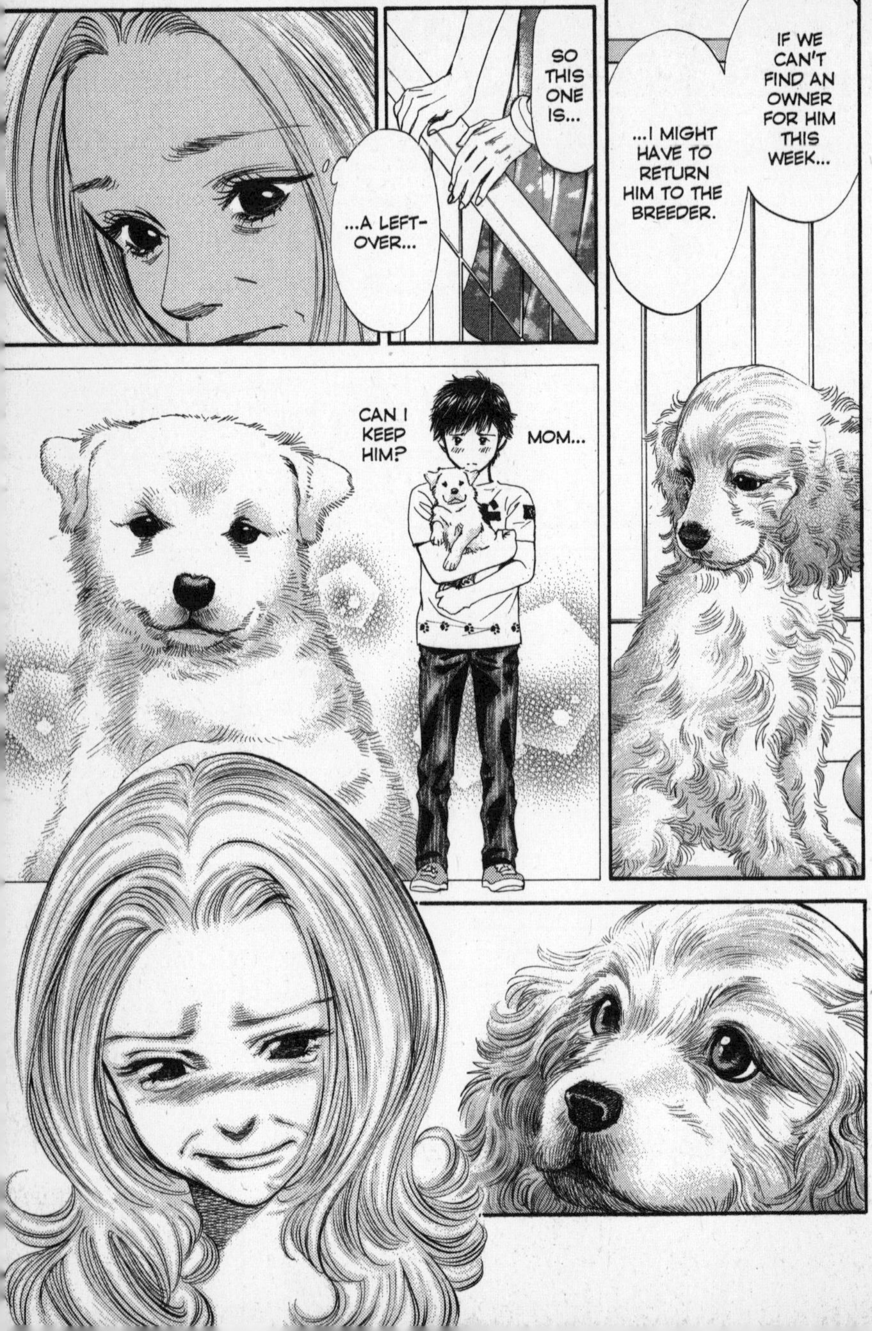
IF WE CAN'T FIND AN OWNER FOR HIM THIS WEEK...
...I MIGHT HAVE TO RETURN HIM TO THE BREEDER.
SO THIS ONE IS...
...A LEFT-OVER...
MOM...
CAN I KEEP HIM?

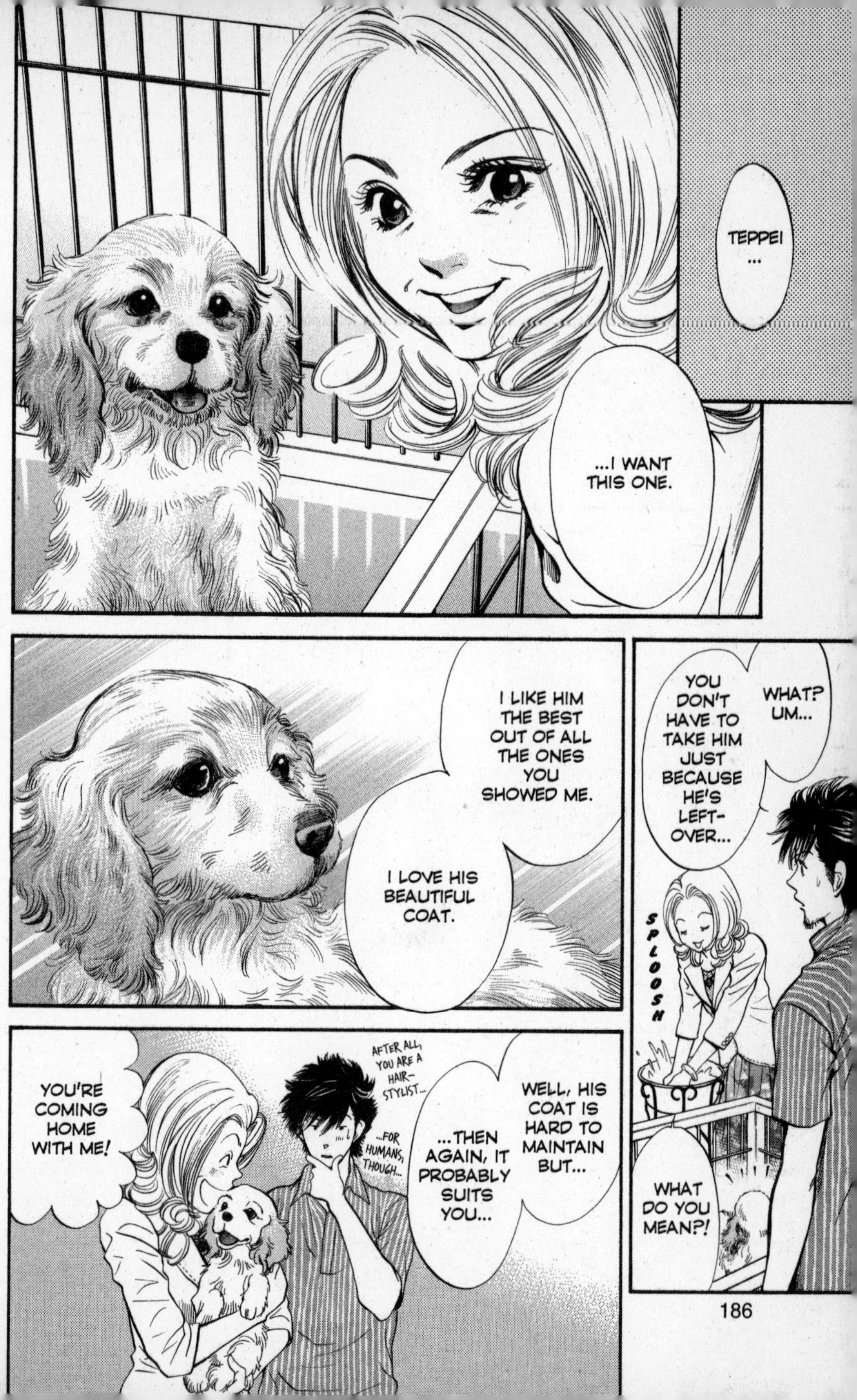
TEPPEI ...
...I WANT THIS ONE.
WHAT? UM...
YOU DON'T HAVE TO TAKE HIM JUST BECAUSE HE'S LEFT-OVER...
SPLOOSH
WHAT DO YOU MEAN?!
I LIKE HIM THE BEST OUT OF ALL THE ONES YOU SHOWED ME.
I LOVE HIS BEAUTIFUL COAT.
WELL, HIS COAT IS HARD TO MAINTAIN BUT...
...THEN AGAIN, IT PROBABLY SUITS YOU...
AFTER ALL, YOU ARE A HAIR-STYLIST...
...FOR HUMANS, THOUGH...
YOU'RE COMING HOME WITH ME!

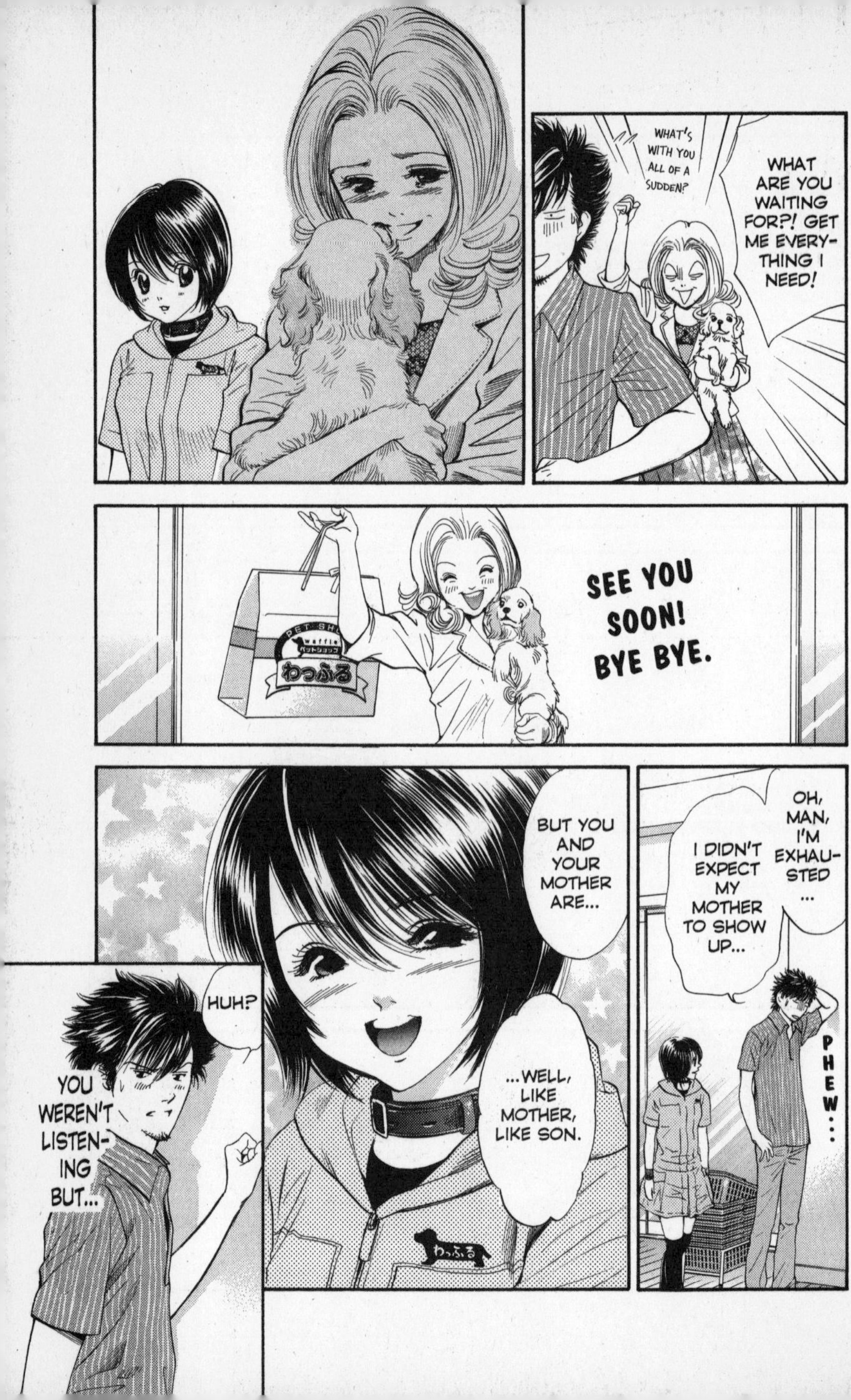
WHAT ARE YOU WAITING FOR?! GET ME EVERYTHING I NEED!
WHAT'S WITH YOU ALL OF A SUDDEN?
PET SHOP
waffle
ペットショップ
わっふる
SEE YOU SOON! BYE BYE.
OH, MAN, I'M EXHAUSTED...
I DIDN'T EXPECT MY MOTHER TO SHOW UP...
PHEW...
BUT YOU AND YOUR MOTHER ARE...
...WELL, LIKE MOTHER, LIKE SON.
わっふる
HUH?
YOU WEREN'T LISTENING BUT...

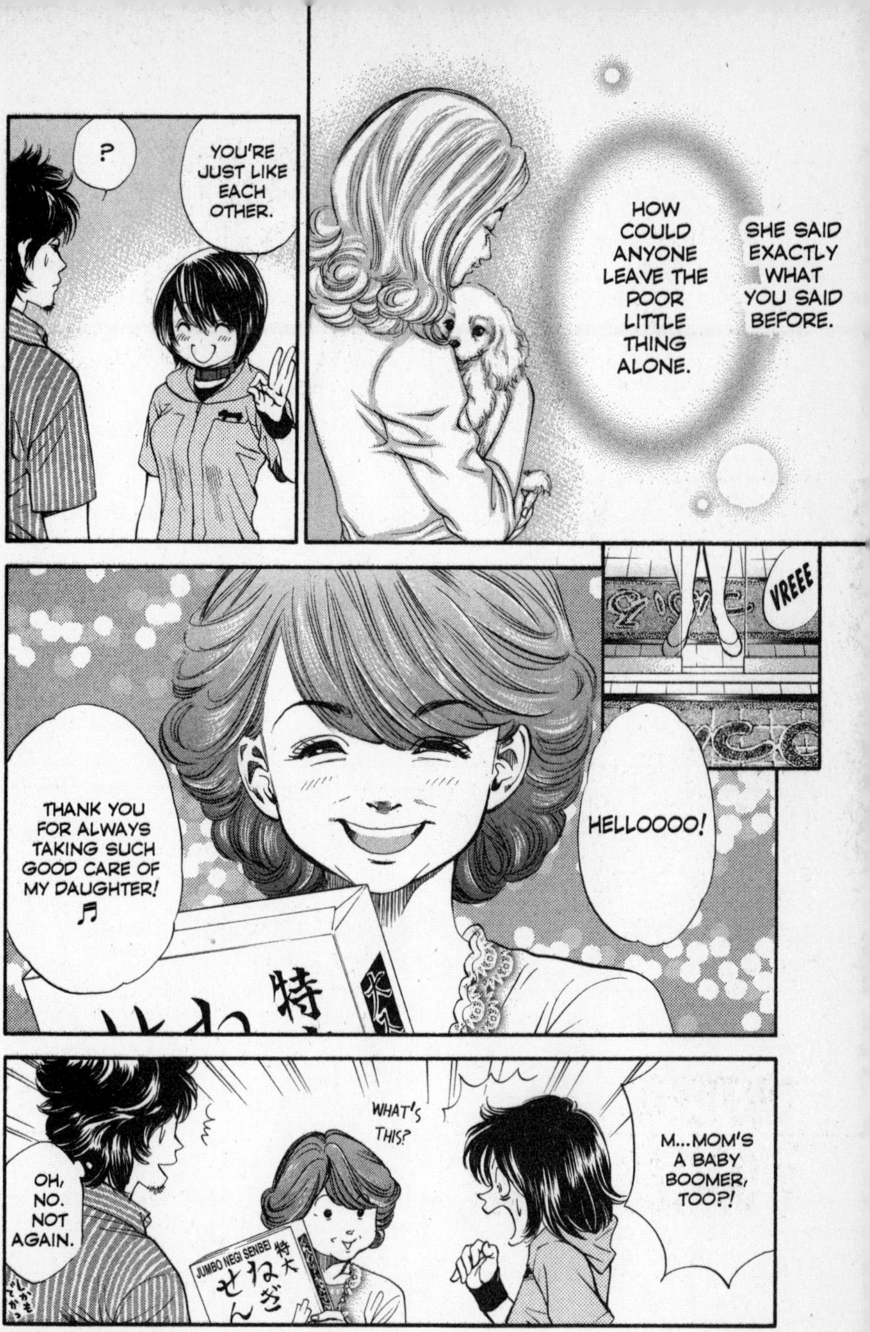
SHE SAID EXACTLY WHAT YOU SAID BEFORE.
HOW COULD ANYONE LEAVE THE POOR LITTLE THING ALONE.
YOU'RE JUST LIKE EACH OTHER.
?
VREEE
HELLOOOO!
THANK YOU FOR ALWAYS TAKING SUCH GOOD CARE OF MY DAUGHTER! ♫
M...MOM'S A BABY BOOMER, TOO?!
WHAT'S THIS?
OH, NO. NOT AGAIN.
JUMBO NEGI SENBEI
特大ねぎせん

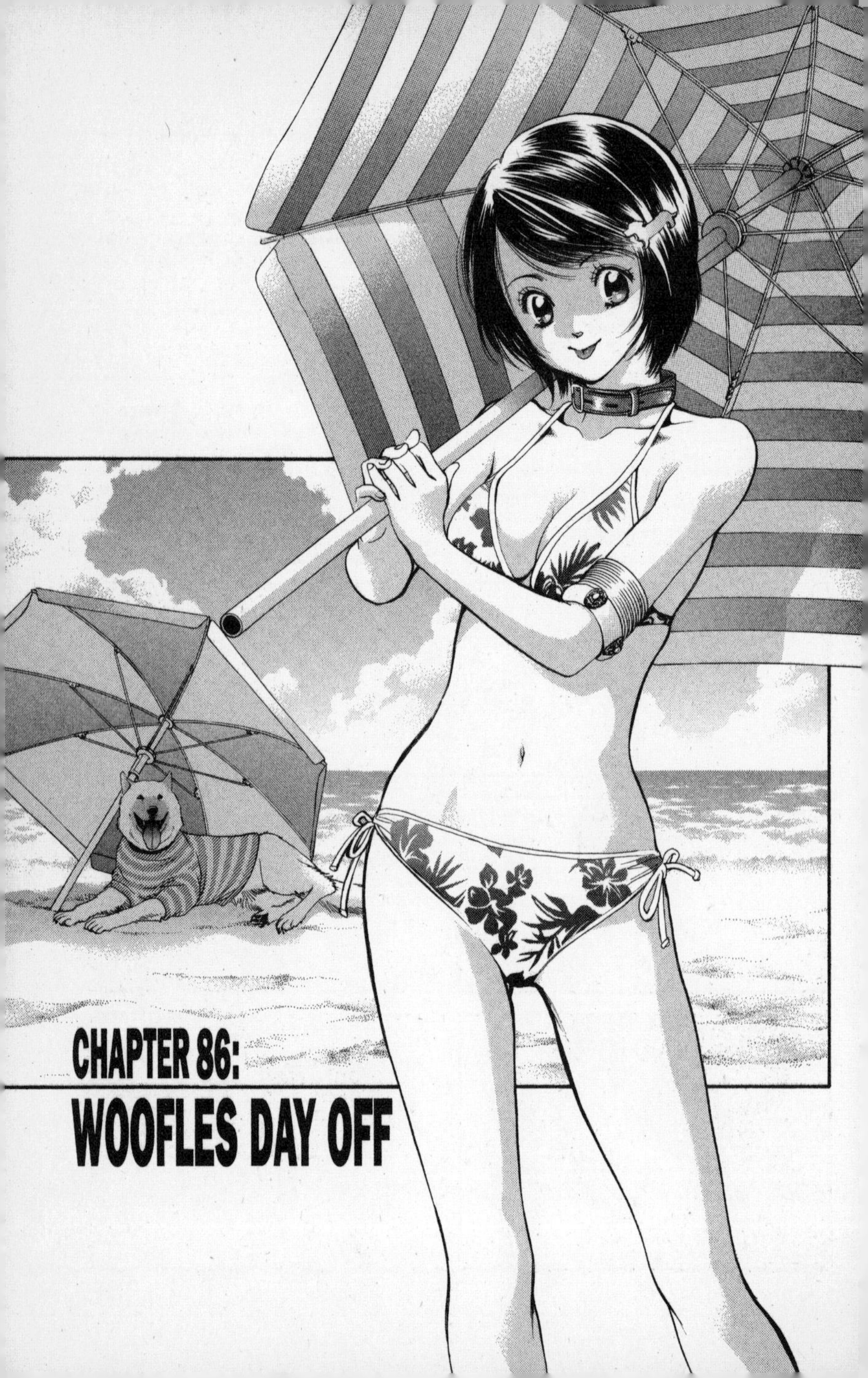
CHAPTER 86:
WOOFLES DAY OFF

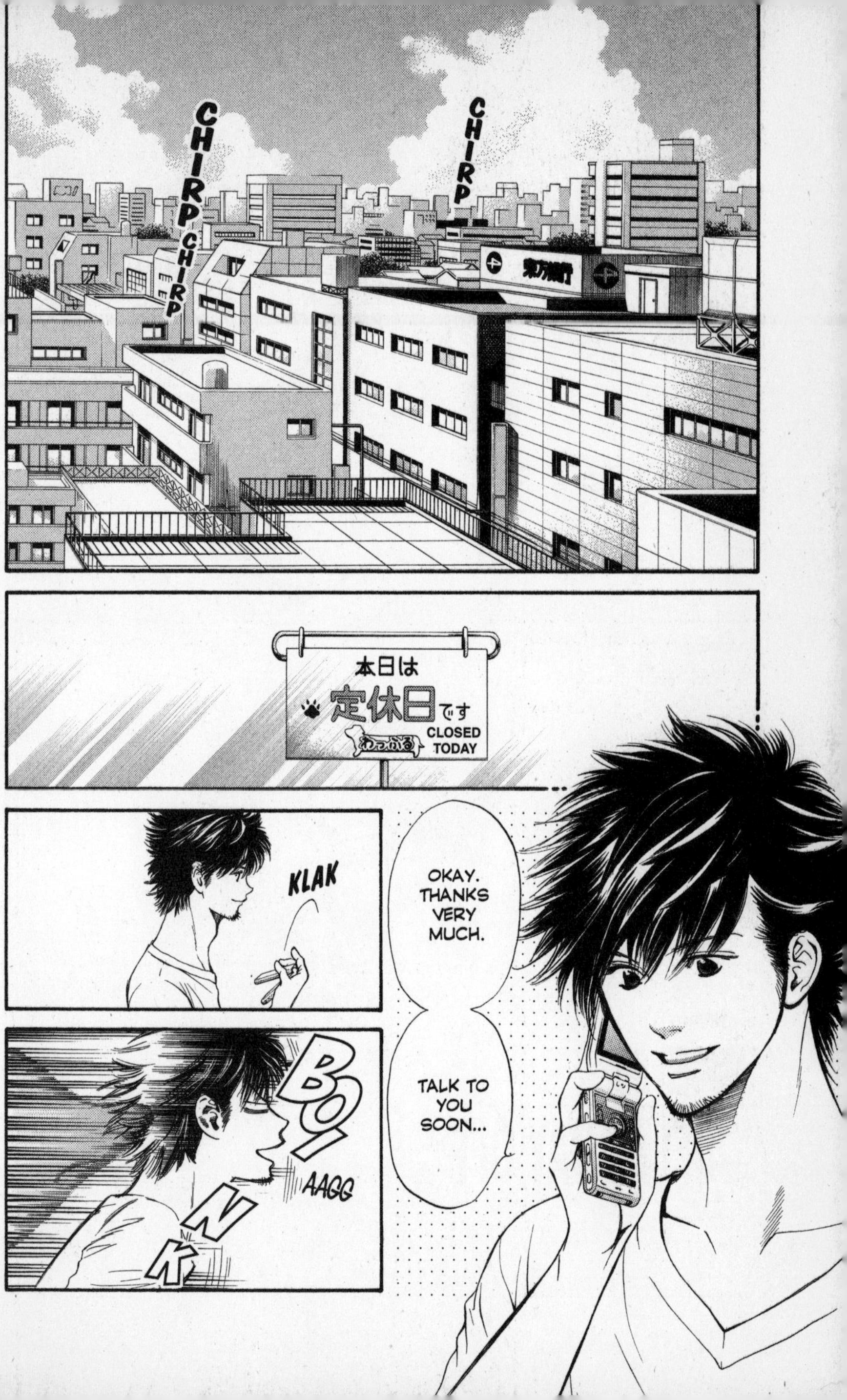
CHIRP
CHIRP CHIRP
本日は
定休日です
わっぷる
CLOSED TODAY
OKAY. THANKS VERY MUCH.
TALK TO YOU SOON...
KLAK
BOINK
AAGG

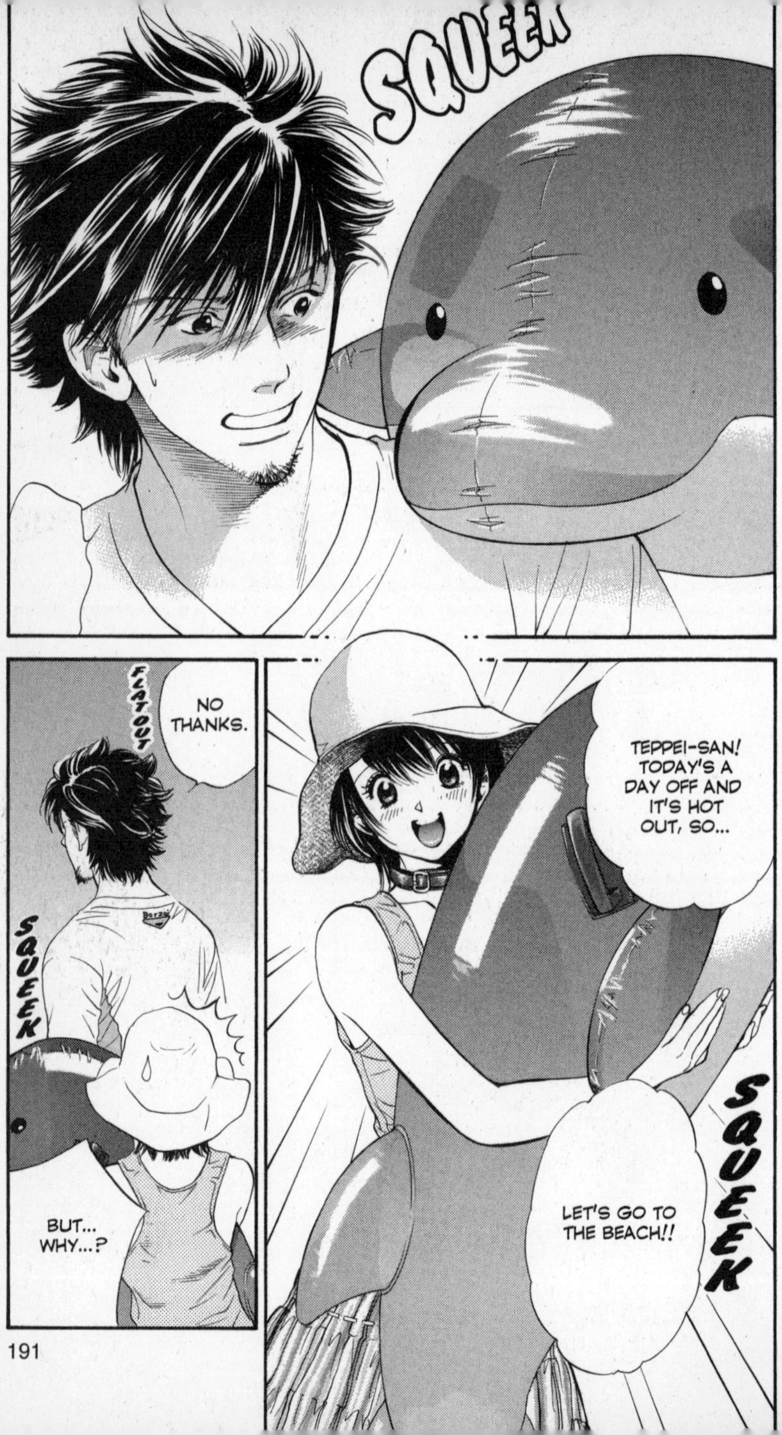
SQUEEK
TEPPEI-SAN! TODAY'S A DAY OFF AND IT'S HOT OUT, SO...
SQUEEEK
LET'S GO TO THE BEACH!!
FLAT OUT
NO THANKS.
SQUEEEK
BUT... WHY...?

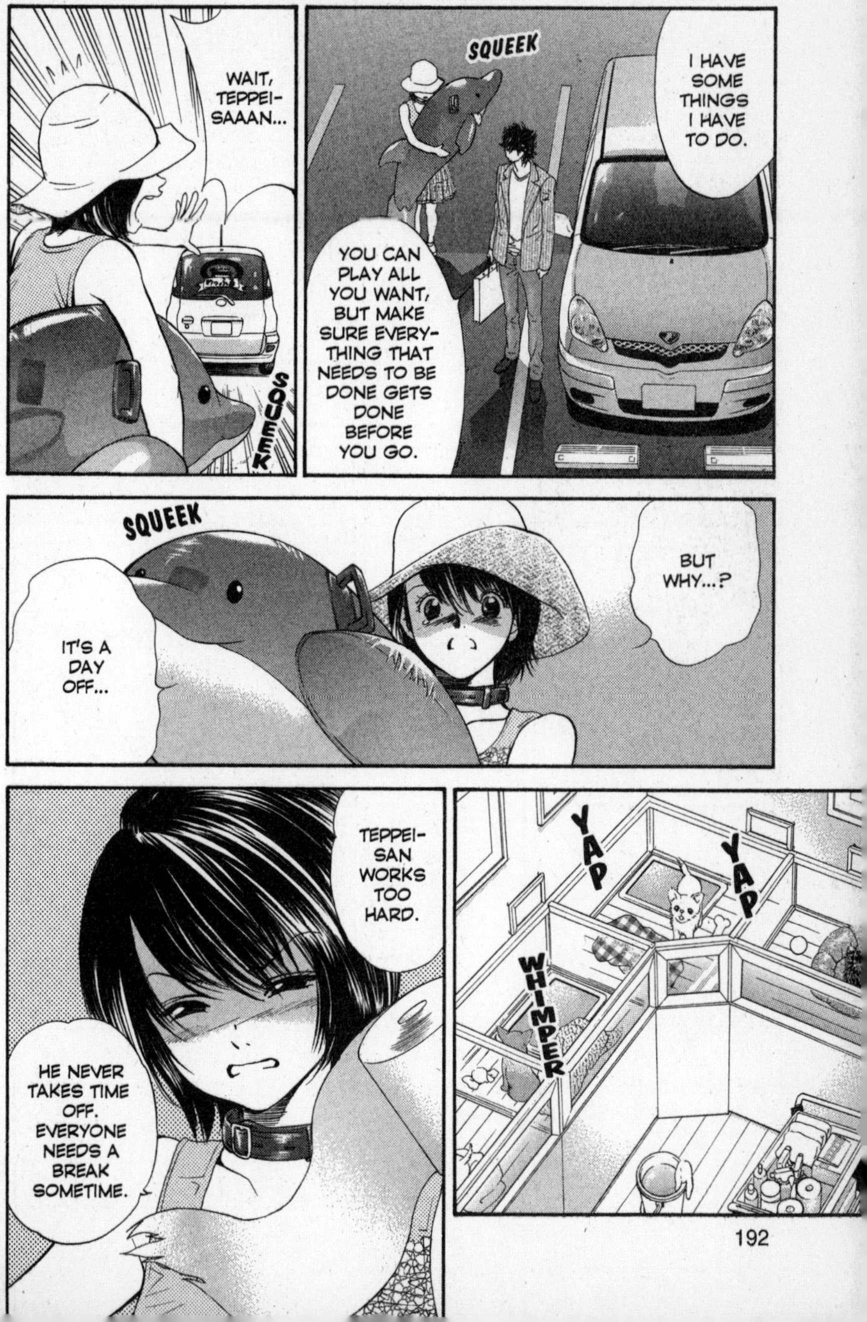
I HAVE SOME THINGS I HAVE TO DO.
SQUEEK
YOU CAN PLAY ALL YOU WANT, BUT MAKE SURE EVERY-THING THAT NEEDS TO BE DONE GETS DONE BEFORE YOU GO.
WAIT, TEPPEI-SAAAN...
SQUEEK
BUT WHY...?
SQUEEK
IT'S A DAY OFF...
YAP
YAP
WHIMPER
TEPPEI-SAN WORKS TOO HARD.
HE NEVER TAKES TIME OFF. EVERYONE NEEDS A BREAK SOMETIME.

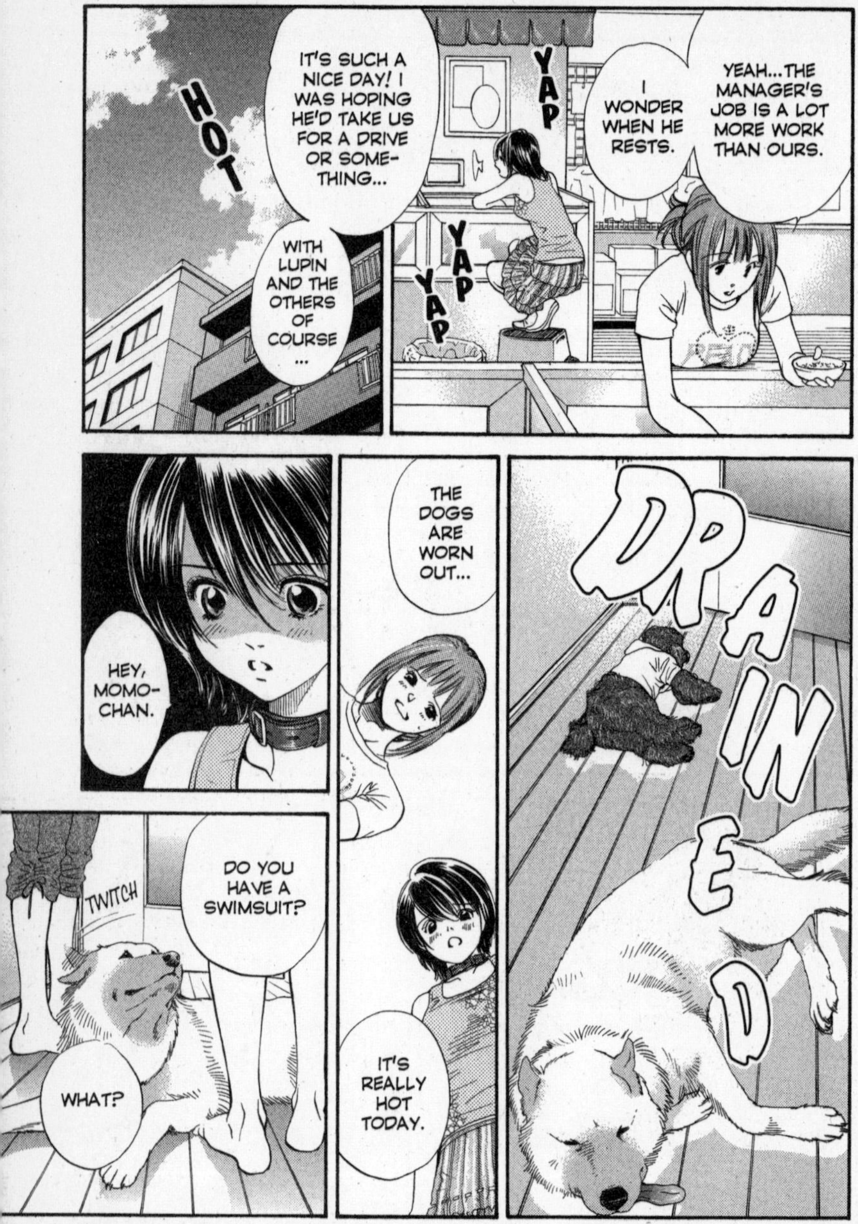
I WONDER WHEN HE RESTS.
YEAH...THE MANAGER'S JOB IS A LOT MORE WORK THAN OURS.
YAP
YAP YAP
YAP
HOT
IT'S SUCH A NICE DAY! I WAS HOPING HE'D TAKE US FOR A DRIVE OR SOME-THING...
WITH LUPIN AND THE OTHERS OF COURSE ...
DRAINED
THE DOGS ARE WORN OUT...
IT'S REALLY HOT TODAY.
HEY, MOMO-CHAN.
DO YOU HAVE A SWIMSUIT?
TWITCH
WHAT?

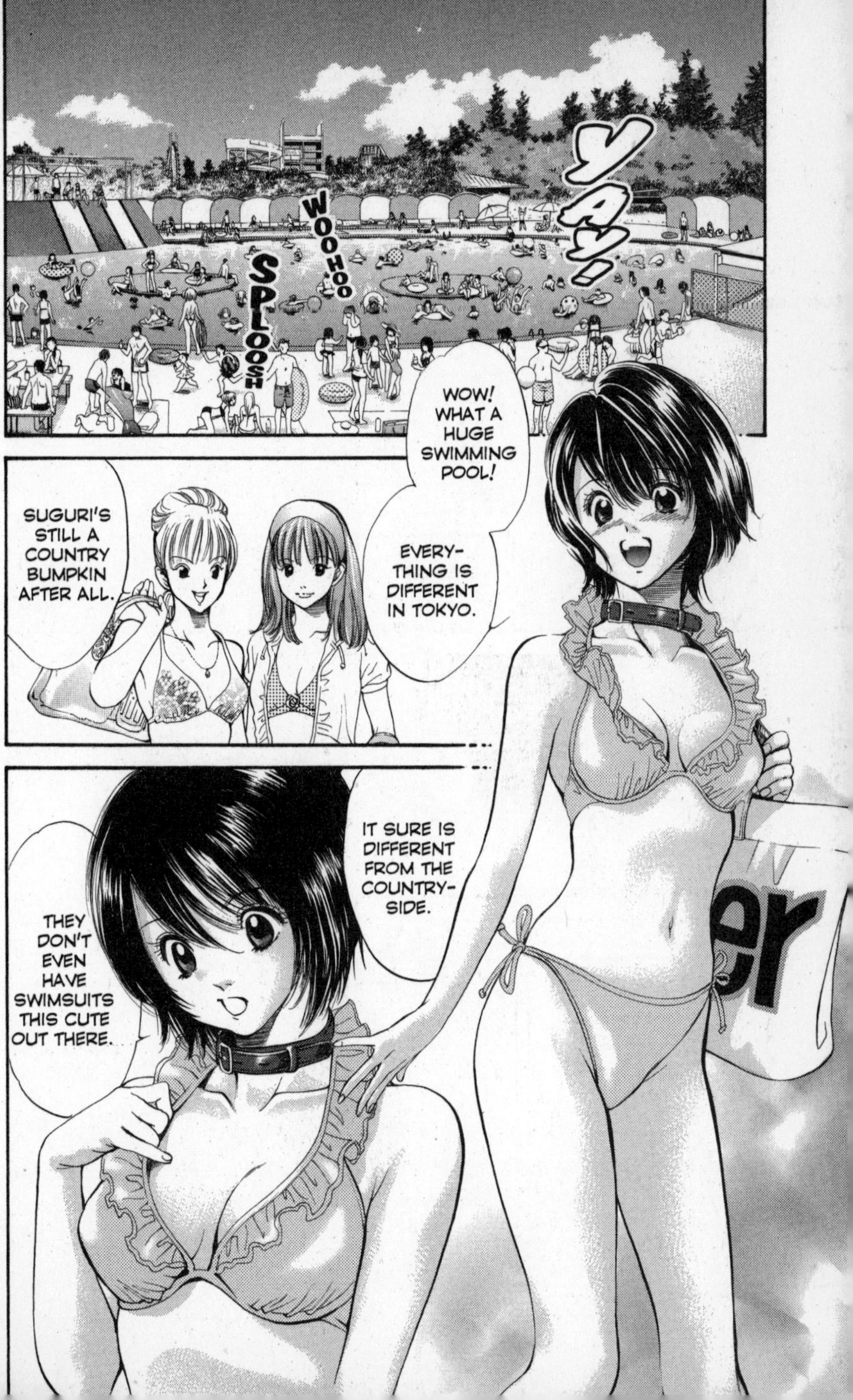
YAY!
WOOHOO
SPLOOSH
WOW! WHAT A HUGE SWIMMING POOL!
EVERY-THING IS DIFFERENT IN TOKYO.
SUGURI'S STILL A COUNTRY BUMPKIN AFTER ALL.
IT SURE IS DIFFERENT FROM THE COUNTRY-SIDE.
THEY DON'T EVEN HAVE SWIMSUITS THIS CUTE OUT THERE...

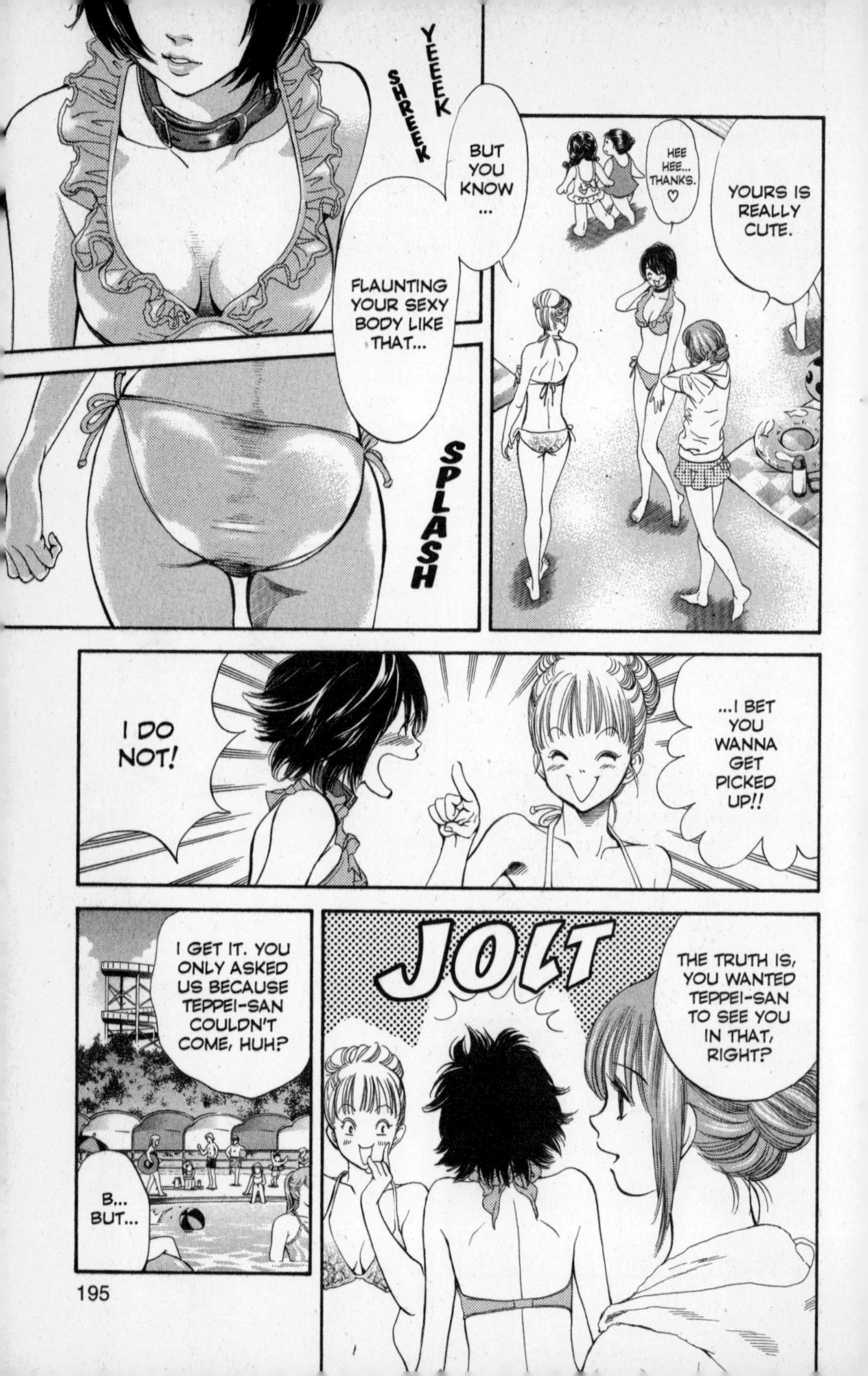
YOURS IS REALLY CUTE.
HEE HEE... THANKS. ♡
YEEEK
SHREEK
BUT YOU KNOW ...
FLAUNTING YOUR SEXY BODY LIKE THAT...
SPLASH
...I BET YOU WANNA GET PICKED UP!!
I DO NOT!
JOLT
THE TRUTH IS, YOU WANTED TEPPEI-SAN TO SEE YOU IN THAT, RIGHT?
I GET IT. YOU ONLY ASKED US BECAUSE TEPPEI-SAN COULDN'T COME, HUH?
B... BUT...

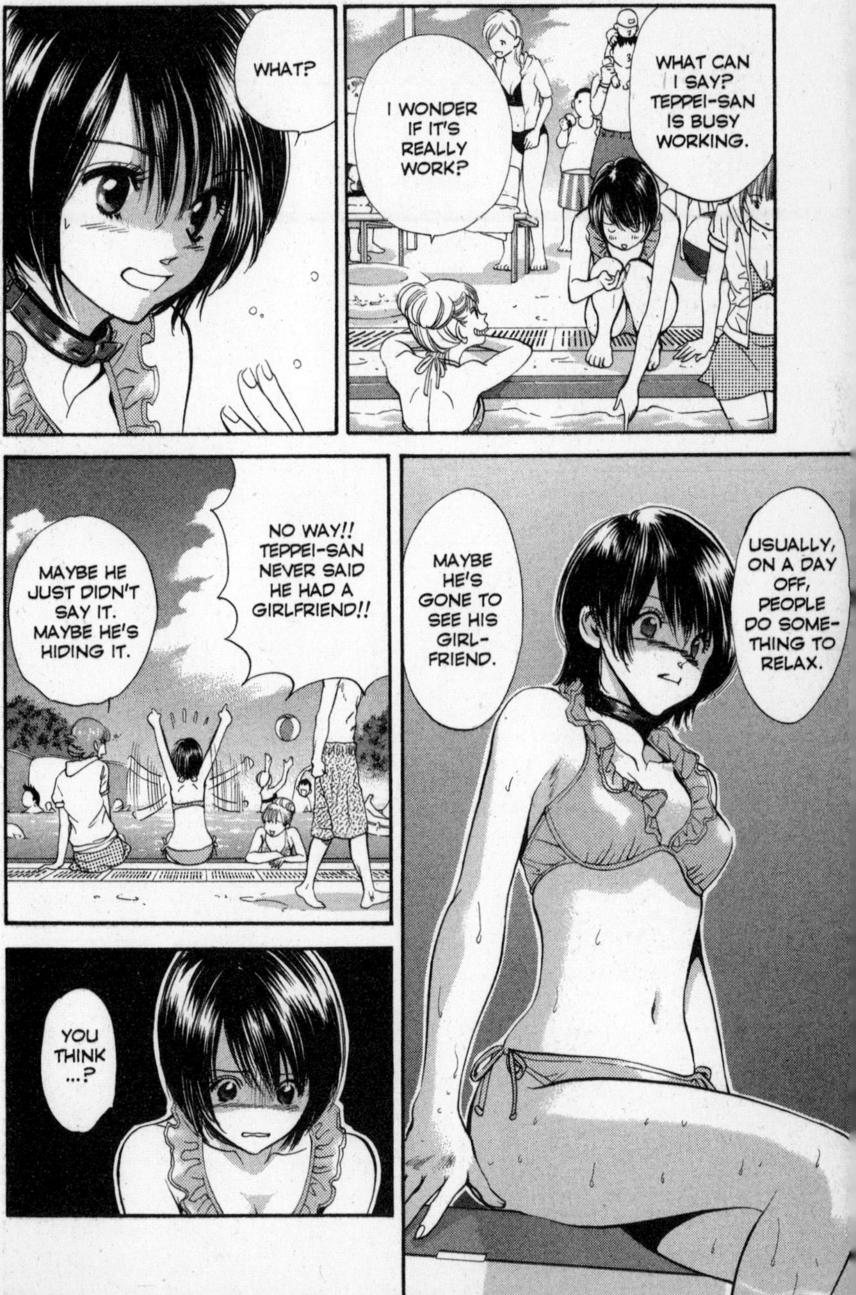
WHAT CAN I SAY? TEPPEI-SAN IS BUSY WORKING.
I WONDER IF IT'S REALLY WORK?
WHAT?
USUALLY, ON A DAY OFF, PEOPLE DO SOME-THING TO RELAX.
MAYBE HE'S GONE TO SEE HIS GIRL-FRIEND.
NO WAY!! TEPPEI-SAN NEVER SAID HE HAD A GIRLFRIEND!!
MAYBE HE JUST DIDN'T SAY IT. MAYBE HE'S HIDING IT.
YOU THINK ...?

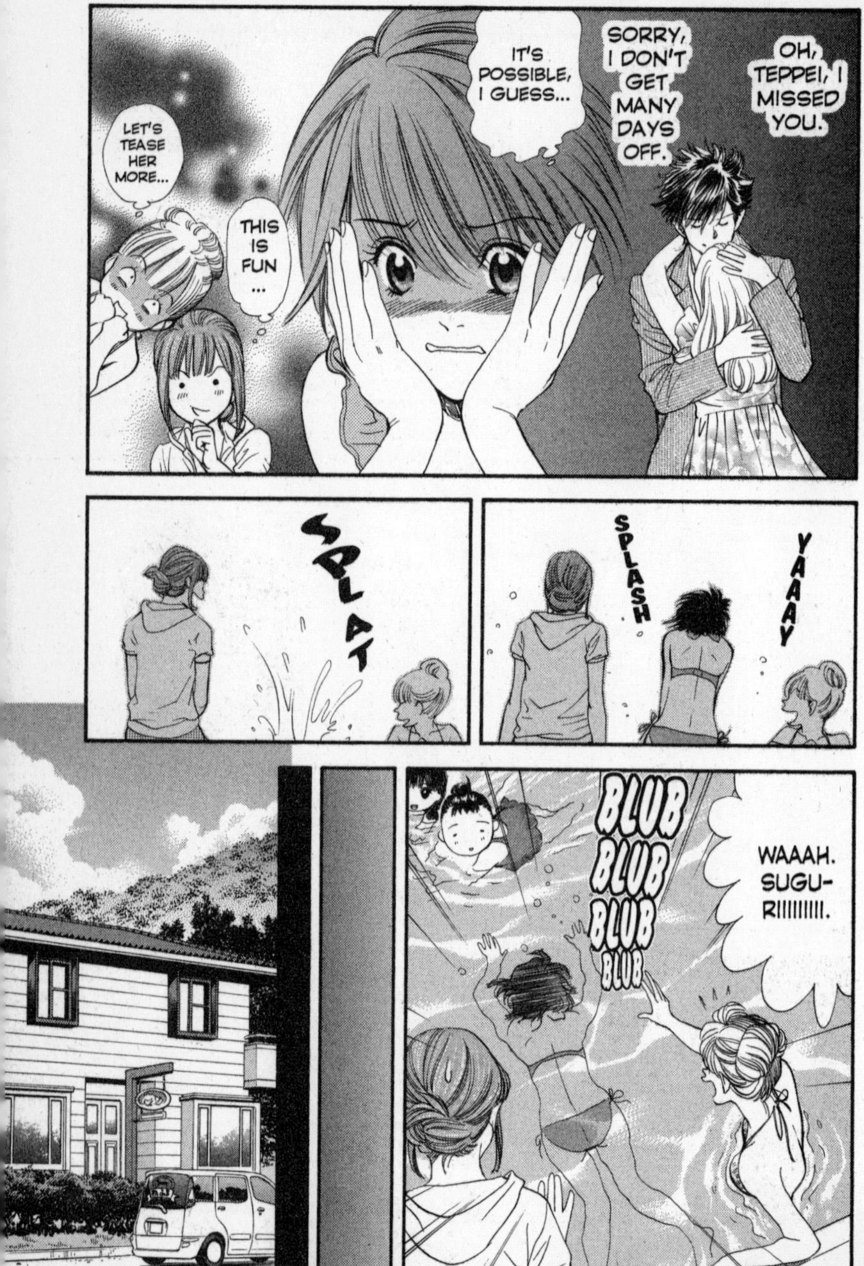
OH, TEPPEI, I MISSED YOU.
SORRY, I DON'T GET MANY DAYS OFF.
IT'S POSSIBLE, I GUESS...
THIS IS FUN ...
LET'S TEASE HER MORE...
YAAAY
SPLASH
SPLAT
BLUB BLUB BLUB BLUB
WAAAH. SUGU-RIIIIIIII.

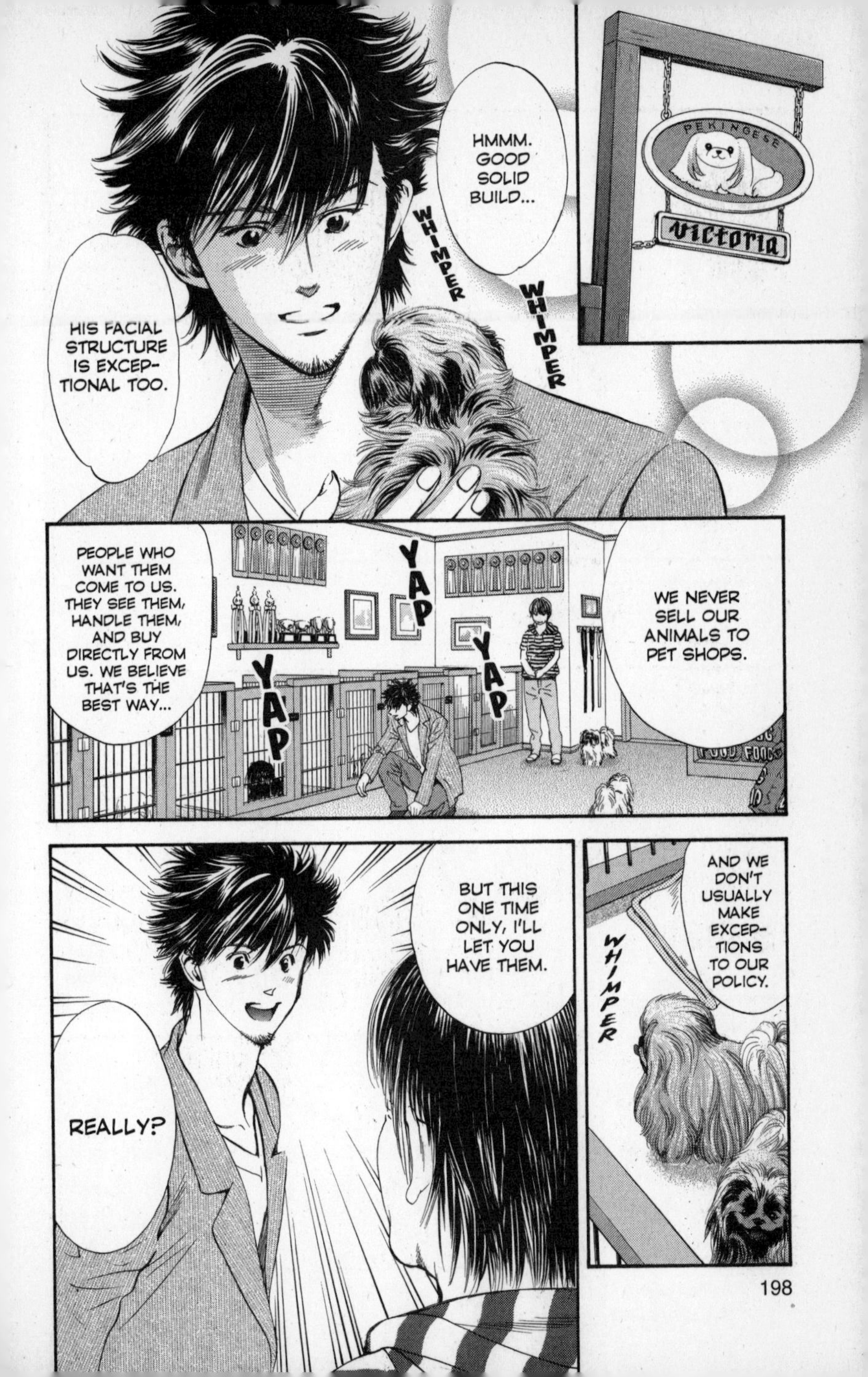
PEKINGESE
victoria
HMMM. GOOD SOLID BUILD...
WHIMPER
WHIMPER
HIS FACIAL STRUCTURE IS EXCEP-TIONAL TOO.
WE NEVER SELL OUR ANIMALS TO PET SHOPS.
YAP
YAP
YAP
YAP
PEOPLE WHO WANT THEM COME TO US. THEY SEE THEM, HANDLE THEM, AND BUY DIRECTLY FROM US. WE BELIEVE THAT'S THE BEST WAY...
AND WE DON'T USUALLY MAKE EXCEP-TIONS TO OUR POLICY.
WHIMPER
BUT THIS ONE TIME ONLY, I'LL LET YOU HAVE THEM.
REALLY?

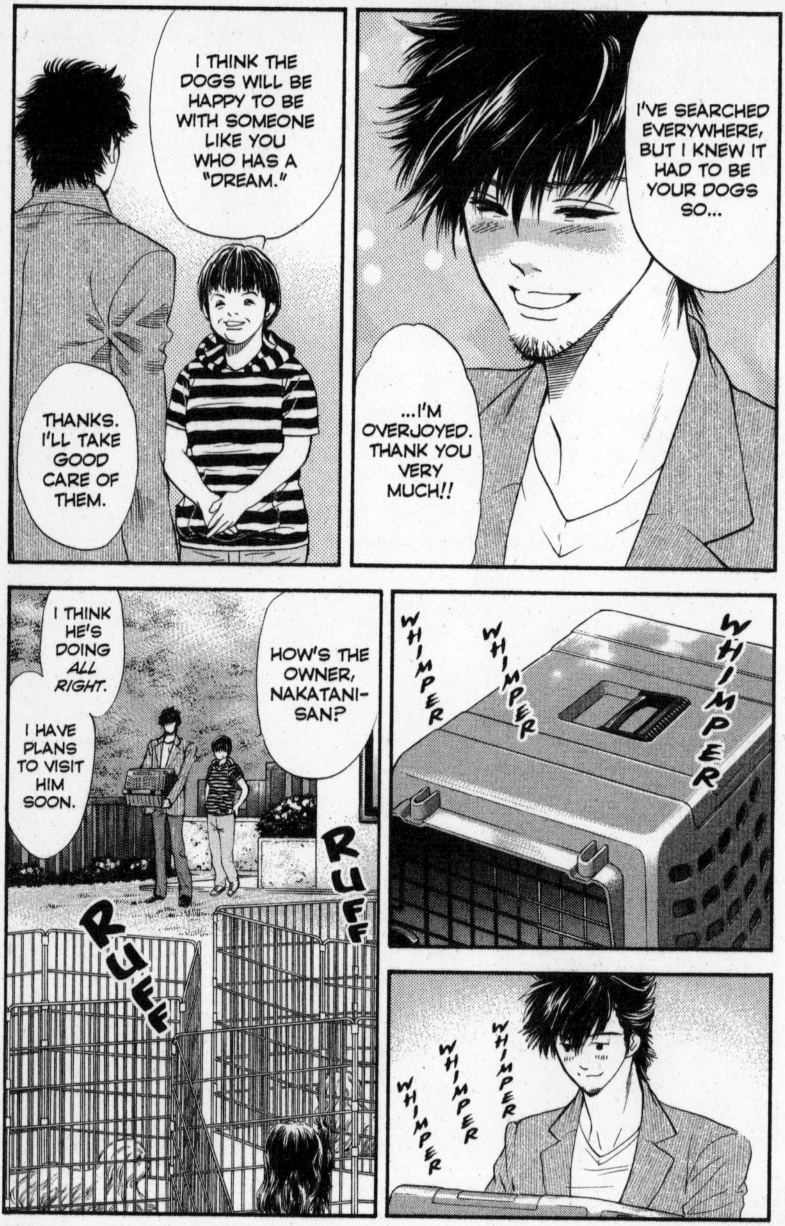
I'VE SEARCHED EVERYWHERE, BUT I KNEW IT HAD TO BE YOUR DOGS SO...
...I'M OVERJOYED. THANK YOU VERY MUCH!!
I THINK THE DOGS WILL BE HAPPY TO BE WITH SOMEONE LIKE YOU WHO HAS A "DREAM."
THANKS. I'LL TAKE GOOD CARE OF THEM.
WHIMPER
WHIMPER
WHIMPER
WHIMPER
WHIMPER
WHIMPER
HOW'S THE OWNER, NAKATANI-SAN?
I THINK HE'S DOING *ALL RIGHT*.
I HAVE PLANS TO VISIT HIM SOON.
RUFF
RUFF

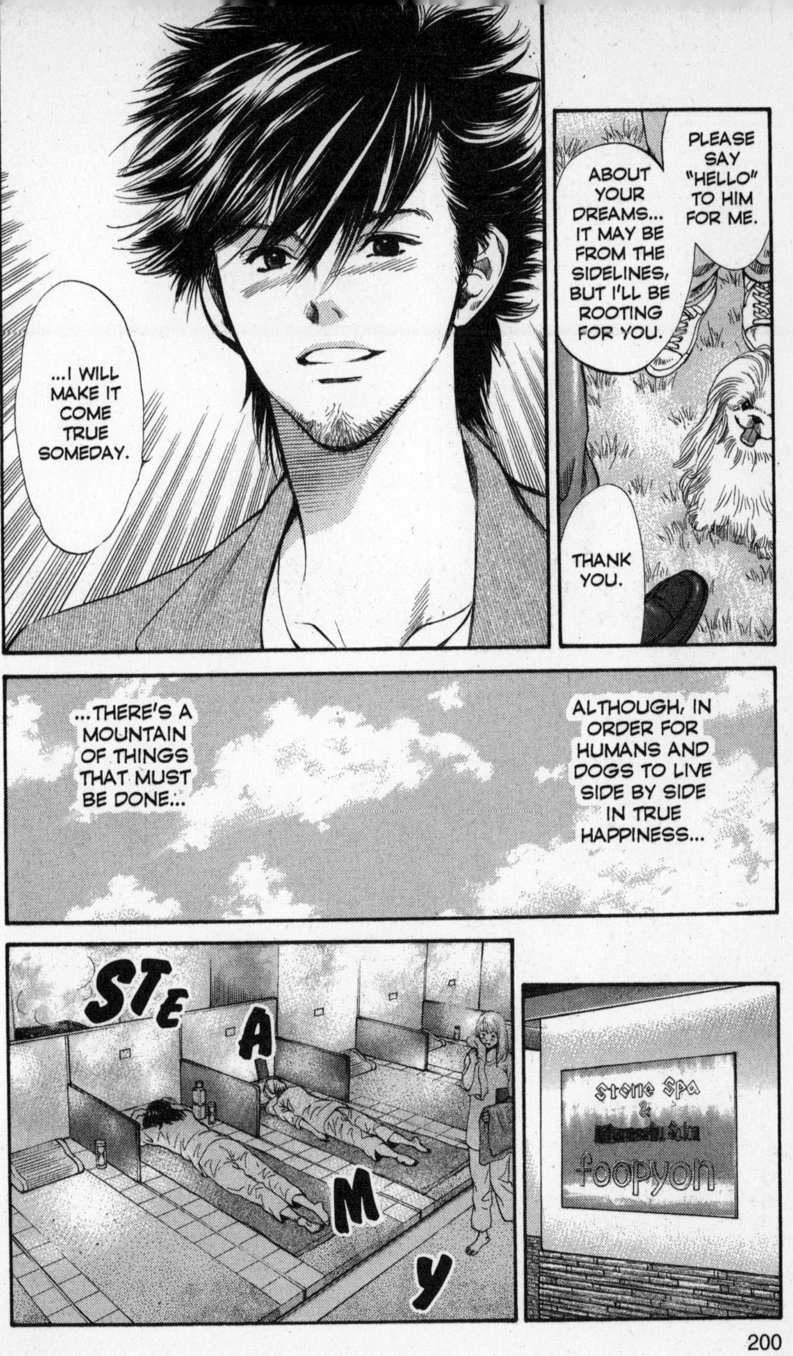
PLEASE SAY "HELLO" TO HIM FOR ME.
ABOUT YOUR DREAMS... IT MAY BE FROM THE SIDELINES, BUT I'LL BE ROOTING FOR YOU.
THANK YOU.
...I WILL MAKE IT COME TRUE SOMEDAY.
ALTHOUGH, IN ORDER FOR HUMANS AND DOGS TO LIVE SIDE BY SIDE IN TRUE HAPPINESS...
...THERE'S A MOUNTAIN OF THINGS THAT MUST BE DONE...
Stone Spa
&
foopyon
STEAMy

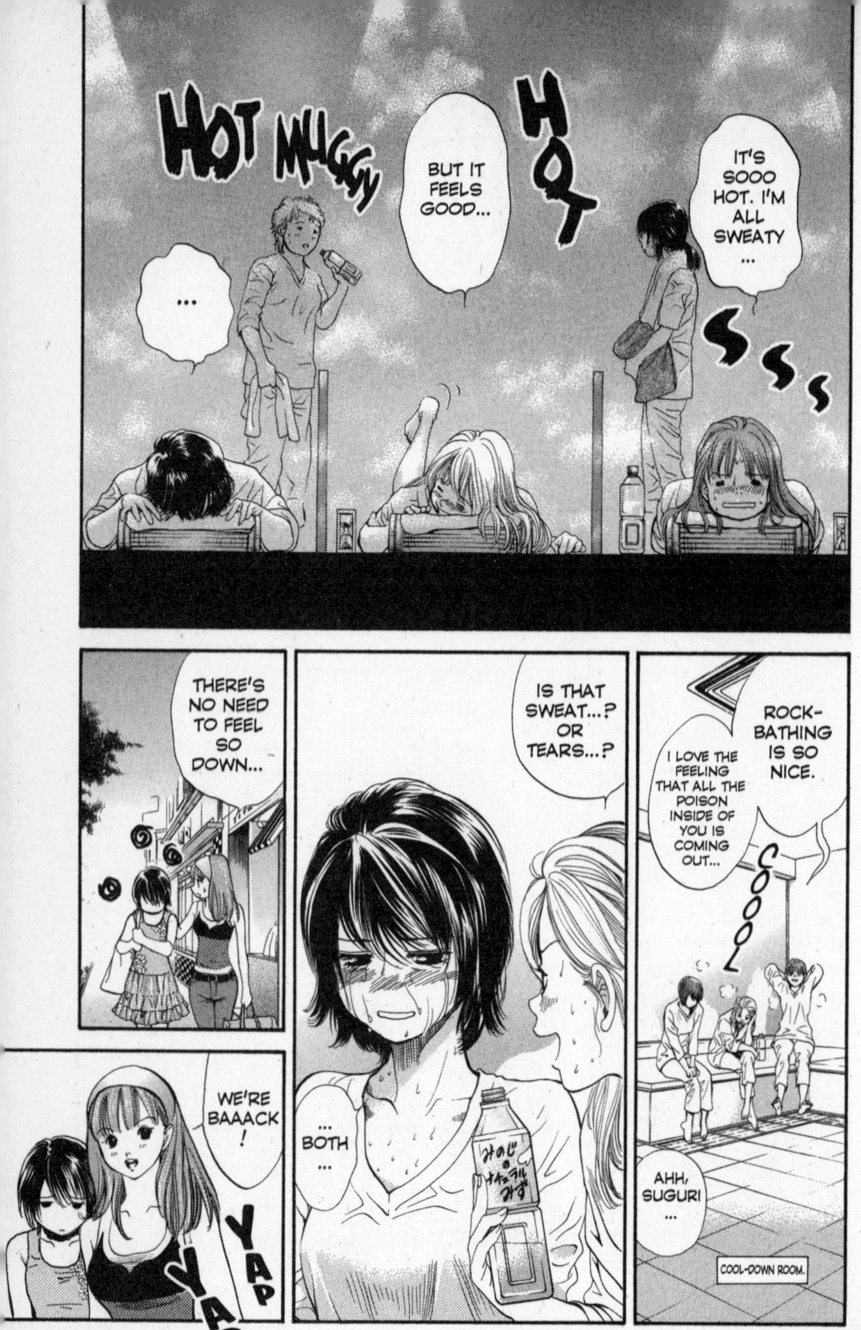
IT'S SOOO HOT. I'M ALL SWEATY ...
SSS
HOT
BUT IT FEELS GOOD...
HOT MUGGY
...
ROCK-BATHING IS SO NICE.
I LOVE THE FEELING THAT ALL THE POISON INSIDE OF YOU IS COMING OUT...
COOOOL
AHH, SUGURI ...
COOL-DOWN ROOM.
IS THAT SWEAT...? OR TEARS...?
... BOTH ...
THERE'S NO NEED TO FEEL SO DOWN...
WE'RE BAAACK!
YAP
YAP

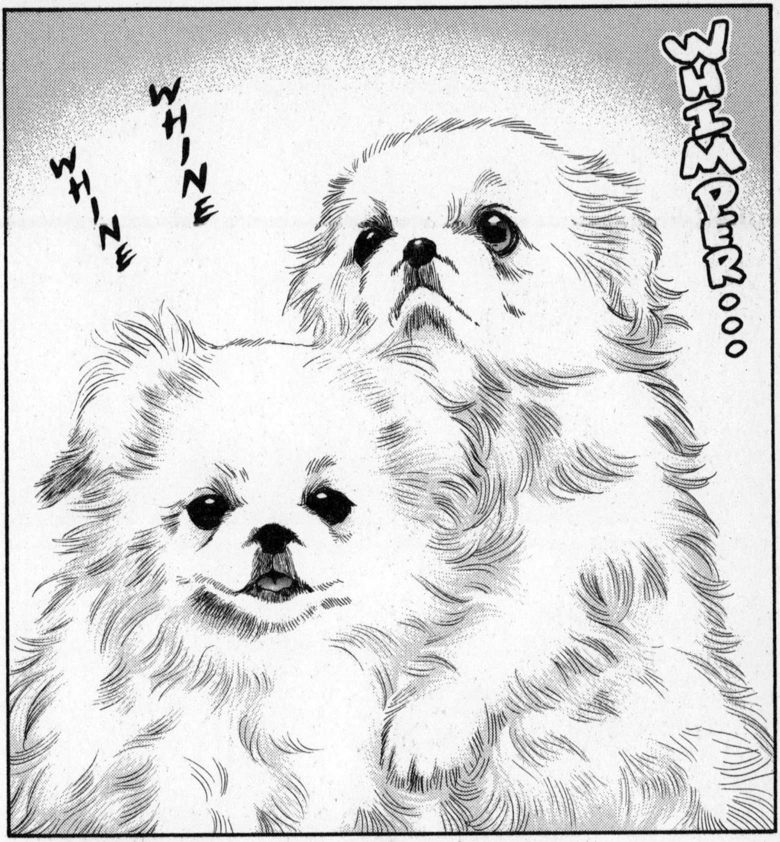
WHIMPER...
WHINE
WHINE

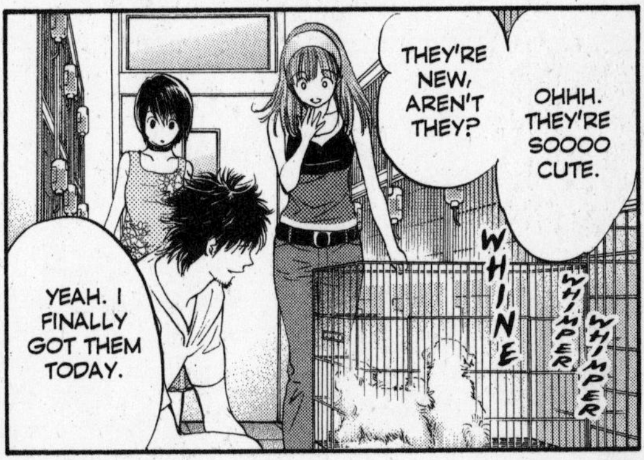
THEY'RE NEW, AREN'T THEY?
OHHH. THEY'RE SOOOO CUTE.
WHINE
WHIMPER
WHIMPER
YEAH. I FINALLY GOT THEM TODAY.

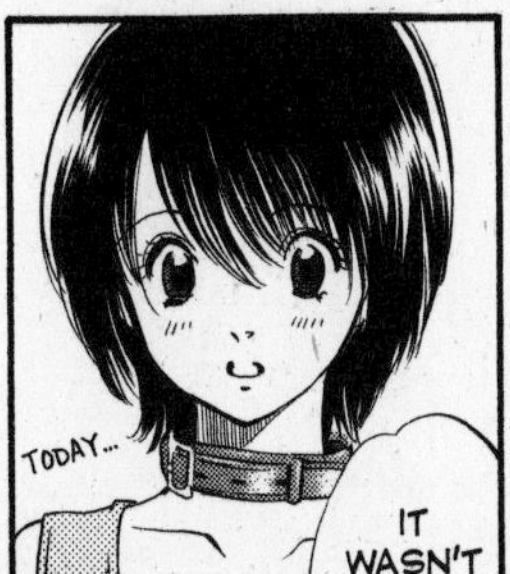
TODAY...
IT WASN'T EASY.

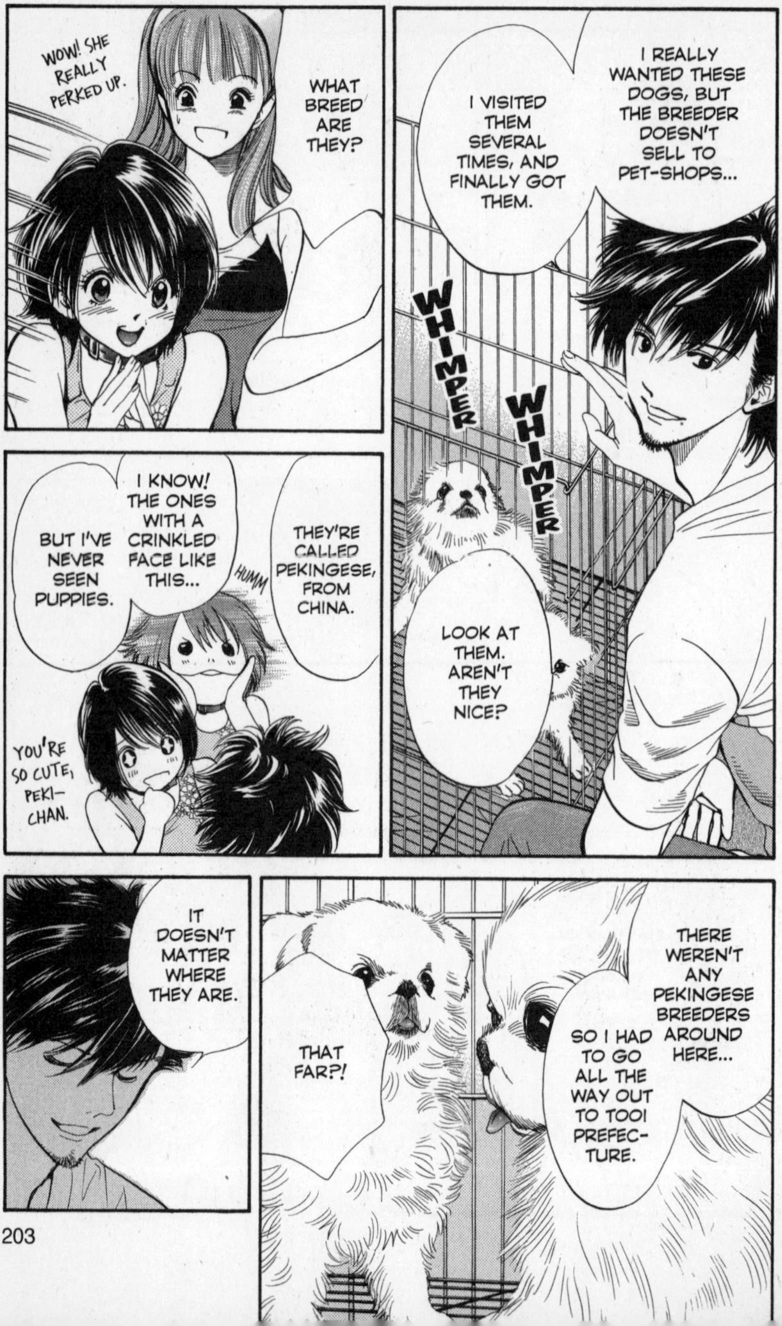
I REALLY WANTED THESE DOGS, BUT THE BREEDER DOESN'T SELL TO PET-SHOPS...
I VISITED THEM SEVERAL TIMES, AND FINALLY GOT THEM.
WHIMPER
WHIMPER
LOOK AT THEM. AREN'T THEY NICE?
WHAT BREED ARE THEY?
WOW! SHE REALLY PERKED UP.
THEY'RE CALLED PEKINGESE, FROM CHINA.
I KNOW! THE ONES WITH A CRINKLED FACE LIKE THIS...
HUMM
BUT I'VE NEVER SEEN PUPPIES.
YOU'RE SO CUTE, PEKI-CHAN.
THERE WEREN'T ANY PEKINGESE BREEDERS AROUND HERE...
SO I HAD TO GO ALL THE WAY OUT TO TOOI PREFECTURE.
THAT FAR?!
IT DOESN'T MATTER WHERE THEY ARE.

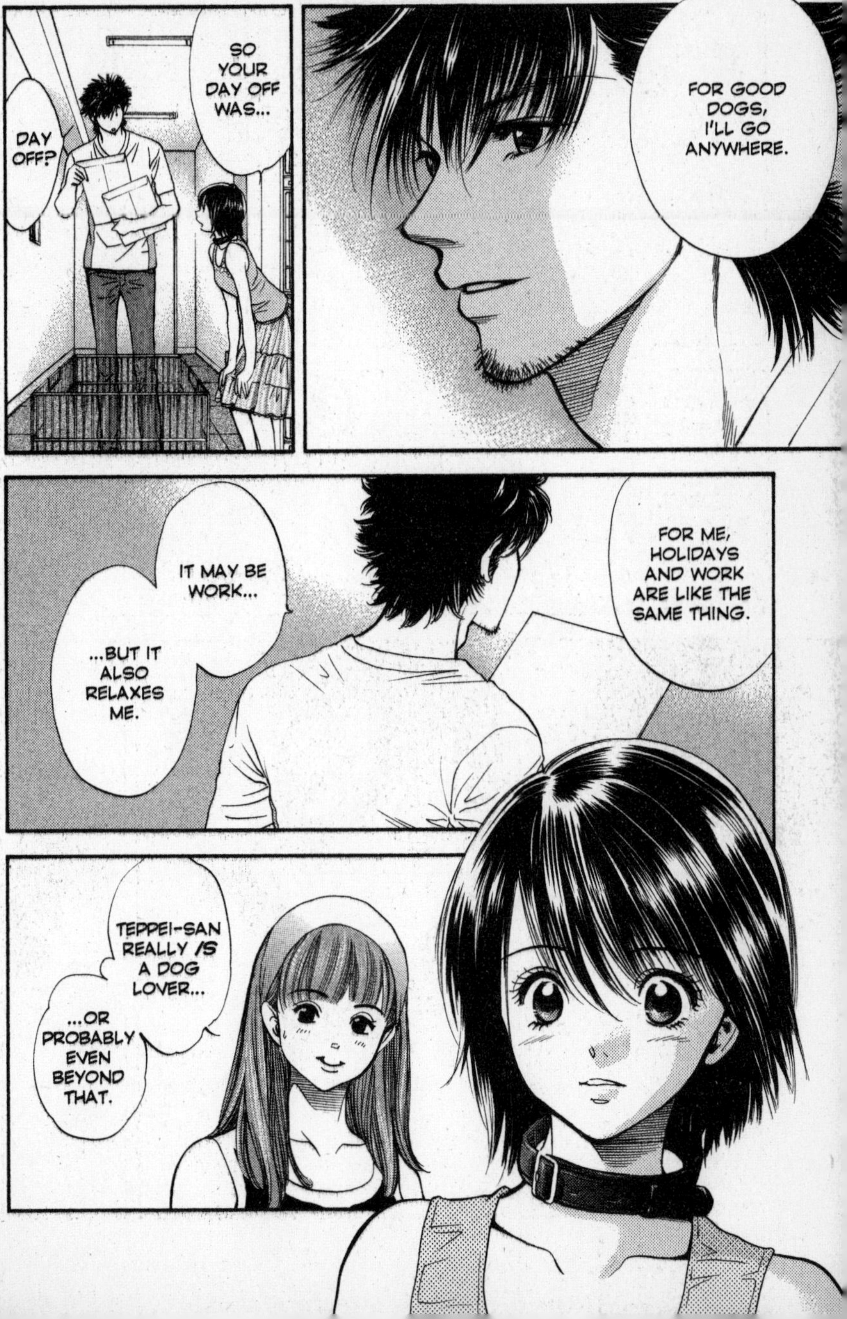
FOR GOOD DOGS, I'LL GO ANYWHERE.
SO YOUR DAY OFF WAS...
DAY OFF?
FOR ME, HOLIDAYS AND WORK ARE LIKE THE SAME THING.
IT MAY BE WORK...
...BUT IT ALSO RELAXES ME.
TEPPEI-SAN REALLY *IS* A DOG LOVER...
...OR PROBABLY EVEN BEYOND THAT.

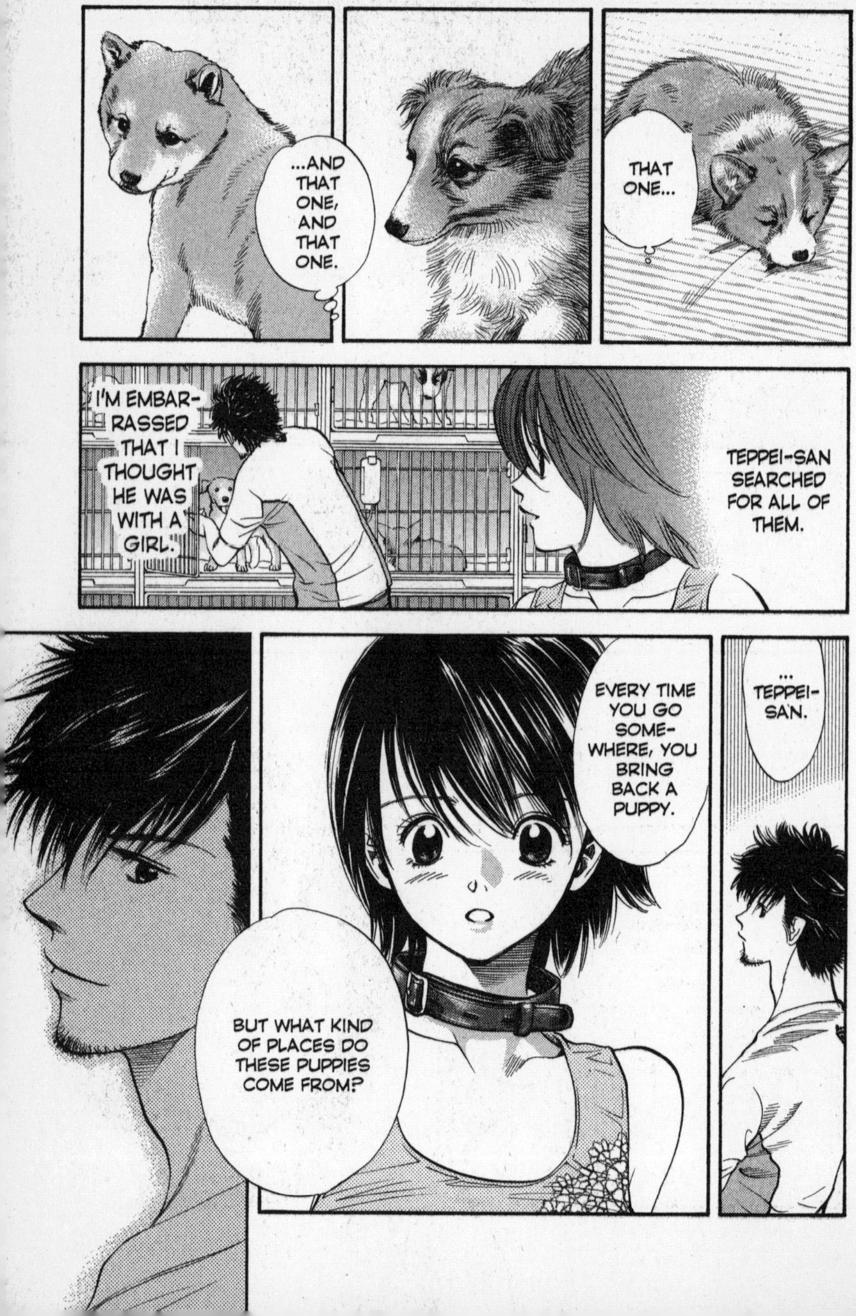
THAT ONE...
...AND THAT ONE, AND THAT ONE.
TEPPEI-SAN SEARCHED FOR ALL OF THEM.
I'M EMBARRASSED THAT I THOUGHT HE WAS WITH A GIRL.
... TEPPEI-SAN.
EVERY TIME YOU GO SOMEWHERE, YOU BRING BACK A PUPPY.
BUT WHAT KIND OF PLACES DO THESE PUPPIES COME FROM?

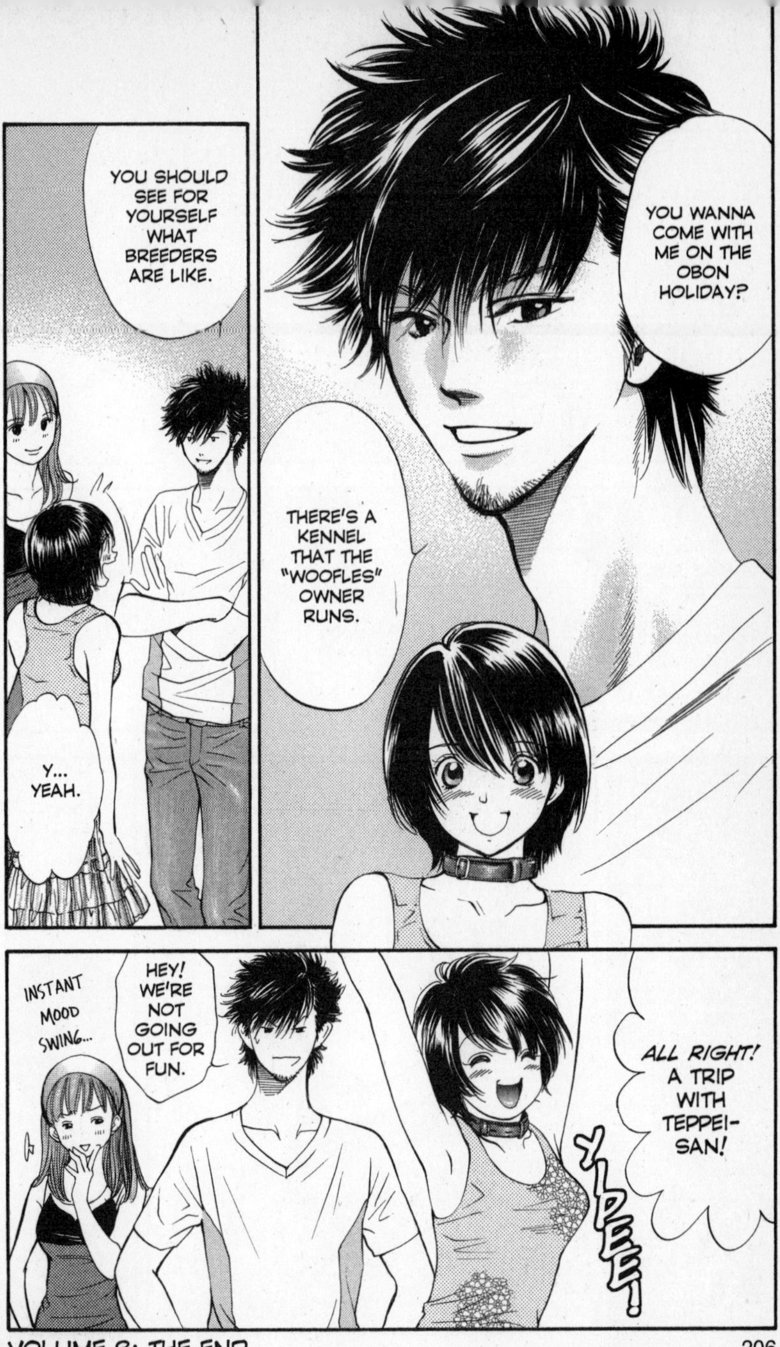
YOU WANNA COME WITH ME ON THE OBON HOLIDAY?
THERE'S A KENNEL THAT THE "WOOFLES" OWNER RUNS.
YOU SHOULD SEE FOR YOURSELF WHAT BREEDERS ARE LIKE.
Y... YEAH.
ALL RIGHT! A TRIP WITH TEPPEI-SAN!
YIPEE!
HEY! WE'RE NOT GOING OUT FOR FUN.
INSTANT MOOD SWING...

VOLUME 8: THE END

INUBAKA

INUBAKA

Everybody's Crazy for Dogs!

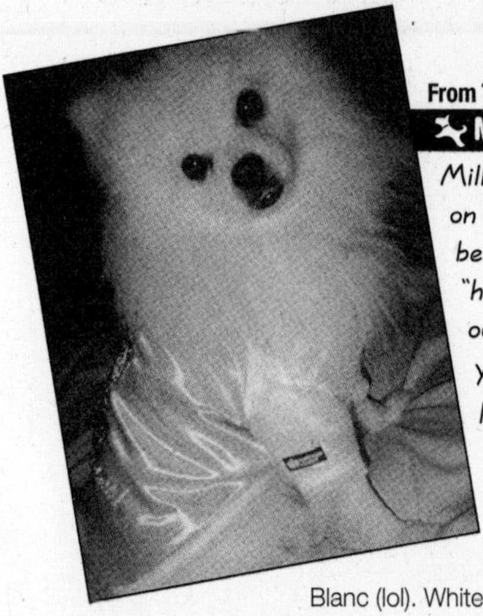

From Tsubasa-san in Kanagawa prefecture

Milky-kun (Pomeranian)

Milky-kun is quite affectionate. Even on hot summer days he stays right beside his owner as the owner says "hoooooooot!" with a smile and a spaced-out look on his face. His hair sticks to you when you're sweaty and can get pretty itchy, but I'm sure Milky-kun will keep on being affectionate.

Yukiya Sakuragi

I was surprised. He looks like my dog, Blanc (lol). White Pomeranians are so adorable! When they have clothes on, they turn into little lions, but that's part of their charm.

From Kotori Meo-san in Saitama prefecture

Lilyn-chan and Kozakura-chan
(Maltese and a long-haired Chihuahua)

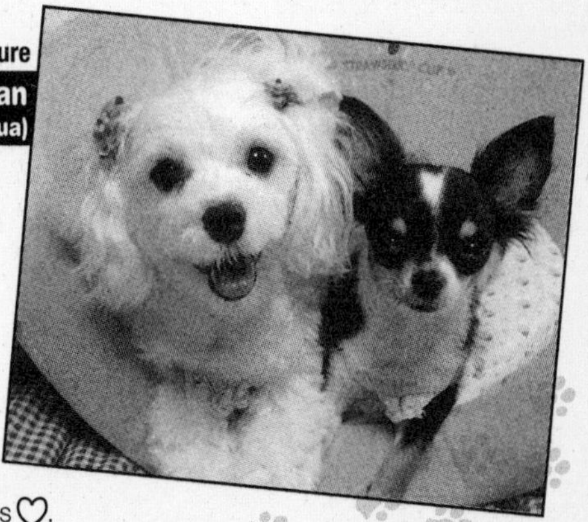

Lilyn-chan and Kozakura-chan wear matching outfits when they go out. Sometimes they fight, but they are close sisters. They're so close that they often cooperate in mischief!

Yukiya Sakuragi

Without a doubt, they look like sisters♡.
So cute… (lol) I'm sure these pretty sisters are popular with the neighbors.

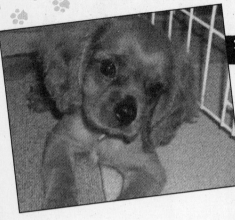

From Tsuchimoto-san in Shizuoka prefecture

🐾 **Stellar-kun**
(Cavalier King Charles spaniel)

He is a very active dog and loves to tug on his rope toy. Because of his ruby (dark brown) colored coat, he's often mistaken for a miniature dachshund. But we love him, so it doesn't bother Stellar-kun.

Yukiya Sakuragi

When I first saw this picture, I thought he was a dachshund too (Sorry). He's so cute!

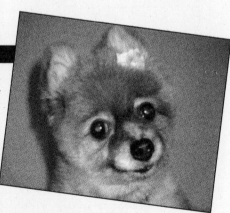

From Ozaki-san in Aichi prefecture

🐾 **Polon-chan (Pomeranian)**

The hair ornament looks lovely on her. She's also very smart. When you talk to her, she will tilt her head from side to side intently like she's trying to understand. Just adorable.

Yukiya Sakuragi

Here it is! The summer hairdo for Pomeranians! Super cute!!
You can't help but want to touch that fluffiness. My dog also tilts his head when I ask "Are you hungry?" It's the cutest thing.

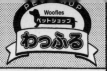

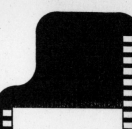

INUBAKA

Yukiya Sakuragi

EDITOR
Jiro Hyuga

COMICS EDITOR
Chieko Miyata

STAFF

Fumiko Tomochika

Ryo Yamane

Toshiaki Kato

PET SHOP
Woofles
ペットショップ
わっふる

PET SHOP
Woofles
ペットショップ
わっふる

Noriko Takahashi

Yuzo Warabi

Mamiko Taguchi

Chie Ishido

Akira Iwaya

Yuya Kanzaki

SPECIAL THANKS TO

YUKIYA'S FAMILY AND BLANC

HIRO & RYÔ

THANK YOU!!

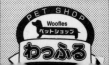

Inubaka
Crazy for Dogs
Vol. #8
VIZ Media Edition

Story and Art by
Yukiya Sakuragi

Translation/Hidemi Hachitori, HC Language Solutions, Inc.
English Adaptation/Ian Reid, HC Language Solutions, Inc.
Touch-up Art & Lettering/Kelle Han
Cover and Interior Design/Hidemi Sahara
Editor/Ian Robertson

Editor in Chief, Books/Alvin Lu
Editor in Chief, Magazines/Marc Weidenbaum
VP of Publishing Licensing/Rika Inouye
VP of Sales/Gonzalo Ferreyra
Sr. VP of Marketing/Liza Coppola
Publisher/Hyoe Narita

Printed in the U.S.A.

Published by VIZ Media, LLC
P.O. Box 77010
San Francisco, CA 94107

10 9 8 7 6 5 4 3 2 1
First printing, April 2008

www.viz.com
store.viz.com

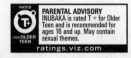

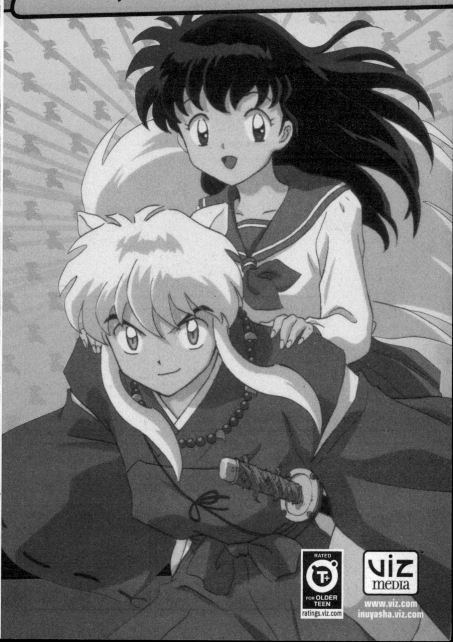

INUYASHA

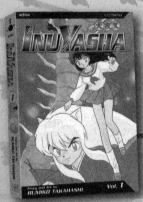

Read the action from the start with the original manga series

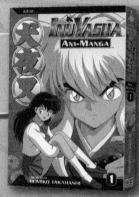

Full color adaptation of the popular TV series

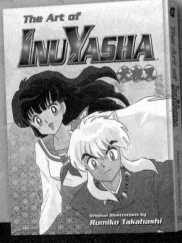

Art book with cel art, paintings, character profiles and more

TV SERIES & MOVIES ON DVD!

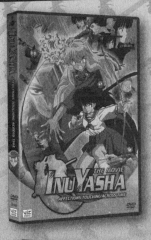
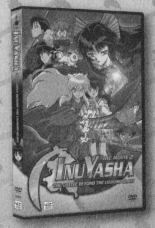
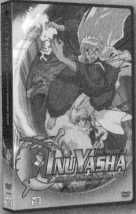
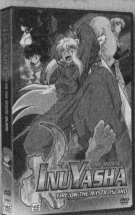

See more of the action in *Inuyasha* full-length movies

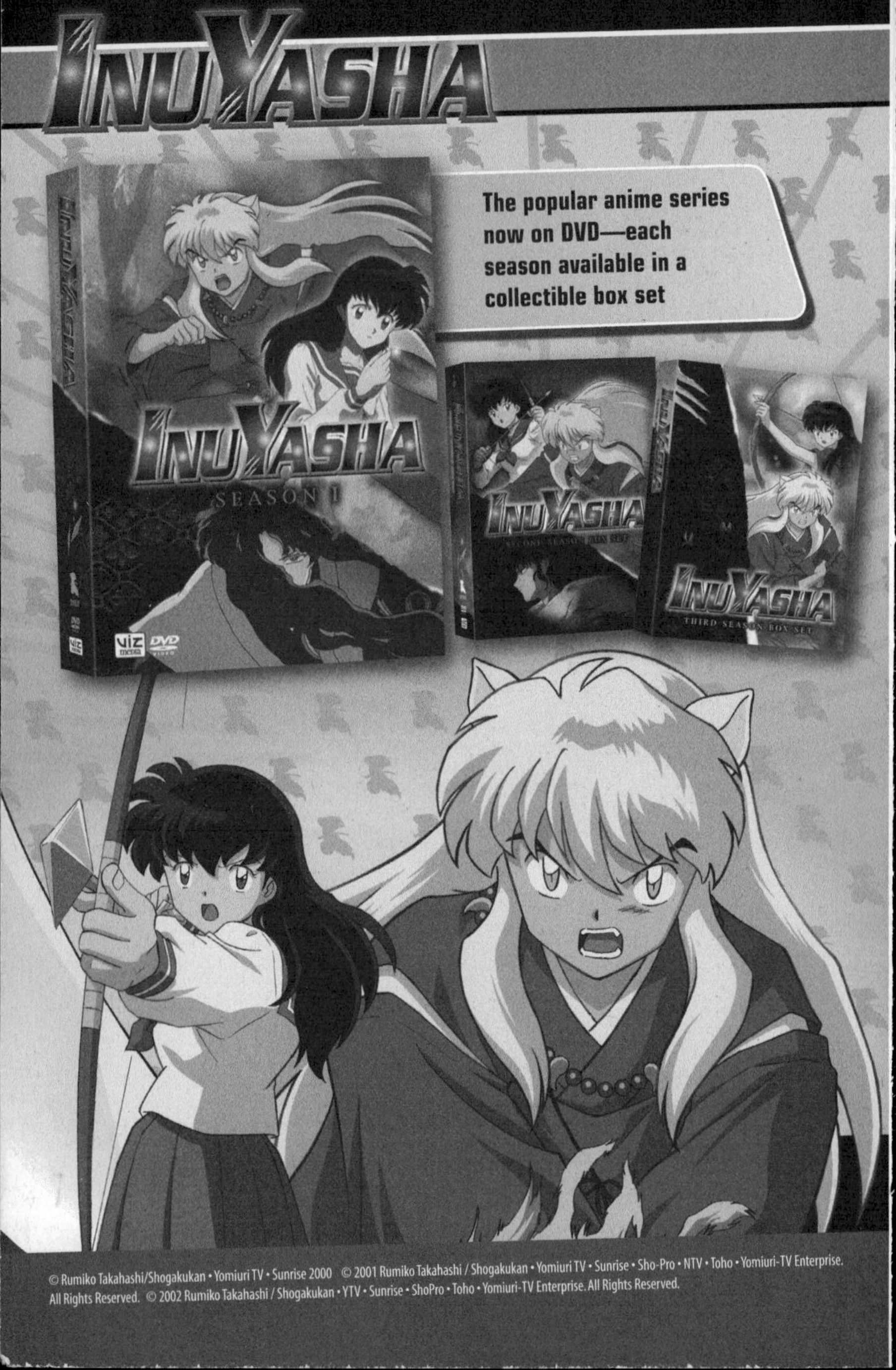
InuYasha
The popular anime series now on DVD—each season available in a collectible box set
InuYasha
SEASON 1
InuYasha
InuYasha
THIRD SEASON BOX SET